T0154069

TEN BOURDES

MIDDLE ENGLISH TEXTS SERIES

GENERAL EDITOR
Russell A. Peck, University of Rochester

ASSOCIATE EDITOR
Alan Lupack, University of Rochester

ASSISTANT EDITOR
Martha Johnson-Olin, University of Rochester

ADVISORY BOARD

Theresa Coletti
University of Maryland

Rita Copeland
University of Pennsylvania

Susanna Fein
Kent State University

Thomas G. Hahn
University of Rochester

David A. Lawton
Washington University in St. Louis

Michael Livingston
The Citadel

R. A. Shoaf
University of Florida

Lynn Staley
Colgate University

Paul E. Szarmach
Western Michigan University

Bonnie Wheeler
Southern Methodist University

The Middle English Texts Series is designed for classroom use. Its goal is to make available to teachers, scholars, and students texts that occupy an important place in the literary and cultural canon but have not been readily available in student editions. The series does not include those authors, such as Chaucer, Langland, or Malory, whose English works are normally in print in good student editions. The focus is, instead, upon Middle English literature adjacent to those authors that teachers need in compiling the syllabuses they wish to teach. The editions maintain the linguistic integrity of the original work but within the parameters of modern reading conventions. The texts are printed in the modern alphabet and follow the practices of modern capitalization, word formation, and punctuation. Manuscript abbreviations are silently expanded, and *u/v* and *j/i* spellings are regularized according to modern orthography. Yogh (ȝ) is transcribed as *g*, *gh*, *y*, or *s*, according to the sound in Modern English spelling to which it corresponds; thorn (þ) and eth (ð) are transcribed as *th*. Distinction between the second person pronoun and the definite article is made by spelling the one *thee* and the other *the*, and final *-e* that receives full syllabic value is accented (e.g., *charité*). Hard words, difficult phrases, and unusual idioms are glossed either in the right margin or at the foot of the page. Explanatory and textual notes appear at the end of the text, often along with a glossary. The editions include short introductions on the history of the work, its merits and points of topical interest, and brief working bibliographies.

This series is published in association with the University of Rochester.

Medieval Institute Publications is a program of
The Medieval Institute, College of Arts and Sciences

WESTERN MICHIGAN UNIVERSITY

TEN BOURDES

Edited by
Melissa M. Furrow

TEAMS • Middle English Texts Series

MEDIEVAL INSTITUTE PUBLICATIONS
Western Michigan University
Kalamazoo

Copyright © 2013 by the Board of Trustees of Western Michigan University
Manufactured in the United States of America

This book is printed on acid-free paper.

Library of Congress Cataloging-in-Publication Data

Ten bourdes / edited by Melissa M. Furrow.
      pages cm. -- (Middle English texts series)
  Ten Bourdes is a fresh edition of the poems found in Ten fifteenth-century comic poems
(New York: Garland, 1985), with one deletion (The Feast of Tottenham) and one addi-
tion (King Edward and the Shepherd). This edition is designed for students. The earlier
scholarly edition was done before the publication of the Linguistic Atlas of Late Mediaeval
English (LALME) with its new information, which has now changed many conclusions
about the place of origin of poems.
  Includes bibliographical references.
  ISBN 978-1-58044-192-6 (pbk. : alk. paper)
  1. English poetry--Middle English, 1100-1500. 2. Humorous poetry, English. 3. English
poetry--Middle English, 1100-1500--History and criticism. 4. Humorous poetry, English-
-History and criticism. I. Furrow, Melissa M., 1954- editor. II. Furrow, Melissa M., 1954- Ten
fifteenth century comic poems.
  PR1195.H8T38 2013
  821'.108–dc23

                                                                      2013001538

ISBN 978-1-58044-192-6

P   5   4   3   2   1

❦ CONTENTS

❧ ACKNOWLEDGMENTS

It is a pleasant task to acknowledge the assistance that has gone into this edition, most immediately that of Peter Chiykowski, who has been deeply involved in research on *King Edward and the Shepherd*, and who has been the latest of those able assistants who have brought a combination of the perspective of a student and the abilities of a researcher and editor to work on these poems. His predecessors Alexandra Rahr and Alison Symons too were an invaluable help in the establishment of the texts and glosses.

Russell Peck first invited me to prepare this edition, and I am grateful for his interest, patience, and support, and the helpfulness of the TEAMS project staff in assembling manuscript microfilm printouts for me to do preliminary checking of texts (notably Rose Paprocki) and formatting the results (John H. Chandler). Additional thank yous go to Alan Lupack, Martha M. Johnson-Olin, Sharon E. Rhodes, and Kara L. McShane. I would also like to thank Patricia Hollahan and her staff at MIP and the National Endowment for the Humanities for funding this project.

Thanks for support received from the Social Sciences and Humanities Research Council of Canada, which allowed my initial trips to England to examine manuscripts, and to a Dalhousie University Sabbatical Leave grant, which allowed trips to Cambridge and to the Huntington Library in California to examine the manuscript of *King Edward and the Shepherd* and the early print of *The Freiris of Berwik*, respectively. Research Development Grants from Dalhousie and the Sabbatical Leave grant have very much facilitated bringing this project to a conclusion.

I am grateful to the libraries housing the manuscripts and early texts concerned and to their librarians who gave me access to the texts and permission to edit and publish them: the British Library for MS Harley 78, fols. 74r–81v, *The Lady Prioress*; and MS Additional 27879 (the Percy Folio Manuscript), pp. 357–68, *John the Reeve*, and pp. 284–87, *The Boy and the Mantle*. Cambridge University Library for MS Ff.5.48, fols. 58r–61v, *The Tale of the Basin*, and 48v–56v, *King Edward and the Shepherd*. The Bodleian Library, University of Oxford, for MS Ashmole 61 (Bodley 6922), fols. 59v–62r, *Sir Corneus*, and 157r–161v, *The King and the Hermit*; for S.Seld.d.45(6), *Dane Hew, Munk of Leicestre*; and for MS Rawlinson C.86 (Bodley 11951), fols. 52r–59r, *Jack and His Stepdame*. The Trustees of the National Library of Scotland for the Bannatyne Manuscript, MS Advocates' 1.1.6, vol. 2, fols. 180v–186v, *The Freiris of Berwik*. I am grateful too to the Huntington Library for permission to examine the early printed edition of *The Freiris of Berwik*.

Some of the work in this edition is indebted to *Ten Fifteenth-Century Comic Poems* (New York: Garland, 1985), and readers are referred to that earlier text if they would like to follow up on scholarly issues. I remain indebted to Elizabeth Edwards, then my research assistant and now my colleague, for her help in the preparation of that edition, particularly the glossary.

# GENERAL INTRODUCTION

Ten Bourdes is a fresh edition of the poems found in my earlier *Ten Fifteenth-Century Comic Poems* (New York: Garland, 1985), with one deletion (*The Feast of Tottenham*) and one addition (*King Edward and the Shepherd*).[1] The edition is completely reconceived — that was a scholarly edition; this is designed in the first instance for students. That was done before the publication of the monumental *Linguistic Atlas of Late Mediaeval English* (*LALME*); this has been done since, with the consequence that many of the conclusions I reached earlier about place of origin of poems have had to be modified in the face of new information. In that edition two poems (*The Freiris of Berwik* and *Jack and His Stepdame*) were edited from multiple source texts by recension; in this edition all poems are based primarily on a single source, manuscript or print, and emendations even for sense or rhyme are more cautious. Like other METS texts, this edition has marginal glosses to make it more accessible to student readers, as well as the glossary at the end, and explanatory and textual notes. The earlier edition had more extensive textual notes and more information on the manuscripts and early printed versions, but that information is apt to be of interest only to scholarly researchers. This edition aims to put funny (or would-be funny) Middle English poems under the eyes of a much broader readership.

What to call this edition became an interesting conceptual problem. There are still ten poems, although two of them are incomplete. But research on *King Edward and the Shepherd* persuaded my research assistant Peter Chiykowski and me that it could be dated quite precisely to the period 1345–47, not the fifteenth century by anyone's reckoning. At the other end of the time span, poems that are preserved only in late manuscripts like *The Boy and the Mantle* in the Percy Folio Manuscript are impossible to date to the fifteenth century with complete conviction unless there are corroborating external references, as there are for *John the Reeve*, another Percy Folio poem. And "comic poems" is not medieval terminology. French had of course the genre term *fabliau* for its comic poems of the twelfth and thirteenth century, a term that is transferable readily to those of Chaucer's *Canterbury Tales* that are clearly imitating them and what they do. But an acquaintance with the ten poems in this collection will quickly reveal that unlike a *fabliau* they all conclude with morality triumphant, provided they still have a conclusion. Wandering spouses are returned to marriages; adulterous clergy are punished and barred from returning to their adultery; at the very least, as in the Arthurian bourdes, adultery at court is exposed; a cruel stepmother is humiliated; and on the rewards side of justice, a little victim is made secure, virtue triumphs, hospitality is rewarded, and money, gifts, and food flow to the good. *Fabliaux* do not

---

[1] *The Feast of Tottenham* is now available edited by Kooper in *Sentimental and Humorous Romances*, pp. 205–11; *King Edward and the Shepherd*, on the other hand, has not been readily available since 1930, in French and Hale's collection *Middle English Metrical Romances*, 2:947–85.

necessarily oppose morality — in them, sometimes the wicked are punished as much as the foolish are — but many a *fabliau* derives its humor from defrauding the innocent. Not so in these comic poems.

Unfortunately, if this is a genre, what is left of it is scant (perhaps a score of poems at the outside) and contemporary commentary on them is apparently nonexistent: there is no one I can find who wrote "comic poems like *The Tale of the Basin* or *The Freiris of Berwik* are a waste of time," a piece of genre criticism that would be immeasurably useful. And certainly "comic poems" is a label that would not have been used by those who wrote them. *Bourdes*, however, is potentially such a label. Three of our poems actually use the term. The earliest, *King Edward and the Shepherd,* uses the term eight times in reference to the entertaining customs of the shepherd in the poem, or to the enjoyment of others in learning of that behavior, but not in a way that makes it refer to the whole poem (see lines 214, 223, 323, 478, 487, 612, 633, and 699). *John the Reeve* describes its origins:

> As I heard tell this other yere,
> A clarke came out of Lancashire;
> A rolle he had reading.
> A bourde written therein he found
> That sometime fell in England
> In Edwardes dayes our king.
> (lines 7–12)

Sir Corneus proclaims

> Of a bowrd I wyll you schew
> That ys full gode and trew,
> That fell sometyme in Ynglond.
> (lines 4–6)

The word is first attested in English in the Auchinleck Manuscript c. 1330, according to *The Middle English Dictionary*, and already there it has several related meanings: an amusing story, fun, an amusing incident. As a small genre, the *bourde* is the immediate predecessor of the *merry jest*, a type discussed by Linda Woodbridge as existing for a short while during the early years of printing, from 1510 to 1534.[2] Two of our tales, *Jack and His Stepdame* (in its print version *The Friar and the Boy*), and *Dane Hew, Munk of Leicestre*, were published as *A Mery Jest* ("Here begynneth a mery geste of the frere and the boye," "Heere beginneth a mery Iest of Dane Hew Munk of Leicestre, and how he was foure times slain and once hanged"). Like the term *bourde*, the term *merry jest* was used both to label the kind of poem and to describe its content, the practical joke, revealing deception, or humiliating exposure that the poems are built upon and that the reader, if not all the characters, is invited to enjoy. Though not all the poets whose work is included here have used the term *bourde* to

---

[2] She identifies nine single jests in verse, one compilation of jests in verse in 1525 (*Twelve Merry Jests of the Widow Edith*), and then six compilations in prose, in *Vagrancy, Homelessness, and English Renaissance Literature*, appendix B, English Renaissance Jest Books, p. 285.

label their work, it seems possible that all ten would have recognized it as an appropriate one. *Ten Bourdes*, then, is what we have here.

The French and English comic genres are best contrasted by how they fail to be funny. A *fabliau* fails by being excessively violent or excessively disgusting in either physical or moral ways: if the reader cannot tolerate the extremes to which a *fabliau* goes, the tale will not strike that reader as amusing. But considering the number of provocations in the genre — the rapes, beatings, castrations, and feculence — it is evident that a *fabliau* is supposed to derive its humor from being shocking enough. A bourde, however, fails by being too morally corrective. A good example would be *The Wright's Chaste Wife*, which involves a similar sort of fleecing of the predatory male to what we see in *Dane Hew, Munk of Leicestre*. But whereas there is a good deal of slapstick humor and misplaced horror in *Dane Hew*, in which no tears are shed for the lascivious monk's death, in *The Wright's Chaste Wife* there is a tedious abundance of lesson-teaching. Three lecherous men are one by one dropped through a trapdoor and forced to do women's work in order to earn anything to eat. They emerge into the custody of the lady married to the highest ranking of the three. Nothing is left concealed, nobody is blackmailed, the chaste wife still gets to keep the enormous amounts of money given to her in anticipation by her three lustful suitors, and the wright ends unscathed and indeed benefited. In a romance, let alone a *fabliau*, he would have been the sort of aged roué married to a young and beautiful woman who deservedly gets cuckolded for shutting her up in a structure that protects her from the attentions of other men. In this story he ends with a virtuous *and* wealthy wife.[3]

A signal of the genre of bourde can be understood to be the demand for laughter, expressed either as an opening signaling that laughter or merriment is expected or an internal observation that some of the characters "laughed and had good game" at others. It is there, for example, in *The Wright's Chaste Wife*, where at the end the wife of the lascivious lord reacts to the plight of her husband and his two fellows:

> The lady lawghed and made good game
> Whan they came owte alle in-same   *together*
> From the swyngylle tre.
>   (lines 601–03)

The lady is, however, probably the only one who laughs. Other genre signals are "Make you mery all and som" (*Lady Prioress*, line 15); "Ever they lough and had good game" (*Jack and His Stepdame*, line 175); "Ever the boye blewe and lewh amonge" (*Jack and His Stepdame*, line 253); "Tho that at souper satte / They had good game and lough therat" (*Jack and His Stepdame*, lines 346–47); "In feyth this was the meryest fytte / That I hard this sewyn yere" (*Jack and His Stepdame*, lines 413–14); "A man may dryfe forth the day that long tyme dwellis / With harpyng and pipyng and other mery spellis" (*Tale of the Basin*, lines 3–4); "When that men be glad and blyth, / Than wer solas god to lyth, / He that wold be stylle" (*King and the Hermit*, lines 7–9); "All that wyll of solas lere, / Herkyns now and ye schall here, / And ye kane understond. / Of a bowrd I wyll you schew / That ys full gode and trew, / That fell sometyme in Ynglond" (*Sir Corneus*, lines 1–6); "And ye wil listyn how hit ferd / Betwene

---

[3] See the edition of *The Wright's Chaste Wife* by Eve Salisbury in her collection *Trials and Joys of Marriage*, pp. 61–84.

Kyng Edward and a scheperd, / Ye shalle lawgh of gyle" (*King Edward and the Shepherd*, 10–12), and the king's promise to his nobles, "Ye shall have gode bourd, in certayne, / Yif that ye will be stille" (*King Edward and the Shepherd*, lines 612–13); "Best is mirth of all solace; / Therfore I hope itt betokenes grace, / Of mirth who hath likinge" (*John the Reeve*, lines 4–6); "The laughed, without doubt, / And soe did all that were about, / To see John on his steede" (*John the Reeve*, lines 778–80); "Heere beginneth a mery Iest of Dane Hew Munk of Leicestre" (*Dane Hew*, title; see Textual Note); "Then every knight / That was in the kinges court / Talked, lauged, and showted / Full oft att that sport" (*The Boy and the Mantle*, lines 73–76). There is no such overt generic signal in *The Freiris of Berwik*, which is rather more like a *fabliau* in the gratuitous harm done the innocent husband in the poem, who accidentally knocks himself out in the flurry of violence as the adulterous friar leaves the building, but more like a bourde in its putting a stop to the ongoing adultery between Alison and Friar John.

Obviously contemporary readers cannot have expectations of a genre unless it exists. But if the genre of bourde did exist when Chaucer wrote, one important implication is the expectation readers would have brought to his comic tales. The Miller's and Reeve's Tales would have seemed by contrast to bourdes startlingly retro, a revisiting and remaking of a genre that had existed in Anglo-Norman a hundred years in the past. Creative forms of humiliation and violence affect the cuckold, the would-be cuckolder, and the actual cuckolder in The Miller's Tale, and the swiving of Simkin the miller's wife and daughter in The Reeve's Tale is presented as a means of getting revenge on Simkin. But the Summoner's and Friar's Tales might have been experienced as tales that fit into the genre of bourde instead, a more comfortably English genre, and one in which comeuppance is highly valued and lack of compassion for the innocent is a punishable offence: a predatory summoner is sent off to hell by the poor widow's curse, a greedy and insensitive friar is given a very noisy fart by a sick peasant whose child has recently died. The Friar's Tale even has a similar generic signal ("I wol yow of a somonour telle a game" [III(D)1279]) though The Summoner's Tale rather conspicuously does not claim "they all laughed" but rather provides an amusingly deadpan reception for Jankin's solution to the problem in arsmetrik. Perhaps that pair of tales could best be considered as belonging to an English rather than a French genre, and meeting the expectations of that genre (indeed helping to shape it) rather than not fitting the other one, or any genre, very well at all. It seems more prudent, because potentially productive of fresh and more accurate insight, to assign a different generic label than *fabliau* to the comic poems of the fifteenth century in English and to follow up the implications of the different expectations such a genre would entail. It is a matter of more doubt whether the genre should be extended backwards into the fourteenth century in our current state of knowledge, given the dating of *King Edward and the Shepherd* but the lack of other similar poems from such an early date.

Readers interested in the comic tale as a genre in Middle English will find the following of use:

Brewer, Derek. "The International Medieval Popular Comic Tale in England." In *The Popular Literature of Medieval England*. Ed. Thomas J. Heffernan. Tennessee Studies in Literature 28. Knoxville: University of Tennessee Press, 1985. Pp. 131–47.
———. "Introduction" to *Medieval Comic Tales*. Second ed. Cambridge: D. S. Brewer, 1996. Pp. xi–xxxiv, especially pp. xxxii–xxxiv.

Busby, Keith. "Conspicuous by its Absence: The English Fabliau." *Dutch Quarterly Review* 12 (1982), 30–41.

Cooke, Thomas. "Middle English Comic Tales." In *A Manual of the Writings in Middle English 1050–1500*. Vol. 9, gen. ed. Albert E. Hartung. New Haven: Connecticut Academy of Arts and Sciences, 1993. Section 24 Tales, pp. 3138–3328, 3472–3592, especially pp. 3151–58.

Furrow, Melissa. "The Middle English Fabliaux and Modern Myth." *ELH* 56 (1989), 1–18.

———. "Comic Tales." In *Medieval England: An Encyclopedia*. Ed. Paul E. Szarmach, M. Teresa Tavormina, and Joel Thomas Rosenthal. New York: Garland, 1998. Pp. 203–04.

Goodall, Peter. "An Outline History of the English Fabliau after Chaucer." *AUMLA: Journal of the Australasian Universities Language & Literature Association* 57 (1982), 5–23.

Hines, John. *The Fabliau in English*. London: Longman, 1993.

Robbins, Rossell Hope. "The English Fabliau: Before and after Chaucer." *Moderna Språk* 64 (1970), 231–44.

Wright, Glenn. "The Fabliau Ethos in the French and English *Octavian* Romances." *Modern Philology* 102 (2005), 478–500.

The Tale of the Basin is grouped together with *Jack and His Stepdame* in this edition because in both poems the plot turns on white magic. Each poem has a benign figure — an old man in *Jack and His Stepdame*, a concerned brother who is also a priest in *The Tale of the Basin* — who intervenes to help the protagonist in his domestic struggles. The brother in *The Tale of the Basin* enchants a chamberpot so that his sister-in-law's lover will not be able to put it down once he picks it up, and a cluster of those who try to help by tugging each other away cannot be broken. The old man in *Jack and His Stepdame* grants three wishes to the kindhearted little boy Jack, and two of those wishes (for a bow and for a pipe) are met with enchanted objects as well: a bow and arrows that cannot miss, a pipe that causes all who hear it to dance uncontrollably. The third wish — that Jack's cruel stepmother should fart thunderously every time she scowls at him — is harder to categorize.

For those accustomed to reading *fabliaux*, the comic tales from medieval French literature of a type made known to later English readers through Chaucer's adaptations of the genre, the husband in *The Tale of the Basin* is a peculiar figure: a hapless and ineffective husband in two senses of the word *husband*, married man and domestic manager, who is nevertheless rescued in the course of the tale by his brother's cleverness instead of ending as a comic victim of the plotting. It is the manly hunk, the adulterous priest, who is humiliated and blackmailed out of the picture, and the erring shrew of a wife is also shamed and reined in sexually and financially by the exile of her lover so that domestic harmony is restored.

The motif of the magic object to which a group of people become stuck is a widespread one in European folklore. It is discussed in an important German article on the story collected by the Grimm Brothers: *Die goldene Gans*, in Johannes Bolte and Georg Polívka's *Anmerkungen zu der Kinder- und Hausmärchen*, 2, article 64. *The Tale of the Basin* seems to be the earliest of the stories in which the sticky situation arises as a punishment for adultery.

Jack and His Stepdame is a peculiarity, not only when read against a background of *fabliaux*, but when read against the background of medieval literature in general. Its protagonist is a child, an ordinary little boy. And the tale itself has a distinctive comic innocence about it: normally a comic plot involving a friar who is the confidant of the wife of the household would hinge upon adultery, but any suggestion of an adulterous relationship between the friar and the wife in this story is brought to it by an experienced reader, not explicit in the story itself. Instead the comedy of the tale derives from slapstick violence and from flatulence, and from the stripping of power away from the threatening figures of the stepmother, who wants to get Jack out of the household, and the friar, who is enlisted by her to beat Jack brutally as revenge for her gassy humiliation.

Jack and His Stepdame became a remarkably popular story. It survives in four medieval manuscripts as well as the later Percy Folio Manuscript and five early printed editions or fragments from London up to 1626. There is a longer version of the story in one of the medieval manuscripts, in the Percy Folio Manuscript, and in all the printed texts, in which the friar retaliates against Jack by having him summoned to court to answer to the "offycyal" for necromancy. In all the printed editions the extended story is titled some variant of *The Friar and the Boy*, and that is the name under which it continued to be known for hundreds of years. It was published as a chapbook, like *Dane Hew, Munk of Leicestre*, and in chapbook form — small, cheap, and portable for chapmen to carry across the countryside for sale — it was disseminated not only from London but from other printing centers in an increasingly wide circle, up into Scotland, over to Ireland, and then to the United States. It was modernized, extended, and given a sequel, which was also widely circulated. After being read, chapbooks could serve as what was indelicately called "bumfodder"; they were a sort of value-added toilet paper. But the unbound chapbook, massprinted on paper, achieved a much more widespread circulation for *The Friar and the Boy* than the laboriously produced manuscript ever could have done for *Jack and His Stepdame*. At one extreme, the literary luminary Robert Burton alluded to it in his immensely learned *Anatomy of Melancholy*, and valued it enough to preserve his copy with some other chapbooks and leave it to the Bodleian Library on his death in 1639/40. At the other, it may have been one of few books ever read by the barely literate. Its childish appeal may mean it was one of the first books read by many.

Recent scholarship on *Jack and His Stepdame* has taken various directions. Nicholas Orme, a historian of medieval education, has written on *Jack and His Stepdame* (under the title *The Friar and the Boy*) as a rare example of medieval literature for children with a protagonist who is a child throughout the story, in "Children and Literature in Medieval England." Brian S. Lee cites Jack as a "pert" child (such children "are those self-conscious enough to be able to articulate their opposition to adult constraints") in "Seen and Sometimes Heard," p. 42. But the American folklorist Carl Lindahl has written on it as the first of the "Jack" folktales, a large group in American folklore describing the adventures of a man named Jack. He argues that folktale Jacks are off-limits to children and women because of the obscenity and scatology of their stories in "Jacks: The Name, the Tales, the American Traditions." This last observation seems better suited to the late nineteenth and early twentieth centuries, in which modernized and bowdlerized versions (versions with the naughty bits taken out) of the story were circulated, than it does to the periods before or since.

Richard Kieckhefer mentions *Jack and His Stepdame* as an exception to the usual role of magic in *fabliaux*, in his *Magic in the Middle Ages*: "The power of Jack's magical pipe might be mysterious, but most magical trickery, even in the *fabliaux*, worked in natural ways" (p. 93). *The Tale of the Basin*, though not mentioned, is a similar exception in that the chamberpot is genuinely enchanted, as are the objects in the two Arthurian bourdes included in this edition. Kieckhefer's section "The Making of a Clerical Underworld" (pp. 153–56) is useful on priests practicing magic.

The Tale of the Basin is mentioned by Peter Goodall in "English Fabliau after Chaucer," especially pp. 9–10, and by Marie Nelson and Richard Thomson in "Fabliau," especially pp. 261–62. As *The Tale of the Pot* it appears modernized in Derek Brewer's *Medieval Comic Tales*, pp. 55–58, and is discussed by him on pp. xxxii–xxxiii. *Jack and His Stepdame* is mentioned by Goodall under the title *The Frere and the Boye*, pp. 9–10. As *The Friar and the Boy* (but in the shorter version of most of the medieval manuscripts) it appears in Brewer's *Medieval Comic Tales*, pp. 58–62, and in the discussion on pp. xxxii–xxxxiii. Both poems are mentioned in the more general generic discussions of Glenn Wright in "Fabliau Ethos in the French and English *Octavian* Romances," p. 479n3; and Melissa Furrow's "Comic Tales."

THE TALE OF THE BASIN: INTRODUCTION

MANUSCRIPT AND SCRIBE

The Tale of the Basin is found in Cambridge University Library MS Ff.5.48, fols. 58r–61v. *The King and the Shepherd*, in the current collection, is also from this manuscript. CUL MS Ff.5.48 has been of interest to a number of scholars; it has been fully described by Manfred Görlach in *Textual Tradition*, pp. 126–27. Janay Y. Downing has edited the whole manuscript as a Ph.D. dissertation, "A Critical Edition of Cambridge University MS Ff. 5.48." My earlier edition, *Ten Fifteenth-Century Comic Poems*, describes the manuscript and lists its principal contents on pp. 45–49. Thomas Ohlgren analyzes it in his chapter "'lewed peple loven tales olde:' *Robin Hood and the Monk* and the Manuscript Context of Cambridge, University Library MS Ff.5.48," in his *Robin Hood: The Early Poems*, pp. 28–67.

The language of the manuscript has been analyzed by the editors of *LALME*, who find that the manuscript has two "hands" (though Hand A, the relevant one to us, is described as having similar, but not identical, language in different places, and it is my belief that there are two principal hands included in this section, A1 for fols. 2r–56v, 58r–66r, and 93r–112r; A2 for fols. 67r–78v, and 112v–the end). Hand A is said in *LALME* to be responsible for fols. 1r–78v, and 93r–135v, including the signature of the scribe, Gilbert Pylkyngton, on fol. 43r (1:67). The language of Hand A is said to be from Derbyshire. Lister Matheson has done a further analysis of the language of *Robin Hood and the Monk* from fols. 128v–135v of the manuscript, using the methodology of *LALME*, and finds the scribal language to be more specifically from West Derbyshire, near the Cheshire or Staffordshire borders. His analysis is part of an appendix to Ohlgren's *Robin Hood: The Early Poems*, "The Dialects and Language of Selected Robin Hood Poems," that seeks to bolster Ohlgren's claim that Gilbert Pilkington was "Hand A"; that he was the Gilbert Pilkington ordained as a subdeacon, then deacon, then priest in 1463–65 in the diocese of Coventry and Lichfield; and that he may have belonged to a family of Pilkingtons from Mellor, Derbyshire (see pp. 194–200). The detective work on Pilkington's identity is convincing and of great interest. That Pilkington was the scribe for the whole manuscript is not probable. Ohlgren himself sees "two main scribal hands: Scribe A (fols. 2r to 78v) and Scribe B (fols. 95r to 135v)";[1] by implication, at least one more hand is involved in fols. 79r to 92v, before the missing fols. 93 and 94. I would argue that there are three principal hands and a couple of minor ones, but I accept as likely that Pilkington was involved with only a small group of people in its planning and production.

---

[1] Ohlgren, *Robin Hood: The Early Poems*, p. 29.

It is not surprising that *The Tale of the Basin* should have survived in a manuscript associated with a parish priest. Like other bourdes, it has a morally corrective conclusion, and the hero of the story, the one who sets matters to rights, is himself a good parish priest, even if the transgressor in the story is also a priest. The tale is lively and amusing enough to have served as attractive sermon material.

AFTERLIFE

The Tale of the Basin appears, with different names as noted below, in the following early or otherwise useful editions:

1806. *The Enchanted Basyn*. Robert Jamieson, ed. *Popular Ballads and Songs*, vol. 1. Edinburgh: Constable. Pp. 272–82.

1829. *The Tale of the Basyn*. Charles Henry Hartshorne, ed. *Ancient Metrical Tales*. London: W. Pickering. Pp. 198–208.

1836. *The Tale of the Basyn*. Thomas Wright, ed. *The Tale of the Basyn and The Frere and the Boy*. London: W. Pickering. N.p.

1866. *The Tale of the Basyn*. William Carew Hazlitt, ed. *Remains of the Early Popular Poetry of England*, vol. 3. London: John Russell Smith. Pp. 42–53.

1969. *The Tale of the Basin*. Janay Y. Downing, ed. "A Critical Edition of Cambridge University MS Ff. 5. 48." Ph. D. dissertation, University of Washington. Pp. 166–75.

1985. *The Tale of the Basin*. Melissa M. Furrow, ed. *Ten Fifteenth-Century Comic Poems*. New York: Garland. Pp. 43–64.

REFERENCE TOOLS

The motif "objects (people, animals) stick to magic object" is listed in *ATU* as 571. *The Tale of the Basin* is 571B, "All Stick Together; Lover Exposed."

The Tale of the Basin is *NIMEV* 2658.

The Tale of the Basin is addressed by Thomas Cooke in volume 9 (1993) of the *Manual of the Writings in Middle English 1050–1500*, section 24 Tales [17], "*The Tale of the Basin* (also *The Enchanted Basin*)."

POET, POETRY, AND LANGUAGE

A brief poem, *The Tale of the Basin* presents few clues as to date and origins, let alone poet. Since the manuscript is late fifteenth-century, the poem can be no later. The poem likely belongs to the North or north Midlands area, as demonstrated by the rhymes *wyfe/stryfe/fyfe* at lines 220–22. Forms of *five* with *–f(f)(e)* are found in those areas (*LALME* Q126). This localization is compatible with the third person singular verb ending *–ys (–is)* seen in rhyme in lines 1–4 (*tellys/ellis/dwellis/spellis*; *LALME* Q59). The form "thou may," in rhyme at lines 148–50 (*fay/may/awey*), suggests a northern origin, though if the poet is from the North, it is surprising that far from treating descendants of Old English long *a* as rhymes with long *a* from other sources, he rhymes them instead with long close *o*.

The stanza form of *The Tale of the Basin* is the same as that of *The Lady Prioress*, rhyming *aaaabcccb*. The four-stressed *a* lines have the rhythm of alliterative long line, with a caesura between the two half-lines. The *c* lines, while they too might have as many as four stressed syllables, sound markedly different because there is no cæsura and there are fewer unstressed syllables, or dips. The *b* lines are short, usually with two stressed syllables. The overall effect of the *bcccb* part of the stanza is like that of the bob and wheel in stanzaic alliterative poetry, although the *a* lines are rhymed rather than alliterative. The poem gives a perfunctory nod to its indebtedness to alliterative poetry in the first line:

Of **ta**lys and **tri**fulles **ma**ny man **tell**ys.

But after that there is little other than occasional decorative alliteration, and there is no attempted concatenation as in *The Lady Prioress*.

THE TALE OF THE BASIN

Of talys and trifulles many man tellys;	*false stories*
Summe byn trew and sum byn ellis.	*are; otherwise*
A man may dryfe forth the day that long tyme dwellis	*spend; lingers*
With harpyng and pipyng and other mery spellis,	*tales*
5 With gle and with gamme.	*fun and games*
Of a person ye mowe here	*parson; will*
(In case that hit soth were),	*Supposing it were true*
And of his brother that was hym dere	
And lovyd well samme.	*And [they] loved each other well*

10 The ton was his fadirs eyre of hows and of lande,	*The one; heir; residence*
The tother was a person as I undurstande.	*The other; parson*
A riche man wex he and a gode husbande,	*grew; manager*
And knowen for a gode clerke thoro Goddis sande,	*through; grace*
And wyse was holde.	*considered*
15 The tother hade littul thoght;	
Of husbandry cowth he noght,	*household management he knew nothing*
But alle his wyves will he wroght,	*wife's desire; did*
. . . .	

A febull husbande was he on as many ar on lyve:	*feeble; one; in life*
20 Alle his wyves biddyng he did it full ryve.	*quickly*
Hit is an olde seid saw, I swere be Seynt Tyve,	*old proverb; by*
Hit shalbe at the wyves will if the husbond thryve,	
Bothe within and withowte.	
A wyfe that has an yvell tach,	*bad habit*
25 Therof the husbond shalle have a smache,	*touch of it*
But yif he loke well abowte.	*Unless he is wary*

Of that yong gentilman was a gret disese:	*cause of distress*
Aftur a yere or two his wyfe he myght not pleese;	
Mycull of his lande lay to the preestis ese.	*Much; served to pamper the priest*
30 Sche taught hym ever among how the katte did snese,	
Right at hir owne wille.	
He that hade bene a lorde	
Was nouther at bedde ne at borde,	*[one] neither; nor at table*

Ne durst onys speke a worde   *dared once*
35   When she bade be stille.   *quiet*

Litull of husbondry the godeman con thynke,   *about; man of the house thought*
And his wyfe lovyd well gode mete and gode drynke.   *food*
She wolde nouther therfore swete ne swynke,   *sweat or labor*
But when the baly was full, lye down and wynke,   *belly; nap*
40   And rest hir nedur ende.   *bottom*
Soo long this life thei ladde
That spende was that thei hadde.   *gone (spent)*
The wife hir husbonde badde
Belyfe forth to wende,   *Quickly*

45   "To the person thi brodur that is so rich a wrech,   *miser*
And pray hym of thi sorow sumdel he wolde slech.   *part; lessen*
Fourty pounde or fyfty loke of hym thou fech.   *see that; fetch*
So that thou hit bryng litull will I rech   *care*
Never for to white."   *repay*
50   To his brother forth he went,
And mycull money to hym he lent,   *much*
And also sone hit was spent: *just as*
Thereof they hade but lyte.   *little*

Micull money of his brother he fette;   *fetched*
55   For alle that he broght he ferd never the bette.   *got on (fared); better*
This person wex wery and thought he wolde hym lette: *stop*
"And he fare long thus he fallis in my dette,   *If he behaves*
And yet he may not the.   *still he can not prosper*
Betwene hym and his wife, iwysse,
60   A drawght ther is drawen amysse.   *The game is being misplayed*
I will wete, soo have I blisse,   *find out, as I hope for happiness*
How that hit myght be."

Yet on a day afterwarde to the person he yede   *Again; went*
To borow moné, and he ne myght spede.   *money; succeed*
65   "Brother," quod the person, "thou takis litull hede
How thou fallis in my dett — therof is all my drede —
And yet thou may not the.   *prosper*
Perdy, thou was my fadurs eyre   *By gosh*
Of howse and lande that was so feyre,
70   And ever thou lyves in dispayre.   *hopelessness*
What devell! How may this be?"   *What the devil*

"I ne wot how it faris, but ever I am behynde.   *in arrears*
For to liffe manly hit come me be kynde.   *generously; comes to me by nature*
I shall truly sey what I thynke in my mynde."
75   The person seyde, "Thou me telle."

"Brother," he seid, "be Saynt Albon,   *by*
Hit is a preest men callis Sir John.
Sich a felow know I non: *Such*
Of felawes he berys the bell.

80 "Hym gode and curtesse I fynde evermoo.
He harpys and gytryns, and synges wel thertoo;   *plays gittern; in addition*
He wrestels and lepis, and castis the ston also."   *is a shot-putter*
"Brother," quod the person, "belife home thou goo,   *quickly*
So as I thee say.
85 Yif thou myght with any gynne   *trick*
The vessell owt of the chambur wynne,   *steal*
The same that thei make watur in,   *pee*
And bryng hit me, I thee pray."

"Brother," he seid blithly, "thi wil shalbe wroght,
90 It is a rownde basyn, I have hit in my thoght."
"As prively as thou may, that hit be hidur broght,   *secretly*
Hye thee fast on thi way. Loke thou tary noght,   *Hurry*
And come agayne anone."   *soon*
Hamwarde con he ride;   *did*
95 Ther no longur wolde he byde.
And then his wife began to chyde
Because he come so sone.

He hent up the basyn and forth can he fare.   *grabbed; out he went*
Till he came to his brother wolde he not spare.   *slack off*
100 The person toke the basyn and to his chaumbur it bare,
And a privé experiment sone he wroght thare,   *made*
And to his brother he seyde ful blithe,   *happily*
"Loke thou where thou the basyn fette,   *Make sure*
And in that place thou hit sett,
105 And than," he seid, "withowtyn lette,   *delay*
Come agayne right swythe."   *quickly*

He toke the basyn and forth went.
When his wife hym saw hir browes she uphent.   *raised*
"Why hase thi brother so sone thee home sent?
110 Hit myght never be for gode, I know it verament,   *truly*
That thou comes home so swythe."
"Nay," he seid, "my swetyng,   *sweetheart*
I moste take a litull thyng,
And to my brother I mot hit bryng,   *must*
115 For sum it shall make blithe."   *it will make somebody happy*

Into his chaumbur prively went he that tyde   *time*
And sett downe the basyn be the bedde side;   *by*

He toke his leve at his wyfe and forth can he ride.   *from*
She was glad that he went and bade hym not abyde.
120   Hir hert began to glade.   *rejoice*
She anon right thoo   *then*
Slew a capon or twoo,
And other gode mete thertoo
Hastely she made.

125   When alle thyng was redy, she sent aftur Sir John
Prively at a posturne yate as stille as any ston.   *side entrance (gate) very quietly*
They eten and dronken as thei were wonte to done   *drank*
Till that thaym list to bedde for to gon,   *they desired*
Softly and stille.
130   Within a litull while Sir John con wake,
And nedis watur he most make.   *necessarily*
He wist wher he shulde the basyn take
Right at his owne wille.   *Whenever he wanted*

He toke the basyn to make watur in.
135   He myght not get his hondis awey all this worde to wyn.   *world to gain*
His handis fro the basyn myght he not twyn.   *separate*
"Alas," seid Sir John, "how shall I now begynne?"
Here is sum wych crafte."
Faste the basyn con he holde,   *Firmly*
140   And alle his body tremeld for colde.   *trembled*
Lever then a hundred pounde he wolde   *Rather*
That hit were fro hym rafte.   *taken*

Right as a chapmon shulde sell his ware   *peddler; merchandise*
The basyn in the chaumbeur betwix his hondis he bare.
145   The wife was agrevyd he stode so long thare   *aggrieved*
And askid why so; hit was a nyce fare   *silly behavior*
So stille ther to stande.
"What, woman!" he seid, "In gode fay,   *faith*
Thou must helpe, gif thou may,   *if you can*
150   That this basyn were awey:
Hit will not fro my honde."   *will not [move]*

Upstert the godewyfe — for nothyng wolde she lette —   *Up jumped; delay*
And bothe hir hondis on the basyn she sette.
Thus sone were thai bothe fast, and he never the bette.   *stuck; better*
155   Hit was a myssefelisshippe a man to have imette,   *bizarre group; [for] anyone; met*
Be day or be nyght.
They began clepe and crye   *shout; call*
To a wenche that lay thaim bye,   *servingwoman*
That she shulde come on hye   *in a hurry*
160   To helpe yif she myght.

Upstert the wench er she was halfe waked   *before*
And ran to hir maistrys all baly-naked.   *mistress; buck-naked*
"Alas," seid hir maistrys, "who hase this sorow maked?
Helpe this basyn wer away that oure sorow were slakyd.   *Help [that]; would be lessened*
165 Here is a sory chaunce."   *painful mischance*
To the basyn this wench she raste   *rushed*
For to helpe hade she caste.   *meant*
Thus were they sone alle thre fast.
Hyt was a nyce daunce.

170 Ther thei daunsyd al the nyght till the son con ryse.
The clerke rang the daybell as hit was his guise.   *custom*
He knew his maisturs councell and his uprise.   *secrets; getting up [time]*
He thoght he was to long to sey his sirvyse,   *too delayed*
His matyns be the morow.   *matins in the morning*
175 Softly and stille thidur he yede.
When he come thidur he toke gode hede
How that his maystur was in grett drede
And brought in gret sorow.

Anon as he Sir John can se he began to call.
180 Be that worde thei come down into the hall.   *During; calling*
"Why goo ye soo?" quod the clerke. "Hit is shame for you alle.
Why goo ye so nakyd? Foule mot yow falle.   *May evil befall you*
The basyn shalle yow froo."
To the basyn he made a brayde,   *grab*
185 And bothe his hondis theron he leyde.
The furst worde that the clerke seyde:
"Alas, what shall I doo?"

The carter fro the halle dure erth can he throw,   *door*
With a shevell in his honde, to make it clene, I trowe.
190 When he saw thaym go rounde upon a row
He wende hit hade bene folys of the fayre (he told hit in his saw).
He seid he wolde assay, iwysse.   *certainly*
Unneth he durst go in for fere.   *Scarcely; dared*
All save the clerke nakyd were.
195 When he saw the wench go there
Hym thoght hit went amysse.   *It seemed to him*

The wench was his speciall that hoppid on the rowte.   *girlfriend; rabble*
"Lette go the basyn er thou shalle have a clowte!"   *wallop*
He hit the wench with a shevell above on the towte.   *rump*
200 The shevyll sticked then fast withowte any dowte,
And he hengett on the ende.   *hung*
The carter, with a sory chaunce,   *with bad luck*
Among thaim alle he led the dawnce.

      In Englonde, Scotland, ne in Fraunce

205   A man shulde non sich fynde.

      The godeman and the person come in that stounde.   *moment*

      Alle that fayre feliship dawnsyng thei founde.   *fellowship*

      The godeman seid to Sir John, "Be cockis swete wounde,

      Thou shalle lese thine harnesse or a hundred pounde.   *equipment*

210   Truly thou shalle not chese."   *you have no choice*

      Sir John seid, "In gode fay,

      Helpe this basyn were awey   *Help [that]*

      And that moné will I pay

      Er I this harnes lese."   *Before*

215   The person charmyd the basyn that it fell thaim fro;

      Every man then hastely on thaire wey can goo.

      The preest went out of contré for shame he hade thoo,

      And then thai levyd thaire lewtnesse and did no more soo,   *left; bad behavior*

      But wex wyse and ware.   *prudent*

220   Thus the godeman and his wyfe

      Levyd togedur withowt stryfe.   *Lived*

      Mary for hir joyes fyfe

      Shelde us alle fro care.

      Finitur   *The end*

EXPLANATORY NOTES TO THE TALE OF THE BASIN

ABBREVIATIONS: **CT**: Chaucer, *The Canterbury Tales*; **MED**: *Middle English Dictionary*; **MS**: manuscript; **OED**: *Oxford English Dictionary*; **NCE**: *The New Catholic Encyclopedia*; **Whiting**: Whiting, *Proverbs, Sentences, and Proverbial Phrases*.

16   *Of husbandry cowth he noght.* This is true in multiple senses of the term *husbandry*: management of his household, farming his father's lands, and (punningly) being a respected spouse.

21   *Hit is an olde seid saw, I swere be Seynt Tyve*: The "olde seid saw" is first cited from c. 1470 (see Speake, *Oxford Dictionary of Proverbs*): "For he that cast hym for to thryve, he must ask offe his wiffe leve." See also Whiting M155 ("A Man may not wive and thrive all in a year") as a variant.
      The New Catholic Encyclopedia lists three St. Ives, one (1253–1303) born in Brittany, the patron saint of lawyers (see "Ivo Hélory, St.," *NCE*); another (c. 1040–1116) an important canonist and bishop of Chartres (see "Ivo of Chartres, St.," *NCE*); and a third from the sixth or seventh century who purportedly left his home in Persia to act as a missionary in Britain (see "Ivo, St.," *NCE*). In addition, *The Oxford Dictionary of Saints* mentions an early Irish missionary, also called Ia of Cornwall (supposedly fifth or sixth century), after whom the Cornish town of St. Ives is named (see "Ives, St.," in Farmer, *Oxford Dictionary of Saints*, p. 201). Ia/Ives was a woman, so perhaps that is a reason (beyond convenience of rhyme) for her invocation in this context.

30   The sole citation for Whiting C106: "To teach one how the Cat sneezes (i.e., put in one's place, bully)."

60   *A drawght ther is drawen amysse.* Under "draught" 3e, "drauen a draught," *MED* gives the meaning "to play a trick, or engage in a deceitful or sinful activity." The metaphor is from the game of chess: "a chess move is made improperly."

76   *be Saynt Albon.* St. Alban was the first British martyr, killed at what is now called St. Alban's in Hertfordshire, where a Benedictine abbey was built to commemorate him. His legend is the subject of Lydgate's poem *St. Alban and St. Amphibalus* (1439).

77   *Hit is a preest men callis Sir John. Sir* was a conventional courtesy title for a priest; *John* was an equally conventional name for one, particularly a lecherous one. Since the early thirteenth century, priests had been required to be celibate.

79   *Of felawes he berys the bell.* That is, like a bellwether among sheep, he is a leader among good fellows.

81   *gytryns*. The gittern was an ancestor of the modern guitar.

126   *Prively at a posturne yate as stille as any ston.* A postern gate is a side or back
            entrance, smaller and less conspicuous than the main public gate. The phrase
            "as still as a stone" can mean both "as motionless as a stone" and, as it does here,
            "as quietly as a stone." See Whiting S772 for many other examples of the phrase.

174   Matins in a parish church were the early morning service, before the Mass.

188   *The carter fro the halle dure erth can he throw.* The cart driver (carter) is not only
            responsible for carrying away material in his cart; here he is clearly responsible
            for arriving very early in the morning and shoveling it into the cart from where
            the servants have dumped it outside the door. I suspect that "earth" here is a
            euphemism for various organics (rushes from the hall floor, perhaps; food
            refuse; but most importantly body waste) and that like the carter in Chaucer's
            Nun's Priest's Tale (*CT* VII[B²]3016–62) his job is to collect, very early in the
            morning, the last day's waste, and to take it out of town for fertilizer. Compare
            the quotation in *MED carter*, 1.(a) (1460) "All carterys and carmen that usyth to
            drawe dung out of the towne."

191   *He wende hit hade bene folys of the fayre (he told hit in his saw).* "He believed they
            were performing fools (that's what he said)." Compare *OED fair* n.1., citation
            1764 "Has he not . . . made himself the fool of the fair?"

208   *Be cockis swete wounde.* A euphemistic swearing by the wounds of Christ, with *cock*
            standing in for *God* as modern *gosh* does. In medieval Christian theology all
            three members of the Trinity are equally God, so Christ can be referred to as
            God just as God the Father can. It is not until 1618 that *OED* cites the word *cock*
            used with the meaning "penis" (see cock n.[1], sense 20), but the often anthol-
            ogized early fifteenth-century lyric "I have a gentil cok" from London, British
            Library MS Sloane 2393 plays upon the reader's dawning recognition that the
            cock in question is not avian. The lyric may mark the early stages of the use of the
            term for the penis. Given that medieval poets liked to pick oaths with particular
            significance, *cock* may well be a pun here, with the sense "penis" playing into the
            following line in which the philandering priest is threatened with loss of his
            "harnesse." We see the same punning combination of euphemistic oath and
            earthy context in Ophelia's lament on sexual treachery in Act 4, scene 5 of
            Hamlet:

                        Young men will do't, if they come to't;
                        By cock, they are to blame.
                                    (lines 59–60)

            On the more solemn aspect of the reference, the Five Wounds of Christ were the
            object of contemplation and veneration in the Middle Ages. They were the wounds
            in hands and feet inflicted by nails during the Crucifixion, and a lance wound
            in the side.

222   *Mary for hir joyes fyfe.* The Five Joys of the Virgin Mary were the Annunciation (of
            the coming birth of Christ), the Nativity, the Resurrection, the Ascension (of
            Christ to heaven), and the Assumption (of Mary herself into heaven).

TEXTUAL NOTES TO THE TALE OF THE BASIN

COPY-TEXT: Cambridge University Library, MS Ff.5.48, fols. 58r–61v.
ABBREVIATION: MS: manuscript, here referring to the copy-text.

title	No title in MS.
1	MS reads: *Off talys and trifulles many man tellys*, in very large letters and underlined, like line 75.
18	The line is missing, with no gap in MS. Some such line as "And did as she hym tolde" is called for.
25	A line is missing to complete the stanza; no gap is in MS.
30	*Sche taught hym ever among how the katte did snese*: the word *katte* is inserted above the line.
47	MS reads: *Fourty pounde of or fyfty loke of hym thou fech*. Emendation for sense.
73	The word *me* is inserted above the line.
75	MS reads: *The person seyde thou me telle*, in very large letters and underlined, like line 1.
103	MS reads: *Loke thou where the basyn fette*. Emendation for sense.
121	After line 120, line 124 appears by mistake but is canceled with a line drawn through it: *Hastely she made*. The verse appears in its proper position as well.
141	MS reads: *Leuer then a C pounde he wolde*.
168	The word *sone* is inserted above the line.
179	MS reads: *Anon as Sir John can se he began to call*. Emendation for sense.
187	MS reads: *Alas ~~why~~ what shall I doo*.
209	MS reads: *Thou shalle lese thine harnesse or a C pounde*.
222	MS reads: *Mary for y hir joyes fyfe*. Emendation for sense.
After 224	*Finitur* in very large letters, like lines 1 and 75.

JACK AND HIS STEPDAME: INTRODUCTION

MANUSCRIPTS, SCRIBES, AND PRINTED TEXTS

The earliest versions of the story of the little boy Jack and his unkind stepmother are in fifteenth- and early sixteenth-century manuscripts. This edition is based on one of them, Oxford, Bodleian Library, MS Rawlinson C.86 (MS Bodley 11951), hereafter called MS R, in which the poem appears on fols. 52r–59r. But it does not have the authority of the original text — we do not have a manuscript that has that authority — and it is by no means the final version of the story, either. The story, especially its ending, changes as it moves from manuscript into the early printed versions and their contemporary manuscripts. The title changes too. *The Tale of Jak and His Stepdame* is wording from MS R. MS Q (Oxford, Balliol College, MS 354) calls it *Jak & His Stepdame & of the Ffrere*. MS E (Cambridge, Cambridge University Library, MS Ee.4.35) calls it *The Cheylde and hes Stepdame*. MS P (Aberystwyth, National Library of Wales, MS Brogynton 10, formerly Porkington 10) does not give it a title at all, and the early printed editions (C, M, D, A, and F) and MS B (the Percy Folio Manuscript, London, British Library, MS Additional 27879; see the introduction to *The Boy and the Mantle* for more information on it) all have variants on the title of edition C from ca. 1510–13: *The Frere and the Boye*. "Frere" was then still the normal version of what has since become "friar"; the switch from one form of the word to the other can be traced in the history of publication of this poem, which by the time of Edward Alde's edition ca. 1584–89 had the spelling "frier." The major change in later versions is to the ending. All the complete versions run as far as line 414 and the end of Jack's playing on his magic pipe to his father and others. MSS R, P, and Q all end shortly thereafter, with two shared stanzas, then two additional moralizing stanzas in P, and a different two tying-up stanzas in R and Q. The other early texts, E, C, M, D, A, F, and B, have an additional episode in which the stepmother and friar complain about Jack as a necromancer to the "offycyall" at court (implicitly an archdeacon presiding over an ecclesiastical court). The official asks Jack to play his pipe to confirm that it compels all hearers to dance uncontrollably. Jack does play, with the predictable chaotic and violent results, until he can negotiate his release in exchange for stopping the music. The additional episode, with its second defeat of the stepmother and friar, is redundant and repetitive.

Julia Boffey and Carole Meale's discussion of MS Rawlinson C.86 ("Selecting the Text") gives interesting context for the early circulation of *Jack and His Stepdame*.[1] The manuscript as it now stands is a combination of four more or less independent parts, but even considering only booklet 2, which contains *Jack and His Stepdame*, there are names written

---

[1] Other useful analyses of the manuscript are Griffiths, "Re-examination," and Boffey, *Manuscripts of English Courtly Love Lyrics*, pp. 125–26.

into the margins that Boffey and Meale have "tentatively traced" to particular merchants and citizens of London of the early sixteenth century (pp. 157–58). They use *Jack and His Stepdame* to argue that "Rawlinson C.86 may be seen as typifying the tastes of middle-class, usually mercantile, readers. The anti-feminist and anti-fraternal tale of *Jack and his Stepdame* in booklet II, for instance, evidently held considerable appeal for this audience" (p. 160). They point to the tale's presence in two other merchant-owned manuscripts with *Jack* in them: Richard Hill, a grocer and citizen of London, owned MS Q (Oxford, Balliol College MS 354); Richard Calle adds his merchant's mark to his manuscript, MS E (Cambridge University Library MS Ee.4.35) (pp. 160–61). MS E also contains the notation "Iste liber constat Ricardo Calle" (This book has been compiled by Richard Calle). In my previous edition of *Jack and His Stepdame*, I argued that this Richard Calle could not be the late fifteenth-century steward of the Paston family in Norfolk because the spelling of the manuscript is quite distinctive and different from that of the steward. Thomas Ohlgren has since made a convincing argument that the manuscript nevertheless probably belonged to that Calle, even though it was not written by him.[2] Boffey and Meale point out that the Calle family too was mercantile — they were grocers, perhaps in Framlingham in Norfolk (see pp. 160–61n54). These three manuscripts then give the researcher an unusually well localized set of contexts for the poem: it was collected in mercantile families, in household miscellanies, homemade rather than professional productions.

The early manuscripts with *Jack and His Stepdame* are also like each other in their miscellaneousness, with a wide variety of types of text included that give fascinating glimpses of the tastes, needs, and opportunities for collection of the households in which they were assembled. Boffey and Meale call MS R "A miscellaneous late medieval collection of secular texts and minor devotional writings, the contents ranging from *The Northern Passion* and religious lyrics, to a unique English translation of the *Polychronicon* and other items concerned with the history and geography of England; and from two unique copies of Arthurian romances, extracts from Chaucer and Lydgate, and Gilbert Banester's courtly adaptation of Boccaccio's tale of *Guiscardo and Ghismonda*, to anti-feminist and scatological verses and tales" ("Selecting the Text," p. 145). MS Q has recipes, remedies, information on the values of goods and exchanges of money, samples of business correspondence in English and French, lists of English fairs, of Lord Mayors of London, and of feast days in that city, rules for movable feasts, and notes on the necessary qualities of a priest and the functions of popes and bishops. There are no romances in it but many lyrics, and a large collection of short and mostly moral tales, including a number from Gower's *Confessio Amantis*, *The Seven Sages of Rome*, *The Siege of Rouen*, *How the Wise Man Taught His Son*, *Stans Puer*, *Little John*, *The Churl and the Bird*, and *The Nutbrown Maid*. MS E has short moralizing and pious tales and lyrics, an account of "The Expenses of flesche at the Mariage of mey ladey Marget þat sche had owt off Eynglande" (probably the marriage of Margaret, sister to Edward IV, in Bruges in 1468), *Robin Hood and the Potter*, and *The King and the Barker*. MS P, which is associated with gentry families near and in Wales, has some scientific tables and tracts, practical instructions on planting trees and making ink, some saints' lives, *The Siege of Jerusalem*, the lyric "Timor mortis conturbat me," several carols, a burlesque, and *Syre*

---

[2] See Ohlgren, "'Pottys, grete chepe!': Marketplace Ideology in *Robin Hood and the Potter* and the Manuscript Context of Cambridge, University Library MS Ee.4.35," in his *Robin Hood: The Early Poems*, pp. 68–96.

Gawene and the Carle of Carelyle. This miscellany format is quite different from the anthology format of the last late manuscript in which the poem appears, the Percy Folio Manuscript (MS B) from the seventeenth century, a manuscript that is entirely filled with a collection of narrative poems and ballads. Among them are *The Boy and the Mantle* and *John the Reeve*, which are included in the current volume. The version in MS B is most closely related to the printed editions A and F, which precede it chronologically. All of the manuscripts, though, even the earliest ones, were written in the age of print; the miscellanies created for and probably in particular households were one alternative, and the cheaply made single text chapbook was another, in which *Jack and His Stepdame* (or *The Friar and the Boy*) was acquired.

The chapbooks that we have remaining are the tip of the iceberg for the numbers that once must have been in print. Manuscripts were not so easily replicated, but there is one other manuscript version that we know for certain to have existed. "The tale of the little boy and the Friar; in old English verse," in MS Cotton Vitellius D.xii, appears in a catalogue of the Cottonian library, but the fire at Ashburnham House in 1731 left that manuscript in fragments.[3] The circulation of the poem must have been large; this was a popular poem.

The chapbooks are all cheap quarto or smaller volumes with woodcuts. The ones I consulted are C, printed by Wynkyn de Worde ca. 1510–13, now article Sel.5.21 in the Cambridge University Library, *RSTC* 14522; M, a fragment printed by William Middleton ca. 1545, now article C.125.dd.15 (7) in the British Library, *RSTC* 14522.5; D, printed by Edward Alde ca. 1584–89 article S.Seld.d.45 in the Bodleian Library, *RSTC* 14522.7; A, printed by Edward Alde ca. 1617, now article Arch.A.F.83 (7) in the Bodleian Library, *RSTC* 14523; and F, printed by Elizabeth Alde under the name of Edward Alde in 1626, now article C.57aa.13 in the British Library, *RSTC* 14524.3. Although the chapbooks were published individually, C, D, and A were subsequently bound with others in a collection. C is part of a collection of twenty-six early chapbooks, all but one printed by de Worde, and that one printed by Richard Pynson ca. 1513. D is part of another collection of twenty-six, one of which was *Dane Hew, Munk of Leicestre*, included in the current edition; the chapbooks that are dated run from 1528 to 1605. A is part of a bound collection of twelve, which was in turn part of the larger library belonging to Robert Burton, who bequeathed it to the Bodleian at his death in January of 1640 (new style).

As for the version in MS R and its scribes in particular, two scribes are responsible for *Jack and His Stepdame* in this manuscript, with the principal scribe having written out the whole poem and the other having replaced the first leaf, running to line 58, after it became lost from the gathering. The principal scribe was from the southern part of England, using southern forms of the third person indicative present tense of verbs (e.g., *gewyth*, line 115; *lokyth*, line 118; *aylith*, line 220; *LALME* Q59), of the third person plural accusative pronoun (*hem*, lines 101, 125, 150, 152; *LALME* Q152) and of the third person plural possessive pronoun (*her*, line 371; *LALME* Q5). The replacement of *v* by *w* (and inversely of *w* by *v*) in syllable initial position in *gewyth* (line 115), *sewyn* (line 414), and *vent* (line 208) helps to locate this scribe in the east. Perhaps he did not come from the same area as the poet, given that he balks at reproducing the rhyme *chere/fyre* at lines 369–72 that is one of the more unusual features of the poet's dialect. Boffey and Meale connect the manuscript to London: "In terms of audience, evidence of various kinds serves to connect each booklet of Rawlinson

---

[3] See Smith, *Catalogue of the Manuscripts*, p. 93, column a.

C.86 with London at an early stage of its existence."[4] But they do not comment on scribal dialect, which would at any rate be difficult to disentangle. They reproduce facsimiles of facing pages from *Jack and His Stepdame*, one by each of the scribes involved, on pp. 150–51 of "Selecting the Text."

AFTERLIFE

The Friar and the Boy, as the poem is known in its chapbook versions, was popular to a degree and for a length of time that are hard to imagine. The poem is alluded to in the Langham Letter, which purports to be by one Robert Langham and describes the entertainments for Queen Elizabeth I at Kenilworth in 1575; in *The Life of Sir John Oldcastle*, ca. 1600; by Arthur Dent in *The Plain Man's Pathway to Heaven*, 1601; in a mock sermon of 1601 in Lincolnshire by John Cradock; and by Robert Burton in *The Anatomy of Melancholy*, 1621. In his edition of the poem, William Carew Hazlitt says Taylor the Water Poet alludes to it in 1622. Francis Kirkman, the seventeenth-century publisher and bookseller, implies that his own career as a lover of books began with "that famous Book, of the Fryar and the Boy" (*The Unlucky Citizen*, 1673), lending some anecdotal weight to the idea that the book appealed to young readers.

It was reprinted again and again, and further and further afield. While the printed chapbooks I consulted for this edition were all published in London, later editions originated from both London and elsewhere. We know of later seventeenth-century editions in London and Glasgow. A second part was printed from at the latest 1720 and onwards which was sometimes bound with, and sometimes separate from, the dozens of eighteenth-century editions of the first part from places as far afield as Dublin, Stirling, and New England. And there were even editions from the nineteenth century, as late as an 1831 edition from New York. These must be only the tip of the iceberg: many such chapbooks were read to pieces and disappeared, as is made clear by the fact that of the copies of *The Friar and the Boy* still extant, many are the sole survival of a printing run. So other printings may well have disappeared altogether from knowledge. There are even early instances in which the poem was registered for printing in the *Stationers' Register* (see Arber, *Transcript of the Registers of the Company of Stationers of London*), but we have no corresponding edition: J. Waley in 1557–58, J. Alde in 1568–69, and Edward White in 1586–87. Later editions of the chapbook have variations in title, such as *Jack the piper, or the pleasant pastime of a fryar and boy* (this is from the 1831 New York edition) or *The friar and boy. Or the merry piper's pleasant pastime . . . Part the first* (from a late eighteenth-century Birmingham edition).

Popular chapbook editions were still being published when the first antiquarian editions began with Ritson in 1791. William Carew Hazlitt published the poem in original form from the first two printed texts in 1866, but he also rewrote it in modern prose and bowdlerized the third gift, making the stepmother subject to uncontrollable laughter; see "The Friar and the Boy," in his *Tales and Legends of National Origin or Widely Current in England from Early Times* (New York: Macmillan, 1891), pp. 17–55. It is this bowdlerized version that Edmund Dulac rewrote and illustrated in *Edmund Dulac's Fairy-book: Fairy Tales of the Allied Nations* (London: Hodder & Stoughton, [1916], reprinted in 1988 by Portland House and 2008 by IndyPublish).

---

[4] Boffey and Meale, "Selecting the Text," p. 156.

Jack and His Stepdame appears, with different names as noted below, in the following early or otherwise useful editions:

1791. *A Mery Geste of the Frere and the Boye.* Joseph Ritson, ed. *Pieces of Ancient Popular Poetry from authentic manuscripts and old printed copies.* London: T. and J. Egerton. Pp. 31–56. [Edition of C, D, and MS E; includes ending of E in addition to the ending of C and D.]

1836. *The Frere and the Boy.* Thomas Wright, ed. *Early English Poetry*, vol. 3: *The Tale of the Basin and the Frere and the Boy.* London: W. Pickering. [Edition of MS E, with emendations from Ritson's edition. This printing does not contain page numbers.]

1855. [no title.] J. O. Halliwell, ed. *Early English Miscellanies, in Prose and Verse.* London: Warton Club. Pp. 46–62. [Edition of MS P.]

1866. *A Mery Geste of the Frere and the Boye.* W. Carew Hazlitt, ed. *Remains of the Early Popular Poetry of England*, vol. 3. London: John Russell Smith. Pp. 93–97. [Edition "a collation" of de Worde text (C) with Alde text D and Wright's edition of 1836.]

1868. *Fryar and Boye.* Frederick J. Furnivall, ed. *Bishop Percy's Folio Manuscript.* Vol. 4: *Loose and Humorous Songs.* London: published by the editor. Pp. 9–28. [Edition of MS B.]

1893. *Jak and his step dame.* Julius Zupitza, ed. *Archiv für das Studium der neuren Sprachen und Literaturen* 90, 57–82. [Edition of MS R, with reference to MS P.]

1907. *Jak & his Stepdame, & of the Frere.* Roman Dyboski, ed. In *Songs, Carols, and other Miscellaneous Pieces from the Balliol MS. 354, Richard Hill's Commonplace Book.* Early English Text Society, e.s. 101. London: K. Paul, Trench, Trübner & Co. Pp. 120–27. [Edition of MS Q.]

1907. Francis Jenkinson, ed. *The Frere and the Boye.* Cambridge: Cambridge University Press. [Facsimile edition of C.]

1985. *Jack and his Stepdame.* Melissa M. Furrow, ed. *Ten Fifteenth-Century Comic Poems.* New York: Garland. Pp. 65–153. [MS R as copy-text; critical edition.]

REFERENCE TOOLS

The motif "boy receives magic object from beggar as reward" is listed in *ATU* as 592, under the heading "The Dance Among Thorns."

Jack and His Stepdame is *NIMEV* 977.

It is addressed by Thomas Cooke in volume 9 (1993) of the *Manual*, section 24 Tales [18], *The Friar and the Boy* (also *Jak and His Stepdame*).

The *RSTC* numbers for the early editions are 14522–24.3.

POET, POETRY, AND LANGUAGE

The early versions of the poem are in six-line loosely accentual stanzas, *aa4b3cc4b3*. With so many versions of the poem, it is plain to see how loosely it was treated by its scribes and printers: there are only two lines in the whole poem that appear just the same in all ten of the earliest versions extant. Later versions (A, B, and F) are modernized in their language and regularized in their meter. Later versions still are further modernized and revised to an *a4b3a4b3* variant of the ballad stanza.

Since scribes and printers are cavalier about revision, much of the residual evidence about the poet's own dialect has undoubtedly been revised out of existence, and the waters muddied considerably. On the face of its manuscript history, the poem was most likely first written in the fifteenth century. As for the area from which the poet originated, there are some quite specific cues:

1. The poem rhymes the verb form *wilte* (*wylte*) with *fytte* twice (at lines 351, 354; and lines 412–13). This suggests an origin in East Anglia: forms of *wilt* without *-l-* are to be found in only a small area, Cambridgeshire, Norfolk, and Suffolk. See *LALME*, Q24. The confusion around lines 88–89 of the poem may stem from the rhyme *wilt/it*; later scribes who did not share the poet's pronunciation, as most, including the R scribe, would not, might have felt compelled to revise the lines.
2. The poet uses the form *goos*, or something similar, for the third singular present tense form of the verb *to go*: *close/goos* (lines 141, 144); *arose/goos* (lines 205–06). *Goos* and *gos* are spellings found in Norfolk, *gos* also in Hereford and Kent (*LALME*, Q138).

The combination of these two restricted forms pinpoints Norfolk as a probable area of origin, and this ascription is compatible with a number of other restricted forms: *fyre* rhymes with *chere* at lines 369, 372; the spelling *fere* is attested in Norfolk more than anywhere else. The rhyme *wete/forgete* at lines 199–200 is dependent on the form *wete* for the infinitive *witen*, *to know*, a form found frequently in Norfolk (*LALME*, Q257). *Tho* (at lines 169–70, rhymes with *goo*) is a form for *then* that was in use in Norfolk (*LALME*, Q30).

JACK AND HIS STEPDAME

	God that died for us all	
	And drank both eysell and gall	*vinegar; bile*
	Bring theym oute of bale	*harm*
	And graunt theym good liff and long	
5	That woll listyn to my song	*will*
	And tend to my tale.	*attend*

	Ther was a man in my contré	
	Which had wyves thre	
	In processe of tyme.	
10	By the fyrst wyff a child he had	
	Which was a propre lad	*all boy*
	And a hasty hyne.	*precocious lad*

	Hys fader loved hym well;	
	And his moder never a dele —	*not a bit*
15	I tell you as I think.	
	All she thought lost, by the rode,	*wasted, by the cross*
	Of all that ever did hym good	
	Of mete or of drynk.	*food*

	Nott half inough therof he had	
20	And yett forsoth it was right bad,	*truly*
	Yett she thought it lost.	
	Therfor evill mott she fare,	*may she suffer*
	For ofte she did hym moch care	*gave him a lot of grief*
	As farforth as she durst.	*As much as she dared*

25	The goodwiff to her husband gan say,	*mistress of the household*
	"For to putt this boye away	
	I rede you in haste.	*advise*
	For in fayth it is a shrewed lad;	*badly-behaved*
	I wold som other man hym had	*wish*
30	That wold hym better chaste."	*discipline*

	The goodman answered agayn,	*master of the household*
	And said, "Dame, I shall thee sayn,	*I shall tell you*

He is butt yong of age.
He shall abide with me a yere
35   Till he be strenger   *stronger*
To wynne better wage.

"We have a man, a strong freke,   *man*
Which kepyth on the feld our nete,   *cattle*
And slepith half the day.
40   He shall com home, be Mary myld;   *by*
The boy shall into the feld
And kepe hem if he may."   *them if he can*

The goodwiff was glad verament   *truly*
And therto sone she assent   *to that; assented*
45   And said, "It is best."
Upon the morowe when it was day
Forth went the litell boye:
To the feld he was preste.   *He was ready for the field*

Upon his bak he bare his staff.   *bore*
50   Of no man he ne gaff: *He cared for nobody's opinion*
He was mery inowgh.
He went forth, the soth to sayn,
Till he com on the playn.   *came; clearing*
His dynner oute he drewe.

55   When he sawe it was so bad
Lytill lust therto he had   *appetite*
And putt it up anon.   *stowed it away at once*
Iwysse, he was nott for to wyte.   *Certainly; not to blame*
He seyde, "I will ete but a lyghte   *little*
60   Tyl nyght that I come home."

Uppon an hill he hym set.
An olde man therwith he met,
Cam walkyng be the wey.
He seide, "God spede, good son."
65   He seide, "Sir, welcome,
The sothe for to saye."   *truth*

The olde man was hungrid sore   *very hungry*
And sayde, "Son, hast thou any mete astore   *saved up*
That thou mayst geve me?"
70   The boye seide, "So God me save,
Thow shalt se suche as I have,
And welcome shalt thou be."

The lytill boye gaffe hym suche as he had   *gave*
And bad him ete and be glad   *encouraged him to*
75   And seide, "Welcome trewly."
The olde man, for to pleise,
He ete and made him at eise,   *made himself comfortable*
And sayde, "Sir, gramarcy.   *thanks*

"For the mete that thow hast geve me   *given*
80   I shall gyffe thee gyftis thre
That shall not be forgete."   *forgotten*
The boye sayde, "As I trowe,   *believe*
It were best that I hadde a bowe
Byrdys for to shete."   *shoot*

85   "Bowe and bolte thou shalt have ryve   *arrow; quickly*
That shall laste thee all thi lyve
And ever alyke mete.   *always equally suitable*
Shete whersoever thou wilt,
Thow shalt never fayle of it: *miss it*
90   The markys thou shalte kepe."   *You will hit the targets*

The bowe anon in hand he felt
And his boltys under his belt.   *arrows*
Lyghtely than he drewe.   *Easily*
He saide, "Had I now a pipe,   *If I had*
95   Thouh it were never so lite   *No matter how little*
Than were I mery inowe."

"A pipe thou shalte have also:
True mesure it shall goo,   *tune*
I put thee owte of dowte.
100 All that ever that pipe dothe here,
They shall not hemself after astere   *restrain themselves afterwards*
But lepe and daunce abowte.

"Let se, what shall that other be?
For thou shalt have yeftis thre   *three gifts*
105 As I thee hyght before."   *promised*
The boye than lowde lowgh
And sayde, "Be my trowth I have inowe;
I will desire no more."

The olde man saide to hym, "Aplyght,   *Truly*
110 Thow shalt have as I thee hyghte.
Therfore sey on, let se."
The lytill boye seyde full sone,

"I have a steppemoder at home.
She is a shrowe to me.   *shrew*

115   "When my fadir gewyth me mete   *gives*
      She wold the devill had me cheke,   *choked*
      She stareth so in my face.
      When she lokyth on me so
      Yef she myght lette a rappe goo   *Grant; a fart*
120   That myght rynge all the place."

      The olde man sayde to him tho,   *then*
      "Yef she loke on thee so   *If*
      She shall begynne to blowe.
      All that maye her heere,
125   They shall hem not astere
      But laugh upon a rowe."   *all together*

      "Farewele," saide the olde man,
      "No more, than, I ne can,   *I can do no more, then*
      But take my leve of thee.
130   Allmyghty God that best may
      Spede yow both nyghte and daye."
      "Gramarcy, syr," sayde he.

      Than aftyrward whan it was nyghte
      Home went the boy full ryght.   *straight*
135   This was his ordinaunce: *arrangement*
      He toke his pipe and began to blow;
      Than all his bestis on a row   *one after another*
      Abowte him begun to daunce.   *began*

      The boye went pypyng thorow the towne.
140   The bestis folowid him be the sowne   *sound*
      Unto his fadirs close.   *enclosure*
      Whan he was come home
      He beshet hem everychone   *shut every one of them up*
      And into the halle he goos.   *hall (main room)*

145   His fader at sooper sat.
      The boye spyed wele that
      And spake to him anoon.
      He seyde, "Welcome.   *He (the father)*
      Where be my bestys, good son?
150   Hast thou broughte hem home?"

      "Ye, fadir, in good faye,   *Yes; in good faith (certainly)*
      I have kepte hem all this daye,

And now they are shet."   *enclosed*
A capons legge he toke him tho   *gave him then*
155   And sayde, "Jak, that is wele do.
Boy, thou shalte fare the bet."   *eat better [because of your good work]*

That grevid his dame herte sore: *annoyed his mother's heart deeply*
Ever she was tenid more and more.   *enraged*
Than she starid in his face.
160   And she let go a gret blaste
That every man therof was agaste
That was in that place.

Ever they lowgh and had good game.   *amusement*
The wyffe wex red for shame;   *turned*
165   She wolde fayne be agon.   *would gladly have been gone*
Jak seide, "Wele I wote   *I well know*
I trow this game were wele smote   *this target would have been well hit*
Though it had be a gon stone."   *Even if it had been [with] a pellet*

Ful egerly lokid she on him tho.   *Very fiercely*
170   Another rappe she let goo;
And ever she awey went.   *each time she turned away*
Jak seid, "Will ye se?
My moder can let a pelet fle   *discharge a missile*
Or ever she astent."   *Before she ever stops*

175   Ever they lough and had good game.   *entertainment*
The wyffe went awaye for shame:
She was in moche sorow.
The goodman seide, "Go thi weye,
For it is tyme, be my faye:
180   Thyn arce is not to borowe."   *Your backside is not a satisfactory witness*

Aftir that, will ye here,
Tho into that howse cam a frere   *Then; friar*
That lay ther al nyghte.
Owre dame thoughth him a saynte.
185   Anon to him she made a pleynte
And tolde to hym anon ryght: *straight away*

"I have a boy that in this howse wons;   *lives*
He is a shrew for the nons.   *brat for sure*
He doth me moche care.   *causes me a lot of trouble*
190   I may not loke ons hym upon   *cannot glance at him once*
But I have a shame, be Seynt Jhon;   *Without being embarrassed*
I telle the how I fare.

  "Mete hym in the fylde tomorow.

  Loke thou bete hym and do hym sorowe   *Make sure*

195 And make the boye lame.

  Iwis it is a cursed byche.   *Certainly*

  I trow the boye be some wycche: *believe*

  He dothe me moche shame."

  The frere seid, "I will wete."   *I will find out [if he is a witch]*

200 She prayde him not forgete,

  "For that will greve me sore."

  The frere seide, "In good faye,

  But I lasshe wele that boye   *Unless*

  Truste me never more."

205 Upon the morow the boye arose

  And into the felde he goos.

  His bestis gan he dryve.

  The frere went oute at the gate;

  He went he had come too late   *believed*

210 And ran aftyr full ryve.   *quickly*

  Whan he cam into that londe   *countryside*

  The lytill boye ther he founde

  And his bestis echon.   *every one*

  He seide, "Boye, God gif thee shame.   *give*

215 What haste thou do to thy dame?

  Have do and tel me anon.   *Stop*

  "But yf thou can escuse thee the bet *Unless you can excuse yourself really well*

  Be my trouth thi narce shall be bete.   *your ass; beaten*

  I will no lenger abyde."   *longer wait*

220 The boye seide, "What aylith thee?   *What is wrong with you*

  My dame farith as wele as ye.

  Thow haste no cause to chyde."

  The boye sayde, "Will thou wite   *Do you want to know*

  How fele byrdis I can shete   *many; shoot*

225 And other thyngis all?

  I trowe though I be but lyght   *believe; only little*

  Yonder birde shall I smyte

  And geve it thee I shall."   *give*

  Ther sat a byrde on a brere.   *brier*

230 "Shete on that," quod the frere,   *Shoot at; said*

  "That lystyth me to se."   *I'd like to see that*

  The boye smote it on the hede

That it felle doune ther dede:
It myghte no lenger flee.   *fly*

235 The frere into the hegge went   *hedge*
     And the birde up he hente   *he picked up*
     As it was for to don.   *As needed to be done*
     The boye leyde aside his bowe
     Full hastly, as I trowe,
240 And tooke his pype sone.

     Whan the frere the pipe herde,
     As a wodman he ferde   *lunatic he behaved*
     And began to lepe abowte.
     Amonge the bowis smale and grete
245 Aboute lyghtly gan he lepe,
     But he cowde nowhere owte.   *But he could nowhere [get] out*

     Bremblis cracched hym in the face   *Brambles scratched*
     And eke in many another place.   *also*
     His body began to blede.
250 He rent his clothis by and by,   *right away*
     His girdill and his chapelery   *belt; scapular*
     And all his other weede.   *clothing*

     Ever the boye blewe and lewh amonge.   *laughed in between*
     How the frere lepe and wronge!   *leapt and twisted*
255 He leped wonder hye.   *amazingly high*
     Than sayed the boye and sware withall,   *swore besides*
     "Be my trowth, here is a sporte ryall   *entertainment fit for a king*
     For any man to se with yee."   *eye*

     Ever the frere hyld up his hande
260 And callid to hym amonge   *at the same time*
     And prayed hym, "Be stylle,   *quiet*
     And here my trowth I plyghte to thee,
     Thou shalte never have harme of me:
     I will do thee non ylle."

265 The boye seide to hym that tyde,   *that time*
     "Crepe owte on that other syde,   *the far side*
     And hye thee thou were go.   *hurry yourself to be gone*
     My dame made a pleynte to thee   *complaint*
     And now I can non other se: *I can see no alternative*
270 Thow must compleyne to her also."

     The frere oute of the hegge wente,
     All to-raged and to-rente   *Very ragged and ripped to shreds*

And torne on every syde.
Unneth he had any clowte   *He hardly had a rag*
275   For to wende hys body abowte   *To twist around his body*
His arsse for to hyde.

Bothe his fyngers and his face
Were crached in many a place   *scratched*
And berayed all with bloode.   *smeared*
280   Every man that hym gan se,
They were hym fayne for to fle.   *glad*
They went the frere had bene woode.   *thought; crazy*

Whan he cam to his oste   *lodging*
Of his jorney made he no boste.   *day's work*
285   He was both tame and tale.   *tame and meek*
Moche sorow in hert he had,
For every man was adrad   *frightened*
Whan he came into the hall.

The goodwyf sayed, "Where hast thou be?
290   In shrewde place as semyth me,   *dangerous*
Me thynke be thyn araye."   *outfit*
He seid, "I have be with thy son;
The devill of helle hym overcom,
For certis I ne maye."   *I certainly can't*

295   Than cam in the goodman.
"Lo, sir," seid the goodwyf than,
"Here is a shrewid araye.   *nasty state of affairs*
Thy son that is to thee so leef and dere   *so beloved*
Hath almoste slayne this holy frere,
300   Alas, and weleaweye."

The goodman seide, "Benedicité!   *Gracious*
What hath my boye don to thee?
Tell me anon blyve."   *right away*
The frere seyde, "Be Seynt Jame,
305   I have dauncid in the devillis name."
The goodman seyde to hym belyve —   *quickly*

These woordis seyde he tho:
"And thou haddist lorne thi lyf so   *If you had lost your life that way*
Thou haddist be in grete synne."   *You would have been*
310   The frere seide, "I shall tell why:
Me thoughte the pipe went so merely   *merrily*
That I cowde not blynne."   *stop*

"Be my trowth," than seide he,   *(i.e., the father)*
"Than is that a mery gle,   *instrument*
315   Or ellys thou art to blame.
That pipe will I here truly."   *I really want to hear*
The frere saide, "So will not I,   *I do not want to*
Be God and be Seynte Jame."

Afterward whan it was nyghte,
320   Homeward went the boy ryght   *directly*
As it was for to done.
As soon as he came into the hall
Anon his fader did hym call
And seide, "Boye, come heder anon."   *hither*

325   "Herke boy, now thou arte here,
What hast thou don to this frere?
Telle me withowte lettynge."   *delay*
"Fader," he seide, "in good faye,
I did ryght not nought to hym this day   *I didn't do a single thing*
330   But pipe him a sprynge."   *dance tune*

"That pipe," he seide, "will I here."
"Nay, for God," quod the frere,   *before; said*
"That were an evill thynge."
The goodman sayde, "Ys, be Goddis grace."   *Yes*
335   The frere seide, "Alas, alas";
His handis he gan wrynge.

"For Goddis love," quod the frere,
"And ye will the pipe here,   *If you want to hear the pipe*
Bynde me to the poste.
340   Iwis I can no better rede: *know no better advice*
I wote I shall be dede.   *know*
My lyffe wyll sone be loste."

Ropys anon they had in hond
And to the poste they hym bond
345   That stode in the hall.
Tho that at souper satte   *Those*
They had good game and lough therat
And seid, "Now the frere shall not fall."

Than spake the goodman.   *spoke up*
350   To his son he seyde than,
"Pipe on what thou wylte."
"All redy, fader," seide he,

"I shall yow shewe of my gle: *some of my music*
Ye shall have a fytte."   *tune*

355   As soon as the pype wente
They myghte not hemselfe stent   *stop themselves*
But began to daunce and lepe.
All that ever myght it here,
They myght not themself asstere,   *control themselves*
360   But worled on a hepe.   *whirled in a throng*

Tho that at souper satte,   *Those*
Over the table anon they lepte
And sterid in that stounde.   *moved; moment*
They that sat on the forme   *bench*
365   Had no tyme hem to turne;
They were borne to the grounde.

The goodman was in dispeyre:
Streyte he sterte owte of the cheyre   *Immediately he bounded*
With an hevy chere.   *sad expression*
370   Som sterte over the stoke   *the post*
And brake her shynnes ageyn the bloke,   *broke their shins against the post*
And som felle in the fyre.

The goodwyfe cam in behynde.
She began to lepe and wynde   *wriggle*
375   And sharpely for to shake.   *quickly*
But when she lokid on litill Jak,
Her arsse to hym spake
And lowde began to crake.   *thunder*

The frere was allmoste loste:
380   He beete his hede ageyne the poste.
He had non other grace.   *luck*
The rope rubbid off the skynne
I woote the blode ranne doune be hym   *on*
In many dyvers place.   *different*

385   The boye went pypyng in the strete
And after hym hoole all the hepe: *the whole crowd*
They myghte never astentt.   *stop*
They went owte at the dore so thyke   *in such a throng*
That eche man fell in others neke,   *neck*
390   So myghtely oute they wente.   *forcefully*

They that dwellyd therby   *nearby*
Harde the pype sekyrly   *certainly*

	In place ther they sat.	*where*
	Anon they lepte over the hacche;	*lower half-door*
395	They had no tome to undo the lacche,	*leisure*
	They were so lothe to lette.	*reluctant to wait*

	And tho that laye in ther bedde,	*those*
	Anon they hyld up ther hede,	*held*
	Bothe the lesse and eke the more.	*Both low-ranking people and also high*
400	In the strete, as I hard saye,	*heard*
	In feyth they toke the ryght waye	
	As nakyd as they were bore.	*born*

	Whan thay wer gaderid all abowte,	*gathered*
	Than was ther a grete route	*assemblage*
405	In the medyll of the strete.	
	Some were lame and myghte not goo,	*walk*
	Yt they hoppid aboute also	*Yet*
	And some began to crepe.	

	The boye sayde, "Fader, wyll ye reste?"	
410	"In feyth," he seide, "I holde it beste,"	
	With ryght a good chere.	
	"Make an ende whan thou wilte.	
	In feyth this was the meryest fytte	
	That I hard this sewyn yere."	*in the last seven years*

415	Whan the pype went no more	
	Than they amerveylid sore	*very much marveled*
	Of the governaunce.	*About the behavior*
	"Seynt Mary," sayde some,	
	"Where is all this myrth become	*What became of all this music*
420	That made us for to daunce?"	

	Every man was of good chere.	
	Thank the goodwyfe and the frere:	*Credit*
	They were all dysmayde.[1]	
	He that hath not all his will,	*He who does not get what he wants*
425	Be it good or be it ylle,	
	He holdyth hym not apayde.	*does not feel satisfied*

	Now have ye herd all insame	*together*
	How Jak pleyde with his dame	
	And pypid before the frere.	
430	Hym lykyd nothyng the boyes lay;	*The boy's tune pleased him not at all*

---

[1] Lines 421–23: That is, *everyone else's pleasure is due to the goodwife and the friar, who are humiliated*

Therfor he toke his leve and went his wey
Somedele with hevy chere.   *With a somewhat sober face*

The goodman norysshyd forth his chylde.   *continued to bring up*
The stepmoder was to hym mylde.
435 And fare wele all in fere: *together*
     That Lorde yow kepe, frendis all,
     That dranke both eysill and gall,
     Holy God in His empere.
                    Amen.

Here endyth the tale of Jak and his stepdame

EXPLANATORY NOTES TO JACK AND HIS STEPDAME

ABBREVIATIONS: **A**: Oxford, Bodleian Library, Article Arch.A.F.83(7) (printed by Edward Alde, ca. 1617); **C**: Cambridge, Cambridge University Library, Article Sel.5.21 (printed by Wynkyn de Worde, ca. 1510–13); **D**: Oxford, Bodleian Library, Article S.Seld.d.45 (printed by Edward Alde, ca. 1584–89); **F**: London, British Library, Article C.57aa.13 (printed by [Elizabeth] Alde, 1626); **M**: London, British Library, Article C.125.dd.15 (7) (fragment printed by William Middleton ca. 1545); **MED**: *Middle English Dictionary*; **MS(S)**: manuscript(s); **MS B**: Percy Folio Manuscript: London, British Library, MS Additional 27879; **MS E**: Cambridge, Cambridge University Library, MS Ee.4.35; **MS P**: Aberystwyth, National Library of Wales, MS Brogynton 10; **MS Q**: Oxford, Balliol College, MS 354; **MS R**: Oxford, Bodleian Library, MS Rawlinson C.86 (MS Bodley 11951); **OE**: Old English; **OED**: *Oxford English Dictionary*.

1–2	Jesus Christ, slowly dying on the cross in the process of crucifixion, would have suffered intolerable thirst as crucified convicts usually did. His executioners held up to him on a pole a sponge soaked in a bitter or sour liquid to torment him further: the alternative was to drink and be sickened, wrenching his body against the nails holding him if he vomited, or resist drinking despite his thirst. The poem talks of "eysell and gall," vinegar and bile, to reconcile the conflicting accounts in the four Gospels of what the liquid was. Matthew 27:34 speaks of wine mixed with bile; Mark 15:36, Luke 23:36, and John 19:29 of vinegar.
14	*his moder*. The mother in question is one of the boy's stepmothers; compare lines 8–10.
25	Here as elsewhere *gan* is a past tense marker, followed by an infinitive: "she gan say" means "she said."
40	*be*. Scribe A sometimes, and Scribe B almost always, uses *be* for *by*; for Scribe B the exception is at line 250, in the phrase *by and by*, in rhyming position.
	Mary myld. "Mary mild" is of course the Virgin Mary, mother of Jesus.
41	Here the verb *shall* implies a verb of motion, as it sometimes does: "the boy shall go."
37–42	The father's proposal is to send his son to replace the herdsman who takes the cattle to the field to graze, stays with them there, and brings them in at night — a light day's work. The man can then be brought back to use his strength in labor all day.

51–54   *inowgh/drewe*. These rhyme words, which do not look as if they rhyme at all and do not rhyme in Modern English (*enough/drew*), could be exact rhymes in Middle English on long *o* or *ou* plus a guttural continuant or could represent a rhyme on *enow/drow* (a form of the past tense of *draw* without its earlier guttural). The "ew" spelling form of *drew* emerged in the fourteenth century, but the "ough" and "ow" spellings and pronunciations of the past tense of *draw* persisted throughout the fifteenth century(see *OED draw* v.). See also the rhymes at lines 93–96 (*drewe/inowe*), and 106–07 (*lowgh/inowe*).

81–84   Again the rhyme *forgete/shete*, representing modern *forgotten/shoot*, looks improbable. But *shete* was the form of the infinitive of the verb derived from OE and died out in the fifteenth century, superseded by *shote*; and *forgete* was one of several possible forms of the past participle of the verb *to forget*.

101   *astere*. Apparently for *stere* (modern "steer"), with a prefix, is not attested in *MED* or *OED* but appears to be deliberate since it is repeated at line 125 below, as well as at line 359, which is supplied from MS Q.

116   *cheke*. This idiosyncratic form of the past participle of *choke* is not attested in *MED* or *OED*.

179–80   *For it is tyme, be my faye / Thyn arce is not to borowe*. These are difficult lines. In idioms such as "Saint John to borowe" the phrase has a legal connotation, the saint being called upon "as witness," "sponsor," or "guarantor." Perhaps the sense here is, "Your backside has a great deal to say but is not a good choice of speaker on your behalf." The St. John being sworn by here and at line 191 is likely the apostle John, who was believed in the Middle Ages to be the same John as the author of the fourth Gospel.

184   *Owre dame*. That is, the woman of the house.

196–97   *byche/wycche*. Apparently both terms could be applied to males at this time: see *MED bicche* 2b, *OED bitch* n.¹, 2b; *MED wicch(e)*, (n.) (a); *OED witch* n.¹. But the evidence is not good beyond this poem for the use of *bitch* for males.

218   The phrase *thin arce* becomes *thi narce* by a process called metanalysis. It is the same process by which *an ekename* became (and stayed) *a nickname*.

229   A brier is a thorny bush, likely a blackberry; this one would form part of a hedge of mixed trees and bushes, mostly thorny, fencing in the field. The boy is very cunning in putting his two first gifts to good use, using the bow and arrow to entice the friar into a vulnerable situation, but the friar is too easily distracted from his mission for any plausibility. However, in defense of the poet, plausibility is not required in a story involving three magic gifts.

285   *both tame and tale*. Tale here seems to have the meaning of *tame*, including *meek* or *humble*. *OED* lists no such definition, but examples under *tall* A. Adj.1. +1 ("Quick, prompt, ready, active") are susceptible to such a reading and *OED* says the sense in its quotations is doubtful. *MED tal* adj. (e) has more and better examples but is still tentative about the meaning "?humble, meek."

300   Like "alas," "wellaway" is a cry of sorrow that has no modern equivalent.

304   *Be Seynt Jame*. The St. James in question is most probably one of the apostles, James the son of Zebedee and brother of the apostle John, or James the son of Alphaeus. But in any case, the name is chosen more for the rhyme than any particular significance.

308–09   The goodman either thinks that death by dancing would have been voluntary, thus suicidal, and therefore the friar would have died in a state of sin, or he takes the friar's "in the devillis name" literally and thinks of the dancing as a form of devil worship or demonic possession. Normally "in the devil's name" would be a simple exclamation or intensifier.

310   That is, "I shall tell why I kept on dancing until I was ragged and bleeding."

332   *for God* is an oath, "before God."

367   *The goodman was in dispeyre*. The experience of being subject to the pipe is apparently unpleasant while it lasts (compare lines 241–61), and its sound is pleasant only in retrospect (lines 311–12, 412–14, 419–21).

414   At this point, the endings of the various manuscripts and printed texts begin to differ from each other. Only three manuscripts, MSS R, Q, and P, have the next two stanzas, and only MSS R and Q have the two after that, while MS P ends instead with the following moralization:

> Hyt ys every good wyffys wone
> For to love hyr husbondes sone
> Yn well and eke yn woo.
> In olde termys it is fownd
> He hat lowythe me lovythe my hound
> And my servaunt also.
>
> So schuld every good child
> Be to hys moder meke and myld.
> Be good yn every degree.
> All women that love her husbondes sone,
> Yn hevyn blys schall be her wone,
> Amen, amen, for charyte.

The other versions end with a redundant court scene where the boy humiliates the friar and stepmother once more. There are many differences among these other texts. MS E, clearly the earliest of them if one accepts Thomas Ohlgren's argument (mentioned in the introduction to the poem, p. 22 above) that the Richard Calle who owned the manuscript was the Pastons' steward, is exceptionally difficult to read and make sense of, and the versions in printed texts C and D, fragment M, and then A and F, with the MS B version based on a text like A and F, differ from each other and from MS E too much to make it possible to represent them all here. Interested researchers can track them down in my Garland edition of *Ten Fifteenth-Century Comic Poems* (1985).

438   *empere*. Empire? Or perhaps an early attempt at Englishing *empyreum*, the Latin term for the uppermost heaven, the fiery dwelling place of God?

TEXTUAL NOTES TO JACK AND HIS STEPDAME

COPY-TEXT: Oxford, Bodleian Library MS Rawlinson C.86 (Bodley 11951), fols. 52r–59r.

ABBREVIATIONS: **C**: Cambridge, Cambridge University Library, Article Sel.5.21 (printed by Wynkyn de Worde, ca. 1510–13); **D**: Oxford, Bodleian Library, Article S. Seld.d.45 (printed by Edward Alde, ca. 1584–89); *MED*: *Middle English Dictionary*; **MS(S)**: manuscript(s); **MS E**: Cambridge, Cambridge University Library, MS Ee.4.35; **MS P**: Aberystwyth, National Library of Wales, MS Brogynton 10; **MS Q**: Oxford, Balliol College, MS 354; **MS R**: Oxford, Bodleian Library, MS Rawlinson C.86 (MS Bodley 11951); *OED*: *Oxford English Dictionary*.

title	The original title in MS R is "The Tale of Jacke and his Stepdame."
16	The word *lost* is missing in MS R, though present in the other versions. Emendation for sense.
38	MS R reads: *Which kepyth on the feld our ~~shepe~~ nete*.
58	This line is at the end of the substitute outer folio and concludes the work of Scribe A.
79	MS R reads: *For the mete this thow has geve me*.
87–89	In this area of the poem MS R is different from all other versions, and for lines 87–89 has the sequence "At euery keyte that thou mete / Loke thou kepe thi pylt / And shote where at thou wylt." If "keyte" is "kite," as *MED* says it is, then "pylt" cannot be "pilt" meaning "thrust," as both *OED* and *MED* say: shooting at a bird with a bow and arrow does not involve thrusting but drawing. Perhaps, since kites are notorious predators of young poultry, the underlying sequence of this puzzling set of lines means "Be careful to guard your poult (young chicken), and shoot wherever you want at any kite that you meet." On this hypothesis, the rhyme would have been on "pulte" and "wult." Reproduced here is line 87 from printed versions C and D. MS Q has "And euery while mete"; MS P has "And euer to the a lyche mete." Both these readings are close in meaning to the line as C and D have it. Lines 88–89 represent MS Q and to a lesser degree are close to MS P. The version in MS R is the least satisfactory. But the gist of all of the versions is that the magical bow and its arrows will hit the target, no matter how bad the aim of the archer is.
107	MS R reads: *And sayde be my be my trowth I haue inowe*. Emendation for sense.
117	*stareth*: MS R reads: *She stare so in my face*. Emendation for sense.
171	MS R reads: *And ~~she~~ euer she a vey went*. Emendation for sense.
175	MS R reads: *Euer they lough and good game*. Emendation for sense.

178	The line begins with "afterwar the," perhaps through eyeskip down to line 181.
194	MS R reads: *Loke thou bete hym an and do hym sorowe.*
208	MS R reads: *vent.* Emendation for sense.
216	MS R missing: *anon.* The word is supplied from all other versions. Emendation for rhyme.
315	A slash mark separates *art/to*; the words are crammed together in MS R.
324	MS R reads: *An seide boye come heder anon.*
352	MS R reads: *All redy fader he seide than he.*
358–60	These lines are missing in MS R, supplied from MS Q.
371	*ageyn the bloke*: MS R reads: *ageyn bloke.* Emendation for sense.
372	MS R reads: *And som in the fyre felle*; all others end the line with the word *fire*, as necessary for the rhyme.
402	MS R reads: *borne*; MSS P, Q, and E have *bore* or *bor*, a possible form that provides an exact rhyme.
414	This is the end of the body of the tale shared by all versions. After this, only MSS R, Q, and P have the next two stanzas, and only MSS R and Q have the two after that. See Explanatory Notes for more details.
427	MS R reads: *Now haue he ye herd all insame.*

FIENDS AND RISEN CORPSES: INTRODUCTION

Three of our tales fall apparently into the realm of necromancy. In *The Lady Prioress* a priest performing a clandestine funeral service is horrified when the devil rushes into the chapel, and further terrified when the corpse jumps up and bolts. *Dane Hew, Munk of Leicestre* is the story of a corpse that will not stay dead and is killed repeatedly, sometimes more than once by the same person. And in *The Freiris of Berwik*, a solemn ceremony of black magic is performed to raise a fiend. In all three tales, however, there is only human ingenuity at work in what is really a purely naturalistic chain of events.

The plot of *The Lady Prioress* combines a widespread story about a woman with multiple unwanted suitors who gets rid of them by assigning each one a role that will frighten the others with another story about the corpse of a man that is forbidden burial because of his unpaid debts. Our heroine sends off the knight who seeks to prove his devotion to lie all night in a chapel in the woods, sewn in a sheet like a corpse; the priest to the same chapel to bury her cousin, whose burial has been forbidden because he owes money; and the burgess, or town merchant, to the chapel dressed as a devil to stop a burial service being held for a man who owes her priory a sum of gold. The suitors terrify each other and fail in their respective tasks; the next day the Prioress sends the three of them packing and also blackmails the third into providing a healthy endowment for her priory.

The story of the multiple suitors has many medieval analogues, the best known today and the earliest being the story of Francesca, Rinuccio, and Alessandro, the first tale of the ninth day in Boccaccio's *Decameron*. Pestered by two suitors, the lady Francesca sends word to one, Rinuccio, to take the place of a corpse which she says is to be carried to her house that night. She sends word to the other, Alessandro, to go fetch the corpse. As Alessandro is carrying Rinuccio in his graveclothes through the dark streets to her house, they are surprised by the watch and both flee, thus forfeiting any claim to Francesca's love by failing to do what she has ordered.

An oral Netherlandish analogue is closer to our tale in that it is the fear of demons and ghosts that afflicts the suitors, unlike the fear of the officers of the watch that scatters Rinuccio and Alessandro. The tale is recorded by Benjamin Thorpe in *Northern Mythology*, vol. 3 (London: Lumley, 1852), pp. 217–18. The Long Wapper (a malicious spirit) takes the form of a promiscuous lady of Antwerp. The first of her lovers is promised her hand if he will go to the churchyard and sit on the transverse of the great cross. The second is sent, with the same promise, to lie in a coffin under the cross. The third is sent to knock three times on the coffin lid, and the fourth must run three times around the cross, rattling an iron chain. The first three lovers drop dead from fright, and the fourth returns to the lady with the news of the three corpses. But the lady knows nothing of the Long Wapper's scheme and kills herself in remorse, and in this respect is considerably unlike the lady of our poem.

There are other early versions of the story that are like our poem in having three wooers (rather than the two or four of the first-mentioned analogues) at the gravesite frightening each other: Johannes Pauli's tale number 220 in his *Schimpf und Ernst* (1522; ed. by Johannes Bolte [Berlin: Stubenraugh, 1924]); Nicholas de Troyes's second tale, *Les Trois galants au cimitière*, in his *Grand parangon des nouvelles nouvelles (choix)* (1536; ed. by Krystyna Kasprzyk [Paris: M. Didier, 1970]); and the anonymous farce *Les Trois amoureux de la croix* in *Recueil de farces (1450–1550)*, ed. Tissier. In none of these stories is the lady a nun: in Pauli she is an ugly but rich widow who knows the suitors to be after her money; in Nicholas she is unmarried; in the farce she is a married woman. The roles played by the suitors vary from version to version: in Pauli a corpse, angel, and devil; in Nicholas a corpse, gendarme, and devil; and only in the farce, as in *The Lady Prioress*, a priest, corpse, and devil. The denouement in Pauli's tale and that in Nicholas are similar to that in *The Lady Prioress*; but in the farce, the suitors eventually recognize each other and give up their folly out of a sense that the lady is not worth having. No clear lines of relationship and ancestry emerge out of the similarities and differences in these stories.

The anonymous poet has taken cues from other literature, the most obvious being from Chaucer for the suggestion of a prioress as an out-of-place romance heroine. Another influence may account for the Prioress's fiction of the man whose corpse is being forbidden burial because of his debts. A corpse who has been denied burial but is then treated reverently by a pious hero is a recurring folklore motif (see *ATU*, motif 505), a motif that goes back at least as far as the book of Tobit. But it is also a prominent feature of *Sir Amadace*, a late fourteenth-century romance of the northwest Midlands. In *The Lady Prioress*, as in *Sir Amadace*, the corpse lies on a bier in the chapel, with two candles burning beside it; in *Sir Amadace* the corpse is refused burial because of debt. It seems likely that the poet had this particular romance in mind as he wrote. In making the knight vow to stay in the chapel all night, the poet may have remembered *The Avowyng of King Arthur*, an early fifteenth-century romance in which the three principal characters make vows, Gawain's being to watch all night at Tarn Wadling. *The Avowyng*, *Sir Amadace*, and *The Awntyrs off Arthur* (a late fourteenth-century alliterative romance with a horrifying ghost returned from the dead and a stanzaic form somewhat like that of *The Lady Prioress*) all appear in the first section of Princeton University, MS Ireland Blackburn. MS Ireland Blackburn probably originated at Hale, southern Lancashire, and is dated in the third quarter of the fifteenth century: see Ralph Hanna's introduction to his edition *The Awntyrs off Arthure at the Terne Wathelyn* (Manchester: Manchester University Press, 1974), pp. 6–7. The last potential influence is the romantic literature of questing knights in general, which provides the knight in this tale with the comically pointless service he has to offer in contrast to the religious function of the priest and the monetary protectionism of the burgess.

Dane Hew, Munk of Leicestre tells of a lecherous monk who is manipulated by a virtuous wife, then murdered by her outraged husband. His corpse is then shuffled furtively by night from the murder scene to his abbey, from his abbey back to the murder scene, and from there towards a millpond in a sack. When the sack containing Dane Hew's corpse is switched with a stolen sack containing the miller's bacon, the thieves promptly return the sack with the corpse to the miller's rafters. In a final blaze of chivalric glory the dead monk, tied to a horse with a lance under his arm, charges the abbot and is dragged from his horse and beaten to death again. The basic folktale motif is of a corpse (often a hunchback, but not so here or in the closest analogues) that is "killed" several times. *Dane Hew* is most closely related to several earlier French *fabliaux*, though none of these is clearly its source: *Le dit dou soucretain* by Jean le Chapelain, *Du Segretain moine*, and *Du Segretain ou du moine*. These stories can be found as number 74 in the *Nouveau recueil complet des fabliaux (NRCF)*, ed. Willem van Noomen (Assen: van Gorcum, 1993), 7:1–189. The French stories differ in certain minor details from the English version, and in every case but one the French stories are more detailed, more rationalized. In the French versions, the wife who is the focus of Dane Hew's lust is given a motive for her pretended yielding to the monk's bribery: she and her husband have fallen into poverty. The monk's corpse is not simply leaned against the abbey wall but perched on a privy in the abbey. The swapping of the corpse for a side of bacon is also more plausibly done in the French versions. But in *Dane Hew*, the horse that carries the monk's corpse onto the grounds of the abbey is after the abbot's mare, so that both his movements and the abbot's terror are more understandable. Because of this detail of the horse's pursuit of the mare, which does not occur in any of the extant French *fabliaux* but which does occur in a late fifteenth-century Italian *novellino* by Masuccio Salernitano (the first in *Il Novellino di Masuccio Salernitano*), Archer Taylor posits a common French ancestor to the English *Dane Hew* and the Italian *novellino* in "Dane Hew, Munk of Leicestre." Taylor also argues that the later occurrences of the tale in English are all descended from Thomas Heywood's story "The Fair Lady of Norwich" in his *History of Women* (1624), and it in turn is descended from Masuccio's *novellino*, retaining features which *Dane Hew* does not. *Dane Hew* has therefore no direct descendants but many analogues.

The Freiris of Berwik is a comparatively long tale, with more richly developed characters and situation than the others in this collection. The plot begins with two friars, old Allane and younger Robert, returning home to Berwick after an excursion into the countryside and seeking lodging at the house of Symon Lawrear when night approaches while they are still well outside the town walls. Symon's wife Alesone refuses them lodging on the grounds that her husband is away from home and she does not want to be blamed for having the friars under her roof in his absence, but old Friar Allane plays upon her sympathies with his fatigue. She agrees to let them stay but insists they must be closed up in the loft. Friar Robert, who is curious, pierces a hole in the floor of the loft and sees her real reason for getting them out of the way: extensive preparations for a feast as she welcomes her lover, Friar Johine, from a rival order. When Symon knocks at the gate shortly after Friar Johine settles in for the evening, Friar Robert sees Alesone hide Johine under a trough and get her maid to stow the rich food and drink in a cupboard. Alesone lets Symon stand and call for a long while before she lets him in and insists she has nothing good for him to eat. A strategic cough from Friar Robert leads to the two friars in the loft being invited down to share Symon's cold leftovers. Friar Robert proposes to amend the meal by practices he has learned in Paris. After a display of his magic procedures, Alesone is visibly surprised to find her cupboard full of excellent food and wine. A night's carousing follows, and then Symon wants to know how Robert did it. He asks to see the fiend who is Robert's servant. Robert reluctantly agrees to bring him forth, dressed as a Black Friar, with his hood pulled over his fiendish face so that Symon will not be too terrified. Robert performs an impressive conjuration, and the fiend arises from under the trough and dashes out the door, while Symon beats him with a cudgel and manages to knock himself out in the hullaballoo.

There are analogues to this tale that have a hidden lover and a stashed-away feast both exposed to an outraged husband, but not until the mid-fifteenth century is there one close to *The Freiris of Berwik* in its dramatic revelation and eating of the food, and release with physical punishment of the hidden lover, both without getting the wife into trouble and betraying her adultery: Hans Rosenblüt's "Von einem varnden Schüler."

The earliest known instance of the tale is the Latin version told in a collection of sermon *exempla* of the mid-fourteenth century, the *Scala Celi* of the Dominican "Johannes Junior," i.e., Johannes Gobius. This is a very brief version, as befits an *exemplum*, and lacks many of the details found in *The Freiris of Berwik*, but there is a clerk fed sour wine and hard bread by the wife, who then hustles him into a separate room because she expects her lover; the husband does come back unexpectedly and bang on the door; the woman gets her lover to hide under a bench; the clerk claims to be student of necromancy; he points to the hidden food; and he conjures the hidden devil to come forth in the form of a monk and leave but orders the husband and wife not to look at him because he is so horrible. No mention is made of such matters as how the clerk sees the assignation, where precisely the food is hidden, or how the lady feels about the situation, nor of the episode in which the husband strikes at the devil. The Latin *Scala Celi* was widely used across medieval Europe as a source of engaging *exempla* of human behavior and misbehavior for preaching friars to use in their sermons. The barebones plots would be expanded as appropriate. Although after some of the *exempla* there is a brief allegorical interpretation, for this one no moral is drawn by Gobius himself: the tale is simply given to be used as the preacher sees fit and is classed under the heading "De Clerico," "About a Clerk." There is an edition by Marie-Anne Polo de Beaulieu, *La Scala coeli de Jean de Gobi*; this tale is number 207.

The relation of the tale to the earlier medieval French genre of *fabliau* and Chaucer's revival of that genre in *The Canterbury Tales* has been the focus of most of the criticism on the poem. W. M. Hart gives a sensitive reading of *The Freiris of Berwik* in the context of genre history in "Fabliau and Popular Literature." C. S. Lewis, in perhaps the most influential comment on the poem, calls it "an excellent fabliau" and considers it "above all other attempts to continue the tradition of the comic *Canterbury Tales*" (*English Literature in the Sixteenth Century*, p. 106). R. D. S. Jack argues that a comparison of the poem and what he calls its closest analogue, the *fabliau Le Povre clerc*, shows "the Scottish author to be following many of the devices initiated or perfected by Chaucer in those of the *Canterbury Tales*, which have obvious connection with the fabliau" (p. 145). But actually the story in the *Scala Celi* is closer than that in *Le Povre Clerc*, where there is no pretense of necromancy, for example; but if the story in the *Scala Celi* is more closely analogous, the way the story is told is, as Jack makes a good case, similar to the way *fabliaux* are. R. James Goldstein follows Jack in placing *The Freiris of Berwik* within the *fabliau* tradition but adds some Lacanian observations and the comment that "The return to a threatened patriarchal order depends on a fiction so preposterous as to reveal the precariousness of that order" (p. 274).

The Freiris of Berwik does differ from the other poems in this collection in being racier, in one passage even obscene, as *fabliaux* characteristically are, and with the hapless husband continuing in his ignorance of his wife's adultery and with his head split open to boot. It is true, though, that as a group the English language comic poems, even this one, end with a correction of moral wrongs, whereas *fabliaux* often (though far from always) leave cleverness triumphant at the expense of virtue. Because *The Freiris of Berwik* is so often identified as a *fabliau*, a couple of important studies of that genre and its circulation are useful in considering how well it fits that designation, though readers need to remember the difference in context between fifteenth-century Scotland and the French-speaking world of the thirteenth century to which most *fabliaux* belong. A good place to begin is Charles Muscatine, *Old French Fabliaux*. For the perennial issue of what audience the genre appealed to, see particularly the discussion "The Social Background" in his chapter 2 (pp. 24–46), which opens with an historical review of the arguments for the genre as a bourgeois one, then an aristocratic one, and develops Muscatine's own persuasive argument that the genre had "a socially heterogeneous and mobile audience" (p. 46). A stringent structural definition of the genre is attempted in Mary Jane Stearns Schenck's monograph *The Fabliaux: Tales of Wit and Deception*. Readers interested in the issues of genre, feminism, and audience of *fabliaux* would do well to consult Simon Gaunt, "Genitals, Gender, and Mobility."

On gender issues specifically within *The Freiris of Berwik* there is an article by Evelyn S. Newlyn, "The Political Dimensions of Desire and Sexuality in Poems of the Bannatyne Manuscript." It is Newlyn's argument that the poem "demonstrates the enforcement of patriarchal control over a woman who attempts sexual autonomy" (p. 85).

Dane Hew (under the title *Dom Hugh*) and *The Lady Prioress* are both addressed by Derek Brewer in "Comedy of Corpses in Medieval Comic Tales." They are modernized by him and included in his *Medieval Comic Tales*, and commented upon in his introduction, specifically pp. xxxii–xxxiii. A useful comparison to some of the analogues of *The Lady Prioress* is to be found in an article by Ben Parsons and Bas Jongenelen, "Play of Three Suitors," especially pp. 60–61 on our poem and its feminist sympathies. All three poems are discussed as "true verse fabliaux" of the period by Peter Goodall in "English Fabliau after Chaucer," especially pp. 8–9 (quotation is from p. 8), and by Marie Nelson and Richard Thomson, "Fabliau," especially pp. 259–64. The three poems are mentioned in the more general generic discussions of Glenn Wright, "The Fabliau Ethos in the French and English *Octavian* Romances," p. 479n3; and Melissa Furrow, "Comic Tales." *The Lady Prioress* is addressed by John Hines, *Fabliau in English*, pp. 207–08; *Dane Hew* at pp. 208–09, and *The Freiris of Berwik* at pp. 209–10. But all of these are very brief and tangential discussions, and for *Dane Hew* and *The Lady Prioress* there is as yet very little criticism.

THE LADY PRIORESS: INTRODUCTION

MANUSCRIPT AND SCRIBE

The Lady Prioress appears in a single manuscript, London, British Library, MS Harley 78, fols. 74r–77v. Harley 78 is a collection of miscellaneous papers; some of the papers are poetry, some are matters of political or historical interest, and the sheets were probably not bound together until they were assembled from various sources by a sixteenth-century collector of old documents, John Stow. The part of the manuscript that concerns us is a booklet of only six leaves, on which are written both *The Lady Prioress*, which takes up six and a half pages of the twelve in the booklet, and a short poem by Lydgate known as "A Ditty against Haste" (which begins "All hast is odyus where as dyscrecyon"). Below the "Ditty" is written the name "lydgatt." Presumably it is Lydgate's name at the end of this booklet that has caused a later reader to understand both poems to have been his, and to have written "Lydgate" over *The Lady Prioress*, which is otherwise untitled in the manuscript. We are left with very little context to speculate on this text's readers and their other interests: the only item compiled with *The Lady Prioress* in the Middle Ages was Lydgate's poem, and we have no evidence of ownership of the little booklet before Stow.

Two scribes are responsible for the booklet, the main one having written both poems, and the second having corrected only *The Lady Prioress*. The main hand is an informal book-hand of the last quarter of the fifteenth century. The corrector's hand is similar and contemporary but his spelling is more conservative, using the symbols þ (thorn) and ȝ (yogh), while the main scribe does not. At lines 24–26, both scribes seem to be struggling to make sense of a damaged exemplar. Sometimes the corrector appears to be emending from conjecture.

The form in which the main scribe wrote out the poem sometimes conceals its stanzaic shape. She or (much more probably) he often divides long lines into two short lines or runs two short lines together. At lines 200–01, where the lineation is particularly confused, the corrector adds a short line (an obviously faulty emendation) to provide a rhyme for a word that ought to fall in the middle of line 201.

The spelling of the main scribe has some distinctive features that allow his location to be pinned down using *LALME*. He has a glide vowel with -*w*-, with -*y*-, and with -*r*-, as in the following examples: *pewer* (line 20), *blowen* (86), *dowen* (111); *begyen* (27), *fayer* (28), *skyen* (170); *thoren* (181), *boren* (183), *scoren* (184). The Appendix of Southern Forms in vol. 4 of *LALME* attests the glide vowel with -*y*- in Devon, Norfolk, and Somerset (p. 319). The glide vowel with -*w*- and with -*r*- is further spread, but both cases appear in manuscripts from Devon and Somerset. These locations in the southwest of England are also compatible with the scribe's use of a double consonant after long vowels, e.g., *fett* (106), *shett* (104), *wyff* (233) (*LALME*, 4:320). The difficult rhyme sequence at lines 208–11 reads *goyth/deth/mette/breth* in the manuscript, for *goeth, death, mead, breath*. The rhyme depends on a widespread form of *mead, meth(e)*, but also a form of *goeth, geth*, that was not the usual one for this scribe, who has switched the spelling to his own *goyth* (compare *doyth* for *doth* in line 7). The spelling *goyth* is attested in *LALME* in five counties, among them Devon and Somerset (Q138).

The corrector evidently came from the same area as the main scribe. He uses the form *softe* for *sought* at line 26; an *f* spelling for the Middle English fricative /x/ is most often found in Somerset or Devon.

AFTERLIFE

The Lady Prioress appears in the following early or otherwise informative editions:

1806. *The Pryorys and her Thre Wooyrs*. Robert Jamieson, ed. *Popular Ballads and Songs, from Tradition, Manuscripts, and Scarce Editions*. Edinburgh: Archibald Constable, and London: Cadell and Davies, and John Murray. 1:249–65.

1840. *The Tale of the Lady Prioress and her Three Suitors*. J. O. Halliwell, ed. *A Selection from the Minor Poems of Dan John Lydgate*. London: Percy Society. Pp. 107–17.

1911. *A Tale of a Prioress and her Three Wooers*. Johannes Prinz, ed. Berlin: E. Felber.

1985. *The Lady Prioress*. Melissa M. Furrow, ed. *Ten Fifteenth-Century Comic Poems*. New York: Garland. Pp. 1–28.

REFERENCE TOOLS

The motif of the corpse denied burial is listed in *ATU* as 505, and "The Three Suitors in the Cemetery" as *ATU* 940.

The Prioress and her Three Suitors is *IMEV* 2441 (see Carleton Brown and Rossell Hope Robbins, *The Index of Middle English Verse* [New York: Columbia University Press, for the Index Society, 1943]); it is not listed in *NIMEV*.

It is addressed by Thomas Cooke in volume 9 (1992) of the *Manual*, section 24 Tales [16], *The Lady Prioress and her Suitors*.

POET, POETRY, AND LANGUAGE

The poet begins ambitiously, attempting the alliterative long line rhymed, in stanzas with a rhyming wheel of five short lines, and an effort at concatenation, or stanza linking by repetition. The nine-line stanzas rhyme *aaaabcccb*, as do those in *The Tale of the Basin* in the current volume, *The Tournament of Tottenham* (another comic poem), and the *Towneley Secunda Pastorum* (a Corpus Christi pageant). A contemporary romance, *The Awntyrs off Arthur*, though it rhymes *abababababcddc* and has only four short lines rather than *The Lady Prioress*'s five, has not only rhyme, alliteration, and a short-line wheel like our poem, but also stanza-linking through the repetition of a part of the last line of one stanza in the first of the next; thus it could have served as a model for our poet. But in *The Lady Prioress* the stanza-linking does not last long, appearing only in lines 9–10, 18–20 (one word only, and skipping a line), and 45–46 (again one word only). And the alliteration is a secondary consideration for the poet: there are many lines which do not alliterate at all, or in which the alliteration does not cross the caesura between the half-lines; and the poet recognizes no restrictions on which lifts, or stressed syllables, can alliterate. Even the rhyme scheme occasionally breaks down as well, and the poet resorts to an *aaAAbcccb* variant, as in lines 55–63, 127–35, and 163–71. In the edition that follows, the long lines are split at the caesura and the second half lines are deeply indented, to allow room for the glosses in the right margin.

The meter of the poem is based on rhythms of late Middle English alliterative verse, the long lines having two lifts in each half-line (but very often with three lifts in the first half-line), and the short lines having two or three lifts. There can be a *clash* between lifts (that is, they can be next to one another), or there can be one, two, or several unstressed syllables making up the *dip* preceding or following a lift. The most common rhythms in *The Lady Prioress* are rising in both half-lines (a rising half-line has dips followed by lifts), and rising-falling in the first half-line (a dip followed by a lift, then a dip, lift, dip sequence):

> rising
>> There was no **hegge** for me to **hey**   line 229a
>
> rising-falling
>> To **meve** you of a **matt**er   line 13a

Less frequent are second half-lines with a single dip
>> **clen** he had for**gett**   line 154b
>
> falling half-lines
>> "**Do** thy de**ver**," the **la**dy sayd   line 100a
>
> and half-lines with a clash
>> The **pryst de**myd them **dev**yllys both   line 156a.

There are, as well, over-heavy lines, such as a four-lift short line
>> Hys **har**tte **ho**ppyd, hys **wyll** to-**woke**   line 96
>
> and a three lift second half-line
>> **busche**, **gryne**, nor **grett**   line 157b.

But the poem sounds unlike more traditional alliterative verse for a number of reasons. It does not use the special vocabulary, the hosts of synonyms beginning with different phonemes (like *burn*, *lede*, *freke*, and *gome* for *man*) that survive only to serve the alliterative poet's needs; nor does it use the convenient alliterative tags like *hardy under helm* or *stiff in stalle*. More traditional verse would have a greater incidence of falling rhythm in both half-lines. In the second half-line, unrhymed alliterative verse would have more rising-falling and fewer rising rhythms: *The Lady Prioress* tends toward masculine rhymes, final -*e* no longer being pronounced.

The date of the poem must be no later than the last quarter of the fifteenth century, given the handwriting of the manuscript, but after some of the important phonological shifts of the fifteenth century, such as the Southumbrian silencing of fricatives (as in the rhyme *lyght/quyt* at lines 167, 171).

The poet's dialect is hinted at by the sequence *goyth/deth/mette/breth* at 208–11. The form *meth(e)* for *mead* is widespread, but *geth* for *goeth* is not so: it appears in *LALME* in various spellings (*geeþ*, *geth*, and *geþ*) from the southwest Midlands to the southeast, but not the scribe's Somerset or Devon (Q138). The poet thus came evidently from somewhere other than the scribe's location. But the restricted areas in which forms like *geth* are used do not match up to the restricted areas in which, among others, *wenter* for *winter* is used (*wyntter* rhymes with *venter* at lines 55–56, and inexactly with *intent* and *precedent* at lines 57–58; see Appendix of Southern Forms): Ely, Norfolk, Suffolk, and Surrey. According to *LALME*, all four are possible areas for *ren-* forms of *run* (*then* rhymes with *ryen* at lines 149, 153; Q208), and Ely, Norfolk, and Suffolk for places where *erd-* forms of *earth* are used (*aferd/sherd/erd* rhyme at lines 159–61; see Q155). The poet's own dialect seems to have been a mixed one, perhaps because he moved around during his life, perhaps because he was happy to draw rhymes from wherever he could get them and was not abashed by inexact rhymes. No safe conclusions can be drawn about the origins of this poet.

THE LADY PRIORESS

O gloryus God oure governer,
    glad in all thys gesttyng,   *rejoice; tale-telling*
And gyfe them joye that wyll here
    whatt I shall saye or syng.
Me were loth to be undernom   *I would hate; reproached*
    of them that byn not connyng: *expert [in poetry]*
Many maner of men there be   *Many kinds of men*
    that wyll meddyll of everythyng,   *meddle with*
5   Of resons ten or twelfe.   *methodologies*
Dyverse men fawttys wyll fele   *sniff out faults*
That knowyth no more then doyth my hele,   *heel*
Yt they thynke nothyng ys well   *Yet*
But yt do meve of themselfe.   *Unless; come from*

10 But yt move of themselfe
    forsoth they thynke yt ryght nowght.
Many men ys so usyd;   *accustomed*
    ther terme ys soen tought.   *their limits are soon seen*
Sympyll ys there consayet   *Foolish; notion*
    when yt ys forth brought.   *brought to light*
To meve you of a matter   *mention*
    forsoth I am bethought,   *it occurs to me*
Declare you of a case:
15 Make you mery all and som,   *one and all*
And I shall tell you of a noone,   *nun*
The fayryst creator under the son,   *creature*
Was pryorys of a plase.   *convent*

The lady that was lovely,
    a lorddys dowter she was,   *daughter*
20 Ful pewer and full precyous   *pure; worthy*
    provyd in every plase.
Lordys and laymen and spryttuall   *clergymen*
    her gan chase.   *pursued*
For her fayer beawté   *beauty*
    grett temtacyon she hase,
Her love for to wynne.

Grett gyftys to here they browghth.

25 Many men lowyth here out of thought.   *love her beyond reason*
How she hereselfe myght kepe from shame she sought;
She wyst not how to begyen.   *knew; begin*

There wooyd a young knyght,   *wooed*
    a fresse lord and a fayer,   *lively*
And a person of a paryche,   *parson; parish*
    a prelet wythouttyn pyre,   *prelate; peer*
30 And a burges of a borrow.   *burgess; town*
    Lyst and ye shall here   *Listen*
How they had layed ther love
    apan the lady dere,
And nooen of other wyst.   *no one*
Evyre more thei went and com,   *came*
Desyryd of here louff soon;   *love*
35 They sware by son and mone
Of here to have there lyste.   *desire*

The young knyght for the ladys love
    narrow tornyd and went;
Many bokkys and dooys   *bucks; does*
    to the lady he sent.
The person present her prevely   *presented*
    (hys matters to amend)
40 Beddys, brochys, and botellys of wyen.   *Rosaries, candles*
    Of his gold and rent
The burges to her broght.
Thus they trobylyd her thorow tene.   *efforts*
She wyst not how hereselfe to mene   *conduct*
For to kepe here soule clene,
45 Tell she her bethought.   *considered*

The young knyght bethought hym mervelously   *resolved incredibly hard*
    wyth the lady for to mell.   *get it on*
He flatteryd her wyth many a fabyll;   *story*
    fast hys tonng gan tell.   *speak*
Lessyngys lepyd out amonge   *Lies; all the while*
    as sowend of a bell: *sound*
"Madam, but I have my lyst of yow   *unless I have my way with*
    I shall myseleff quell: *kill*
50 Youre loufe unto me graunt.
In batyll bolde I there abyde,   *fearlessly I dare*
To make the Jues there heddys hyde,
With gret strokes and bloddy syd,
And sle many a grette gyaunt.

55 "All ys for your love, madame;
    my lyfe wold I venter,   *venture*
So that ye wyll graunt me   *Provided that*
    I have desyryd many a wyntter,   *[what] I*
Underneth your comly cowle   *cloak*
    to have myn intent."
"Syr," she sayd, "ye be ower lord,   *our*
    ower patron, and ower precedent: *head*
Your wyll must nedys be do,
60 So that ye wyll goo thys tyde   *at a certain time*
Dowen to the chapyll under the woodsyde   *Down*
And be rewlyd as I wyll ye gyde."   *ruled*
"All redy," sayde he thoo.   *then*

"Dowen in the wode there ys a chapell:
    ryght as I you hett   *command*
65 Therein must ye ly all nyght,
    my love and ye wyll gett.   *if you want to*
Ly there lyke a ded body
    sowyd in a shett —   *sewed; sheet*
Than shall ye have my love,
    myn awen hony swett —   *own sweetheart*
Unto morow that yt be lyght."   *Until*
"Madame," he sayed, "for your love
70 Yt shall be don, be God above!   *by*
Ho sayeth 'naye,' here ys me glove   *Whoever; my*
In that quarrell for to fyght."

That knyght kyssyd the lady gent;   *noble*
    the bargen was made.
Of no bargen syght he was borne   *since*
    was he never halfe so glade.
75 He went to the chapell
    as the lady hym bad,
He sowyd hymselfe in a shett.
    He was nothyng adred;   *not at all frightened*
He thought apon no sorrow.   *harm*
When he com there he layed upryght   *flat on his back*
Wyth two tapers bornynge bryght:
80 There he thought to ly all nyght,
To kys the lady on the morrow.

As soon as the knyght was go
    she sent for Syr John.
Well I wott he was not long: *know*
    he cam to her anon.   *at once*
"Madam," he sayd, "what shall I do?"

She answeryd to hym than:	
85 "Syr," sche sayd,	
"I schall tell you my conssell sone,	*private business right away*
Blowen yt ys so brode.	*It is so well known [anyway]*
I have a cosyn of my blode	
Lyeth ded in the chapyll wood;	
For owyng of a som of good	*sum of money*
90 Hys beryng ys forbode.	*burying; forbidden*
"We be not abyll to pay	
the good that men do crave;	*demand*
Therfore we send for you	
ouer worshype for to save.	*good name*
Say hys dorge and masse	*dirge*
and laye hym in hys grave —	
Wythin a whyle after	
my love shall you have —	
95 And truly kepe consell."	*keep it secret*
Hys hartte hoppyd, hys wyll to-woke,	*entirely woke*
To do all thys he undertoke.	
To say hys servys apon a boke	*service from the missal*
He sware be hevyn and hell.	*by*
100 "Do thy dever," the lady sayd,	*duty*
"as farforth as thou may.	*far*
Then shalt thou have thy wyll of me."	
And serten I thee saye,	*certainly I tell you*
Syr John was as glad of this	
as ever was fowle of daye.	
Wyth a mattake and a showyll	*mattock; shovel*
to the chapyll he takyth the waye,	
Where he lay in hys shett.	*he [the knight]*
105 When he cam ther he made hys pett	*pit*
And sayed hys dorge at hys fett.	*feet*
The knyght lyeth styll and dremyd hyt:	
That "my loffe" whas hys swett.	*his sweetheart had become "my love" [to him]*
As soen as the pryst was gon	
the yong knyght for to bery,	
110 She sent after the marchaunt.	
To her he cam full mery.	*merrily*
"Dowen in the wode ther ys a chapell,	
ys fayer under a pere;	*directly; pear tree*
Therin lyeth a ded corse;	*corpse*
therfore must ye stere ye	*bestir yourself*
To helpe us in ower ryght.	
He owyth us a som of golde;	

115   To forbyd hys beryng I am bolde.
       A pryst ys theder, as yt ys me tolde,   *[gone] to that place*
       To bery hym thys nyght.

       "Yf the corse beryd be
            and ower mony not payed
       Yt were a fowlle sham for us
            so for to be bytrayed.
120   And yf ye wyll do after me   *what I tell you*
            the pryst shall be afrayed:
       In a devellys garment
            ye shall be arayed   *dressed*
       And stalke ye theder full styll.   *quietly*
       When ye se the pryst styre   *stir*
       To bery hym that lyeth on bere   *bier*
125   Lepe in at the quyer dore   *choir (quire)*
       Lyke a fend of hell."

       "Madam, for your love
            soen I shall be tyryd,   *dressed*
       So that ye wyll graunt me
            that I have ofte desyryd."
       "Syr," she sayd, "ye shall yt have,
            but fyrst I wyll be sewryd   *assured*
130   That ower cownsell ye wyll kepe,
            that they be not dyscuryd.   *revealed*
       Tell tomorow that yt be day   *Till*
       Yf thou voyed or ellys flee   *go away*
       Forever thow lesyst the love of me."   *lose*
       "I graunt, madame," sythe sade he,   *agree; then*
135   And on wyth ys araye.   *his costume*

       He dyght hym in a dyvellys garment.   *dressed*
            Furth gan he goo;
       He cam in at the chyrch dore
            as the dyrge was doo,
       Rynnyng, roryng wyth hys rakyls   *Running; chains*
            as devyllys semyd to doo.   *suited devils to do*
       The pryst brayed up as a boke.   *jumped; buck*
            Hys hartt was allmost goo.
140   He demyd hymselfe but ded.   *considered*
       He was aferd he was to slowe.
       He rose up he wyst not howe
       And brake out at a wyndow,
       And brake fowle ys heed.   *badly split his head*

145	But he that bod all the brunt,	*endured the worst of it*
	how sherwly he was egged,	*badly; provoked*
	For to here hys dyrge do	
	and se hys pet deggyd.	*grave dug*
	"I trow I had my damys curse:	*believe; mother's*
	I myght have byn better beggyd,	*located*
	For now I am but lost,	*no better than destroyed*
	the lyghtter but I be leggyd."	*unless I am faster legged*
	And up rose he then.	
150	The devyll se the body ryse;	*saw*
	Then hys hart began to gryse —	*shudder*
	I trow we be not all wyse —	
	And he began to ryen.	*run*

	Hys ragys and hys rakylys	
	clen he had forgett;	*completely*
155	So had the yong knyght	
	that sowyed was in the shett.	
	The pryst demyd them devyllys both;	
	wyth them he wolde not mett.	*meet*
	He sparyd nother hyll nor holt,	*woods*
	busche, gryne, nor grett.	*grassy land, nor gravel*
	Lord, he was fowle scrapyd!	
	The other twayen was ell aferd;	*two; badly*
160	They sparyd nether styll ne sherd.	*stile nor gap [in a hedge]*
	They had lever then mydyll erd	*rather; this world*
	Ayther from other have scapyd.	*Either*

	The pryst toke a bypathe;	
	wyth them he wolde not mett.	
	Yt ys hed was fowle brokyn;	*Still his*
	the blod ran dowen to ys fett.	
165	He ran in a fyrryd gowen:	*furred*
	all hys body gan reke.	
	He cast off all hys clothys	
	to the bare breke	*underpants*
	Because he wolde goo lyght.	*wanted to travel light*
	He thought he harde the devyll loushe;	*dash*
	He start into a bryer boushe	*jumped; briar bush*
170	That all hys skyen gan rowsshe	*So that; skin began to rush*
	Off hys body quyt.	*Quite off*

	The knyth he ran into a wood	*knight*
	as fast as he myght weend.	*go*
	He fell apon a stake	
	and fowle hys lege gan rentt.	*lacerated*
	Therefore he toke no care;	*attention*

          he was aferd of the fend.

175   He thought yt was a longe waye
          to the pathes end,
     But then cam all hys care: *suffering*
     In at a gape as he glent,   *gap; darted*
     By the medyll he was hent;   *caught*
     Into a tretope he went
180   In a bokys snarre.   *buck's snare*

     The marchaunt ran apon a laund,   *an open space*
          there where growyth no thoren.
     He fell apon a bollys bake: *bull's back*
          he causte hym apon hys horn.   *threw*
     "Out, alas!" he sayd,   *Oh, no*
          "that ever I was boren,
     For now I goo to the devyll
          bycause I dyd hym scoren,
185   Unto the pytt of hell."
     The boll ran into a myre.
     There he layed ower fayer syer.   *our handsome sire*
     For all the world he durst not stere   *stir*
     Tyll that he herde a bell.

190   On the morrow he was glad
          that he was so scapyd.
     So was the pryst also,
          thoo he was body nakyd.   *though; stark naked*
     The knyght was in the tretope:
          for dred sore he quaked.
     The best jowell that he had,   *jewel*
          fayn he wolde forsake yt
     For to com dowen.
195   He caught the tre by the tope;
     Ye, and eke the calltrape.   *Yes, and also the calltrop*
     He fell and brake hys foretope   *crown*
     Apon the bare growend.

     Thus they went from the game
          begylyd and beglued.   *beguiled; deluded*
200   Nether on other wyst;   *None of the three knew another*
          hom they went beshrewyd.   *abused*
     The person tolde the lady on the morrow
          what myschyf ther was shewed,   *shown*
     How that he had ronne for her love;
          hys merthys wer but lewed,   *entertainments; bad*
     He was so sore dred of deth.
     "When I shuld have beryd the corse,

205 The devyll cam in, the body rose:
    To se all thys my hart grose; *shuddered*
    Alyffe I scapyd unneth." *hardly*

    "Remember," the lady sayth,
        "what mysschyfe heron geth: *what evil follows from this*
    Had I never lover yt *yet*
        that ever dyed good deth."
210 "Be that lord," sayd the pryst,
        "that shope both ale and methe, *made; mead*
    Thow shaltte never be wooed for me
        whylyst I have spech or breth,
    Whyle I may se or here."
    Thus they to mad ther bost: *two said their say*
    Furthe he went wythout the corse.
215 Then com the knyght for hys purpos
    And told her of hys fare. *doings*

    "Now I hope to have your love
        that I have servyd youre, *deserved for a long time*
    For bought I never love soo dere *paid for; dearly*
        syth I was man ibore." *since; born a human*
    "Hold they pese," the lady sayd.
        "Therof speke thou no more,
220 For by the newe bargen
        my love thou hast forlore *lost*
    All thys hundryth wynter." *Forever*
    She answered hym; he went hys way.
    The marchaunt cam the same day;
    He told her of hys grett afray *fright*
225 And of hys hygh aventure.

    "Tyll the corse shulde beryd be *was supposed to be*
        the bargen I abod. *endured*
    When the body ded rise,
        a grymly gost aglood, *grim-looking; glided up*
    Then was tyme me to stere; *bestir myself*
        many a style I bestrood. *strode across*
    There was no hegge for me to hey, *hedge; too high*
        nor no watter to brod *broad*
230 Of you to have my wyll."
    The lady said "Pese" full blyffe. *quickly*
    "Neer," she said, "whylle thou art man on lyffe, *Never; alive*
    For I shall shew yt to they wyff *thy*
    And all the contré yt tyll, *to*

235   "And proclaym yt in the markyt towen
         they care to encrese."
     Therwyth he gave her twenty marke
         that she shold hold her pese.
     Thus the burges of the borrowe,
         after hys dyses,   *decease*
     He endewed into the place   *endowed*
         wyth dedys of good relese   *deeds; conveyance*
     In fee forever more.   *By heritable right*
240   Thus the lady ded fre: *nobly*
     She kepyth hyr vyrgenyté,
     And indewed the place with fee,   *money*
     And salvyd them of ther soore.   *cured; suffering*

       Explycyt   *The End*

EXPLANATORY NOTES TO THE LADY PRIORESS

ABBREVIATIONS: *CT*: Chaucer, *Canterbury Tales*; *MED*: *Middle English Dictionary*; *OED*: *Oxford English Dictionary*.

18   A prioress was a leader of nuns, either the superior in a daughter house or the second in command to the abbess in a mother house. This prioress is the superior in a daughter house, a particular "plase."

19–20   Like a heroine of romance, the prioress is lovely and well born. But nuns, particularly those in positions of power, often did come from noble families.

21   *Gan* is a past tense marker in this poem: *gan chase* means "chased."

37   *narrow tornyd and went*. Literally, "turned this way and that in tight circles" (from the phrase "turn and wind," with confusion from the verb "wend").

38–41   The wooers are clearly differentiated from each other, down to the presents they bring: the knight brings game, the parson rosaries, candles, and wine, and the merchant brings "gold and rent." In *The Long Wapper* they are not distinguished at all; in *Les Trois galants au cimetière* there is no systematic distinction, and in the *Decameron* and the farcical *Trois amoureux de la croix* the lovers are distinguished only by name. In *Schimpf und Ernst* they are distinguished only by status (a student, a nobleman, and a burgess's son who belongs to a regiment).

52   *To make the Jues there heddys hyde*. Saracens were more usual adversaries, since they held the Holy Land throughout most of the medieval period. Compare *Les Trois galants au cimetière*, in which the young woman says to the first lover "vous me promettès tant de bien et mesmes pour aller en Jerusalem" (pp. 33–34) [you promised me much and even to go to Jerusalem]. The last abortive crusade began and ended in 1464 when its leader, Pope Pius II, died before his ship left port at Ancona. The combination of Jews and huge giants as the knight's potential adversaries must have seemed comically odd, like a boast now that one will fight Belgians and space invaders.

77   The boastfully fierce knight, eagerly sewing himself into a winding sheet to be like a corpse ready for burial, has turned himself into a comic figure. Since a winding sheet could have been wound and knotted rather than stitched, perhaps the stitching here is reminiscent of the young man Amans at the beginning of the French text that did so much to define *fin' amours* for northern Europe, the thirteenth-century *Roman de la rose* by Guillaume de Lorris. In a dream vision, Amans goes off to find love on a fine spring morning, and as he walks along he

stitches his sleeves to make them fashionably tight around his arms. Sewing was not a usual pursuit among men of the gentry, and both stitching one's sleeves while wearing them and stitching oneself into a winding sheet involve improbable contortions.

82   *Syr John*. The conventional title and name for a priest.

90   *Hys beryng ys forbode*. Refusing burial to a corpse because of debt was a literary theme, not a historical reality. See the introduction to *The Lady Prioress* for an instance of the theme in contemporary romance.

121   *In a devellys garment ye shall be arayed*. The devil's garment here is made of rags, as implied in line 154. In contemporary art the devil was usually portrayed as bestial, with shaggy fur, and costumes in contemporary plays undoubtedly tried for the same effect. In 1393 Charles IV of France and five of his lords were acting as "hommes sauvages" in a "ludus" at court, and imitated the fur also associated with the wild men by coating themselves with pitch and, stuck in that, frayed linen. The results were tragic: the duke of Orléans brought a torch too close to one, trying to guess who he was, and a fire spread among them, killing four of the courtiers. Probably a costume made of real fur was more usual (and safer). The Lucifer in *Les Actes des apôtres* (played at Bourges in 1536) "estoit vestu d'une peau d'ours, ou à chaucun poil pendait une papillotte" [was clothed in a bearskin, where from each hair hung a curl of paper] (cited by Gustave Cohen, *Histoire de la mise en scène dans la théâtre religieux français du moyen age*, second ed. [Paris: Libraire Honoré Champion, 1951], p. 95). But perhaps the merchant's rags formed a cloak meant loosely to suggest rough fur.

138   *Rynnyng, roryng wyth hys rakyls as devyllys semyd to doo*. The merchant carries chains, a symbol of the bonds of hell, as do the pretended devils in *The Long Wapper* and the *Trois amoureux de la croix*. In the account book of expenses for the playing of the mystery of the Passion at Mons in 1501, a major expense is for the devil's chains: "Item pour iii kaisnes de fer, pesant ensemble cxx livres, servant pour le deable Lucifer d'Enfer en hault, à iii s. la livre, xviii l." [Item, for three iron chains, weighing together 120 pounds, serving for the devil Lucifer of Hell above (?), at three sous the pound, 18 livres] (ed. Gustave Cohen, *Le Livre de conduite du régisseur*, Publications de la Faculté des Lettres de l'Université de Strasbourg 23 [1925], p. 507).

180   *In a bokys snarre*. A snare was not a usual way of catching bucks. Snares were set for birds and for small animals, but deer were hunted by driving them into enclosures or by shooting with bow and arrows. But this snare has to be big enough to catch a man, and so it is a buck's snare.

184   *For now I goo to the devyll bycause I dyd hym scoren*. Feeling the bull's horns, the priest assumes he is being carried off to hell on a devil's back, as Vices traditionally were in morality plays. The priest also assumes that he has offended the devil by daring to imitate him.

189   *Tyll that he herde a bell.* A bell was a sanctified object, and its ringing had power against demons. The bell would have been heard from the church or the convent, ringing to signal a service.

196   *Ye, and eke the calltrape.* The precise sense is unclear, since a caltrop is usually a spiky trap on the ground. The general sense must be that the knight accidentally undoes or detaches the snare that has hauled him up into the tree top, and so he will fall out of the tree and crash to the ground. Likely the line is corrupt in its current form.

208–09   The prioress of course speaks with double meaning: she has never had a lover who died a good death, in God's grace, because she has never had a lover, but the unprincipled and superstitious priest is quick to swear off pursuing her any further because he now sees his night's misadventures as diabolic retribution for his attempt to violate a nun's vows of chastity.

228–35   The merchant makes a last-ditch attempt to turn his flight from the risen corpse into a demonstration of his love for the prioress: no hedge is too high, no body of water too broad, for him to cross to win her. Her response is a brusque instruction to be quiet, and a threat of exposing him to his wife and the people on whom his business depends, those in the countryside and the local market town.

236   *Therwyth he gave her twenty marke that she shold hold her pese.* A mark was a large unit of money, worth two-thirds of a pound.

TEXTUAL NOTES TO THE LADY PRIORESS

ABBREVIATIONS: MS: London, British Library, MS Harley 78, fols. 74r–81v; **MED**: *Middle English Dictionary*; **OED**: *Oxford English Dictionary*.

title	No title in the MS. Instead appears the heading: *Lydgate.*
5	MS reads: *Of resons x or xii.*
24–26	This area is a mess, with layered conjectures trying to restore an unrecovered original text. The main scribe has written this:

> *Grett gyftys to here they put*
> *Many men lowyth here out of mynd*
> *How here selfe myght from shame shytt*

The corrector has made insertions and deletions:

> *Grett gyftys to here they ~~put~~ browghth*
> *Many men lowyth there ~~out of mynd~~ thei hir softe*
> *How here selfe myght from them shame shytt wrowthe*

Accepting that "brought" is probably a good guess by the corrector as to what the original might have read before the line endings in this area were damaged, I have made highly conjectural emendations to the other two lines, trying to make sense of them, guided by the rhyme scheme and the first parts of the lines.

28	This line is written as two separate lines, broken after *knyght*. In the first half of the poem many long lines after this are similarly broken. They are: 37, after *love*; 46, after *mervelously*; 58, after *lord*; 64, after *chapell*; 65, after *nyght*; 73, after *gent*; 74, after *borne*; 76, after *shett*; 82, after *go*; 84, after *do*; 101, after *me*; 102, after *this*; 103 after *showyll*; 109, after *gon*.
33	*Evyre more thei went and com.* This is inserted by the corrector. The main scribe has: *They goo and com.* The corrector's version restores a consistency of tenses: "went," "came," "desired." Agreement of tenses is not necessary in Middle English, but it is plausible that the main scribe read *com* as present tense and thus changed to *goo* from *went*, but that the corrector habitually used *com* as a past tense. Middle English *com* as a past tense had long *o* (unlike the more central vowel in *com* as a present tense or infinitive), which would have rhymed with the vowel in *moon* and *soon*.
40	MS reads: *beddys brochys and botellys of wyen he to the lady sent.* The second part of the line virtually repeats the second part of line 38. The sense requires naming the presents that the burgess offers. The emendation is conjectural.
42	MS reads: *Thus they trobylyd her thorow tene*; "her" added above the line by the corrector.

46	MS reads: *The young knyght bethought hym mervelously wyth lady for to mell*. Emendation for sense.
48	MS reads: *lessyngys lepyd out of amonge as sowend of a bell*.
49	*Madam but I haue my lyst of yow I shall myseleff quell*: added between lines by the corrector.
51	MS reads: *In batyll bolde there abyde*. Emendation for sense, taking *there* as a form of the verb *tharf* (*OED;* confused with *dare v.¹*), *thurven* (*MED*, def. 8).
52	MS reads: *To make the ~~Iude~~ Iues there heddys hyde*. "Iues" added above the line by the main scribe.
53	*With gret strokes and bloddy syd*: added between lines by the corrector.
64	MS reads: *Dowen in the wode there ys a chapell / ryght as I you hyght lett*. The word *lett* is in the hand of the corrector, but *hyght* is not canceled. The form *hyght* (instead of *hett*) is doubtless influenced by the appearance of *nyght* at the end of the half line immediately below.
72	*In that quarrell for to fyght*: *for* inserted above the line.
79	MS reads: *Wyth ij tapers bornynge bryght*.
85	MS reads: *Syr sche sayd hyt schall tell you my conssell sone*. *It* is added by the corrector between lines, and emended for sense.
90	MS reads: *hys beryng ys for ~~good~~ bode*.
92	MS reads: *therfore we send for you ouer worshype for to save*. *for* is inserted above the line.
96	MS reads: *hys hartte hoppyd hys wyll toworke worke*. An *r* is added in the corrector's hand between the *o* and *k* of *towoke*; then the whole word *worke* is added in the corrector's hand beside the line.
101	MS reads: *and serten to I the saye*. The word *to* is added above the line.
103	MS reads: *Wyth a mttake and a showyll*.
107	MS reads: *The knyght lyeth styll and dremyd byt*. The *b* of *byt* is corrected to *h* with an exaggerated downstroke.
112	MS reads: *Therin lyeth a ded corse; thefore must ye stere ye*.
113–14	These lines are written as one line in the MS. After this point no more long lines are broken in half by the scribe, but short lines are combined into one. They are lines 122–23; 124–25; 131–32; 133–35; 140–41; 142–43; 149–50; 151–52; 158–59; 160–61; 168–69; 170–71; 176–77; 178–79; 186–87; 188–89; 193–94; 195–96; 197–98; 203–04; 205–06; 212–13; 221–22; 223–24; 230–31; 232–33; 238–39; 240–41; 242–43.
119	MS reads: *Yt were a fowlle sham for us so for to be bytrayed*. The *by* of *bytrayed* has been inserted above the line.
122	The word *full* has been added above the line.
127	MS reads: *Madam for your love soen I ~~ye~~ shall be tryed tyryd*. The corrector adds *tyryd* above the line but does not cancel *tryed*. The *I* is squeezed in after *soen*; *ye* is scraped to obliterate.
134	The words *sade he* are added above the line in the corrector's hand.
138	MS reads: *Rynnyng ~~raoryng~~ wyth hys rakyls as devyllys semyd to doo*.
139	MS reads: *The pryst brayed up as a boke hys hartt was all ~~a~~ most goo*. The word *most* is added above the line.
143	The word *at* is added above the line.

147   MS reads: *I trow I had my damys curse I myght haue byn better beddyd*. Emended for rhyme.

150   MS reads: *the devyll se the ~~rose~~ body rose*. Emended for rhyme.

154   MS reads: *Hys Ragys and hys Rattellys clen he had forgett*. Emendation for sense (compare line 138).

158   MS reads: *lord he was fowle scrapyd*. The second *r* is added above the line.

160   MS reads: *they sparyd nethe styll ne sherd*. Emendation for sense.

165–67   MS reads:
> *he ran in a fyrryd gowen he cast of all hys clothys all hys body gan reke*
> *to the bare breke be cause he wolde goo lyght.*

Emended to restore stanza form and sense.

182   MS reads: *he fell apon a bollys bake he causte hym apon hys hornys*. Emendation for rhyme.

183–85   These lines are broken in the wrong places. MS reads:
> *Out alas he sayd that euer I was boren for now I goo to the devyll*
> *by cause I dyd hym scoren vnto the pytt of hell.*

193–94   MS reads: *the best jowell that he had fayn he wolde for sake for to com dowen*. Emendation (the addition of *yt*) for rhyme.

199   Above *be gylyd and be glued* appears in the corrector's hand: *by feldys and by felldys and by forrow*.

200–01   The four half-lines appear in scrambled order in the MS, with a caret and line running up between the two pairs as an attempt to indicate the right order. Here is how they appear in the MS:
> *nether on other wyst \ the person tolde the lady on the morrow*
> *hom they went be shrewyd ^ what myschyf ther was shewed.*

Emendation to restore stanza form and sense.

206   MS reads: *To se all thys my hart grese*. Emendation for rhyme.

208   MS reads: *Remember the lady sayth / what mysschyfe heron goyth*. Emendation for rhyme, and removal of what seems to be a meaningless penstroke.

209   MS reads: *had I neuer louer yt that euer dyed good ~~the~~ deth*.

210   MS reads: *be that lord sayd the pryst that shope both ale and mette*. Emendation for rhyme and sense.

214–16   These lines are misdivided in the MS. They appear thus:
> *ffurthe he went wyth out the corse then com the knyght*
> *for hys purpos and told her of hys fare.*

Emendation to restore stanza form.

225   MS reads: *And of hys hyght aventure*.

227   MS reads: *when the body ded rise a grymly gost agleed*. Emendation for sense and rhyme.

231   MS reads: *the lady said f pese full bleth*. Emendation for sense and rhyme.

234–37   These lines are misdivided in the MS, ignoring the stanza break altogether. They appear thus in the MS:
> *And all the contre yt tyll and proclamytte in the markyt towen*
> *they care to encrese ther wyth he gaue her xx marke*
> *that she shold hold her pese thus the burges of the borrowe after hys dyses.*

Emendation to restore stanza form and (for *proclamytte* to *proclaym yt*) sense.

DANE HEW: INTRODUCTION

Dane Hew is article S.Seld.d.45(6) in the Bodleian Library, Oxford. Its printer, John Alde, has not dated it. According to Arber's *Stationers' Register*, Alde (Alday or Aldee in the *Register*) printed books between 1560 and 1584 and so those dates can be taken as the earliest and latest possible dates for that edition (see Arber, *Transcript of the Registers*). The *RSTC* estimates "1560?"

Dane Hew belongs to a group of twenty-six chapbooks, formerly bound together while in the collection of John Selden (1584–1654). Of the twenty-six in Selden's collection, many are medieval stories that have been revised to fit the chapbook format and to modernize the language for a sixteenth-century audience, for example, *Kynge Richarde cuer du lyon* (published by Wynkyn de Worde in 1528) and *Syr Bevis of Hampton* (published by Thomas East around 1582).

The first page of *Dane Hew* is headed "Heere beginneth a / mery Iest of Dane Hew Munk of Lei- / cestre, and how he was foure times slain / and once hanged." The rest of the page is taken up with a large woodcut (12.5 by 9.5 cm) divided into five compartments, each with a picture of one of the slayings or the hanging. The bottom picture, which represents the jousting scene, is twice as wide as the others.

The colophon reads "Imprinted at Lon / don at the long Shop adioyning onto Saint Mildreds Churche in the / Pultrie, by John Alde."

TEXT AND PRINTER

Dane Hew appears in the following early or informative editions:

1812. *Heere beginneth a mery Iest of Dane Hew Munk of Leicestre, and how he was foure times slain and once hanged.* J[oseph] H[aslewood], ed. In *The British Bibliographer*, ed. Sir Egerton Brydges and Joseph Haslewood. London: R. Triphook. 2:593–601.

1829. *Heere beginneth a mery Iest of Dane Hew Munk of Leicestre, and how he was foure times slain and once hanged.* Charles Henry Hartshorne, ed. *Ancient Metrical Tales*. London: W. Pickering. Pp. 316–29.

1866. *A Mery Jest of Dane Hew Munk of Leicestre.* William Carew Hazlitt, ed. *Remains of the Early Popular Poetry of England*. London: John Russell Smith. 3:130–46.

1985. *Dane Hew, Munk of Leicestre*. Melissa M. Furrow, ed. *Ten Fifteenth-Century Comic Poems*. New York: Garland. Pp. 155–74.

REFERENCE TOOLS

Dane Hew is not listed in *NIMEV*.

It is addressed by Thomas Cooke in volume 9 (1992) of the *Manual*, section 24 Tales [23], *Dane Hew, Munk of Leicestre*.

It is number 13257 in *RSTC*.

The motif "the corpse killed five times" is listed in *ATU* as 1537.

POET, POETRY, AND LANGUAGE

The meter of this poem is exceptionally ragged. The rhymed couplet format is a simple one, but lines range from six syllables ("He is foorth of the town," line 71) to thirteen ("And when the day began to appeer in the morning," line 61), and no accentual pattern is easily picked out. The rhyming, even with allowance made for variant and dialectal forms of words, still takes a great deal of license: *anon/bacon* (lines 229–30), *lusty/fansy* (7–8), *houre/door* (63–64), *town/noon* (71–72), *him/time* (179–80), and so on.

Any attempt to pin down the date of the composition of the poem by the state of its language is confounded by inconsistencies. For example, the form *thore* for *there* is in rhyming position at line 224 with *sore*. It is last cited in *OED* in 1470. But on the other hand, the word *vow* in line 164 is earliest cited by *OED* in the sense used in the poem in 1593. (Further analysis of the language of the poem is in my earlier edition, pp. 160–62.)

A hypothesis that accounts for both the awkward poetry and chronologically inconsistent language in the poem is that *Dane Hew* as we have it is a sixteenth-century printer's-shop modernization of a fifteenth-century poem. This conjecture gains support from the fact that a similar fate befell *Jack and His Stepdame*, which as *The Friar and the Boy* was modernized between printed version D (1584–89) and printed version A (1617), both printed by John Alde's son Edward. *The Friar and the Boy* (1584–89) is another one of the chapbooks in Selden's collection. But the modernization of *Dane Hew* is inept. Sometimes archaic forms are left, particularly where required by the rhyme, like *thore*; sometimes alterations destroy the rhyme and the metrical coherence.

A priori, the first two lines of the poem give the best clues as to its time and date of composition:

> In olde time ther was in Lecester town
> An abbay of munks of gret renown . . .

On the face of them, these lines might put the composition of the poem well after the dissolution of the monasteries in 1539 and would suggest that the poet was writing in or near Leicester. But as the introduction to *The Freiris of Berwik* argues, that poem was not written in Berwik, and there is no real reason to believe this poem had to come from Leicester. Perhaps a nearby rival town of comparable importance, such as Nottingham or

Lincoln, is a possibility for its origins. And if we accept the hypothesis that the poem was revised, it would be the revision that places the abbey in the past.

There is little reliable dialectal information left in the poem as we have it, but the rhyme *sore/thore* at lines 223–24 is likely to preserve the poet's usage. *Thore* and variant spellings with the vowel *o* are forms used for *there* in a restricted area of the North and Midlands of England: *LALME* lists Yorkshire, its North and West Riding, Lincolnshire, Nottinghamshire, Lancashire, and northern Middle English (unspecified) as places in which these forms occur. The rhyme *first/list* at lines 79–80 suggests forms such as *frist* or even *fist* for *first*; such forms are found in the Midlands and North but overlap with the *thore* forms in Yorkshire, its North and West Riding, Lincolnshire, Nottinghamshire, and northern Middle English (unspecified). These locations provide a field of possibilities for the origin of the poem.

DANE HEW, MUNK OF LEICESTRE

In olde time there was in Lecester town
An abbay of munks of great renown,
As ye shall now after heer.
But amongst them all was one there
5   That passed all his brethern, iwis: *brothers, certainly*
His name was Dane Hew, so have I blis.   *Master Hugh*
This munk was yung and lusty
And to fair women he had a fansy,
And for them he laid great wait indeed.   *lurked in ambush*
10   In Leicester dwelled a tayler, I reed,   *read*
Which wedded a woman fair and good.
They looved eche other, by my hood,
Seven yeer and somwhat more.
Dane Hew looved this taylers wife sore   *very much*
15   And thought alway in his minde
When he might her alone finde,
And how he might her assay,   *have intercourse with*
And if she would not say him nay.   *If*
Upon a day he said, "Fair woman free,   *noble*
20   Without I have my pleasure of thee   *Unless*
I am like to go from my wit."   *likely to go out of my mind*
"Sir," she said, "I have many a shrewd fit   *vigorous romp*
Of my husband every day."
"Dame," he said, "say not nay.
25   My pleasure I must have of thee
Whatsoever that it cost mee."
She answered and said, "If it must needs be,
Come tomorow unto me,
For then my husband rideth out of the town.
30   And then to your wil I wil be bown,   *bound*
And then we may make good game.
And if ye come not, ye be to blame.
But Dane Hew, first tel thou me
What that my rewarde shal be."
35   "Dame," he said, "by my fay,   *faith*
Twenty nobles of good money,   *gold coins*
For we wil make good cheer this day."

And so they kist and went their way.
   The tayler came home at even tho,   *in the evening then*
40   Like as he was wunt to doo,   *Just as; accustomed*
And his wife tolde him all and some   *the whole story*
How Dane Hew in the morning would come,
And what her meed of him should be.   *reward*
   "What! Dame, thou art mad, so mot I thee.
45   Wilt thou me a cuckolds hood give?
That should me shrewdly greeve."   *severely*
   "Nay, sir," she said, "by sweet Saint John,
I wil keep myself a good woman
And get thee money also, iwis.
50   For he hath made therof a promisse,
Tomorow earely heer to be:
I know wel he will not fail me.
And I shall lock you in the chest
That ye out of the way may be mist.   *missed*
55   And when Dane Hew commeth hether early,   *here*
About five of the clock truely —
For at that time his houre is set
To come hether then without any let —   *delay*
Then I shall you call ful lightly.   *quickly*
60   Look that ye come unto me quickly."
   And when the day began to appeer in the morning,
Dane Hew came thitherwarde fast renning: *running*
He thought that he had past his houre.
Then softly he knocked at the taylers door.
65   She rose up and bad him come neer,
And said, "Sir, welcome be ye heer."
   "Good morow," he said, "gentle mistris;
Now tel me where your husband is,
That we may be sure indeed."
70   "Sir," she said, "so God me speed,
He is foorth of the town   *out of*
And wil not come home til after noon."
   With that Dane Hew was wel content,
And lightly in armes he did her hent   *take*
75   And thought to have had good game.
   "Sir," she said, "let be for shame.
For I wil knowe first what I shall have:
For when I have it I wil it not crave.   *beg for*
Give me twenty nobles first,
80   And doo with me then what ye list."   *you please*
   "By my preesthood," quoth he than,
"Thou shalt have in golde and silver anon;
Thou shalt no longer crave it of me.
Lo, my mistresse, where they be."

85	And in her lap he it threw.	
	"Gramercy," she said unto Dane Hew.	*Thank you*
	Dane Hew thought this wife to assay.	*expected to; grope*
	"Abide, sir," she said, "til I have laid it away,"	
	For so she thought it should be best.	
90	With that she opened then a chest.	
	Then Dane Hew thought to have had her alone,	
	But the tayler out of the chest anon,	
	And said, "Sir Munk, if thou wilt stand,	*stand still*
	I shall give thee a stroke with my brand	*sword*
95	That thou shalt have but little lust unto my wife."	
	And lightly without any more strife	
	He hit Dane Hew upon the hed	
	That he fel down stark dead.	
	Thus was he first slain indeed.	
100	"Alas," then said his wife, "with an evil speed	*bad luck*
	Have ye slain this munk so soone?	
	Whither now shall we run or gone?"	
	"There is no remedy," then said he,	
	"Without thou give good counsail to me	*Unless*
105	To convay this false preest out of the way,	*remove secretly*
	That no man speak of it ne say	
	That I have killed him or slain,	
	Or els that we have doon it in vain."	
	"Yea, sir," she said, "let him abide	
110	Til it be soon in the eventide;	*early in the evening*
	Then shall we him wel convay,	
	For ye shall beare him into the abbay	
	And set him straight up by the wall,	
	And come your way foorthwithall."	*immediately*
115	The abbot sought him all about,	
	For he heard say that he was out,	
	And was very angry with him indeed,	
	And would never rest, so God me speed,	
	Until Dane Hew that he had found,	
120	And bad his man to seek him round	
	About the place, and to him say	
	That he come "speak with me straightway."	
	Foorth went his man til at the last,	
	Beeing abrode, his eye he cast	*outside the monastery*
125	Aside where he Dane Hew did see,	
	And unto him then straight went he.	
	And thinking him to be alive	
	He said, "Dane Hew, so mut I thrive,	*as I hope to*
	I have sought you and mervel how	
130	That I could not finde you til now."	
	Dane Hew stood as stil as he that could not tel	

What he should say. No more he did, good nor il.
   With that the abbots man said with good intent,
"Sir, ye must come to my lord, or els you be shent." *disgraced*
135 When Dane Hew answered never a dele *not a bit*
He thought he would aske some counsail;
Then to the abbot he gan him hye. *he hurried*
   "I pray you, my lord, come by and by *right away*
And see where Dane Hew stands straight by the wall,
140 And wil not answere, whatsoever I call,
And he stareth and looketh upon one place
Like a man that is out of grace,
And one woord he wil not speak for me."
   "Get me a staf," quoth the abbot, "and I shall see
145 And if he shall not unto me answere." *If*
   Then when the abbot came there
And saw him stand upright by the wall,
He then to him began to call
And said, "Thou false bribour, thou shalt aby. *vagabond; pay*
150 Why keepest thou not thy service truely?
Come hether," he said, "with an evil speed." *blast you*
   But no woord than Dane Hew answered indeed.
   "What, whoreson!" quoth the abbot. "Why spekest not thou?
Speak, or els I make God a vow
155 I wil give thee such a stroke upon thy head
That I shall make thee to fall down dead."
   And with that he gave him such a rap
That he fel down at that clap. *whack*
   Thus was he the second time slain,
160 And yet he wroght them much more pain,
As ye shall afterwarde heer ful wel.
   "Sir," quoth the abbots man, "ye have doon il,
For ye have slain Dane Hew now
And suspended this place, I make God a vow." *profaned*
165 "What remedy?" quod the abbot than. *i.e., there is no remedy*
   "Yes," quoth his man, "by sweet Saint John,
If ye would me a good rewarde give,
That I may be the better while that I live."
   "Yes," quoth the abbot, "forty shillings thou shalt have
170 And if thou can mine honor save." *If*
   "My lord, I tel you, so mot I thee,
Unto such a taylers house haunted he *a certain; frequented*
To woo his pretty wife certain,
And thither I shall him bring again,
175 And there upright I shall him set
That no man shall it knowe or wit. *find out*
And then every man wil sain
That the tayler hath him slain,

For he was very angry with him
180 That he came to his wife so oft time."
    Of his counsail he was wel appaid. *satisfied*
And his man took up Dane Hew that braid *minute*
And set him at the taylers door anon
And ran home as fast as he might gone.
185   The tayler and his wife were in bed
And of Dane Hew were sore afraid
Lest that he would them bewray, *expose*
And to his wife began to say, *[the tailor]*
"All this night I have dreamed of this false caitife, *scoundrel*
190 That he came to our door," quoth he to his wife.
    "Jesus," quoth his wife, "what man be ye
That of a dead man so sore afraid ye be?
For me thought that you did him slo." *it seemed to me that you slew him*
    With that the tayler to the door gan go,
195 And a polax in his hand,
And saw the munk by the door stand,
Whereof he was sore afraid.
And stil he stood and no woord said
Til he spake unto his wife:
200 "Dame, now have I lost my life
Without I kil him first of all." *Unless*
Foorth he took his polax or mall *hammer*
And hit Dane Hew upon the head
That he fel down stark dead.
205   And thus was Dane Hew three times slain,
And yet he wrought him a train. *still; played a trick on him*
    "Alas," quoth the taylers wife,
"This caitife dooth us much strife." *causes; trouble*
    "Dame," he said, "what shall we now doo?"
210 "Sir," she said, "so mote I go, *as I hope to be able to walk*
The munk in a corner ye shall lay
Til tomorow before the day.
Then in a sack ye shall him thrast *thrust*
And in the mildam ye shall him cast. *milldam*
215 I counsail it you for the best, surely."
    So the tayler thought to doo, truely.
In the morning he took Dane Hew in a sack
And laid him lightly upon his back.
Unto the mildam he gan him hye, *hurried*
220 And there two theeves he did espye
That fro the mil came as fast as they might.
But when of the tayler they had a sight
They were abashed very sore,
For they had thought the miller had come thore,
225 For of him they were sore afraid,

That their sack there down they laid
And went a little aside, I cannot tel where.
And with that the tayler saw the sack lye there;
Then he looked therin anon
230 And he saw it was ful of bacon.
Dane Hew then he laid down there
And so the bacon away did beare
Til he came home. And that was true.
    The theeves took up the sack with Dane Hew
235 And went their way til they came home.
    One of the theeves said to his wife anon,
"Dame, look what is in that sack, I thee pray,
For there is good bacon, by my fay;
Therfore make us good cheer lightly."   *a good meal quickly*
240   The wife ran to the sack quickly,
And when she had the sack unbound
The dead munck therein she found.
Then she cryed "Out!" and said "Alas!   *"Oh no!"*
I see heer a mervailous case   *astonishing*
245 That ye have slain Dane Hew so soon.
Hanged shall ye be if it be knowen."
    "Nay, good, dame," said they again to her,
"For it hath been the false miller."
    Then they took Dane Hew again
250 And brought him to the mil certain
Where they did steale the bacon before.
And there they hanged Dane Hew for store.   *in storage*
    Thus was he once hanged indeed.
And the theeves ran home as fast as they could speed.
255   The millers wife rose on the morning erly
And lightly made herself redy
To fetch some bacon at the last.
But when she looked up she was agast
That she saw the munk hang there.
260 She cryed out and put them all in fere,   *fear*
And said, "Heer is a chaunce for the nones,   *bad luck for sure*
For heer hangeth the false munk, by cocks bones,
That hath been so lecherous many a day
And with mens wives used to play.
265 Now somebody hath quit his meed ful wel —   *paid him back*
I trow it was the devil of hell —   *think*
And our bacon is stolne away.
This I call a shrewd play.   *dirty trick*
I wot not what we shall this winter eate."
270   "What, wife," quoth the miller, "ye must all this forget,
And give me some good counsail, I pray,
How we shall this munk convay

And privily of him we may be quit."   *be rid*
   "Sir," she said, "that shall you lightly wit.   *quickly find out*
275 Lay him in a corner til it be night
     And we shall convay him or it be daylight.   *before*
     The abbot hath a close heer beside;   *enclosed field*
     Therein he hath a good horse untide.   *untied*
     Go and fetch him home at night
280 And bring him unto me straight,
     And we shall set him thereupon indeed,
     And binde him fast, so God me speed,
     And give him a long pole in his hand
     Like as he would his enmies withstand,   *As if*
285 And under his arme we wil it thrust
     Like as he would fiercely just.   *joust*
        For," she said, "as ye wel knowe,
     The abbot hath a mare, gentle and lowe,   *meek*
     Which ambleth wel and trotteth in no wise.   *not at all*
290 But in the morning when the abbot dooth rise
     He commaundeth his mare to him to be brought,
     For to see his workmen, if they lack ought,
     And upon the mare he rideth, as I you tel,
     For to see and all things be wel.   *if*
295 And when this horse seeth this mare anon,
     Unto her he wil lightly run or gone."
        When the miller this understood
     He thought his wives counsail was good,
     And held him wel therwith content,   *very satisfied with it*
300 And ran for the horse verament.   *truly*
     And when he the horse had fet at the last   *fetched*
     Dane Hew upon his back he cast
     And bound him to the horse ful sure
     That he might the better indure
305 To ride as fast as they might ren.   *run*
     Now shall ye knowe how the miller did then:
     He tooke the horse by the brydle anon —
     And Dane Hew sitting theron —
     And brought him that of the mare he had a sight.
310 Then the horse ran ful right.   *in a straight line*
        The abbot looked a little him beside
     And saw that Dane Hew towarde him gan ride,
     And was almoste out of his minde for feare
     When he saw Dane Hew come so neere.
315   He cryed, "Help, for the loove of the Trinité,
     For I see wel that Dane Hew avenged wil be.
     Alas! I am but a dead man."
     And with that from his mare he ran.
        The abbots men ran on Dane Hew quickly

320   And gave him many strokes lightly
       With clubs and staves many one.
       They cast him to the earth anone;
       So they killed him once again.
          Thus was he once hanged and foure times slain,
325   And buried at the last, as it was best.
       I pray God send us all good rest.
                      Amen.

EXPLANATORY NOTES TO DANE HEW

2　　　　*An abbay of munks of great renown.* Historically, there was an abbey of Augustinian canons in Leicester (living under a rule, like monks, but in holy orders as priests). They were attached to the church of St. Mary of the Fields (Sancte Marie de Pratis) in Leicester. It was an extraordinarily wealthy establishment, valued at over 960 pounds at the time of the dissolution in 1539. Records of the bishop's visitation to St. Mary's in 1440 survive (see A. H. Thompson, ed., *Visitations of Religious Houses in the Diocese of Lincoln*, Canterbury and York Series, vol. 24 [London: Canterbury and York Society, 1919], 2:206–17). At many abbeys or churches there were grievous complaints of sexual licentiousness among the monks or canons, but (according to the records of the bishop's visit) St. Mary's was not among them, at least in 1440, despite Dane Hew's flouting of the rule of chastity. Although it uses the vocabulary of monasticism (*abbot, abbey, monk* rather than *dean, church, canon*), the poem does seem to be about a canon, since Hew swears by his priesthood at line 81 and is called a "false preest" at line 105, and he lives in a town rather than the countryside, where monasteries were built in relative isolation.

6　　　　*His name was Dane Hew, so have I blis.* "His name was Dan Hew, as I hope to have the joy of heaven." *Dan* was a courtesy title used for monks and other learned men; ultimately it comes from the Latin word *dominus*.

12　　　*by my hood.* A very mild assertion of the truth of what is being said.

36　　　*Twenty nobles of good money.* A noble was a gold coin worth half a mark, or six shillings and eight pence.

44　　　*so mot I thee.* "As I hope to prosper."

45　　　*Wilt thou me a cuckolds hood give?* Hoods and hats were readily visible signs of status and occupation (for example, physicians' hoods, cardinals' hats). The cuckold's hood (or as in *Sir Corneus*, line 186, his hat) is an imaginary sign of shame, like the horns referred to by Renaissance writers.

47　　　*sweet Saint John.* The probable reference is to St. John, the apostle said to be particularly loved by Christ in the account in the Gospel of John; medieval tradition considered John the apostle, John the evangelist, and John the author of the book of Revelation to be the same person. But there were many other saints named John, including John the Baptist.

70　　　*so God me speed.* "as I hope God will give me success."

92   *But the tayler out of the chest anon.* A verb of motion is understood.

150   *Why keepest thou not thy service truely?* "Why are you not performing your canonical duties properly?" Dane Hew is absent when he should be available with his brethren for the performance of the services at the canonical hours of the church day.

163–64   *ye have . . . suspended this place.* By killing a man inside the precincts of the monastery, the abbot has profaned it and caused it to be unfit for worship until it is cleared by the Church. But as the conversation goes on to reveal, their concern is for public knowledge and open condemnation, not for the act of profanation, which they hope to conceal.

188   *And to his wife began to say.* "And to his wife the tailor began to say." The speaker is not specified, but such switches of subject are common in Middle English.

195   *polax.* A poleaxe was a weapon used for close-up fighting, with a shaft for handle and a head that was either hammer or axe-blade on one side and a point on the other.

214   *And in the mildam ye shall him cast.* The milldam is the body of deep water above a dam, used for running a mill wheel.

252   *And there they hanged Dane Hew for store.* The thieves hanged Dane Hew where the bacon had been stored as food for the winter.

262   *by cocks bones.* A euphemistic form of "by God's bones." It is perhaps not by chance that the wife swears by "cocks bones" when talking of the lecherous Dane Hew. See the note to *The Tale of the Basin*, line 208.

TEXTUAL NOTES TO DANE HEW

ABBREVIATION: J: Oxford, Bodleian Library, Article S.Seld.d.45(6), printed by John Alde.

Title	*Dane Hew, Munk of Leicestre.* No title appears at the head of the text. The first page of the chapbook reads: *Heere beginneth a mery Iest of Dane Hew Munk of Leicestre, and how he was foure times slain and once hanged.*
18	*And if she would not say him nay.* J: *And if she would not to say him nay.* Emendation for sense.
152	*But no woord than Dane Hew answered indeed.* J: *But no woord that Dane Hew answered indeed.* Emendation for sense.
162	*"Sir," quoth the abbots man, "ye have doon il.* J: *Sir quoth the abbots an ye have doon il.* Emendation for sense.
169	*"Yes," quoth the abbot, "forty shillings thou shalt have.* J: *Yes quoth the abbot xl shillings thou shalt haue.*
210	*"Sir," she said, "so mote I go.* J: *Sir she said so mote go.* Emendation for sense.
226	*That their sack there down they laid.* J: *That the sack there down they laid.* Emendation for sense.
287	*For," she said, "as ye wel knowe.* J: *Fo (she said) as ye wel knowe.*

THE FREIRIS OF BERWIK: INTRODUCTION

MANUSCRIPTS, SCRIBES, AND PRINTED TEXT

There are three extant early texts of *The Freiris of Berwik*: one in the Bannatyne Manuscript (MS B, finished in 1568), one in the late sixteenth-century Maitland Folio Manuscript (MS M), and a chapbook from 1622 now in the Henry Huntington Library (H). This edition is based on MS B, the Bannatyne Manuscript, Edinburgh, National Library of Scotland, MS Advocates' 1.1.6, fols. 348r–354v. In it the poem is headed "Heir begynnis The Freiris of Berwik." MS M, the Maitland Folio Manuscript, is Cambridge, Magdalene College, MS Pepys 2553, in which the poem appears on pp. 113–29. The poem is untitled, but it concludes with "ffinis the freiris of Berwik." The Maitland Folio Manuscript, like Bannatyne, is a compilation written out for a particular household, in this case that of Sir Richard Maitland (d. 1586) of Lethington, Haddington. H is article 88850 in the Henry Huntington Library, San Marino, California: *The Merrie Historie of the Thrie Friers of Ber[wi]cke*, Printed at Aberdene, by Edward Raban, for David Melvill, 1622. Of these three, MS M and H are more closely related to each other than they are to MS B.

Almost all of the writing in MS B is that of one person, George Bannatyne, a young Edinburgh merchant. He wrote out the manuscript in Forfarshire in the last three months of 1568, when he was forced by the plague to stay away from his normal business life in town.

The three different late sixteenth- and early seventeenth-century texts in which *The Freiris of Berwik* survives give us information on the appeal of the poem to different kinds of readers: MS B was written by a merchant for his household's use; MS M was compiled by a prominent jurist and public functionary, the Keeper of the Great Seal of Scotland, Sir Richard Maitland, for his household's use; and H was a chapbook, printed on cheap paper and offered for sale by a printer who calculated that it would sell to a wide enough public to make it profitable for his print shop. This is truly a heterogeneous readership.

For those interested in the Bannatyne Manuscript, a good starting place is Alasdair A. MacDonald, "Cultural Repertory"; MacDonald there gives an analysis of the circumstances of production of the collection by Bannatyne and draws on work done by Priscilla Bawcutt for her then-not-yet-published article "Scottish Manuscript Miscellanies." It would be more accurate to call the Bannatyne Manuscript an anthology, for it is a carefully planned collection of literary texts organized by theme, rather than a miscellany, a grouping together of assorted texts of very different types and functions from narration to horse medicine, such as we see in some other of the household manuscripts where other works in this volume appear. For a sense of the whole manuscript and its organization, see the facsimile edition, *Bannatyne Manuscript*, introduced by Denton Fox and W. A. Ringler. The introduction by

Fox and Ringler gives information on the history and contents of the manuscript. There is an edition of the manuscript transcribed into print by W. Tod Ritchie, *Bannatyne Manuscript*.

Notes on the language in MS B may be helpful, not to localize the manuscript (which we already know to have to have been written by Bannatyne), but to help readers new to the distinctive (and perhaps initially daunting) features of a text in Middle Scots. A more scholarly discussion is to be found in my 1985 critical edition of the poem in *Ten Fifteenth-Century Comic Poems*, pp. 321–26. Despite the setting of the poem in the southeast corner of Scotland, its language suggests that it was written elsewhere, but certainly in Scotland. The language of MS B in part represents Bannatyne's usage and in part the earlier language of the poet and scribes of intervening versions of the poem. In MS B these are recurring features that a reader needs to recognize:

- *Quh-* is at the beginning of words that in modern English have *wh-*:
  quha: who
  quhair: where
  quhairfoir: wherefore, because of that
  quhairof: whereof, of what
  quhatkin: whatever
  quhen: when, once meaning "though" (at line 180)
  quhilk: which
  quhill: while, till
- The pronoun *scho* is always used for "she." *Thir* is an adjective meaning "these."
- The prepositions *into* and *intill* are very frequent, and they mean "in." *Our* can mean "over" and *owttour* means "over" or "across."
- *Woundir* is used as an intensifier, with no attention paid to its semantic meaning, like today's "incredibly." *Richt*, *verry*, and *full* are other frequent intensifiers in the poem.
- Present participles end in *-and* instead of *-ing*: *bydand* is "biding." But gerunds end, like ours, in *-ing*: *with fair hailsing and bekking*.
- Third person singular present indicative verbs end in *-is* or *-ys*, less frequently in *-es*. Past tense weak verbs end in *-it* rather than *-ed*. *Come* is the past tense of "to come." The present tense is *cum*. "Will be" and "shall be" are regularly contracted to *wilbe* and *salbe* in this text. "Shall" is always *sal*. *Hes* and *wes* are "has" and "was." *Haif* is "have."
- *That* is often omitted, not only where we would omit it (when it is a conjunction), but also where we would not (when it is a relative pronoun):
  lines 470–71: *Ye sall him se in liknes of a freir*
  In habeit blak it was his kynd to weir.
  line 111: *Intill a loft, wes maid for corne and hay.*
- Long *a* sounds are often spelled *ai*, and words that in Old English had long *a*, but in southern Middle English changed to long *o*, will still usually have long *a* in this text: e.g., *baith* for "both," *mair* for "more," *stane* for "stone," *ga* for "go." But sometimes there are *o* spellings, and these often have *oi* to indicate the long vowel: *moir* for "more." *Ane* is the usual form for both "a" and "an," even before a consonant (compare line 6, but also line 5). But *mony* and *ony* are the usual forms of "many" and "any."

- In midword, *-d-* or *-dd-* appears where now *-th-* appears: *bruder, bredir, hidder, togidder,* and most frequently, *uder* for "brother," "brothers," "hither," "together," and "other."
- Words that in modern English have *-gh-* will probably have *-ch-* in this text, and the *-ch-* would still be sounded as a palatal or velar continuant: *licht, thocht* for "light," "thought."
- In this edition, *u* and *v* have been regularized to modern usage, but *w* has not, and appears in place of both *u* and *v*: *selwer* is "silver," and *ws* is "us," for example.

A<small>FTERLIFE</small>

The Freiris of Berwik has been very often published, at first usually attributed to William Dunbar, and appears in the following important editions that are particularly early, informative, or recent. See also the editions of the Bannatyne Manuscript mentioned above.

1786. *The Freiris of Berwik, a tale.* John Pinkerton, ed. *Ancient Scotish Poems.* London: C. Dilly. 1:65–85. [Edition of MS M, silently bowdlerized.]

1802. *The Freirs of Berwik, A Tale.* J. Sibbald, ed. *A Chronicle of Scottish Poetry from the Thirteenth Century to the Union of the Crowns.* Edinburgh: J. Sibbald. 2:372–90. [Edition based upon Pinkerton's, "collated with" MS B; silently bowdlerized.]

1832. *The Freiris of Berwik.* David Laing, ed. *The Poems of William Dunbar, Now First Collected.* Edinburgh: Laing and Forbes. 2:3–23. [Edition of MS B, silently euphemized.]

1894. *The Freiris of Berwik.* Jakob Schipper, ed. *The Poems of William Dunbar,* vol. 5: *Anonymous Early Scottish Poems Forming a Supplement to the Poems of William Dunbar.* Denkschriften der Kaiserlichen Akademie der Wissenschaften 43. Vienna: K. Akademie der Wissenschaften. Pp. 389–432. [Edition based on MS M, amended from MS B; acknowledged bowdlerization.]

1955. *The Freiris of Berwik.* W. Mackay MacKenzie, ed. *The Poems of William Dunbar.* Second ed. London: Faber and Faber, 1955. Pp. 182–95. [Edition based on MS B; acknowledged bowdlerization. Poem acknowledged as an "attribution" to Dunbar.]

1985. *The Friars of Berwick.* Melissa M. Furrow, ed. *Ten Fifteenth-Century Comic Poems.* New York: Garland, 1985. Pp. 313–62. [MS B as copy-text; critical edition.]

1997. *The Freirs of Berwik.* R. D. S. Jack and P. A. T. Rozendaal, eds. *The Mercat Anthology of Early Scottish Literature 1375–1707.* Edinburgh: Mercat. Pp. 152–65. [MS B as copy-text, emended from MS M.]

R<small>EFERENCE</small> T<small>OOLS</small>

The Freiris of Berwik is addressed by Florence H. Ridley in volume 4 (1973) of the *Manual,* section 10: Middle Scots Writers [112], *The Freiris of Berwick.*

The motif "Trickster Surprises Adulteress and Lover" is listed in *ATU* as 1358, and *The Freiris of Berwik* belongs under 1358C, "Trickster Discovers Adultery: Food Goes to Husband instead of Lover."

The *RSTC* number for H, the 1622 Aberdeen edition of *The Merrie Historie of the Thrie Friers of Berwicke*, is 7349.5.

POET, POETRY, AND LANGUAGE

The poet of this, as of all the other poems in the current edition, is unknown, but this one is an admirable writer. The *fabliau* plot is handled adroitly; the iambic pentameter couplets are skillful and by contrast to the other poems in this edition remarkably free of padding and fillers to make up a line and provide a rhyme; the speeches sound like men and women with distinct personalities and private agendas talking; and the physical setting is vividly imagined.

On the face of it, the most natural place of origin for the poem would be Berwick itself, where Scotland met England on the eastern coast. The poem was clearly written by someone familiar with the setting, buildings, and fortifications of the town, and with the fact that the four main orders of friars all had foundations there. But a few linguistic points cast doubt on this guess. The first of these is the frequent use of the prepositions *intill* and *into* for ME *in*, a usage which belongs to the center and northeast of Scotland, according to *OED*. It might be scribal, however: Bannatyne was from Edinburgh, Maitland's family from Haddington, and the printed text from Aberdeen, all within the area where *intill* and *into* were used. Yet the two-syllable prepositions are required by the scansion, and thus likely to be authorial. Another point is the use of the noun *pleiss* at line 408. No other medieval citation for the noun exists, but the *Scottish National Dictionary* gives modern citations of the phrase *to hae a please*, attributing it to northeast Scotland and Angus. But the third and most convincing point is that the *ai* diphthong in *stair* has gone to long *a*, rhyming with *mair* ("more") at lines 557–58. The change of *ai* to *a* takes place everywhere in Scotland *except* the southeast, where Berwick is (see Jordan, *Handbook of Middle English Grammar*, p. 132, and Luick, *Historische Grammatik der englischen Sprache*, p. 434).

This evidence that the poem (or at least the poet) originates in an area outside Berwickshire has implications for its date as well. Berwick passed permanently to England in 1482, after centuries of conquest and reconquest. If the poem were written by a Scot elsewhere in Scotland (as opposed to a native of Berwick who had changed his nationality but not his language), it is inconceivable to me that he could have written the entirely laudatory account of Berwick's defenses and other advantages after the town had passed into the hands of the English, without at least some expression of regret or hint of irony. If the poem was written to the north of Berwickshire, then it must have been written between 1461 and 1482, years in which Berwick was in Scottish hands.

Trying to date a medieval poem by its language is a very dubious matter in the current state of knowledge, so at best we can say that there is nothing in the language of this poem that rules out the dates 1461–82. There are words in it not attested that early in *DOST* or *OED*, but also words attested no later than around 1500 in *OED*, *DOST*, and *MED*. The inflectional endings *-is* and *-it* can still be pronounced as full syllables, as signaled by the meter, though they are not always pronounced as full syllables. The loss of the vowel in those syllables had begun before the fifteenth century in the north, according to Jordan (p.

291). The older pronunciation with a vowel could still be retained in poetry in the sixteenth century in the -*es* ending of nouns and the -*ed* ending of verbs and adjectives (see Dobson, *English Pronunciation 1500–1700*, 2:312 and 315) but *not* in the third singular ending of verbs (Dobson 2:313), as it is for example in line 241: "Scho stertis up and gettis licht in hy." Pronunciation of the vowel in these verbs, clearly mandated by the meter in a poem that is metrically careful, suggests no later than a fifteenth-century date; its absence in other contexts, for example in line 165 ("Scho sayis, 'Ye ar full hertly welcome heir'"), suggests not much earlier than a fifteenth-century date.

A further historical point may have some bearing on the provenance of the poem. The poet is clearly confused on the colors pertaining to the different orders of friars. Allane and Robert are Jacobins (line 29). The Jacobins (or Dominicans) are not White Friars, as the poem suggests ("The Jacobene freiris of the quhyt hew," line 24), but Black Friars. The Carmelites were known as the White Friars (from their white habit), the Minors or Franciscans as the Gray Friars (from their gray habit). Most likely, Friar Johine was a Franciscan, members of that order being traditionally foes of the Jacobins. Certainly Robert's refusal to let the fiend, as requested, appear in "our habeit quhyt," on the grounds that it would be a disgrace to "our ordour" if he did so (lines 465–66), makes clear that the poet thinks of Robert and Allane as in an order with white habits, while Johine is in an order with black habits: he is called a Black Friar or dressed in black (at lines BH126, B471, B502), though Black Friar was the usual name for the Jacobins themselves, from their black cloaks worn over white habits. In MS M and H, he is called a Gray Friar or dressed in gray at lines M126, MH 471, MH502). Either the poet made one mistake here or two. He might have mistakenly believed the Jacobins to be White Friars, and correctly called Johine a Gray Friar, in which case Bannatyne and (inconsistently) H made Johine a Black Friar to enhance his demonic appearance. Or the poet might have mistakenly believed the Jacobins to be White Friars, and though intending Johine to belong to another order than the Jacobins, have mistakenly called him a Black Friar, in which case Maitland and (inconsistently) H have corrected the poem, changing him to a Gray Friar. The latter case is the more likely, since two independent factual corrections (M and H both noticing that Johine cannot be a Black Friar because Allane and Robert are Jacobins, who are really Black Friars) are more likely than two independent esthetic improvements (M and H both thinking that black would be symbolically better than gray). The changes by M and H have to be independent because H is inconsistent; if a shared ancestor had gray, then H would not likely have accidentally reverted to black at line 126.

In either event, the poet himself was confused about the orders of friars. Perhaps he had seen the Jacobins wearing their white inner habits without their black cloaks over them, and thought they were White Friars. Certainly his confusion implies that he was not familiar with the orders. Two explanations are possible. First, that he was writing in Berwick after 1539 (the date of the dissolution of major religious foundations in England). But this explanation is implausible for the linguistic and historical reasons given above on dating. Second, that he lived in an area of Scotland other than Berwick (which was the most important center for friars in all of Scotland), one to which the Jacobins had no frequent access. This second explanation seems preferable.

THE FREIRIS OF BERWIK

	As it befell and happinnit into deid,	*in fact*
	Upoun a rever the quhilk is callit Tweid —	
	At Tweidis mowth thair standis a nobill toun,	
	Quhair mony lordis hes bene of grit renoune,	*have been; great*
5	Quhair mony a lady bene fair of face,	
	And mony ane fresche lusty galland wass —	*well-dressed handsome gentleman*
	Into this toun, the quhilk is callit Berwik	
	(Upoun the sey thair standis nane it lyk,	*sea; none*
	For it is wallit weill abowt with stane,	*well walled*
10	And dowbill stankis castin, mony ane,	*double moats dug, many a one*
	And syne the castell is so strang and wicht,	*then; strong and well-built*
	With strait towris and turattis he on hicht,	*narrow; turrets high above*
	The wallis wrocht craftely withall,	*skillfully fashioned as well*
	The portcules most subtelly to fall	*portcullises*
15	Quhen that thame list to draw tham upoun hicht,	*When it pleases them to pull them up*
	That it micht be of na maner of micht	*So that it cannot be possible*
	To win that houss be craft or subteltie;	*by; trickery*
	Quhairfoir it is maist gud all-utirly,	*For which reason; entirely*
	Into my tyme, quhairevir I haif bene,	
20	Moist fair, most gudly, most plesand to be sene:	*Most*
	The toune, the wall, the castell, and the land,	
	The he wallis upoun the upper hand,	*high*
	The grit Croce Kirk, and eik the masonedew,	*Cross Church, and also the hospice*
	The Jacobene freiris of the quhyt hew,	*Jacobin; white hue*
25	The Carmeleitis, Augustinianis, and als the Minouris eik —	*also*
	The four ordouris wer not for to seik,	*not hard to find*
	Thay wer all in this toun dwelling),	
	So appinnit in a May morning	*It so happened*
	That twa of the Jacobyne freiris	*two*
30	(As thay wer wont and usit mony yeiris	*accustomed; years*
	To pass amang thair brethir upaland),	*brethren in the country*
	Wer send of thame best practisit and cunnand:	*by those most experienced and able*
	Freir Allane, and freir Robert the uder.	*other*
	Thir silly freiris with wyffis weill cowld gluder.	*These; flatter women well*
35	Rycht wondir weill plesit thai all wyffis	
	And tawld thame tailis of haly sanctis lyffis,	*holy saints' lives*
	Quhill on a tyme thay purposit to pass hame,	*Till; go home*

Bot verry tyrit and wett wes freir Allane, *tired; wet*
For he wes awld and micht nocht wele travell, *old; might not*
40　And als he had ane littill spyce of gravell. *touch of kidney stones*
Freir Robert wes young and verry hett of blude, *hot of blood*
And be the way he bure both clothis and hude *along the way he carried; hood*
And all thair geir, for he wes strong and wicht. *gear; robust*
　　Be that it drew neir towart the nicht, *By the time that*
45　As thay wer cumand towart the toune full neir, *coming*
Freir Allane said than, "Gud bruder deir,
It is so lait, I dreid the yet be closit, *I fear the gate will be closed*
And we ar tyrit, and verry evill disposit *exhausted; ill prepared*
To luge owt of the toun bot gif that we *lodge; unless*
50　In sume gud houss this nycht mot herbryt be." *might be sheltered*
　　Swa wynnit thair ane woundir gude hostillar *So there resided; innkeeper*
Without the toun intill a fair manar, *Outside; manor*
And Symon Lawrear wes his name.
Ane fair blyth wyf he had of ony ane, *He had a wife, fairest and merriest of anyone*
55　Bot scho wes sumthing dynk and dengerous. *she; somewhat dressy and haughty*
The silly freiris quhen thay come to the houss *came*
With fair hailsing and bekking courteslye, *greeting; bowing*
To thame scho answerit agane in hye. *in haste*
Freir Robert sperit eftir the gudman, *inquired after the host*
60　And scho agane answerit thame thane:
"He went fra hame, God wait, on Weddinsday, *from home, God knows*
In the cuntré for to seik corne and hay, *oats*
And uthir thingis quhairof we haif neid." *whereof*
　　Freir Robert said, "I pray grit God him speid
65　Him haill and sound into his travell." *safe*
And hir desyrit the stowp to fill of aill *[he] asked; tankard; ale*
"That we may drink, for I am wondir dry."
With that the wyfe went furth richt schortly *quickly*
And fillit the stowp and brocht in breid and cheiss. *brought*
70　Thay eit and drank and satt at thair awin eiss. *ease*
　　Freir Allane said to the gudwyf in hye, *mistress of the household*
"Cum hiddir, deme, and sett yow doun me bye; *dame; by me*
And fill the cop agane anis to me." *once again*
　　Freir Robert said, "Full weill payit sall ye be." *shall*
75　　The freiris wer blyth, and mirry tailis cowld tell.
And even with that thay hard the prayer bell *at the same time as that*
Of thair awin abbay, and than thay wer agast
Becauss thay knew the yettis wer closit fast *gates were closed firmly*
That thay on na wayiss micht gett entré. *no way*
80　Than the gudwyfe thay prayit for cheritie *the love of God*
To grant thame herbrye that ane nicht. *lodging*
　　Bot scho to thame gaif answer with grit hicht: *haughtiness*
"The gudman is fra hame, as I yow tald; *told*
And God it wait, gif I durst be so bald *God knows, if I dared; bold*

85 To herbry freiris in this houss with me,	
Quhat wald Symon say — ha, benedicité! —	*gracious*
Bot in his absence I abusit his place?	
Our deir lady Mary keip mee fra sic cace	*such a case*
And keip me owt of perrell and of schame."	
90 Than auld freir Allane said, "Na, fair dame,	
For Godis saik heir me quhat I sall say.	
In gud faith, we will both be deid or day.	*before*
The way is evill, and I am tyrit and wett.	*difficult*
Our yettis ar closit that we may nocht in gett,	
95 And to our abbay we can nocht win in.	*get*
To causs ws peireiss but help ye haif grit syn.	*[to] perish without*
Thairfoir of verry neid we mon byd still,	*must stay*
And ws commit alhaill into your will."	*wholly*
The gudwyf lukit unto the freiris tway	*looked at; two*
100 And at the last to thame this could scho say:	
"Ye byd nocht heir, be Him that ws all coft,	*abide; redeemed*
Bot gif ye list to lig up in yone loft	*Unless you please to lie*
Quhilk is weill wrocht into the hallis end;	*built*
Ye sall fynd stray, and clathis I sall yow send;	*straw; bedclothes*
105 Quhair, and ye list, pass on baith in feir,	*Where, if you please; both together*
For on no wayiss will I repair haif heir."	*company*
Hir madin than scho send hir on befoir,	
And hir thay followit baith withowttin moir.	*without [saying] more*
Thay war full blyth, and did as scho thame kend,	*told*
110 And up thay went into the hallis end,	
Intill a loft, wes maid for corne and hay.	*[that] was*
Scho maid thair bed, syne past doun but delay,	*without*
Closit the trop, and thay remanit still	*trapdoor*
Into the loft. Thay wantit of thair will.	*They lacked what they wanted*
115 Freir Allane lay doun as he best micht.	
Freir Robert said, "I hecht to walk this nicht.	*I vow to stay awake*
Quha wait? Perchance sum sport I ma espy."	*Who knows? Perhaps*
Thuss in the loft latt I thir freiris ly,	*these*
And of the gudwyf now I will speik mair.	
120 Scho wes richt blyth that thay wer closit thair,	*enclosed*
For scho had maid ane tryst that samyn nicht	*date; same*
Freir Johine hir luvis supper for to dicht.	*prepare*
And scho wald haif none uder cumpany	
Becauss freir Johine that nicht with hir sowld ly,	*should*
125 Quha dwelland wes into that samyne toun,	*Who was living*
And ane blak freir he wes of grit renoun.	
He governit alhaill the abbacy.	*the whole estate of the abbot*
Silwer and gold he had aboundantly.	
He had a prevy posterne of his awin	*private gate*
130 Quhair he micht ische, quhen that he list, unknawin.	*issue*
Now this, into the toun I leif him still,	*this [one]*

	Bydand his tyme, and turne agane I will	
	To thiss fair wyfe, how scho the fyre cowld beit,	*make*
	And thristit on fatt caponis to the speit,	*thrusted; spit*
135	And fatt cunyngis to fyre did scho lay,	*rabbits (conies)*
	Syne bad the madin "in all the haist thow may"	
	To flawme and turne and rost thame tenderly;	*baste*
	And to hir chalmer so scho went in hy.	*room; in haste*
	Scho pullit hir cunt and gaif hit buffetis tway	*two slaps*
140	Upoun the cheikis, syne till it cowd scho say,	*to it did she*
	"Ye sowld be blyth and glaid at my requeist:	*should; request*
	Thir mullis of youris ar callit to ane feist."	*These lips of yours are invited*
	Scho cleithis hir in a kirtill of fyne reid;	*clothes; gown of fine red cloth*
	Ane fair quhyt curch scho puttis upoun hir heid;	*white kerchief*
145	Hir kirtill wes of silk and silwer fyne,	*fine silver thread*
	Hir uther garmentis as the reid gold did schyne.	*red*
	On every finger scho werrit ringis two:	*wore*
	Scho was als prowd as ony papingo.	*parrot*
	The burde scho cuverit with clath of costly greyne;	*board; covered; green*
150	Hir napry aboif wes woundir weill besene.	*table linen; appointed*
	Than but scho went to se gif ony come,	*out she went; if anyone came*
	Scho thocht full lang to meit hir lufe freir Johine.	*thought [it] very long; love*
	Syne schortly did this freir knok at the yett.	
	His knok scho kend and did so him in lett.	*knew; accordingly let him in*
155	Scho welcomit him in all hir best maneir.	
	He thankit hir and said, "My awin luve deir,	
	Haif thair ane pair of bossis gud and fyne —	*leather wine bottles*
	Thay hald ane gallone full of Gascone wyne —	
	And als ane pair of pertrikis, richt now slane,	*partridges, just now killed*
160	And eik ane creill full of breid of mane.	*basket; white bread*
	This haif I brocht to yow, my awin luve deir;	
	Thairfor, I pray yow, be blyth and mak gud cheir.	
	Sen it is so that Semon is fra hame,	*Since*
	I wilbe hamely now with yow, gud dame."	*wish to be familiar*
165	Scho sayis, "Ye ar full hertly welcome heir	
	At ony tyme quhen that ye list appeir."	*you choose*
	With that scho smylit woundir lustely;	*smiled; willingly*
	He thristit hir hand againe richt prevely.	*squeezed; in response; discreetly*
	Than in hett luve thay talkit uderis till.	*hot; to [each] other*
170	Thus at thair sport now will I leif thame still	
	And tell yow of thir silly freiris two	
	Wer lokit in the loft amang the stro.	*[Who]; straw*
	Freir Allane in the loft still can ly;	*lay still*
	Freir Robert had ane littill jelosy,	*suspicion*
175	For in his hairt he had ane persaving,	*perception*
	And throw the burdis he maid with his botkin	*boards; bodkin (dagger)*
	A littill hoill. On sic a wyiss maid he	*He made [it] in such a manner*
	All that thay did thair doun he micht weill se,	

And every word he herd that thay did say.

180 Quhen scho wes prowd, richt woundir fresche and gay,[1]

Scho callit him baith hert, lemmane, and luve. *both; lover*

Lord God, gif than his curage wes aboif! *boldness; at a higher level*

So prelatlyk sat he into the chyre, *like a prelate; chair*

Scho rownis than ane pistill in his eir, *whispers; story*

185 Thuss sportand thame and makand melody. *enjoying themselves*

And quhen scho saw the supper wes reddy,

Scho gois belyfe and cuveris the burde annon, *quickly; table soon*

And syne the pair of bossis hes scho tone, *leather wine bottles; taken*

And sett thame doun upoun the burde hir by.

190   And evin with that thay hard the gudman cry, *just then*

And knokand at the yett he cryit fast. *vigorously*

Quhen thay him hard they wer than both agast, *amazed*

And als freir Johine wes in a fellone fray. *also; huge fright*

He stert up fast and wald haif bene away.

195 Bot all for nocht: he micht no way win owt. *get out*

     The gudwyfe spak than with a visage stowt: *furious face*

"Yone is Symone that makis all this fray *noise*

That I micht thol it full weill had bene away. *stand it very well [if he]*

I sall him quyt, and I leif half a yeir, *pay him back, if I live*

200 That cummert hes ws thus in sic maneir, *Who has got in our way thus*

Becauss for him we may nocht byd togidder. *stay*

I sar repent, and wo is ye come hidder, *sorely; it's a terrible thing that you*

For we wer weill gif that ye wer away." *would be well off if*

     "Quhat sall I do? Allace," the freir can say.

205   "Hyd yow," scho said, "quhill he be brocht to rest. *until*

Into yone troich, I think it for the best. *the trough over there*

It lyis mekle and huge in all yone nwke, *big; the whole corner over there*

It held a boll of meill quhen that we buke." *six bushels of (oat?)meal; baked*

Than undir it scho gart him creip in hy *made him crawl in a hurry*

210 And bad him lurk thair verry quyetly.

Scho closit him and syne went on hir way, *covered*

     "Quhat sall I do, allace!" the freir can say.

     Syne to hir madin spedyly scho spak:

"Go to the fyre and the meitis fra it tak. *foods*

215 Be bissy als and slokkin out the fyre. *careful; extinguish*

Ga cloiss yone burd and tak away the chyre, *Go hide*

And lok up all into yone almery, *lock; cupboard*

Baith meit and drink, with wyne and aill put by. *food*

The mayne breid als, thow hyd it with the wyne.

220 That being done, thow sowp the houss clene syne, *sweep*

That na apperance of feist be heir sene,

---

[1] *Though she was gorgeous, very elegantly dressed up, and showy*

Bot sobirly our selffis dois sustene."[1]
And syne withowttin ony mair delay
Scho castis off haill hir fresch array,   *entirely her fancy clothing*
225 Than went scho to hir bed annone,
And tholit him to knok his fill, Symone.   *allowed*
     Quhen he wes for knoking tyrit wes and cryid,   *shouted*
Abowt he went unto the udir syd,   *other side [of the house]*
And on Alesone fast cold he cry.   *steadily shouted to Alison*
230 And at the last scho anserit crabitly: *crossly*
"Ach, quha be this that knawis sa weill my name?
Go henss," scho sayis, "for Symon is fra hame,   *hence*
And I will herbry no gaistis heir, parfey.   *guests; truly*
Thairfoir I pray yow to wend on your way,   *go*
235 For at this tyme ye may nocht lugit be."   *lodged*
     Than Symone said, "Fair dame, ken ye nocht me?   *recognize*
I am your Symone, and husband of this place."   *farmer of this piece of land*
     "Ar ye my spous Symone?" scho sayis; "Allace,
Be misknawlege I had almaist misgane.   *misunderstanding; made a mistake*
240 Quha wenit that ye sa lait wald haif cum hame?"   *knew; so late*
     Scho stertis up and gettis licht in hy   *jumps; gets light in a hurry*
And oppinit than the yet full haistely.
Scho tuk fra him his geir at all devyiss,   *took his gear from him completely*
Syne welcomit him on maist hairtly wyiss.   *most affectionate manner*
245 He bad the madin kindill on the fyre,   *light*
"Syne graith me meit, and tak thee all thy hyre."   *prepare me food; recompense*
     The gudwyf said schortly, "Ye me trow,   *Believe me*
Heir is no meit that ganand is for yow."   *appropriate*
     "How sa, fair deme? Ga gait me cheiss and breid.   *get*
250 Ga fill the stowp. Hald me no mair in pleid,   *tankard. Don't keep me arguing*
For I am verry tyrit, wett, and cauld."   *cold*
     Than up scho raiss and durst nocht mair be bauld,   *rose; audacious*
Cuverit the burde, thairon sett meit in hy,
Ane sowsit nolt fute and scheip heid haistely   *pickled cow's foot; sheep's head*
255 And sum cauld meit scho brocht to him belyve,   *food; quickly*
And fillit the stowp. The gudman than wes blyth.
     Than satt he doun and swoir, "Be all hallow,   *By all saint[s]*
I fair richt weill and I had ane gud fallow.   *I'd be doing; if I had a companion*
Dame, eit with me and drink, gif that ye may."
260 Said the gudwyf, "Devill in the tim may I;   *I can't at this ungodly hour*
It wer mair meit into your bed to be   *more suitable*
Than now to sit desyrand cumpany."   *asking for*
     Freir Robert said, "Allace, gud bruder deir,
I wald the gudman wist that we wer heir.   *I wish the goodman knew*
265 Quha wait? Parchance sum bettir wald he fair,   *he would eat (fare) somewhat better*

---

[1] Lines 221–22: *So that no appearance of a feast be seen here, / But [the appearance is that] we eat soberly*

For sickerly my hairt will ay be sair — *certainly my heart will always be sore*
Gif yone scheipheid with Symon birneist be — *sheep's head is polished clean by Simon*
Sa mekill gud cheir being in the almerie." — *So much good food; cupboard*
And with that word he gaif ane hoist anone. — *cough*

270 The gudman hard and speirit, "Quha is yone?" — *asked; over there*
The gudwyf said, "Yone ar freiris tway."
Symone said, "Tell me, quhat freiris be thay?"
"Yone is freir Robert and silly freir Allane,
That all this day hes travellit with grit pane. — *effort*

275 Be thay come heir it wes so very lait — *By [the time that] they came*
Curfiw wes rung and closit wes thair yait, — *Curfew; gate*
And in yond loft I gaif thame harbrye."
The gudman said, "So God haif part of me,
Tha freiris twa ar hairtly welcome hidder. — *Those*

280 Ga call thame doun that we ma drink togidder."
The gudwyf said, "I reid yow lat thame be; — *advise*
Thay had levir sleip nor sit in cumpanye." — *rather sleep than*
The gudman said unto the maid thone, — *then*
"Go pray thame baith to cum till me annone." — *to*

285 And sone the trop the madin oppinit than, — *trapdoor*
And bad thame baith cum doun to the gudman.
Freir Robert said, "Now be sweit Sanct Jame, — *sweet*
The gudman is verry welcome hame.
And for his weilfair dalie do we pray.

290 We sall annone cum doun, to him ye say."
Than with that word thay start up baith attone, — *jumped up both at once*
And doun the trop delyverly thay come, — *ladder quickly*
Halsit Symone als sone as thay him se; — *Greeted; saw*
And he agane thame welcomit hairtfullie,

295 And said, "Cum heir, myne awin bredir deir, — *brothers*
And sett yow doun sone besyd me heir,
For I am now allone, as ye may se.
Thairfoir sitt doun, and beir me cumpanye, — *keep*
And tak yow part of sic gud as we haif." — *such*

300 Freir Allane said, "Ser, I pray God yow saif, — *God save you*
For heir is now annwch of Godis gud." — *enough*
Than Symon anserit, "Now be the rud, — *by the cross*
Yit wald I gif ane croun of gold, for me, — *Nevertheless; gold coin*
For sum gud meit and drink amangis ws thre."

305 Freir Robert said, "Quhat drinkis wald ye craif, — *ask for*
Or quhat meitis desyre ye for to haif?
For I haif mony sindry practikis seir — *many different methods*
Beyond the sey in Pareiss did I leir — *[That] beyond the sea in Paris; I learned*
That I wald preve glaidly for your saik, — *demonstrate; sake*

310 And for your demys, that harbry cowd ws maik. — *wife's, who gave us shelter*
I tak on hand, and ye will counsale keip, — *I undertake, if you will keep it quiet*
That I sall gar yow se or ever I sleip — *shall make; before*

Of the best meit that is in this cuntré,   *[Some] of*
Of Gascone wyne, gif ony in it be,   *if any is in it*
315 Or be thair ony within ane hundreth myle,
It salbe heir within a bony quhyle."   *in good time*
The gudman had grit marvell of this taill
And said, "My hairt neir be haill   *never be whole*
Bot gif ye preve that practik or ye parte,   *Unless; before you leave*
320 Be quhatkin science, nigromansy, or airt,   *whatever learning, witchcraft, or skill*
To mak ane sport."   *entertainment*
          And than the freir uprais: *rose up*
He tuk his buk and to the feir he gais.   *fire he goes*
He turnis it our and reidis it a littill space   *over; little while*
And to the eist direct he turnis his face;   *east straight*
325 Syne to the west he turnit and lukit doun,   *Then*
And tuk his buk and red ane orisoun.   *prayer*
And ay his eyne wer on the almery   *always; eyes; cupboard*
And on the troch quhair that freir Johine did ly.
Than sat he doun and kest abak his hude: *threw back*
330 He granit and he glowrit as he wer woid,   *groaned; glowered as if; crazy*
And quhylis still he satt in studeing,   *sometimes*
And uthir quhylis upoun his buk reding.
And with baith his handis he wald clap,
And uthir quhylis wald he glour and gaip,   *glower; gape*
335 Syne in the sowth he turnit him abowt
Weill thryiss and mair, than lawly cowd he lowt   *Fully thrice and more; bowed low*
Quhen that he come neir the almery.
Thairat our dame had woundir grit invy,   *hostility*
For in hir hairt scho had ane parsaving   *perception*
340 That he had knawin all hir govirning.   *conduct*
Scho saw him gif the almery sic a straik,   *slap*
Unto hirself scho said, "Full weill I wait
I am bot schent: he knawis full weill my thocht.   *absolutely ruined*
Quhat sall I do? Allace that I wes wrocht!
345 Get Symon wit, it wilbe deir doing."   *Should Simon find out*
          Be that the freir had left his studeing   *By then*
And on his feit he startis up, full sture,   *stern*
And come agane and seyit all his cure   *said [that] all his business*
"Now is it done, and ye sall haif playntie   *plenty*
350 Of breid and wyne, the best in this cuntré.
Thairfoir, fair dame, get up deliverlie   *quickly*
And ga belyfe unto yone almerie
And oppin it, and se ye bring ws syne
Ane pair of boissis full of Gascone wyne.   *leather wine bottles*
355 Thay had ane galloun and mair, that wait ws weill.   *hold*
And bring ws als the mayne breid in a creill,   *white bread; basket*
Ane pair of cunyngis fat and het pypand,   *rabbits; piping hot*
The caponis als ye sall ws bring fra hand,   *at once*

	Twa pair of pertrikis — I wait thair is no ma —	*partridges; more*
360	And eik of pluveris se that ye bring ws twa."	*plovers*
	The gudwyf wist it wes no variance.	*discrepancy*
	Scho knew the freir had sene hir govirnance.	*conduct*
	Scho saw it wes no bute for to deny.	*no use*
	With that scho went unto the almery	
365	And oppinit it, and than scho fand thair	
	All that the freir had spokin of befoir.	
	Scho stert abak as scho wer in afray	*jumped back as if; alarmed*
	And sanyt hir, and smyland cowd scho say,	*crossed herself*
	"Ha, banadicitie! Quhat may this bene?	*be*
370	Quhaevir afoir hes sic a fairly sene,	*before; wonder*
	Sa grit a marvell as now hes apnit heir?	*happened*
	Quhat sall I say? He is ane haly freir.	
	He said full swth of all that he did say."	*complete truth*
	Scho brocht all furth, and on the burd cowd lay	
375	Baith breid and wyne, and uthir thingis moir:	
	Cunyngis and caponis, as ye haif hard befoir.	
	Pertrikis and pluveris befoir thame hes scho brocht.	
	The freir knew weill and saw thair wantit nocht,	*nothing was missing*
	Bot all wes furth brocht evin at his devyiss.	*command*
380	And Symone saw it appinnit on this wyiss;	
	He had grit wondir, and sweris be the mone,	*moon*
	That freir Robert weill his dett had done.	*what he promised*
	"He may be callit ane man of grit science	
	Sa suddanly that all this purviance	*supply of food*
385	Hes brocht ws heir, throw his grit subteltie,	*cunning*
	And throw his knawlege in filosophie.	
	In ane gud tyme it wes quhen he come hidder.	
	Now fill the cop that we ma drink togidder	
	And mak gud cheir eftir this langsum day,	*long*
390	For I haif riddin ane woundir wilsome way.	*dreary*
	Now God be lovit, heir is suffisance	*praised; sufficient supply*
	Unto ws all, throw your gud govirnance."	*deed*
	And than annone thay drank evin round abowt	*equally in turn*
	Of Gascone wyne; the freiris playit cop-owt.	*(see note)*
395	Thay sportit thame and makis mirry cheir	*amused themselves; are very cheerful*
	With sangis lowd, baith Symone and the freir.	
	And on this wyiss the lang nicht thay ourdraif.	*drove away*
	Nothing thay want that thay desyrd to haif.	*lack*
	Than Symon said to the gudwyf in hy,	
400	"Cum heir, fair dame, and sett you doun me by	
	And tak parte of sic gud as we haif heir,	
	And hairtly I yow pray to thank this freir	
	Of his bening grit besines and cure	*benign; diligence; care*
	That he hes done to ws upoun this flure;	*(see note)*
405	And brocht ws meit and drink haboundantlie,	*abundantly*

Quhairfoir of richt we aucht mirry to be."   *ought*
  Bot all thair sport, quhen thay wer maist at eiss,   *most at ease*
Unto our deme it wes bot littill pleiss,   *pleasure*
For uther thing thair wes into hir thocht.
410 Scho wes so red hir hairt wes ay on flocht   *frightened; in a flutter*
That throw the freir scho sowld discoverit be.   *exposed*
To him scho lukit ofttymes effeiritlie,   *fearfully*
And ay disparit in hart was scho,   *the whole time despairing*
That he had witt of all hir purveance, to.   *information about her preparations, too*
415 This satt scho still, and wist no udir wane: *Thus; she; alternative*
Quhatevir thay say scho lute him all allane.   *let; alone*
Bot scho drank with thame into cumpany
With fenyeit cheir, and hert full wo and hevy.   *feigned enjoyment; miserable*
  Bot thay wer blyth annwche, God watt, and sang,   *enough*
420 For ay the wyne was rakand thame amang,   *going quickly*
Quhill at the last thay woix richt blyth ilkone.   *Till at last they all got pretty elevated*
  Than Symone said unto the freir annone,
"I marvell mikill how that this may be,   *very much*
Intill schort tyme that ye sa suddanlye
425 Hes brocht to ws sa mony denteis deir."   *so many expensive delicacies*
  "Thairof haif ye no marvell," quod the freir,
"I haif ane pege full prevy of my awin,   *servant; confidential*
Quhenevir I list will cum to me unknawin   *[Who]; without being noticed*
And bring to me sic thing as I will haif.   *want to have*
430 Quhatevir I list, it nedis me nocht to craif.   *I don't need to ask*
Thairfoir be blyth, and tak in pacience,   *accept [the situation]*
And trest ye weill I sall do diligence: *trust; exert myself*
Gif that ye list or thinkis to haif moir,   *If you like or have a mind to*
It salbe had, and I sall stand thairfoir.   *and I shall insist on it*
435 Incontinent that samyn sall ye se.   *Immediately that very thing*
Bot I protest that ye keip it previe.   *demand; secret*
Latt no man wit that I can do sic thing."
  Than Symone swoir and said, "Be Hevynnis King,
It salbe kepit prevy as for me.
440 Bot bruder deir, your serwand wald I se,   *servant*
Gif it yow pleiss, that we may drynk togidder,
For I wait nocht gif ye ma ay cum hidder,
Quhen that we want our neidis, sic as this."   *lack our necessities, such as this*
  The freir said, "Nay, so mot I haif hevynis bliss,   *as I hope to have*
445 Yow to haif the sicht of my serwand —   *sight*
It can nocht be, ye sall weill undirstand,
That ye may se him graithly in his awin kynd,   *properly in his own form*
Bot ye anone sowld go owt of your mynd,   *But; would*
He is so fowll and ugly for to se.
450 I dar nocht awnter for to tak on me   *venture to take the responsibility*
To bring him hidder, heir into our sicht,   *here*
And namely now, so lait into the nicht,   *especially*

Bot gif it wer on sic a maner wyiss: *Unless; in such a way*
Him to translait or ellis dissagyiss   *transform or else disguise*
455 Fra his awin kynd into ane uder stait."
    Than Symone said, "I mak no moir debait.
As pleisis yow, so likis it to me,   *so it pleases me*
As evir ye list, bot fane wald I him se."   *Just as you like, but gladly*
    "Intill quhat kynd sall I him gar appeir?"   *form; cause to appear*
460   Than Symone said, "In liknes of a freir,
In quhyt cullour richt as yourself it war,   *the color white just as if it were you*
For quhyt cullour will nabody deir."   *harm*
    Freir Robert said that swa it cowld nocht be,
For sic caussis as he may weill foirse,   *foresee*
465 "That he compeir into our habeit quhyt;   *appear*
Untill our ordour it wer a grit dispyte   *To our order it would be; outrage*
That ony sic unworthy wicht as he   *creature*
Intill our habeit men sowld behald or se.
Bot sen it pleissis yow that ar heir,   *since*
470 Ye sall him se in liknes of a freir
In habeit blak it was his kynd to weir,   *[that] it; nature*
Into sic wyiss that he sall no man deir,   *In such a way; harm*
Gif ye so do and rewll yow at all wyiss   *restrain yourself in all ways*
To hald yow cloiss and still at my devyiss: *hidden and silent; command*
475 Quhatevir it be ye owdir se or heir,   *either*
Ye speik no word, nor mak no kynd of steir,   *movement*
Bot hald yow cloiss quhill I haif done my cure."   *hidden till; my job*
Than said he, "Semon, ye mone be on the flure   *must*
Neirhand besyd, with staff into your hand.   *Close at hand*
480 Haif ye no dreid: I sall yow ay warrand."   *protect*
Than Symon said, "I assent that it be swa."   *so*
And up he start and gat a libberla   *got a cudgel*
Into his hand, and on the flure he stert,
Sumthing effrayit, thoch stalwart was his hart.   *Somewhat frightened*
485   Than to the freir said Symone verry sone,
"Now tell me, maister, quhat ye will haif done."
    "Nothing," he said, "bot hald yow cloiss and still.
Quhatevir I do, tak ye gud tent thairtill,   *pay close attention to it*
And neir the dur ye hyd yow prevely.   *door*
490 And quhen I bid yow stryk, strek hardely: *tell you to hit, hit boldly*
Into the nek se that ye hit him richt."   *directly*
    "That sall I warrand," quod he, "with all my micht."   *guarantee*
    Thuss on the flure I leif him standand still,
Bydand his tyme, and turne agane I will
495 How that the freir did take his buke in hy   *[To tell]*
And turnit our the levis full besely   *turned over*
Ane full lang space, and quhen he had done swa,   *time*
Towart the troch withowttin wordis ma
He goiss belyfe, and on this wyiss sayis he:

500 "Ha, how, Hurlybass, now I conjure thee
That thow upryss and sone to me appeir,   *rise up*
In habeit blak, in liknis of a freir.
Owt of this troch quhair that thow dois ly
Thow rax thee sone and mak no dyn nor cry.   *rouse yourself*
505 Thow tumbill our the troch that we may se,   *tumble over*
And unto ws thow schaw thee oppinlie,   *show*
And in this place se that thow no man greif,   *hurt*
Bot draw thy handis boith into thy sleif,
And pull thy cowll doun owttour thy face.   *cowl down across*
510 Thow may thank God that thow gettis sic a grace.
Thairfoir thow turss thee to thyne awin ressett.   *be off to your own dwelling*
Se this be done, and mak no moir debait.   *resistance*
In thy depairting, se thow mak no deray   *harmful disturbance*
Unto no wicht, bot frely pass thy way.
515 And in this place se that thow cum no moir
Bot I command thee, or ellis thee charge befoir.   *Unless; order*
And our the stair se that thow ga gud speid;   *across the flight of stairs; speedily*
Gif thow dois nocht, on thy awin perrell beid."   *bide (stay)*
        With that the freir that under the troch lay,
520 Raxit him sone, bot he wes in afray.   *Stretched; frightened*
And up he raiss and wist na bettir wayn,   *expedient*
Bot off the troch he tumlit, our the stane.   *tumbled, over the millstone*
Syne fra the samyn quhairin he thocht him lang[1]
Unto the dur he preisit him to gang,   *hurried himself to go*
525 With hevy cheir and drery countenance,
For nevir befoir him hapnit sic a chance.
        And quhen freir Robert saw him gangand by,   *going*
Unto the gudman full lowdly cowd he cry,
"Stryk, stryk herdely! For now is tyme to thee."   *now is your time*
530   With that Symone a felloun flap lait fle: *let fly a fierce blow*
With his burdoun he hit him on the nek.   *cudgel*
He wes sa ferce, he fell outtour the sek   *over the sack [of corn]*
And brak his heid upoun ane mustard stane.
Be this freir Johine attour the stair is gane   *over*
535 In sic wyiss that mist he hes the trap   *has missed the ladder*
And in ane myr he fell, sic wes his hap,   *luck*
Wes fourty futis of breid under the stair;   *feet in breadth*
Yeit gat he up with clething nothing fair.   *Again; not at all clean*
Full drerelie upoun his feit he stude,   *miserably*
540 And throw the myre full smertly than he yude,   *went*
And our the wall he clam richt haistely   *climbed*
Quhilk round abowt wes laid with stanis dry.   *Which*
Of his eschaping in hairt he wes full fane.   *escaping; glad*

---

[1] *Then from the same [trough] wherein he thought he had been a long time*

I trow he salbe laith to cum agane.   *believe; loath*
545   With that freir Robert start abak and saw
Quhair the gudman lay sa woundir law   *low*
Upoun the flure, and bleidand wes his heid.   *bleeding*
He stert to him and went he had bene deid   *thought*
And clawcht him up withowttin wordis moir   *snatched*
550   And to the dur delyverly him bure;   *bore*
And fra the wind wes blawin twyiss in his face,   *from [the time when]; blown twice*
Than he ourcome within a lytill space.   *recovered*
And than freir Robert franyt at him fast   *asked; earnestly*
Quhat ailit him to be so sair agast.
555   He said, "Yone feynd had maid me in effray."   *terrified me*
      "Latt be," quod he, "the werst is all away;   *Let it be; the worst is over*
Mak mirry, man, and se ye morne na mair.   *worry no more*
Ye haif him strikin quyt owttour the stair.   *knocked him right over*
I saw him slip, gif I the suth can tell: *truth*
560   Doun our the stair intill a myr he fell.   *over*
Bot lat him go — he wes a graceles gaist —   *wicked*
And boun yow to your bed, for it is best."   *get ready for*
      Thuss Symonis heid upoun the stane wes brokin,
And our the stair the freir in myre hes loppin   *leapt*
565   And tap our taill he fyld wes wounder ill,   *top over tail; dirtied*
And Alesone on na wayiss gat hir will.   *got*
This is the story that hapnit of that freir:
No moir thair is, bot Chryst ws help most deir.
      Finis.

EXPLANATORY NOTES TO THE FREIRIS OF BERWIK

ABBREVIATIONS: *CT*: Chaucer, *Canterbury Tales*; *DOST*: *Dictionary of the Older Scottish Tongue*; **H**: Henry Huntington Library, San Marino, California, Article 88850, printed at Aberdeen by Edward Raban; *MED*: *Middle English Dictionary*; **MS B**: Bannatyne Manuscript, Edinburgh, National Library of Scotland, MS Advocates' 1.1.6; **MS M**: Maitland Folio Manuscript, Cambridge, Magdalene College, MS Pepys 2553; **OE**: Old English; *OED*: *Oxford English Dictionary*.

1–27   The poem opens in high rhetorical fashion, with this description of the fortified town of Berwick. But if the opening fits a rhetorical strategy for Latin texts described by Ernst Curtius, the description of the fortifications, R. D. S. Jack points out, belongs to *fabliau*. Curtius says, "The rules for eulogies of cities were developed in detail by late antique theory. The site had first to be treated, then the other excellencies of the city, and not least its significance in respect to the cultivation of the arts and sciences. In the Middle Ages this last topos is given an ecclesiastical turn" (*European Literature and the Latin Middle Ages*, trans. Willard R. Trask, Bollingen Series, 36 [New York: Pantheon Books, 1953], p. 157). In this poem the description of the site beside the River Tweed and the description of the town are mixed in lines 1–23; the orders of friars living there are listed in lines 24–27. That the lines are a standard topos is made evident by the fact that they have nothing to do with the events of the poem, which take place well outside the town walls. The opening seems to have little relevance, as in his Prologue Chaucer's Clerk says Petrarch's description of the valley of the Po does at the beginning of his version of the tale of Griselda. But as Jack points out, "the Scottish author has used the impregnability of the walls and gates of Berwick (historically due to that town's vulnerable position in border warfare) as an ironic counterpoint for the open walls and gates of Alesone's house and person" ("*Freiris of Berwik* and Chaucerian Fabliau," p. 146). Certainly the defenses are impressive: in lines 9–14, the town is walled and double-ditched; the castle has towers and turrets and battlements; the portcullises are designed so that if an attacking party slips in as far as the opening to the castle, the first attackers will be caught within the gate tower, between the lower portcullises and an inner gate.

1   *into*. The prepositions *into* and *intill* are used throughout with the meaning "in."

2   *the quhilk*. The relative pronoun *the quhilk* is used throughout with the meaning "which" or "that."

4   *mony lordis hes bene*. The form *hes* was used for the plural of *have* from the fifteenth century in Scotland.

24–26   The four orders of friars were, as the poem implies, the Jacobins or Dominicans, the Carmelites, the Hermit Friars of St. Augustine, and the Franciscans or Friars Minor. Berwick was the only town in Scotland to have all four orders (see Cowan, *Medieval Religious Houses*), and the fact is a testimony to the importance of the place in the later Middle Ages. See the introduction to *The Freiris of Berwik* for a discussion of why the poet calls the Jacobins white, and see note to line 126, below.

28   Fair May mornings are the conventional settings for romance, lyric, and allegory alike, a timing used here even though the action proper begins on a cold, wet evening.

34   *silly freiris. Silly* is used as a recurring epithet, carrying more or less ironic connotations of "holy" from the older form *sely*, and also meaning "pitiable" or "harmless."

77   *abbay.* Friars did not live in abbeys; their dwellings were called cloisters or simply houses, and later, convents. The poet here shows a lack of familiarity with the mendicant orders.

87   *Bot in his absence I abusit his place.* The general sense is clear enough, but not whether the goodwife means that Simon would think that she abused his manor by lodging the friars in it in his absence or whether she betrayed his role as husband by lodging friars in his absence.

116   *I hecht to walk this nicht.* "I vow to walk like a ghost tonight"? More likely, the *l* of *walk* simply indicates a long *a*, and the verb is *wake* (watch, stay awake) in a Scottish spelling.

126   *And ane blak freir he wes.* The poet is confused about the orders of friars and the colors normally associated with them. The Black Friars were the Jacobins; but Allane and Robert are Jacobins, and the poet calls them White Friars. Friar Johine is probably meant to be a Franciscan, since Jacobins and Franciscans were archenemies. Franciscans were known as Gray Friars, and it was the Carmelites who were White Friars. But for this poet, Allane and Robert are Jacobins and White Friars, and Johine is a Black Friar. See the introduction to the poem for further discussion of this confusion.

127   *He governit alhaill the abbacy.* Again, the terminology is wrong: friars were not governed by abbots.

149–50   *The burde scho cuuerit with clath of costly greyne; / Hir napry aboif wes woundir weill besene.* The term *burde* has caused confusion in MS B and also in H, where it is taken to refer to a table the goodwife is covering in the bedroom. But later (line 187) she covers one in the hall, in preparation for the supper. Here the *burde* was probably originally meant as an embroidered ornamental strip of cloth that the goodwife is putting on herself; see *MED* bord(e) and *DOST* burd(e) n². MS M reads:

          and of ane burde of silk richt costlie grein
          hir tusche wes with silwer weill besene

But instead of a silk scarf of very costly green material, the tissue well provided with silver, the goodwife is in version B dealing with a table that she covered with cloth of costly green material; her table linen above was very well appointed.

158   *Gascone wyne*. Gascony was the wine-growing area on the continent that belonged to England until 1453 and had well-established trade with the British Isles.

160   *breid of mane*. I.e., pandemain, fine bread made of white wheat flour.

184   *Scho rownis than ane pistill in his eir*. Compare Chaucer's Wife of Bath's Tale, *CT* III(D)1021 ("Tho rowned she a pistel in his ere"). But in The Wife of Bath's Tale, the term *pistel* has only the sense "narration"; here, in the context of line 183, it also carries suggestions of the epistle as part of the divine service, with the goodwife as reader and Friar Johine as prelate.

185   *makand melody*. Compare the sexual implications of the term *melodie* in Chaucer's Miller's Tale, *CT* I(A)3652 and 3306.

206   *yone troich*. The trough is a kneading trough, stored upside down, probably to keep it clean, and kept on the floor in a corner. As described in the lines that follow, it is amply big enough to hide a man if it held a boll of flour when they baked, given that a boll is a measure equivalent to six imperial bushels. The perplexity is, what did they do with all that bread? While the household undoubtedly runs on more than the sporadic income from innkeeping, there is no other indication that they are running a commercial bakery. And there is some indication that they are not: Friar Johine brings a loaf of wheat bread when he comes to supper (line 160). But this is probably not a detail that is thought through, and the point is simply that there is a very big trough tucked away in the shadows, handy for the friar to hide under.

216   *Ga cloiss yone burd and tak away the chyre*. Literally "Go close yonder board"; probably the table is a board on trestles, and it is to be dismantled and put away. "Chyre" is probably the chair on which John has been sitting, and certainly the spelling in H, *chayre*, suggests that understanding.

246   *and tak thee all thy hyre*. "And receive a good recompense"?

278   *So God haif part of me*. Roughly, "As I hope for God to have an interest in me."

287   *be sweit Sanct Jame*. The St. James sworn by here is probably one of the apostles, James the son of Zebedee. But the choice of saints in this instance probably has most to do with the convenience of the rhyme on *Jame* (a usual medieval form of the name), especially in Scottish and northern dialect where it can rhyme on words like *hame* (for *home*).

292   The phrase *doun the trop* implies a distinctively Scottish meaning of *trap*: "b. A ladder or stair giving access to a trap-door" (*Dictionary of the Scottish Language*, *trap* n.[1]). But the term applies in this poem more generally to "a ladder or moveable flight of steps leading to a loft or the like" (*OED*, *trap* n.[3]), if "the like" is understood to include the entry to the house, as at line 535.

297   He is *allone* in the sense that his wife has refused to sit and eat with him.

330   R. D. S. Jack comments on the "wry depiction of the necromantic art, its practices and vocabulary, although there is no equivalent for this in the French analogue. It is connected with madness in the Scots story ('he granit and he glowrit as he wer woid'), as was astrology in Chaucer's Miller's Tale ('this man is falle, with his astromye, in some woodnesse')." See *"Freiris of Berwik* and Chaucerian Fabliau," p. 149.

345   *Get Symon wit. To get wit* is a phrase meaning "to obtain information." See *OED wit n.* 11c.

          deir doing. The general sense is clear enough, though it is not clear whether *deir* represents the poetic adjective from OE *déor*, meaning "severe, grievous," or whether it represents the ordinary adjective *dear* from OE *déore*, in some ironic sense.

358   *fra hand*. A Scottish phrase meaning "at once" (*DOST* hand *n* 8.b.).

361   *it wes no variance*. There is no discrepancy between the food and drink in the cupboard and what Friar Robert is now claiming to have conjured into it. The plovers in line 360 have not been mentioned before, but they are not meant as an exception.

368   *sanyt hir*. Alesone crosses herself for protection from the magic that must have produced all this food out of nowhere.

369–73   Alesone's apparent amazement and enthusiastic admiration for Friar Robert's holiness and truth constitute her acceptance of a tacit deal with him: his story keeps any blame off Alesone, and she is agreeing to go along with his version of events and give him credit for supernatural powers. If he exposes her now, he will expose himself as a fraud at the same time.

394   *playit cop-owt*. To play cop-out meant to drain the cup. See *OED* cop, *n.*[1], 1.b. The phrase is attested by *DOST* from Dunbar's poems (c. 1500) to Robert Sempill's (1583).

396   *the freir*. Presumably *freir* is singular for the sake of the rhyme.

404   *upoun this flure*. The term *floor* is used oddly in this poem, as if it were a location within the room rather than underlying the entire area (see also lines 478, 483, 493, and 547). Probably there is a raised wooden floor at one end of the room, a dais on which the table would be set. Later we learn that the room is not at ground level but that there is an external flight of stairs leading to the entry door; so there must be a floor of some kind, not just beaten earth, throughout the room. But the term *floor* seems to apply only to the dais.

414   *That he had witt of all hir purveance, to*. Alesone is concerned that Robert knows not only that the food exists but also about her preparations to entertain Friar Johine.

471   *habeit blak*. The fiend naturally wears black rather than the white of harmless spirits because a black habit shows his evil nature: Robert's dig at the Black Friars and therefore Johine.

474   *To hald yow cloiss and still at my devyiss.* The raising of demons was thought to be perilous. If the conjurer stepped out of his charmed circle, or said the wrong thing, he could be seized. Simon is to remain still and silent until ordered to move.

486   *maister.* The term of respect could imply several things: that Robert is the leader in this enterprise, that Robert is an expert in necromancy, or that Robert has a Master's degree, probably in Divinity.

500   *Hurlybass* (MS M *Hurlbasie,* H *Hurls-baigs*) is the demon's name. The only other citation of Hurlbasie in *DOST* is from William Dunbar, as "a fanciful term of endearment" ("My belly huddrun, my swete hurle bawsy; Dunb. lxxv. 38"). *Hurl-* is probably from the verb, with the meaning "hurtle"; *-basie* probably represents *bausy,* adjective, likely meaning "large and clumsy"; the compound *Bausy Broun* was used, also by Dunbar, as a fiend's name. See *DOST bausy* adj: "Than all the feyndis lewche, . . . Blak Belly and Bawsy . . . Brown; Dunb. xxvi.30"). *DOST* cites from *The Poems of William Dunbar,* ed. John Small, Scottish Text Society, first series, 5 vols. (Edinburgh: Blackwood for STS, 1893), but the contemporary reader can more easily find the poems in John Conlee's edition, *William Dunbar: The Complete Works* (Kalamazoo, MI: Medieval Institute Publications, 2004). "My swete hurle bawsy" is in 72, *In a Secret Place* [*Ye brek my hart, my bony ane*], and Bausy Brown in 77, *The Dance of the Seven Deadly Sins.*

508–10   *Bot draw thy handis boith into thy sleif, / And pull thy cowll doun owttour thy face. / Thow may thank God that thow gettis sic a grace.* Friar Robert pretends to be protecting his companions from the sight of any part of the horrible fiend that is Friar Johine. The cowl was a hooded cloak worn by monks; here it is imagined as being part of the friar's habit. Friar Johine may well thank God he is getting such a grace from Friar Robert: he has the opportunity to escape from Symon without being recognized.

532–33   "[Simon] was so fierce, he fell over the sack and cracked open his head on the mustard stone." As elsewhere in the poem, domestic objects are prominent: the stone beside the trough, the sack (of grain waiting to be ground?), and a mustard stone, which may be the same as the stone mentioned above, or more likely is a smaller one, since mustard would be pounded or ground in much smaller quantities than grain.

534–37   Johine goes over some upper stairs and misses the movable steps, or trap, below them, falling into a broad patch of mud. This makes sense if one imagines a landing outside the door, then a few fixed stairs running partway down the side of the building, followed by a ladder that can be drawn up, very roughly like a modern fire escape. As instructed, Johine rushes out through the door and goes "our" the stair, straight out and over the edge rather than turning to maneuver down the ladder. Retractable stairs would be a useful means of discouraging small raiding parties from taking a lonely dwelling on the outskirts of one of the most hotly contested places on the Scots/English border.

541–42   The wall around the house is an outer ring of defense, with the mire serving as a rudimentary moat between the wall and the building. The wall is made of dry stones, that is to say, more or less flat stones fitted on top of each other without mortar. Note that at line 153, after nightfall, Johine has to knock at the gate to gain admittance, and Simon too has to have the gate opened from within to admit him at line 242. Yet the desperate Johine manages to scramble over the wall to escape.

TEXTUAL NOTES TO THE FREIRIS OF BERWIK

ABBREVIATIONS: *DOST*: *Dictionary of the Older Scottish Tongue*; **H**: Henry Huntington Library, San Marino, California, Article 88850, printed at Aberdeen by Edward Raban; **MS B**: Bannatyne Manuscript, Edinburgh, National Library of Scotland, MS Advocates' 1.1.6; **MS M**: Maitland Folio Manuscript, Cambridge, Magdalene College, MS Pepys 2553.

title	No title appears at the head of the text. The first page reads: *Heir begynnis The Freiris of Berwik.*
3–4	The lines are in reverse order in MS B.
25	MS B reads: *The carmeleitis and the monkis eik.* But the context clearly calls for the naming of the other two orders of friars in this line. The wording *Augustinianis, and als the Minouris eik* is supplied from MS M. Metrically, "Augustinianis" would need to be pronounced as "Austins," a usual pronunciation.
45	MS B reads: *As thay wer cumand towart the tovne ~~in~~ full neir.*
50	MS B reads: *sume gud ~~g~~ houss.*
88	MS B reads: *keip fra sic cace.* The pronoun and its spelling are supplied from H.
94	MS B reads: *ar ~~cols~~ closit.*
113	MS B often reads *trop,* a Scottish spelling for *trap.* But note the rhyme *trap / hap* at lines 535–36. See *DOST* trap *n.*[1]
135	MS B reads: *cuning.*
142	The version in MS M has four additional lines following line 142:
	scho said till it and softlie at scho leucht
	he did nocht ill that fand yow half aneuche
	and or I sleip I think ye salbe pleisit
	your appetyt and myn sall both be easit
200	MS B reads: *this.*
204	MS B reads: *allace <...> the.*
228	MS B reads: *the ~~th~~ udir.*
255	MS B original "belyth" corrected to "belyve."
260	MS B reads: *Said the gudwyf devill inthe tim ~~I~~ may I.*
276	MS B reads: *Curfiw wes ~~yo~~ rung and closit wes thair yait.*
305	MS B reads: *Freir robert said quhat drinkis wald ye ~~haif~~ craif.*
312	MS B reads: *ever <...> I.*
320	Missing in MS B; supplied from MS M.
321	MS B reads: *to mak ane sport and than the freir vpstart.* This version provides the missing rhyme for line 319 (on *parte*), but leaves line 322 without a rhyme for *gais.*

322	MS B reads: *freir*.
351	MS B reads: *deliuverlie*.
353	MS B reads: *oppinit it*.
384	MS B reads: *suddanly maid*.
390	MS B reads: *ffor I haif riddin ane* ~~*langsum*~~ *woundir wilsome way*.
413–14	*And ay disparit in hart was scho*
	That he had witt of all hir purveance to

This is a problematic couplet, metrically defective. MS M has no equivalent lines, and H has the following lines instead:

> *And in her heart shee did despare lyke-wyse*
> *That they did eate her Dainties in that guyse.*

There may well have been damage to a common source manuscript at this point.

472	MS B repeats line 470: *Ye sall him se in liknes of a freir*. Line supplied from MS M.
496	MS B omits the verb; *turnit* is supplied from MS M.
500	MS B reads: *ha how Hurlybass ł now I coniure the*.
512	MS B reads: *and ⟨..⟩ mak*.
555	MS B reads: *Yone freir hes maid me thussgait say*. The words *feynd had maid me in effray* supplied from MS M.
556	MS B reads: *the* ~~*wes*~~ *werst*.
561	MS B reads: *Bot ⟨...⟩ lat*.

ARTHURIAN BOURDES: INTRODUCTION

Both *Sir Corneus* and *The Boy and the Mantle* take a very cynical view of King Arthur's court and its sexual honor, seeing adulterous love at court as laughable, widespread, and embarrassing rather than rare and elevating.

Sir Corneus, called in some previous editions *The Cokwolds Dance*, tells of King Arthur's humiliation of the cuckolds at his court, and the consequences when a magic drinking horn reveals to him for the first time that he is one of their number. It is a transition text in the symbolizing of cuckoldry in English culture. In England medieval cuckolds were given a hood by their wives, as putting a hood on someone was symbolic of any sort of trickery; Renaissance cuckolds notoriously had horns or perhaps wore willow garlands or hats. A willow garland was symbolic of forsaken love, as in John Heywood's "Ballad of the Green Willow" (published with his works in 1562) or Desdemona's song in *Othello*, 4.3.[1] Lydgate's phrasing in his translation of Boccaccio's *Fall of Princes* in the mid-fifteenth century suggests that the horned cuckold was still a foreign concept at the time:

> a certeyn knyht
> Giges callid, thyng shamful to be told,
> To speke pleyn Inglissh, made hym a cokold.
>
> Alas I was nat auysid weel beforn,
> On-cunnyngli to speke such language;
> I sholde ha said, how that he hadde an horn,
> Or souht sum teerme with a fair visage
> Texcuse my rudnesse off this gret outrage,
> As in sum land Cornodo men them call,
> And summe afferme how such folk haue no gall.[2]

And in his *Payne and Sorowe of Evyll Maryage*, Lydgate combines both old and new symbols of cuckoldry:

---

[1] For instances of the hat, and instances of medieval uses of the hood, see Williams, *Dictionary of Sexual Language*, under *cap*.

[2] "How Candalus kyng of Lide was made Cokewold and aftir slayn," *Lydgate's Fall of Princes*, ed. Bergen, part 1, book 2, lines 3358–67.

And yf so be he be no spereman good,
Hit may well hap he shall have an horn,
A large bone to stuff wythall his hood.[3]

In our poem cuckolds wear garlands of willow on their heads at King Arthur's behest; at line 186 they rejoice that now King Arthur will have to wear a "cokwoldes hate"; and the poem is named *Sir Corneus* after its pretended author, a knight who served at Arthur's court (see lines 244–49). The Latin adjective *corneus* means "of horn." And of course the magical object that diagnoses cuckoldry in the poem is itself a horn, taken from the head of a wild ox and used for drinking, though that is true in much earlier analogues of this story without any suggestion that the horn drinking vessel has any relation to the figurative cuckold's horn.

The most familiar story of the chastity-testing horn for a late fifteenth-century readership in England would have been the story in book 8, chapter 34 of Caxton's edition of Sir Thomas Malory's *Le Morte Darthur* (1485), where Morgan le Faye spitefully sends a magic drinking horn to King Arthur's court, but the knight carrying it is intercepted by Sir Lamerok and made to carry it to King Mark of Cornwall's court instead. King Mark makes his queen, Isolde, drink from the horn, and a hundred other ladies of the court as well. Those who have been false to their husbands cannot drink from the horn without spilling. Only four succeed in drinking (Isolde is of course not among them, because of her love of the king's nephew, Sir Tristram). King Mark wants to burn the guilty women to death, but his barons object that they will not have their ladies burned for a horn made by sorcery. King Arthur's court is never tested by this horn, but the fidelity rate at King Mark's court is comically low, and the noblemen (who presumably are themselves participants in this busy extramarital sexual interchange) are determined to leave well enough alone and to close their eyes to any indication that their wives are unfaithful to them. The comedy and cynicism of the passage are uncharacteristic of Malory's depiction of adultery at King Arthur's court, where it is instead serious and elevated. *Sir Corneus* trains the cynicism and comedy directly at Arthur.

Like *Sir Corneus*, *The Boy and the Mantle* is the story of a chastity test at Arthur's court that produces embarrassing results. Or rather *The Boy and the Mantle* is a series of three chastity tests involving three magic objects — mantle, knife, and drinking horn — instead of the one object of *Sir Corneus*. But *The Boy and the Mantle* is more thoroughly Arthurian: the naming of Guenever herself as well as Kay and Craddock links the poem more specifically to the romances of Arthurian tradition. Whereas the queen is the only female character of *Sir Corneus* and she barely appears there, there are other women tested in *The Boy and the Mantle*. Nevertheless it is clear in *The Boy and the Mantle*, as it is in *Sir Corneus*, that humiliation is being visited on the men of Arthur's court as well as their women. The tests of the knife and the horn are tests that the men take. Craddock wins by passing the tests, though his winning is dependent on his wife's behavior. In other words, in medieval fashion, a man's honor is dependent on his wife's sexual honor.

Various features of *The Boy and the Mantle* are found, some in one analogue and some in another, but no analogue includes all these features. It is possible that there was an original version of the tale combining these features, now lost. For *The Boy and the Mantle*, the most detailed tracing of analogues in print is still the introduction to the poem in

---

[3] Edited by Salisbury in *Trials and Joys of Marriage*, lines 85–87.

Francis Child's *English and Scottish Ballads*, vol. 1.2 (1884), # 29. Child's work was originally published as ten volumes in five (Houghton, Mifflin, 1882–98) and continues to be readily available as a reprint (Dover Publications). Naturally there have since appeared more modern editions of the various analogues that he describes.

The closest of the analogues for *Sir Corneus* is the Anglo-Norman Robert Biket's late twelfth-century *Lai du cor*: see *The Anglo-Norman Text of "Le Lai du cor,"* ed. C. T. Erickson. Erickson's introduction contains a clear and systematic comparison of the various early versions of the Arthurian chastity-test stories involving both horns and mantles: the Old French *Livre de Carados* in the First Continuation of Chrétien de Troyes's *Perceval* (*Conte de Graal*), Heinrich von dem Türlin's Middle High German *Diu Krône* (*The Crown*), the Old French *Prose Tristan*, a French text that is the source of the same scene in Malory's *Morte Darthur* (all the preceding for horn stories); the Middle High German *Lanzelet* by Ulrich von Zatzikhoven; the Old French *Le Mantel mautaillié*; and the Middle High German *Der Mantel*, also thought to be by Heinrich von dem Türlin. A recent edition of both *Le Lai du cor* and *Le Mantel mautaillié* is to be found, together with translations into modern French and a commentary in French, in *"Le Lai du cor" et "Le Manteau mal taillé," Les dessous de la Table Ronde*, ed. Nathalie Koble. The more problematic question of the priority and relation of Welsh analogous stories of Caradog and his beloved Tegau has yet to be resolved: Welsh allusions to the mantle story, discussed by Jane Cartwright in "Virginity and Chastity Tests," are all late, no earlier than the fifteenth century. But as Erickson points out, Tegeu or Tegau is named earlier in an English poem as connected with Cradoc; in the thirteenth-century "Annot and Johon" the beloved is "Trewe as Tegeu in tour" and a few lines later "Cuð ase Cradoc in court carf þe brede," as well known as Cradoc who carved the roasted flesh at court.[4] These lines imply the presence of the story in England in the thirteenth century *from a Welsh source* because of the name Tegau (as opposed, for example, to the Guignier of the First Continuation of *Perceval* or the nameless heroine of *The Boy and the Mantle*). And they add the notion of carving, the third chastity test incorporated into the ballad.

Relatively little besides the tracing of their analogues and potential sources is to be found specifically on the English texts of *The Boy and the Mantle* and *Sir Corneus*, but for *The Boy and the Mantle*, Gwendolyn A. Morgan, *Medieval Balladry and the Courtly Tradition*, argues that the ballad "presents the commoner's prosaic perception of the Arthur myth" (p. 61). George Shuffelton's explanatory notes for *Sir Corneus* in his edition of *Codex Ashmole 61* are very useful (see his notes, pp. 481–84). Readers interested in analysis of gender politics of the two tales should consider, with due attention to the differences between the poems and their analogues, Peggy McCracken on the Old French analogues in her *Romance of Adultery*, especially p. 52–83, and R. Howard Bloch on the genre of the Arthurian *fabliau* in *Medieval Misogyny and the Invention of Western Romantic Love*, especially p. 94–97. An analysis of analogous Arthurian chastity tests in various languages including Robert Biket's *Lai du cor* and Malory's *Morte Darthur* as well as the Italian *Tristan* and the German *Diu Crône* is to be found in Kathleen Coyne Kelly's *Performing Virginity and Testing Chastity*.

---

[4] Erickson's introduction, p. 2; for "Annot and Johon" see Brown, *English Lyrics of the XIIIth Century*, p. 138.

SIR CORNEUS: INTRODUCTION

Sir Corneus is one of many poems in Oxford, Bodleian Library, MS Ashmole 61, the only manuscript in which it survives, and where it appears on fols. 59v–62r. The manuscript as a whole has been recently described and edited by George Shuffelton, *Codex Ashmole 61*. Many of the poems in the manuscript are "signed" by someone named Rate; *Sir Corneus* is not, but the poem immediately before it in the manuscript, *Lybeaus Desconus*, ends "Amen quod Rate." Rate would be the name of the scribe rather than the poet. It should be noted that Rate uses abbreviations frequently and flexibly: a raised *u* can mean *ou*, *ur*, even *nour*, or just *r*; a raised *a* can mean *ra* or just *a*. He uses the grapheme *y* for both thorn and the vowel, sometimes distinguishing the vowel by an accent mark. I have represented his consonantal *y* with *th*. A fish and flower design that recurs, usually with Rate's name, but by itself at the end of *Sir Corneus*, is not yet satisfactorily explained. Shuffelton accepts (as "highly conjectural" but "the most persuasive") the argument by Lynn Blanchfield that it may be a representation of the badge of the Corpus Christi guild in Leicester,[1] but the pictures by Rate are quite varied in the form of the flower (it usually looks something like a rose or roses) and do not look a great deal like the guild symbol to my eye. It may be that, as I speculated in my earlier edition, the picture is a rebus alluding to where Rate was living or where he was born. I suggested as an example a name like Rosgill in Westmoreland County, which has nothing to do etymologically with either roses or fish gills. But I have no evidence to support that solution to the riddle, and it remains an interesting puzzle to solve. The whole manuscript is in one hand, described in correspondence by Albinia de la Mare of the Bodleian Library as "a mixed cursive hand of probably the second half [of the] . . . fifteenth century, basically anglicana but containing secretary elements." Since there are at least three batches of paper involved, with three different watermarks, the manuscript was probably compiled over a stretch of time, one man's (perhaps a merchant's) personal or household collection of romances and moral or religious pieces.

The scribal language of MS Ashmole 61 has been analyzed in the *LALME* (see vol. 3, Linguistic Profile 71, pp. 233–34 for details of the criterial features) and has been determined to come from Leicestershire. On the scribe Rate see *Codex Ashmole 61*, ed. Shuffelton, pp. 4–6, and Lynn S. Blanchfield, "Romances in MS Ashmole 61"; also Blanchfield, "Rate Revisited." In the first of these two chapters Blanchfield reports records (a will, an entry in the First Hall Book of the Merchant Guild, 1447–1553, an arbitration

---

[1] *Codex Ashmole 61*, ed. Shuffelton, p. 5, in reference to Lynn Blanchfield, "'An Idiosyncratic Scribe': A Study of the Practice and Purpose of Rate, the Scribe of Bodleian Library MS Ashmole 61," D.Phil. dissertation, University of Wales, Aberystwyth, 1991, pp. 151–57.

agreement, a land grant) of a father and son William Rate in Leicester and a William Rot(t)e who was an ironmonger in 1480 (see "Romances in MS Ashmole 61," pp. 85–86). The paper of the manuscript is dated on watermark evidence between 1479 and 1488, according to Blanchfield ("Romances in MS Ashmole 61," p. 79, citing notes by Bruce Barker-Benfield). Blanchfield is looking for an ecclesiast to be our scribe, since she contends that the manuscript is strongly religious and didactic in focus, but it is no more so than other merchants' manuscripts (for example, Oxford, Balliol College, MS 354, compiled by Richard Hill, grocer of London in the years following 1500). An ironmonger or other merchant in Leicester in the last years of the fifteenth century would be a plausible candidate for our Rate.

AFTERLIFE

Sir Corneus appears, with different names as noted below, in the following early or otherwise useful editions:

1829. *The Cokwolds Daunce*. Charles Henry Hartshorne, ed. *Ancient Metrical Tales*. London: W. Pickering. Pp. 209–21.

1854. *The Horn of King Arthur*. Francis Child, ed. *English and Scottish Ballads*, vol. 1. Boston: Little, Brown and Company. This was the earliest edition by Child. *The Horn of King Arthur* continued to be included in new editions of *English and Scottish Ballads* but was dropped in the later, more substantially revised *English and Scottish Popular Ballads*. The earliest I have seen is the second edition of 1866 in which *The Horn of King Arthur* is the second of the texts, at pp. 17–27. Child says the text "was furnished from the manuscript by J. O. Halliwell" (p. x).

1864. *The Cokwolds Daunce*. William Carew Hazlitt, ed. *Remains of the Early Popular Poetry of England*, vol. 1. London: John Russell Smith. Pp. 35–49.

1985. *Sir Corneus*. Melissa M. Furrow, ed. *Ten Fifteenth-Century Comic Poems*. New York: Garland. Pp. 271–91.

2008. *Sir Corneus*. George Shuffelton, ed. *Codex Ashmole 61: A Compilation of Popular Middle English Verse*. Kalamazoo, MI: Medieval Institute Publications. Pp. 164–70.

REFERENCE TOOLS

Sir Corneus is *NIMEV* 219.

It is addressed by Thomas Cooke in volume 9 (1993) of the *Manual*, section 24 Tales [13], *The Romance of Syre Corneus* (also *Sir Corneus* or *The Cokwold's Dance*).

POET, POETRY, AND LANGUAGE

We have no linguistic evidence to place the composition of *Sir Corneus* much earlier than the late fifteenth-century manuscript in which it appears, and nothing to identify its poet.

Its treatment of cuckoldry (the implication of the horn in the title discussed above) suggests that the poet may be contemporary to Lydgate.

Some features of the poet's original language are still discernible in rhyming position, where they could not be changed without ruining the rhyme. These include two features that together suggest the poem came originally from Lincolnshire or the West Riding or northwest of Yorkshire:

> The rhyme *sykerlyke/baskefysyke* at lines 115–16 depends on the *-lik(e)* types of ending for *-ly*. *LALME* shows that these are to be found in the North and the east Midlands (Q278).

> The rhyme *senne/amen* at lines 252 and 255 depends on *-en* forms of *since*. *LALME* shows that *sen* and *sene* forms of *since* are to be found in Lincolnshire, the West Riding of Yorkshire, and the North Riding of Yorkshire (Q39), all of these also being places where the *-lik(e)* types of ending are to be found.

These areas are also compatible with other dialectally restricted rhymes in the poem:

> *therby/sey* at lines 28–29 depends upon the *be* form of *by* (Q92) and a *se(e)* form of the past tense of *see* (Q211).
> *yknow/saw* at lines 9, 12 depends upon a past participle of a strong verb without an *-n* ending (Q160). *(Y)know* must also have an *-aw* form to rhyme with the noun *saw*.

One other rhyme might restrict the area of origin still further:

> *redd/glad* at lines 121–22 probably depends upon a pronunciation of *glad* with *-e-*; in the etymology of *glad*, *MED* posits that Old English **gled* is Mercian. Lincolnshire is within the territory that was Mercian, but Yorkshire is not.

The stanza of *Sir Corneus* is the six-line, *aabccb* stanza seen in *John the Reeve* and *Jack and His Stepdame*, usually with four stresses in the *a* and *c* lines, and three in the *b* lines. Half the length of the twelve-line tail-rhyme stanza of *The King and the Hermit* and *King Edward and the Shepherd*, it is otherwise similar in construction. The rhyming is usually exact, with small licenses in rhyming *m/n* (as in *herme/wern* at lines 111 and 114, and *tyme/fyne* at lines 184–85) and greater ones in rhyming stressed and unstressed syllables (e.g., *thyng/lesyng* at lines 15 and 18, *lesyng/kyng* at lines 61–62, and *kyng/dansyng* at lines 141 and 144).

SIR CORNEUS

	All that wyll of solas lere,	*want to learn about entertainment*
	Herkyns now and ye schall here,	*hear*
	And ye kane understond.	*If*
	Of a bowrd I wyll you schew	*funny story; show*
5	That ys full gode and trew,	
	That fell sometyme in Ynglond.	*happened once*
	Kynge Arthour was of grete honour,	*domain*
	Of castelles and of many a toure,	*tower*
	And full wyde yknow.	*widely known*
10	A gode ensample I wyll you sey,	*lesson*
	What chanse befell hym onne a dey:	
	Herkyn to my saw.	*story*
	Cokwoldes he lovyd, as I you plyght:	*Cuckolds; assure*
	He honouryd them both dey and nyght	
15	Yn all maner of thyng.	
	And as I rede in story,	
	He was kokwold, sykerly:	*certainly*
	Forsothe, it is no lesyng.	*lie*
	Herkynes, sires, what I sey:	
20	Her may ye here solas and pley,	*Here; jest*
	Yff ye wyll take gode hede.	
	Kyng Arthour had a bugyll-horn	*wild-ox horn*
	That evermour stod hym beforn	
	Werso that ever he yede.	*Wheresoever; went*
25	For when he was at the bord sete,	*table*
	Anon the horne schuld be fette,	*Immediately; fetched*
	Therof that he myght drynke.	
	For myche crafte he couth therby,	*he could [do] much cunning by means of it*
	And oftetymes the treuth he sey:	*saw*
30	Non other couth he thynke.	*could*
	Yff any cokwold drynke of it,	
	Spyll he schuld withouten lette:	*pause*

118

Therfor thei wer not glade.
Gret dispyte thei had therby,   *indignation*
35   Because it dyde them vilony   *disgrace*
And made them ofttymes sade.

When the kyng wold hafe solas,
The bugyll was fett into the plas,
To make solas and game.   *fun*
40   And than changyd the cokwoldes chere.   *expression*
The kyng them callyd, ferre and nere,
Lordynges, by ther name.   *Gentlemen*

Than men myght se game inowghe,
When every cokwold on other leughe: *laughed*
45   And yit thei schamyd sore.   *felt shame painfully*
Wherever the cokwoldes wer sought,   *pursued*
Befor the kyng thei were brought,
Both lesse and more.   *those of low rank and high*

Kyng Arthour than, verament,   *truly*
50   Ordeynd throw hys awne assent   *Ordered; own*
(Ssoth as I yow sey)   *Truth*
The tabull dormonte, withoute lette,   *fixed table, without delay*
Therat the cokwoldes wer ssette,
To have solas and pley.

55   For at the bord schuld be non other
Bot every cokwold and hys brother:
To tell treuth I must nedes.
And when the cokwoldes wer sette
Garlandes of wylos schuld be fette   *willow*
60   And sett upon ther hedes.

Of the best mete, withoute lesyng,   *[Some] of; food; lying*
That stode on bord befor the kyng,
Both ferr and nere,
To the cokwoldes he sente anon,
65   And bad them be glad everychon,   *each one*
For his sake make gode chere,

And seyd, "Lordynges, for your lyves,
Be never the wrother with your wyves,   *angrier*
For no maner of nede.
70   Of woman com duke and kyng;   *From; came*
I yow tell without lesyng,
Of them com owre manhed."   *humanity*

     So it befell, serteynly,

     The Duke of Gloseter com in hyghe   *in a hurry*

75   To the courte with full gret myght.

     He was reseyved at the kynges palys   *greeted*

     With mych honour and grete solas,

     With lordes that were wele dyght.   *By; dressed*

     With the kyng ther dyde he duell,

80   Bot how long I cannot tell:

     Thereof knaw I non name.   *I cannot name the length of time*

     Of Kyng Arthour a wonder case,

     Frendes, herkyns how it was,

     For now begynnes game.

85   Uppon a dey, withouten lette,   *interruption*

     The duke with the kyng was sette

     At mete with mykell pride.   *great pomp*

     He lukyd abowte wonder faste: *very earnestly*

     Hys syght on every syde he caste

90   To them that sate besyde.

     The kyng aspyed the erle anon   *espied*

     And fast he lowghe the erle upon   *laughed*

     And bad he schuld be glad.

     And yit for all hys grete honour,

95   Cokwold was Kyng Arthour,

     Ne galle non he hade.   *spirit to resist injury*

     So at the last, the duke he brayd,   *broke into speech*

     And to the kyng these wordes sayd

     (He myght no lenger forbere):

100 "Syr, what hath these men don

     That syche garlondes thei were upon?   *wear*

     That skyll wold I lere."   *reason*

     The kyng seyd the erle to,

     "Syr, non hurte thei have do,

105 For this was thrught a chans.   *through a mischance*

     Sertes, thei be fre men all.   *generous*

     For non of them hath no gall,

     Therfor this is ther penans.   *penance*

     "Ther wyves hath be merchandabull   *saleable*

110 And of ther ware compenabull: *companionable [with their commodities]*

     Methinke it is non herme.

     A man of lufe that wold them crave,   *[Whatever] man; love; beg*

Hastely he schuld it have,
For thei couth not hym wern.   *refuse*

115 "All ther wyves, sykerlyke,   *certainly*
     Hath usyd the baskefysyke   *(see note)*
     Whyll these men wer oute,
     And oft thei have draw that draught,   *made that move*
     To use wele the lecheres craft
120 With rubyng of ther toute.   *rump*

     "Syr," he seyd, "now have I redd.   *explained*
     Ete we now and make us glad
     And every man sle care."   *drown his sorrows*
       The duke seyd to hym anon,
125 "Than be thei cokwoldes everychon?"
       The kyng seyd, "Hold thee there."   *I.e., Hold your tongue*

       The kyng than after the erlys word
     Send to the cokwoldes bord
     (To make them mery among)   *meanwhile*
130 All maner of mynstralsy,   *minstrels*
     To glad the cokwoldes by and by   *right away*
     With herpe, fydell, and song,

     And bad them, "Take no greffe,   *Suffer; grief*
     Bot all with love and with 'Leffe,'   *fondness; Friend*
135 Every man with other."
       For after mete, without distans,   *discord*
     The cokwoldes schuld together danse,
     Every man with hys brother.

     Than began a nobull gamme: *splendid*
140 The cokwoldes together samme   *assemble*
     Befor the erle and the kyng.
     In skerlet kyrtells ever one   *tunics of rich cloth all the same*
     The cokwoldes stodyn everychon   *each one*
     Redy unto the dansyng.

145   Than seyd the kyng in hye,   *in haste*
     "Go fyll my bugyll hastely,   *horn*
     And bryng it to my hond.
     Y wyll asey with a gyne   *test; device*
     All these cokwoldes that her be in;
150 To knaw them wyll I fonnd."   *identify; try*

       Than seyd the erle, "For charyté,
     In what skyll, tell me,   *By; reason*

A cokwold may I know?"
  To the erle the kyng ansuerd,
155 "Syr, be my hore berd,   *by; gray*
  Thou schall se within a throw."   *moment*

  The bugull was brought the kyng to hond.
    Than seyd the kyng, "I understond,
  Thys horne that ye here se,
160 Ther is no cokwold fer ne nere
  Hereof to drynke hath no power,
  As wyde as Crystianté,   *Throughout the Christian world*

  "Bot he schall spyll on every syde.
  For any cas that may betyde,
165 Schall non therof avanse."   *succeed*
  And yit for all hys grete honour,
  Hymselfe noble Kyng Arthour   *[To]*
  Hath forteynd syche a chans.   *happened; mischance*

    "Syr Erle," he seyd, "take and begyn."
170 He seyd, "Nay, be Seynt Austyn:
  That wer to me vylony.   *That would disgrace me*
  Not for all a reme to wyn   *realm*
  Befor you I schuld begyn,
  For honour of my curtassy."

175   Kyng Arthour, ther he toke the horn
  And dyde as he was wont beforn,
  Bot ther was yit gon a gyle.   *But yet there happened a trick*
  Bot he wend to have dronke of the best.   *expected*
  Bot sone he spyllyd on hys brest,
180 Within a lytell whyle.

    The cokwoldes lokyd yche on other
  And thought the kyng was ther awne brother,
  And glad thei wer of that:
  "He hath us scornyd many a tyme
185 And now he is a cokwold fyne,
  To were a cokwoldes hate."   *wear; hat*

    The quene was therof schamyd sore.
  Sche changyd hyr colour lesse and mour,
  And wold have ben awey.
190 Therwith the kyng gan hyr behold,   *look at*
  And seyd he schuld never be so bold
  The soth agene to sey.   *To speak against [i.e., deny] the truth*

"Cokwoldes no mour I wyll repreve,   *taunt*
For I ame one, and aske no leve,[1]
195 For all my rentes and londys.
Lordynges all, now may ye know
That I may dance in the cokwold row
And take you by the handes."

Than seyd thei all at a word   *at once*
200 That cokwoldes schuld begynne the bord
And sytt hyest in the halle.
"Go we, lordinges, all samme,   *together*
And dance to make us gle and gamme,
For cokwoldes have no galle."

205   And after that, sone anon,
The kyng causyd the cokwoldes ychon
To wesch, withouten les.   *wash, truly*
For ought that ever may betyde,
He sett them by hys awne syde,
210 Up at the hyghe dese.   *high dais*

The kyng hymselff a garlond fette:
Uppon hys hede he it sette,
For it myght be non other,   *there could be no other way about it*
And seyd, "Lordynges, sykerly,   *certainly*
215 We be all of a freyry: *brotherhood*
Y ame your awne brother.

"Be Jhesu Cryst that is aboffe,
That man aught me gode loffe   *(see note)*
That ley by my quene.
220 Y wer worthy hym to honour,   *I am obliged*
Both in castell and in towre,
With rede skerlyt and grene.   *With rich clothing in red and green*

"For he me helpyd when I was forth,   *away from home*
To cher my wyfe and make her myrth,
225 For women lovys wele pley.
And therfor, sirys, have ye no dowte
Bot many schall dance in the cokwoldes rowte,
Both by nyght and dey.

"And therfor, lordynges, take no care.
230 Make we mery: for nothing spare,

---

[1] That is, *"I do not need to ask anyone's permission to be one."*

All brether in one rowte."   *brothers; group*
   Than the cokwoldes wer full blythe,
And thankyd God a hundred syth,   *times*
For soth withouten doute.

235   Every cokwold seyd to other,
"Kyng Arthour is owr awne brother:
Therfor we may be blyth."
   The Erle of Glowsytour, vereament,
Toke hys leve and home he went,
240 And thankyd the kyng fele sythe.   *many times*

Kyng Arthour left at Skarlyon   *stayed; Caerleon*
With hys cokwoldes everychon
And made both gamm and gle.
   A knyght ther was, withouten les,
245 That servyd at the kinges des:
Syr Corneus hyght he.   *was named*
He made this gest in hys gamm,   *story as a joke*
And namyd it after hys awne name,
Yn herpyng or other gle.   *instrumental music*

250 And after, nobull Kyng Arthour
Lyved and dyghed with honour,   *died*
As many hath don senne,   *since*
Both cokwoldes and other mo.
God gyff us grace that we may go
255 To hevyn. Amen, amen.

EXPLANATORY NOTES TO SIR CORNEUS

ABBREVIATIONS: *MED*: *Middle English Dictionary*; *ODNB*: *Oxford Dictionary of National Biography*.

31–32   *Yff any cokwold drynke of it, / Spyll he schuld withouten lette*. The verbs are both subjunctive, and the tenses mixed. Modern agreement of the tenses would put "drynke" in the past.

52   *The tabull dormonte, withoute lette*. A seat at a table dormant or fixed table (as opposed to removable boards on trestles) would be comparatively a position of honor in the king's hall.

59   *Garlandes of wylos schuld be fette*. A willow garland was symbolic of forsaken love, as in John Heywood's "Ballad of the Green Willow." See the introduction for further discussion of the symbols of cuckoldry.

74   The duke of Gloucester meant here may be Duke Humphrey (duke from 1414 to his death in 1447), who is remembered as an important scholar, having donated a large collection of books to Oxford University. More importantly to this context, however, both of his wives had complicated personal histories. The first, Jacqueline, countess of Hainault, declared her unhappy marriage to John IV, duke of Brabant, annulled so that she would be free to marry Humphrey, which she did secretly in 1422 or 1423. But her efforts to reclaim her territory in Hainault from her uncle led to her capture and imprisonment in 1425. In her absence, Humphrey had a sexual relationship with the beautiful Eleanor Cobham, her lady-in-waiting, and failed to send troops to Jacqueline's rescue until 1427. The troops were unsuccessful. Once the pope declared in 1426 that Jacqueline's marriage to her prior husband was still valid and confirmed again in 1428, after John IV died, that her marriage to Humphrey was therefore invalid, the duke of Gloucester married Eleanor Cobham. (By 1432 Jacqueline herself was married again, to Frank von Borselen.) Eleanor's sexual and personal history was if anything more problematic than Jacqueline's. Jacqueline, who technically was involved in an adulterous relationship with Humphrey himself while she was living in what she maintained to be marriage with him, appears to have been a woman more sinned against than sinning, and there is evidence that the English people liked and sympathized with her in her difficulties. Some women of London went in support of her to Parliament in 1428 and "handed letters to Gloucester, the two Archbishops and other lords there, censuring the duke for not taking steps to relieve his wife from her danger, and for leaving her unloved and forgotten in captivity, whilst he was

125

living in adultery with another woman, 'to the ruin of himself, the kingdom, and the marital bond'" (Vickers, *Humphrey, Duke of Gloucester*, p. 203). John Lydgate, who had written a poem celebrating the impending marriage of Humphrey and Jacqueline, wrote a sympathetic "Complaint for my Lady of Gloucester and Holland" — or perhaps it was another contemporary poet who did so. But Eleanor on the other hand was Humphrey's mistress during his marriage to the unfortunate Jacqueline; then she was accused along with others of treasonable necromancy in the service of killing the king, Humphrey's nephew Henry VI, to whose throne Humphrey was by then the heir. What she appears to have been guilty of is having the king's horoscope cast to find out the likelihood of his death (which would make her queen of England), and she also admitted to using potions got from the Witch of Eye to enable her impregnation by the duke. The witch, Margery Jourdemayne, was burned. Eleanor was only forcibly divorced from Humphrey, compelled to do public penance, and imprisoned for the rest of her life. (See G. L. Harriss, "Eleanor, duchess of Gloucester (c.1400–1452)," *ODNB*). Despite the forced divorce, however, Humphrey's political influence was hurt by Eleanor's fall, and he died of a stroke about six years later, after being arrested (see G. L. Harriss, "Humphrey, duke of Gloucester (1390–1447)," *ODNB*).

The other possible references, if a real duke of Gloucester is being alluded to, are the earlier duke, Thomas of Woodstock (duke 1385–97), son of Edward III, murdered in prison in 1397 while awaiting trial for treason against his nephew Richard II, and the later one, Richard of Gloucester (duke 1461–83, at which point he took the throne from his young nephew Edward V, declaring him illegitimate; the boy and his brother soon thereafter disappeared, and Richard of Gloucester reigned as Richard III). Thomas of Woodstock, however sensational his political machinations and subsequent death, was married to a woman of unremarkable sexual history, Eleanor de Bohun, who was married to him as a child, bore him five children, and entered a convent when he died. Richard of Gloucester was married to Anne Neville, a widowed princess of Wales, in 1472, and there were not as far as I know rumors of impropriety attached to her. All three dukes had many political enemies as well as admirers. But because of his relations with his two wives, Duke Humphrey seems the most likely referent in a poem about sexual scandal at court, and that being the case, a date for the poem after Jacqueline's marriage to someone else was officially declared as valid (1426) would be the earliest likely one, and a date after the disgrace of Eleanor Cobham more likely. A date before there was another duke of Gloucester to confuse the reference (that is, before 1461) is also more likely. The duke of Gloucester in this poem never actually takes the test and tries to drink from the horn: he defers to Arthur and lets him go first, and once Arthur does so it is no longer of such interest to him whether the duke is a cuckold. And indeed it is not a cuckold that Duke Humphrey's alliance with Jacqueline or enchantment with Eleanor would make him. It remains entirely possible that no particular duke of Gloucester is meant, and the title was used because there was no contemporary holder of the title to be offended.

91   *erle*. The poem is inconsistent about Gloucester's title, whether duke or earl, although by the fifteenth century Gloucester was always a ducal title.

96   Here and at lines 107 and 204, a cuckold is identified as someone who has no gall: that is to say, someone who is so meek and mild as not to object to being cheated on.

116   *Hath usyd the baskefysyke*. From *bask* or *baisk*, "bitter," and *fisike* or modern *physic*, "medicine." In the sole other citation for this word in *MED* (under *bask-fisik*), the bitter treatment implied there too may be sexual intercourse: "Do alle youre men be war of the furst frutes and wyne, the whiche be right lustye ate the beginning and hynderyng to mennes hele; and so is a thing called basfysike."

118   *And oft thei have draw that draught*. This is a metaphor taken from chess. "They have often made that move."

119   *To use wele the lecheres craft*. This may be a pun on *lecher* and *leecher* (a physician).

170   *Seynt Austyn*. Perhaps the bishop of Hippo (354–430), but more likely the local St. Augustine (d. 604) who founded the Christian church in southern England and was the first archbishop of Canterbury.

186   *To were a cokwoldes hate*. Hoods were the usual symbols of cuckolds in the English Middle Ages. See the introduction for a discussion of the newer symbols the poem uses.

188   *Sche changyd hyr colour lesse and mour*. "Lesse and mour" is a tag useful in rhyming position, frequent in this poem, often meaning no more than "everybody" or "everything"; here it suggests that the queen's blushes came and went.

190   *gan* is a marker of the past tense in this poem. *The kyng gan hyr behold* = the king beheld her, looked at her.

200–01 *That cokwoldes schuld begynne the bord / And sytt hyest in the halle*. That is, cuckolds are to take the most honorable position of all, where the king normally sits: at the head of the table on the dais.

207   The king gets the cuckolds to wash. Before eating, at least in gentry households and noble ones, those dining would customarily be brought water and towels with which to wash their hands. There is a hint here of being washed free of shame as the cuckolds are shown to be no worse than the king and raised to a much higher status at table than they are used to.

218   *That man aught me gode loffe*. This is an ambiguous line. It means "that man showed pure friendship for me" but also "that man was bound to render (or owed) friendly behavior to me." In other words, Arthur is overtly acknowledging that his wife's lover has done him a great favor by entertaining his wife, but in another interpretation, implying that his wife's lover must have sworn allegiance to Arthur (yet has betrayed him).

241–49 This nine-line stanza is the one deviation from the standard stanzaic pattern of the poem. It is not noticeably weaker (or stronger) poetically than the other stanzas, though, and so may well be original. The filler "withouten les" (line 244) to rhyme with "kinges des" (line 245) is no worse than "vereament" to rhyme with "home he went" in the preceding stanza (lines 238–39), and "gle" (line 243, meaning "entertainment") to rhyme with "gle" (line 249, meaning "instrumental music") is very little worse than "ever one" (line 142, meaning "all the same") to rhyme with "everychon" (line 143, meaning "each one"). As a variant on the regular pattern, the stanza might be taken to be bringing the poem to a satisfying conclusion, but its position in second-last place weakens that effect.

As George Shuffelton points out, though, Rate's scribal practice is rolling revision as he transcribes (see *Codex Ashmole 61*, pp. 5–6); so the many empty fillers in the poem and this odd stanza form might be attributable to him.

247–49 That is, to bear that name whenever the story is performed, to a harp or other instrument.

TEXTUAL NOTES TO SIR CORNEUS

ABBREVIATIONS: see Explanatory Notes.

title	No title in MS, but compare lines 246–48.
14	MS reads: *He hoouryd them both dey and nyght.*
19	MS reads: *Herkynges sires what I sey.*
98	MS reads: *And to the kyng these wordes spake.* Emendation for rhyme.
149	MS reads: *All these cokwold that her is in.* The abbreviation for *this* is identical to that for *these* in this scribe's work. Emendation for sense.
206	MS reads: *The kyng causyd the the cokwoldes ychon.* Emendation for sense.
233	MS reads: *And thankyd god a C syth.*
239	MS reads: *Toke hys leve and home he wentet.* The final *–et* may be by another hand.
248	MS reads: *And manyd it after hys awne name.* Emendation for sense.

THE BOY AND THE MANTLE: INTRODUCTION

MANUSCRIPT AND SCRIBE

The Boy and the Mantle is in the famous Percy Folio Manuscript (London, British Library, MS Additional 27879, p. 284–87), the collection of early poetry rescued by a young Thomas Percy from its fate: it was being used by housemaids to kindle the parlor fire in a house in Shiffnal, Shropshire, to which Percy had chanced to be invited. But since Percy had already begun a career of publishing older poetry by the time he chanced upon the manuscript in his friend's house, it is possible that this version of the story is a romanticized one and that his friend Humphrey Pitt had invited him to the house with the idea in mind of introducing him to the manuscript. Percy's publication of *The Reliques of Ancient English Poetry* in 1765 was an important precursor to the Romantic movement; Percy's *Reliques* reproduced, among others, many poems from the manuscript, though heavily edited and even added to by Percy. The manuscript itself was compiled in the seventeenth century by someone with antiquarian interests, and many of the contents are sole surviving versions of medieval poems, as is the case with both *The Boy and the Mantle* and *John the Reeve* in the current collection. A version of *Jack and His Stepdame* also appears in the Percy Folio Manuscript, but it is probably transcribed from one of the early seventeenth-century print versions of *The Friar and the Boy* and so gives an interesting example of the intermingling of manuscript and print cultures for many decades after the introduction of print.

AFTERLIFE

The Boy and the Mantle was published in the following early or otherwise useful editions:

1765. Thomas Percy, ed. *The Reliques of Ancient English Poetry*, vol. 3. London: J. Dodsley. Pp. 1–11. This had several editions.

1854. Francis Child, ed. *The English and Scottish Ballads*, vol. 1. Boston: Little, Brown and Company. This was the earliest of many editions by Child, the later ones incorporating successive additions to his scholarly prefaces. The earliest I have seen is the second edition of 1866 in which *The Boy and the Mantle* is the first of the texts, at pp. 3–16.

1868. John W. Hales and Frederick J. Furnivall, eds. *Bishop Percy's Folio Manuscript: Ballads and Romances*. London: N. Trübner. 2:301–11.

1884. Francis Child, ed. *The English and Scottish Popular Ballads*, vol. 1, part 2. Boston: Houghton, Mifflin and Co. Pp. 257–74. This is one of Child's later editions and incorporates much research on the chastity test analogues.

1985. Melissa M. Furrow, ed. *Ten Fifteenth-Century Comic Poems*. New York: Garland. Pp. 293–311.

REFERENCE TOOLS

The Boy and the Mantle is not indexed in the *NIMEV*.

It is briefly mentioned by David C. Fowler in volume 6 (1980) of the *Manual*, section 15 Ballads [17], among "nine substantial ballads from the Percy Folio MS that probably have a medieval origin" (p. 1782).

POET, POETRY, AND LANGUAGE

The Boy and the Mantle is in common ballad form, with short two- or three-stress lines in four- or six-line stanzas rhyming *abcb(db)*. But it is also influenced by late medieval alliterative long line, with each of the current lines representing a half line. The pattern is still clearly recognizable in sequences like lines 53–54:

She **curst** the **wea**ver and the **wal**ker / That **cloth**e that had **wrought**.

The long line shows *abb ab* alliteration. However, the alliteration is often purely decorative, not crossing the cæsura:

It was from the **top** to the **toe** / As **sheeres** had itt **shread**.
  (lines 39–40)

And in most cases there is no alliteration.
  Like many ballads, it is loose in its rhyming. Because so much time has elapsed between the poem's composition and its recording in the Percy Folio Manuscript, some of the more startling inexactnesses of rhyme can be accounted for by changes in the language. This is most obviously true at line 72, where the manuscript says "buttockes" in a context where the racier fourteenth- and fifteenth-century synonym *tout* is called for by the rhyme with *about*. A scribe who did not blink at calling Guenever a "bitch" (line 147) and a "whore" (line 148) would not have declined to use the word *tout*, especially when the rhyme required it, except if it had fallen out of use so much that he could not expect his audience to recognize it. By the time that the Percy Folio Manuscript was written out, its scribe could no longer expect that recognition, and so he or she replaced *tout* with *buttockes*. Beyond such very general indications, the date of the original poem cannot be pinned down by the language. There is one hint as to the original dialect of the poem, and that is a rhyme of *knee/eye/see* at lines 184, 186, 188; this must depend on a form of *eye* ending in stressed *-e(e)*, such as *LALME* shows in many locations across the map of the northern part of England (Q115, dot map 750).
  No external medieval allusion to the poem is known.

THE BOY AND THE MANTLE

In the third day of May
To Carleile did come
A kind curteous child   *well-born*
That cold much of wisdome.   *knew*

5   A kirtle and a mantle   *tunic*
This child had uppon,   *on*
With brouches and ringes
Full richelye bedone.   *adorned*

He had a sute of silke   *livery*
10   About his middle drawne.
Without he cold of curtesye
He thought itt much shame.[1]

   "God speed thee, King Arthur,
Sitting att thy meate,   *meal*
15   And the goodly Queene Guenever —
I canott her forgett.

"I tell you, lordes in this hall,
I hett you all heed: *order*
Excepte you be the more surer,   *Unless; secure*
20   Is you for to dread."   *you should be afraid*

   He plucked out of his potener   *pouch*
(And longer wold not dwell),
He pulled forth a pretty mantle
Betweene two nutshells.

25   "Have thou here, King Arthure,   *Here, take [this]*
Have thou heere of mee.
Give itt to thy comely queene
Shapen as itt bee.   *However it may be shaped*

---

[1] Lines 11–12: *He would have thought it shameful not to be conversant with courtesy*

	Itt shall never become that wiffe	*suit a wife*
30	That hath once done amisse."	
	Then every in the kings court	*every [man]*
	Began to care for his.	*be uneasy about*

	Forth came Dame Guenever;	
	To the mantle shee brayd.	*For; grabbed*
35	The ladye, shee was newfangle,	*fickle*
	But yett shee was affrayd.	

	When shee had taken the mantle,	
	Shee sttode as shee had beene madd.	
	It was from the top to the toe	
40	As sheeres had itt shread.	*As if; shredded*

	One while was itt goule,	*red*
	Another while was itt greene;	
	Another while was itt watchet:	*light blue*
	Ill itt did her beseeme.	*suit*

45	Another while was it blacke	
	And bore the worst hue.	
	"By my troth," quoth King Arthur,	
	"I think thou be not true."	

	Shee threw downe the mantle	
50	That bright was of blee.	*face*
	Fast with a rudd redd	*complexion*
	To her chamber can shee flee.	*did*

	She curst the weaver and the walker	*fuller*
	That clothe that had wrought,	*who had made*
55	And bade a vengeance on his crowne	*head*
	That hither hath itt brought.	

	"I had rather be in a wood	
	Under a greene tree	
	Then in King Arthurs court	
60	Shamed for to bee."	

	Kay called forth his ladye	
	And bade her come neere,	
	Saies, "Madam, and thou be guiltye,	*if*
	I pray thee hold thee there."	*stay there*

| 65 | Forth came his ladye | |
| | Shortlye and anon; | *at once* |

Boldlye to the mantle
Then is shee gone.

When shee had tane the mantle   *taken*
70 And cast it her about,
Then was shee bare
All above the toute.   *rump*

Then every knight
That was in the kinges court
75 Talked, lauged, and showted
Full oft att that sport.   *Very*

Shee threw downe the mantle
That bright was of blee.
Fast with a red rudd   *face*
80 To her chamber can shee flee.

  Forth came an old knight
Pattering ore a creede,   *Repeatedly reciting*
And he proferred to this litle boy
Twenty marks to his meede,   *as recompense*

85 And all the time of the Christmasse
Willinglye to feede,   *Willingly to feed [him]*
Forwhy this mantle might   *Because*
Doe his wiffe some need.   *Supply his wife with something she needed*

  When shee had tane the mantle
90 Of cloth that was made
Shee had no more left on her
But a tassell and a threed.
Then every knight in the kings court
Bade evill might shee speed.   *Prayed she would come to grief*

95 Shee threw downe the mantle
That bright was of blee,
And fast with a redd rudd
To her chamber can shee flee.

  Craddocke called forth his ladye
100 And bade her come in,
Saith, "Winne this mantle, ladye,
With a little dinne.   *Without any fuss*

  "Winne this mantle, ladye,
And it shal be thine,

105 If thou never did amisse
    Since thou wast mine."

      Forth came Craddockes ladye
    Shortlye and anon,
    But boldlye to the mantle
110 Then is shee gone.

    When shee had tane the mantle
    And cast itt her about,
    Upp att her great toe
    Itt began to crinkle and crowt.   *push*
115   Shee said, "Bowe downe, mantle,
    And shame me not for nought.

    "Once I did amisse,
    I tell you certainlye,
    When I kist Craddockes mouth
120 Under a greene tree,
    When I kist Craddockes mouth
    Before he marryed mee."

      When shee had her shreeven   *confessed*
    And her sines shee had tolde,
125 The mantle stoode about her
    Right as shee wold,   *Just as she wanted*

    Seemelye of coulour,
    Glittering like gold.
    Then every knight in Arthurs court
130 Did her behold.

      Then spake Dame Guenever
    To Arthur our king:
    "She hath tane yonder mantle
    Not with wright but with wronge.

135 "See you not yonder woman
    That maketh herselfe soe cleane: *Who pretends to be so virtuous*
    I have seene tane out of her bedd
    Of men fiveteene,

    "Preists, clarkes, and wedded men
140 From her bydeene;   *one after another*
    Yett shee taketh the mantle
    And maketh herselfe cleane."

Then spake the litle boy
That kept the mantle in hold;   *possession*
145   Sayes, "King, chasten thy wiffe.
Of her words shee is to bold.

"Shee is a bitch and a witch
And a whore bold.
King, in thine owne hall
150   Thou art a cuchold."

The litle boy stoode
Looking over a dore.
He was ware of a wyld bore
Wold have werryed a man.   *[That] would, made war upon*
155   He pulld forth a woodkniffe:
Fast thither than he ran.
He brought in the bores head
And quitted him like a man.   *acquitted himself*

He brought in the bores head
160   And was wonderous bold.
He said there was never a cucholds kniffe
Carve itt that cold.   *could*

Some rubbed their knives
Uppon a whetstone;
165   Some threw them under the table
And said they had none.

King Arthur and the child
Stood looking them upon:
All their knives edges
170   Turned backe anon.

Craddocke had a litle knive
Of iron and of steele:
He britled the bores head   *cut up*
Wonderous weele,
175   That every knight in the kings court
Had a morssell.

The litle boy had a horne
Of red gold that ronge.
He said there was noe cuckolde
180   "Shall drinke of my horne
But he shold itt sheede   *spill*
Either behind or beforne."   *in front*

Some shedd on their shoulder,
And some on their knee:
185 He that cold not hitt his mouth
Put it in his eye,
And he that was a cuckold,
Every man might him see.

Craddoccke wan the horne   *won*
190 And the bores head;
His ladye wan the mantle
Unto her meede.   *As; reward*
Everye such a lovely ladye,
God send her well to speede.   *grant her success*

Finis.   *The End*

EXPLANATORY NOTES TO THE BOY AND THE MANTLE

ABBREVIATION: *CT*: Chaucer, *Canterbury Tales*.

1–2   *In the third day of May / To Carleile did come.* The third of May is a recurrent date in Chaucer's writing: the third night of May is when Palamon breaks prison and escapes to the woods where he fights Arcite (*CT* I[A]1462–63), the third day of May is the day on which Chauntecleer falls to (but escapes) the fox (*CT* VII[B²]3187–91), and it is the inauspicious opening day of Book 2 of *Troilus and Criseyde* (2.56). *The Boy and the Mantle* may be simply following Chaucer in making May 3 a dangerous date for the servants of Venus or may be following directly whatever tradition Chaucer himself followed (assuming that Chaucer's use of the date was not a merely personal reference, a wedding anniversary or the like). An article by Alfred Kellogg and Robert C. Cox, "Chaucer's May 3 and Its Contexts," reports the various reasons that have been suggested for Chaucer's choice of that particular date. Among the most useful of the explanations suggested is D. W. Robertson, Jr.'s, that May 3 is the date of St. Helena's Invention of the Cross and consequent casting down of the idol of Venus ("Chaucerian Tragedy," p. 19). May 3 was also the last day of the Roman feast of Floralia; as described in Ovid's *Fasti*, Book 5, it was a sexually uninhibited public celebration of fertility, exactly what we would expect the prudish boy with the mantle to disapprove of.

         Carlisle is a setting for Arthur's court in some medieval works: *The Awntyrs off Arthure at the Terne Wathelyne*, for example, or a couple of occasions in Malory's *Morte Darthur*, of most relevance here the catastrophic open accusation of Lancelot's adultery with Guenever and his entrapment in her chamber. The opening lines are thus an economical evocation of prior English literary history.

         In the analogues in which a time is specified it is Pentecost (*Le Lai du cor*, *Le Livre de Carados*, *Le Mantel mautaillié*, and Ulrich von Zatzikhoven's *Lanzelet*). That feast day, above all others, was one on which Arthur conventionally would not eat until some great adventure had befallen.

24   *Betweene two nutshells.* In the analogues, the mantle usually emerges from a magically small container.

44   *Ill itt did her beseeme.* Blue was the color of truth, chastity, and loyalty, and was commonly associated with the Virgin Mary (see Ferguson, *Signs and Symbols*, p. 272).

53   *walker.* The walker or fuller compressed cloth (sometimes by trampling) and cleaned it after it was woven.

57–60   Guenever is expressing a deliberately shocking preference: to live in the uncivilized forest without any comforts, luxuries, or honors rather than to stay in Arthur's court and be humiliated as she has been.

82   *Pattering ore a creede.* The knight is reciting a formula of Christian beliefs, probably the Apostles' Creed or the Nicene Creed, both of which were learned by laypeople in England in the Middle Ages.

100   *And bade her come in.* As in some of the analogues (*Le Mantel mautaillié* and Ulrich von Zatzikhoven's *Lanzelet*), the successful lady is not present while the others are trying the mantle.

152   *Looking over a dore.* The door is evidently a half door.

TEXTUAL NOTES TO THE BOY AND THE MANTLE

ABBREVIATIONS: see Explanatory Notes.

title	The MS reads: *Boy and Mantle*. The title and the initial "In" (which appears in the margin) were both added after the MS was bound, since they leave a mirror image trace on the opposite leaf.
7	MS reads: *With brauches and ringes.*
18	MS reads: *I hett you all heate.* Emendation for rhyme and sense.
21	MS reads: *He plucked out of his potewer.*
24	MS reads: *Betweene 2 nutshells.*
28	MS reads: *Shapen as itt is alreadye.* The MS line fits the stanza form badly and makes little sense: the mantle changes its shape to fit its wearer, hence the appropriateness of the subjunctive *be*.
32	MS reads: *Began to care for his wiffe.* Emendation for rhyme.
34	MS reads: *To the mantle shee her biled.* Emendation for sense and rhyme.
41	MS reads: *One while was itt gaule.* Emendation for sense and rhyme.
43	MS reads: *Another while was itt wadded.* Emendation for sense (other terms in the stanza are color terms).
72	MS reads: *All aboue the buttockes.* Emendation for rhyme. *Toute* was a fourteenth- and fifteenth-century word for the rump.
84	MS reads: *20 marks to his meede.*
86	MS reads: *willignglye.*
136	MS reads: *That maketh herselfe soe cleare.* Emendation for rhyme.
151	MS reads: *A litle boy stoode.* Emended for sense.
151–58	The lines are evidently corrupted. Percy adds lines after 152 (both in the MS's margin and in his edition), to complement lines 150–51 and make a stanza with them:
	And there as he was looking
	He was ware of a wyld bore.
156	MS reads: *Fast thither that he ran.* Emendation for sense.
163	MS reads: *Some rubbed their knies.* Emendation for sense.
169	MS reads: *All their knies edges.* Emendation for sense.
170	MS reads: *Turned backe againe.* Emendation for rhyme.

KINGS AND COMMONERS: INTRODUCTION

There are three king and commoner poems in this collection: *King Edward and the Shepherd*, *John the Reeve*, and *The King and the Hermit*. Only one of these, *John the Reeve*, is complete. The other two poems break off before their ending. The three, together with the fifteenth-century Scottish poem *Rauf Coilyear*, share the motif of a king incognito meeting the humblest of his subjects. The king takes on an assumed name and usually is reluctantly entertained by a poor man (though in *King Edward and the Shepherd*, Adam the Shepherd invites the sympathetic merchant to his home). The subject is initially prickly but warms up to his guest and eventually feeds him good wine and rich foods, including venison poached from the king's forest. In return for his host's hospitality, the king invites the peasant to court, where the latter realizes his guest's identity and fears punishment for poaching the king's deer. But instead he is rewarded. *King Edward and the Shepherd* is incomplete, ending before Adam the Shepherd is rewarded; *The King and the Hermit* breaks off even earlier, before the hermit friar goes to court.

King Edward and the Shepherd and *The King and the Hermit* are alike in that the king in both stories has to learn a nonsensical drinking salute: "passilodion" has to be answered by "berafrynd" in *King Edward and the Shepherd*, "fusty bandyas" by "stryke pantner" in *The King and the Hermit*. This feature of the story goes back to the early thirteenth-century *Speculum Ecclesiæ* by Geraldus Cambrensis, in which a Cistercian abbot entertains an incognito Henry II, and abbot and monarch toast each other with "pril" and "wril."[1] In both Geraldus and *King Edward and the Shepherd*, and also presumably in the lost ending of *The King and the Hermit*, the unusual toasts are given again at court. In *Rauf Coilyear* and *John the Reeve* there is no such exchange, but in these poems too the king is introduced to new customs: he is scolded for lack of courtesy, a charge brought on by Charlemagne's excessive and out-of-place condescension to his host in *Rauf Coilyear* and by Edward's speaking in Latin to his companions in *John the Reeve*. The humor of the pieces derives not only from the churlishness, suspicion, and discourtesy of the commoners (from the point of view of those used to admiration for the manners of the court) but also from the awkwardness of the king introduced into a society with social rules he does not yet know and has some trouble learning.

Other English stories of a king and commoner, whether contemporary to these (like the fifteenth-century *King and the Barker*) or later (like the sixteenth- and seventeenth-century versions of *The King and the Tanner* and the seventeenth-century *King Henry II and the Miller of Mansfield*), differ in deriving their humor entirely from the rusticity of the peasants. For an account of the English king and commoner poems, see F. J. Child, *English and Scottish*

---

[1] See *Geraldi Cambrensis Opera*, ed. J. S. Brewer, Rerum Britannicarum Medii Ævi (Rolls Series) 21, vol. 4 (London: Longmans, 1873), pp. 213–15.

Popular Ballads, 5.1 (Boston: Houghton, Mifflin and Co., 1894), article 273. Elizabeth Walsh discusses the analogues, including *Rauf Coilyear*, in "King in Disguise."

For all the similarities in their stories, the three versions collected here vary in their degree and focus of social satire. *King Edward and the Shepherd* is probably earliest and is by far the most directly tied to current events, specifically concerns of the English court of Edward III in the mid-to late 1340s. It is apparently an occasional poem, written for one of Edward's many court celebrations and including prominent members of the court in its storyline. It appears to be indebted to the Latin *Speculum Regis Edwardi III* by William of Pagula, a pair of open letters from 1331 and 1332 that castigate Edward and his court for abuses of purveyancing. William was a parish priest in Winkfield, about three miles from Windsor.

John the Reeve also mentions a specific king, Edward Longshanks, who was Edward I, and two prominent nobles, the bishop of Durham (who had extraordinary civil powers in northern England rivaling those of the king) and the earl of Gloucester. But the lines that give us the identity of the king also make clear that the poem was written long after his rule:

Of that name were kinges three,
But Edward with the long shankes was hee.
    (lines 16–17)

Edward I died in 1307; his grandson Edward III died in 1377, and the poem must have been written between the latter's death and the accession of Edward IV in 1461. After a lapse of more than seventy years, the circumstances of the rule of Edward I, and a specific earl and bishop, are not being portrayed. But there may be hints of the concerns of the period of Richard II, notably the common man voicing resentment of the use of Latin:

Speake English, everyche one,
Or else sitt still, in the devilles name:
Such talke love I naught.
Lattine spoken amongst lewd men —
Therin noe reason doe I ken;
For falshood itt is wrought.
    (lines 493–98)

The insubordination of John is also reminiscent of the newfound resistance to exploitation of the peasantry expressed in the revolt of 1381. Rachel Snell quotes the chronicler Henry Knighton's account of the aspiration of Wat Tyler, one of the leaders of the revolt, that

throughout the kingdom the poor as well as the rich should be free to take game in water, fishponds, woods and forests as well as to hunt hares in the fields — and to do these and many other things without impediment.[2]

---

[2] Snell, "Undercover King," p. 147. Her source is *Chronicon Henrici Knighton*, 2, 137, translated in R. B. Dobson, ed., *The Peasants' Revolt of 1381* (London: Palgrave Macmillan, 1970), p. 186.

But both the resistance to Latin and the desire for freedom from restrictive legislation continue beyond Richard's reign into the next century. The poem voices a series of John's complaints about restrictions governing what he is free to eat and drink (lines 136–59, 199–205, 482–86), even to burn (lines 193–98), but they are not easily identified with specific legislation, despite John's reference to "statutinge" (line 155). He resists subordination to lords (lines 115–20), to his guests (172–74), to courtiers and porters (656–93, 724–73), to the queen (782–86), and to the king himself. Characteristically, John's first reaction to the discovery of his guest's identity is irony (lines 782–86). His second (lines 787–95) is to stand on his rights and claim what the king has promised. Only after the king shows generosity to him does he finally kneel (lines 811–13).

John the Reeve, unlike *King Edward and the Shepherd*, is no more tied to a specific place than it is to a specific time. Both poems are explicitly set near and at Windsor, but there is nothing about Windsor or its area exploited by the poem, except that it is a likely setting for a king and for some implied poaching and fuel-gathering in a royal forest; the village where John lives is apparently jointly owned by the bishop of Durham, the earl of Gloucester, and the king (lines 178–79, 125), an unlikely combination in the south of England.

The King and the Hermit has another Edward ("god Edwerd," line 13) as king, perhaps meaning Edward III. Its hermit is not a peasant but a friar, and thus likely originally of a noble or gentry family rather than a peasant one. The poem is set in Sherwood Forest, known to some medieval readers and most modern ones as the home of Robin Hood. Here the setting is chosen because, like Windsor Forest, Sherwood Forest was one of the many royal forests of England, protected by legislation from hunting and harvesting. The hermit's clandestine diet of bread, broiled meats, and alcohol is a good deal more basic than the rich foods of both *John the Reeve* and *King Edward and the Shepherd*, and clothing and fuel-gathering are not an issue at all. But the hermit is very suspicious of his guest's attempts to draw him out on hunting in the king's forest:

> The armyte seyd, "So mote thou go,
> Hast thou any other herand than so
> Onto my lord the kynge?"
>   (lines 250–52)

He is doubtless aware that by the late Middle Ages the main function of Forest Law was to provide an income to the king in the form of fines.[3]

Given the class opposition that is explicit in these poems, with their kings and members of the court on one hand and their rustic peasants on the other, the two sides having very different expectations of social behavior, the question of readership is particularly interesting. Are these poems for the gentry, so that they can look down their noses and sneer at the churls? Are they poems for the downtrodden peasantry, so that they can laugh at the king out of his element and rejoice that their oppression is being expressed aloud? Of the three, *King Edward and the Shepherd* is probably the earliest. It was composed by someone who was familiar with the court of Edward III, probably to use at an entertainment for that court. It would have been an entertainment with a satirical edge to it, but also flattering to Edward in that it shows him doing what an admirable king does, listening to his people. And it

---

[3] Birrel, "Medieval English Forest," p. 80.

carefully shows him as Edward II's beloved son, papering over Edward III's own role, as an adolescent, in removing his father from the throne of England. It also reminds us that Isabelle is Edward's mother, glossing over the fact that Isabelle is still alive (d. 1358) but imprisoned for her role in the deposition and murder of Edward II; it is through Isabelle that Edward III was, at time the poem was being written, claiming the throne of France. Because it does a political job of supporting Edward and his dynastic legitimacy, and because its criticisms of oppressions such as purveyancing and failure to keep order within the kingdom are deflected from accusations against Edward himself, who in the poem does not know what is going on, and who promises to fix the situation when he finds out, it is a poem that would have been more than acceptable as an entertainment at one of Edward's many feasts and tourneys. But oddly enough, the poem is preserved not quite complete only in a manuscript owned or read more than a century later by a priest in Staffordshire, Gilbert Pilkington, in the same manuscript miscellany that contains *The Tale of the Basin*, at a time and place in which the poem's original immediate political context could have been of little interest. *The King and the Hermit*, very similar to *King Edward and the Shepherd* in its drinking game, its poaching, and its comic pitting of the culture of the king's court against the culture of the poor, has none of the earlier poem's specific references to political context. It is found in a Leicestershire manuscript of around 1500, MS Ashmole 61, in which *Sir Corneus* also appears. This miscellany manuscript was compiled by someone named Rate who was likely a middle-class guildsman in Leicester. The other king and commoner poem edited here, *John the Reeve*, survives only in the very late Percy Folio Manuscript, so the manuscript gives us no clues as to what sort of medieval readers found it interesting. But the poem was alluded to, among other well-known poems, by Scottish poets, despite its approving references to "our king," "Edward with the long shankes" (*John the Reeve*, lines 12 and 17). Since Edward Longshanks also bore the nickname "The Hammer of the Scots" this is an odd readership. Looked at as a group, the poems evidently enjoyed a very broad audience: royal and noble, clerical, bourgeois; Windsor, Staffordshire, Leicestershire, Scotland.[4]

These three poems, with greatest emphasis on *King Edward and the Shepherd*, are discussed as romances by Rachel Snell in "Undercover King," noted above. Glenn Wright discusses *King Edward and the Shepherd* as having "a foot in the world of romance" but also "a conspicuous kinship with the complaint tradition" (pp. 652–54; quotation p. 652), and *John the Reeve* as "a jovial romp that casts no shadow" (pp. 654–56; quotation p. 656), in his "Churl's Courtesy." Thomas Ohlgren explores similarities of *King Edward and the Shepherd* and *The King and the Hermit* to Robin Hood poems in *Robin Hood: The Early Poems, 1465–1560*, pp. 148–49. George Shuffelton discusses all three in his explanatory notes on "King Edward and the Hermit" in his edition *Codex Ashmole 61*, pp. 590–96, esp. pp. 591–92. All three poems are mentioned by Melissa Furrow, "Comic Tales."

---

[4] For discussions of the manuscripts and their ownership, see the introduction to *The Tale of the Basin* for Cambridge University Library MS Ff. 5. 48, and Ohlgren, "'lewed peple loven tales olde'"; the introduction to *Sir Corneus* for Oxford, Bodleian Library MS Ashmole 61, and the discussions by Shuffelton (*Codex Ashmole 61*, pp. 4–6) and Blanchfield ("Romances in MS Ashmole 61"); also Blanchfield, "Rate Revisited"; for the Percy Folio Manuscript, see the introduction to *The Boy and the Mantle*. For the allusions by Scottish poets Gavin Douglas, William Dunbar, and Sir David Lyndsay, see the introduction to *John the Reeve*. The three poets themselves all had connections to the Scottish court.

KING EDWARD AND THE SHEPHERD: INTRODUCTION

King Edward and the Shepherd is in Cambridge University Library, MS. Ff.5.48, fols. 48v–56v. *The Tale of the Basin*, from the current collection, also appears in this manuscript, and a discussion of the manuscript and its scribal language can be found in the introduction to that poem. The same hand, from Derbyshire, transcribed both poems.

AFTERLIFE

King Edward and the Shepherd appears, with different names as noted below, in the following early or otherwise useful editions:

1829. *A Tale of King Edward and the Shepherd.* Charles Henry Hartshorne, ed. *Ancient Metrical Tales.* London: W. Pickering. Pp. 35–80.

1930. *King Edward and the Shepherd.* Walter Hoyt French and Charles Brockway Hale, eds. *Middle English Metrical Romances.* New York: Prentice-Hall. Pp. 949–85.

1969. *A Tale of King Edward and the Shepherd.* Janay Y. Downing. "A Critical Edition of Cambridge University MS Ff. 5. 48." Ph. D. dissertation, University of Washington. Pp. 116–59.

REFERENCE TOOLS

King Edward and the Shepherd is *NIMEV* 988.

It is addressed by Thomas Cooke in volume 9 (1993) of the *Manual*, section 24 Tales [8], *A Tale of King Edward and the Shepherd.*

POET, LANGUAGE, DATE, METER

The dating of the poem hinges on its content. Close inspection of its allusions to members of the court reveals a depiction of its principals as they would have been in the period 1345–47: the younger Edward (b. 1330) still an adolescent "with the whene" (line 109), still too young to know everything as his father points out (lines 926–28) but a prince (he was made Prince of Wales in 1343, and was the only one of Edward's sons ever to be styled a prince); the king's second cousin Henry of Grosmont already earl of Lancaster (he inherited the earldom of Lancaster in 1345) but not yet a duke (he became one in 1351); John de Warenne, earl of Surrey, of an older generation, and an advisor bold enough to have faced down the angry king in Parliament, still living (he died at the end of June 1347); Sir Ralph of Stafford a valued retainer but not one of the "erles tweyne" mentioned in line 611. (He is called an "erle balde" at line 644, but given that he is distinguished from the earls earlier, and also not styled earl of Stafford, it seems to me probable that the appellation "earl" was a later alteration as the poem was retranscribed after his elevation to an earldom in 1351).

The poem is a graceful combination of requests for attention to the more serious domestic problems of the earlier part of Edward's reign and a celebration of his reign. To take the latter first: the continuity and legitimacy of his kingship are repeatedly stressed by the insistence on the love that the previous (deposed and murdered) Edward bore to Joly Robyne (lines 104–06, 578–80), and honor continues to be paid to the previous Edward (line 884). Edward III's interest in the well-being of his poor subjects is exemplified. He asks Adam's opinion of the king (lines 50–51) and wants to know about the king's men and their behavior (lines 58–59); he takes on the mission of getting the royal household's debt to Adam paid back and refuses compensation (Adam's suggestion that it wouldn't hurt for Joly Robyne to spend some money on his clothing at lines 798–99 is amusing but also subtly flattering from the point of view of fiscal prudence, not usually Edward's strong suit); and at the end of the poem is about to launch a protective strike against the robbers. (It is later claimed in Hoccleve's *Regiment of Princes*, 1412, that Edward III "ofte" used to travel in plain clothes into the countryside and ask the people what they thought about the king.)[1] Edward allows Adam's poaching, is amused by his cheekiness, insists that his courtiers treat Adam well (lines 863–65), and resolves "Hit shalle hym meve al to gode" (line 1064), even though a squire suggests that his power is unlimited and he could have the peasant torn limb from limb (lines 1073–75). The moment when Adam finally takes off his hood is a delayed but satisfying recognition of Edward's power.

But as would be appropriate to a Mirror for Princes, the poem makes clear that there are social abuses that need attention by the king. The court is accused of predatory behavior, and the accusation is substantiated at lines 782–88 where it is clear that the steward would not recognize Adam's tally stick and repay the money owed him if it were not for Edward's intervention. The *Speculum Regis Edwardii III*, or *Mirror of Edward III* (written by William of Pagula, an Oxford-trained theologian and a parish priest in Winkfield, a small village about five miles from Windsor) in the form of open letters to Edward dating from 1331 and 1332, had addressed the issue of purveyance for the king's household, exactly where the king is vulnerable to criticism in *King Edward and the Shepherd* more than a decade later: "[M]en of your court . . . and various subordinates of your court . . . seize many goods by violence from the owners of those goods, namely they seize bread, beer, fowls, cocks, beans, oats and many other things, for which practically nothing is paid; and because of extortions of this kind, many poor people will not have what they need to sow their fields."[2] Worse still, a gang of robbers terrorizes Adam and his family, ousting husband and wife from their house and violating their daughter, though whether the latter is an instance of gang rape (as it seems to be at line 166) or of the daughter's having a lover among them (as

---

[1] Hoccleve, *Regiment of Princes*, lines 2556–62.

[2] William of Pagula, *Mirror of King Edward III*, p. 204.

seems to be the case at line 597 and perhaps at line 830) is not clear, and perhaps simply not consistent. Outlaw gangs were a terrible problem in the England of the late 1320s and early 1330s, particularly the two most audacious gangs, the Folvilles and the Coterels, in Nottinghamshire, Derbyshire, Leicestershire, and Rutland; a massive crackdown in 1332 proved ineffective, and the wars in Scotland and France were more successful in absorbing the gang members than the law was in capturing or convicting them. But in 1346 Eustace Folville "[took] the opportunity of the king's going overseas to resort once more to violence."[3] Since Eustace was "the worst of the brothers . . . with five murders and a score of other felonies" alleged against him, including rape, his resumption of a life of violent crime was a concern, though he died of natural causes a year later.[4]

The poem, then, is clearly set in the 1345–47 period, but of course the events of the poem could not have actually happened, not least because, of the five great lords named in the poem, four were overseas, triumphant leaders in the French war: Edward himself, his son the prince, and to a lesser degree Sir Ralph Stafford at Crécy and Calais; Henry of Lancaster in Aquitaine and at Poitiers. With their return to England in October 1347 we can imagine a suitable occasion for the performance of the poem to the court at Windsor, as part of the "round of court festivities that continued through the winter [of 1347–48] and on into the spring of and summer of 1348."[5] It is very much a Windsor poem and thus fits well with Edward's revived interest in his birthplace Windsor Castle in the 1340s as a significant royal dwelling. Despite its criticisms of the state of the realm, the poem is complimentary to Edward: Joly Robyne disavows the predatory practices of the court purveyors (lines 37–39) and speaks at length about the innocence of the king (lines 133–44). His apparently poor subject is nevertheless a reassuringly rich subject, and a decidedly nonsubmissive one. Adam has faith that the king would permit him to retaliate against the predators if approached properly (lines 836–38); Edward goes one better and proposes to send out a strike force (lines 840–50). It also takes cachet from, and in return gives it back to, the great lords named by memorializing them in a poem: the prince, the earl of Lancaster, Sir Ralph of Stafford, and in a graceful remembrance, the venerable earl of Surrey, John de Warenne, who had recently died. The poem is unlikely to have been composed much later than 1348, given the degree of specificity of the poet's knowledge of the king's household and the events of the period. At any rate the arrival in England of the plague and the death of Edward and Queen Philippa's infant son in the summer of 1348 meant that the latter half of the year was a sadder time without opportunities for festive performance at court.

Who was the poet, and how unusual was he? He appears to be an exceptionally early instance of an English poet writing at least one piece for the royal court, and writing in English to boot. Edward III was keenly aware of the value of managing culture and used tournaments and games at his court to bolster its prestige. He is not known as a literary patron, but Juliet Vale's *Edward III and Chivalry* makes clear that the records that would show such patronage were not kept.[6] Henry of Lancaster is remembered in part for his *Livre des Seintz Medicines*, a devotional treatise in Anglo-French; so poetry was not necessarily undervalued among even Edward's greatest nobles. Other English poetry of the period —

---

[3] Stones, "Folvilles of Ashby-Folville," p. 130.

[4] Stones, "Folvilles of Ashby-Folville," pp. 118 and 120.

[5] Ormrod, "For Arthur and St George," p. 19.

[6] Vale, *Edward III and Chivalry*, p. 48.

specifically, Laurence Minot's celebrations of Edward's victories and the debate poem *Wynnere and Wastoure* — are suitable in one way or another for court performance. Sophisticated *belles lettres* were still normally in French, but early 1348 would have been a particularly satisfying time to be writing in English after the defeat of the French enemy at Crécy and Calais. It is probable that we have lost most evidence that there were earlier poets than Chaucer and Gower who had court connections and wrote occasionally for the royal court or its members.

The language of the poem suggests that, despite the northernisms in the manuscript, the poet originated in East Anglia. The salient points from *LALME* are the following:

> The rhyme of *thou wylt/sitt* at lines 530–31. Forms of *wilt* without -*l*- are to be found in a small area, Cambridgeshire, Norfolk, and Suffolk. See *County Dictionary*, p. 44. This tiny detail is consonant with other more pervasive features of the poet's language.

> But problematically, the rhyme set *ware/mare/are/care* at lines 63, 66, 69, 72 implies that words originating in Old English long *a* (*more, ore*) continue to be pronounced with an *a* rather than an *o*. And this feature is seen recurrently, as in the rhyme *Ya!/ga* at lines 821–22. This feature is usually and strongly associated with the North, but *LALME* does show one instance of its occurrence in Norfolk as a minority form. See *County Dictionary*, p. 85. Note that the rhyme set *soore/thore/hore/more* at lines 171, 174, 177, 180, because *hore* comes from Old English *horh*, implies an *o* pronunciation for *sore* and *more* (both from Old English long *a*), the more usual pronunciation for East Anglia.

Two other features of the poet's language are consonant with an East Anglian origin and not with a northern one:

1. The rhyme set *Adam/thedame/came/man* at lines 1033, 1036, 1039, 1042 implies an /a/ in the past tense of the verb *come* (as opposed to usual northern /o/).
2. Another recurring feature is apparent rhymes on -*ynde* and -*ende*
     mynde/wende/kynde/frende 255, 258, 261, 264
     ende/Berafrynde/kynde/hende 361, 364, 367, 370
     frende/kynde 389–90
     hynde/Berafrynde/wende/unkynde 505, 508, 511, 514
     frynde/ende/wende/fende 865, 868, 871, 874
     ende/berafrynde 968–69
   In other words, descendants of Old English -*y*- (*mynd, ʒecynde*) rhyme with descendants of Old English -*e*- (*wendan, ende, ʒehende*) and of Old English -*éo*- (*féond, fréond*). All of these are exact rhymes for the poet on -*end*. Forms with -*e*- for *kind* and *mind* are attested for (among other eastern areas) Norfolk, Suffolk, and Cambridgeshire, *County Dictionary*, pp. 204–05.

Metrically, the poem is in the common twelve-line tail rhyme stanza, *aabccbddbeeb*, with the usual four stresses in the couplets and three in the *b* lines. It is accentual rather than accentual-syllabic, and it is a form to be heard in contemporary Middle English romances. Occasionally the rhyme scheme breaks down (e.g., *filled/begynne*, lines 455–56; *sawe/lawe/sale/bale*, lines 1081, 1084, 1087, 1090), but rarely enough to suggest loss and scribal conjecture rather than the poet's lack of resourcefulness. Usually the prosody is competent.

KING EDWARD AND THE SHEPHERD

	God that sittis in Trinité	
	Gyffe thaym grace wel to the	*Give; well to prosper*
	That listyns me a whyle.	
	Alle that lovys of melody	*All who love melody*
5	Of hevon blisse God graunte thaim party	*Of heaven's; part*
	(Theyr soules shelde fro peryle)	*shield from peril*
	At festis and at mangery,	*banquet*
	To tell of kyngis that is worthy	
	Talis that byn not vyle.	*Tales; are*
10	And ye wil listyn how hit ferd	*If; went*
	Betwene Kyng Edward and a scheperd,	
	Ye shalle lawgh of gyle.	*trickery*

	Oure kyng went hym in a tyde	*one time*
	To pley hym be a ryver side	*by*
15	In a mornyng of May.	
	Knyght ne squyer wold he non	*nor squire*
	But hymself and a grome,	*servingman*
	To wende on that jorney.	*go; day trip*
	With a scheperde con he mete,	*he met*
20	And gret hym with wordis swete,	*greeted*
	Without any delay.	
	The scheperde lovyd his hatte so well,	*hat*
	He did hit off never a dele,	*took it off not a bit*
	But seid, "Sir, gud-day."	

	The kyng to the herde seid than,	*herdsman*
25	"Of whens art thou, gode man,	
	Also mot I the?"	*As I hope to prosper*
	"In Wynsaure was I borne.	*Windsor*
	Hit is a myle but here beforne;	*just in front of here*
30	The town then maist thou see.	*can*
	I am so pylled with the kyng	*pillaged by*
	That I most fle fro my wonyng,	*must; dwelling*
	And therfore woo is me.	*woe*
	I hade catell; now have I non;	*livestock*

35 Thay take my bestis and don thaim slone,   *animals; have them slain*
        And payen but a stik of tre."   *pay only a stick of wood*

    The kyng seid, "Hit is gret synne
    That thei of sich werkis wil not blynne,   *deeds; stop*
        And Edward wot hit noght.   *knows*
40 But come tomorne when it is day   *tomorrow*
    Thou shalbe sirvyd of thi pay.   *supplied with; deserts*
        Therof have thou no thoght.   *don't worry*
    For in your towne born I was.
    I have dwellid in diverse place   *various places*
45   Sithe I thens was broght.   *Since; thence*
    In the courte I have sich a frende: *a certain*
    The treserer, or then I wende,   *treasurer, before I leave*
        For thi luffe shalle be soght."   *love*

    This gret lord the herd con frayne,   *asked*
50 "What wil men of your kyng seyne?   *say*
        Wel litull gode, I trowe."   *believe*
    The herd onsweryd hym right noght,
    But on his schepe was all his thoght,
        And seid agayn, "Char, how!"   *Turn back, ho*
55 Then loogh oure kyng and smyled stille: *laughed; quietly*
    "Thou onsweris me not at my will;   *as I would like*
        I wolde thai were on a lawe!   *in a lake*
    I aske thee tythyngis of oure kyng,   *you information about*
    Of his men and his wyrkyng;   *performance*
60   For sum I have sorow.

    "I am a marchant and ride aboute,   *merchant*
    And fele sithis I am in dowte   *many times; fear*
        For myn owne ware.   *commodities*
    I tell it thee in priveté,   *confidentially*
65 The kyngis men oon to me   *owe*
        A thousand pounde and mare.   *more*
    Owe he ought mycull in this cuntré?   *very much*
    What silver shall he pay thee,   *ought he to pay you*
        For Goddis haly are?   *holy grace*
70 Sith thou art neghtbur myne,   *neighbor*
    I wil my nedis do and thyne;   *business*
        Tharof have thou no care."

    "Sir," he seid, "be Seynt Edmonde,   *by*
    Me is owand four pounde   *[To] me is owed*
75   And odde twa schillyng.   *two odd shillings*
    A stikke I have to my witness.   *as*
    Of hasill I mene that hit is;   *hazel I complain*

I ne have no nother thyng.   *I have no other*
And gif thou do as thou has me hote,   *if; promised*
80   Then shall I gif thee a cote,   *give; coat*
        Withowt any lesyng;   *lie*
     Sevon schelyng tomorne at day   *Seven shillings*
     Whan I am sirvyd of my pay."   *provided with*
        "Graunte," seid oure kyng.   *Agreed*

85   "Tel me, sir, what is thi name,
     That I for thee have no blame,
        And where thi wonnyng is."
     "Sir," he seid, "as mot I the,   *prosper*
     Adam the scheperde men callen me,
90   For certan soth iwysse."   *indeed*
     The scheperde seid, "Whos son art thou of oure towne?
     Hat not thi fadur Hochon,   *Isn't your father called*
        Also have thou blisse?"   *As you hope to have*
     "No, for God," seid oure kyng,
95   "I wene thou knowist me nothyng;   *believe; not at all*
        Thou redis alle amysse.   *guess all wrong*

     "My fadur was a Walsshe knyght;   *Welsh*
     Dame Isabell my modur hyght,   *was called*
        Forsothe as I tell thee.
100 In the castell was hir dwellyng
     Thorow commaundment of the kyng,   *By*
        Whene she thar shuld be.
     Now wayte thou wher that I was borne.   *you know*
     The tother Edward here beforne,   *The other*
105   Full well he lovyd me,
     Sertanly withowte lye.   *Certainly*
     Sum tyme I live be marchandye,   *trade*
        And passe well ofte the see.   *cross; sea*

     "I have a son is with the whene;   *[who] is; queen*
110 She lovys hym well, as I wene;   *believe*
        That dar I savely say.   *dare; safely*
     And he pray hir of a bone,   *If; for a boon*
     Yif that hit be for to done,   *possible*
        She will not onys say nay;   *once*
115 And in the courte I have sich a frende,
     I shalbe sirvyd or I wende,   *before*
        Withowt any delay.
     Tomorne at undur speke with me;   *nine*
     Thou shalbe sirvyd of thi moné   *provided with; money*
120   Er than hye mydday."   *Before high noon*

"Sir, for Seynt Thomas of Ynde,   *India*
In what place shall I thee fynde,
        And what shalle I thee calle?"
"My name," he seid, "is Joly Robyn;
125   Ilke man knowes hit well and fyne,   *Every; very well*
        Bothe in bowre and halle.   *private and public*
Pray the porter, as he is fre,   *Ask; noble*
That he let thee speke with me,
        Soo faire hym mot befalle.   *good things*
130   For fer owtward shall I not be;   *far away*
Sumquer I trow thou shall me see,   *Somewhere*
        Within the castell wall.

"For thou and other that lene your thyng,   *lend; goods*
Wel ofte sithes ye banne the kyng,   *times; curse*
135   And ye ar not to blame;
Hit er other that do that dede;   *It is others*
Thei were worthy, so God me spede,   *make me prosper*
        Therfor to have gret shame.
And if I wist whilke thei were,   *knew which*
140   Hit shulde come the kyng to ere,   *to the king's ear*
        Be God and be Seynt Jame.
Then durst I swere thei shuld abye   *dare; pay for it*
That dose oure kyng that vilanye,   *do*
        For he berys all the fame."   *reputation*

145   The herd onswerd to the kyng,
"Sir, be Seynt Jame, of this tithyng   *information*
        Thou seist therof right well: *speak of it*
Thei do but gode, the kyngis men;
Thei ar worse then sich ten   *ten times worse*
150   That bene with hym no dell.   *are; not at all*
Thei goo aboute be eight or nyne   *go around in a group of*
And done the husbondis mycull pyne,   *farmers great suffering*
        That carfull is theire mele.   *[So] that anxious; their [every] meal*
Thai take geese, capons, and henne,
155   And alle that ever thei may with renne,   *run with*
        And reves us oure catell.   *rob from us; property*

"Sum of theim was bonde sore,   *tightly tied up*
And afturwarde hanget therfore,   *hanged for it*
        Forsoth, as I yow say.
160   Yet ar ther of theim nyne moo,   *more*
For at my hows thei were also   *house*
        Certis yisturday.   *Certainly*
Thei toke my hennes and my geese
And my schepe with all the fleese,

165 And ladde theim forth away.   *led*
    Be my doghtur thei lay al nyght;
    To come agayne thei have me hyght;   *promised*
      Of helpe I wolde yow pray.

    "With me thei lefte alle their thyng,
170 That I am sicur of theire comyng,   *[So] that I am sure*
      And that me rewes soore.   *makes me very unhappy*
    I have fayre chamburs thre,   *rooms*
    But non of theim may be with me   *can [stand to]*
      While that thei be thore.   *there*
175 Into my carthaws thei me dryfe;   *cart-house; drive*
    Out at the dur thei put my wyfe,   *door*
      For she is olde gray hore.   *barnyard muck*
    Had I helpe of sum lordyng,   *lord*
    I shulde make with thame recknyng;   *reckoning*
180   Thei shulde do so no more.

    "For other thre felowes and I,
    We durst wel take party   *dare; part*
      These nyne for to mete.
    I have slyngus smert and gode   *slings stinging*
185 To mete with theim yif thei were wode,   *even if; violent*
      And reve hem her lyves swete.   *take from them their*
    The best archer of ilkon,   *the lot (each)*
    I durst mete hym with a stone,
      And gif hym leve to schete.   *give; leave to shoot*
190 Ther is no bow that shall laste
    To draw to my slynges caste,   *amount to; distance of shot*
      Nought be feel fete.   *Not by many feet*

    "Ther is non archer in this lande,   *i.e., who could compete*
    And I have my slyng in hande.   *If*
195   For I dar lay with hym ale   *bet*
    That whoso sonyst hittis a bauke   *soonest; target?*
    For to have the tother haut   *the other['s] hawk?*
      To what thyng he will hale —   *draw back the arrow*
    That whoso furst smytis a thyng   *hits*
200 Of his bow or my slyng   *With*
      Undurstande my tale —
    Be the deth that I shall dye,
    Therto my hed then dar I ley,
      Now sone in this swale."   *shade*

205 With talis he made the kyng to dwell,
    With mony moo then I can tell,
      Till hit was halfe-gatis prime. *early morning was half over*

His hatte was bonde undur his chyn;
He did hit nothyng off to hym: *didn't take it off*
210   He thoght hit was no tyme.
"Robyn," he seid, "I pray thee
Hit is thi will: come hom with me,   *[That] it*
A morsell for to dyne."   *To have a bite to eat*
The kyng list of his bourdis lere;   *wanted to learn his funny customs*
215   "Gladly," he seid, "My lefe fere,   *dear companion*
I wil be on of thyne."   *I'm your man*

As thei hamward con gon,
The kyng saw conyngis mony on;   *many a rabbit*
Therat he can smyle.
220   "Adam," he seid, "Take up a ston
And put hit in thi slyng anon;
Abyde we here a while.
Gret bourde it wold be   *fun*
Of theim to slee twoo or thre,   *kill*
225   I swere thee be Seynt Gyle."
"Do way!" quod Adam, "Let be that!   *Give up; Forget it*
Be God, I wolde not for my hat
Be takyn with sich a gyle.   *trick*

"Hit is alle the kynges waren;   *rabbit warren*
230   Ther is nouther knyght ne sqwayne   *swain*
That dar do sich a dede,
Any conynges here to sla   *slay*
And with the trespas awey to ga,   *go*
But his sidis shulde blede.
235   The warner is hardy and fell;   *man in charge; ruthless*
Sirtanly, as I thee tell,
He will take no mede.   *bribe*
Whoso dose here sich maistrye,   *such a feat*
Be thou wel sicur he shall abye   *pay the penalty*
240   And unto prison lede.   *[be] led*

"Ther is no wilde foule that will flyne
But I am sicur hym to hittyne;   *sure; hit*
Sich mete I dar thee hote   *food; promise*
Yif hit be so my slyng will last.
245   Yif I fayle of hym a caste,   *shot*
Brok than welle my cote.   *Enjoy*
When we come and sitten insame,   *together*
I shalle tech thee a gamme;
I can hit wel be rote.   *know; by heart*
250   Then shal thou se my slyng slaght,   *game killed with my sling*

| | And of the best take us a draght, | *drink* |
| | And drynk well right be note." | *by token* |

	The scheperde hows ful mery stode	
	Undur a forest fayre and gode,	
255	Of hert and hynde gret mynde.	*[With a] great amount of hart and hind*
	The kyng seid, "Be God Almyght,	
	In thy hert thou may be light	*heart; happy*
	Hamward when thou shall wende;	
	I thee swere, be Goddis grace,	
260	And I had here sich a place,	*If*
	I shulde have of that kynde;	*some of that species*
	Outher on even or on morneng,	*Either; evening*
	Sum of theim shuld come to ryng,	*join the dance*
	Therwith to make me a frende."	

265	The herd bade, "Let soch wordis be!	*Don't talk like that*
	Sum man myght here thee;	
	Thee were bettur be still.	*better to be quiet*
	Wode has erys, fylde has sight;	
	Were the forster here now right,	
270	Thy wordis shuld like thee ille.	*not please you at all*
	He has with hym yong men thre;	
	Thei be archers of this contré,	
	The kyng to sirve at wille,	
	To kepe the dere bothe day and nyght,	
275	And for theire luf a loge is dight	*for their sake a lodge is built*
	Full hye upon an hill.	*high*

	"I wolde have here no standyng,	*I don't want us to stand here*
	But ride now forth in my blessyng	*with my*
	And make us wel at ese.	*[let's] make; ease*
280	I am glad thou come with me;	*came*
	Goo sit now wher thi willes be,	*where you prefer*
	Right at thine owne ese;	
	Though sumdel of my gode be lorne,	*part; lost*
	I shall have more; and God beforne,	*by God*
285	He may hit wel increse;	
	And I shall tech thee play —	
	When tyme comys, thou shalt asay	*test*
	Whilke play be not lese."	*Which play is not a trick*

	A fayre cloth on the borde he leyd;	*table*
290	Into the boure he made a brayde,	*back room; dash*
	Gode mete for to fette.	*food; fetch*
	Brede of whete bultid small,	*sifted fine*
	Two peny ale he brought withall:	*also*

Therof wolde he not lett;   *refrain*
295 A fesaunde brid and therwith a crane.   *young pheasant*
Other fowles were ther gode ane   *in abundance*
     Before the kyng he sette.   *[that] he*
"Adam," quod the kyng, "blessed thou be:
Here is bettur then thou heghtist me,   *promised*
300   Today when that we mette."

"Sir," he seid, "do now gladly;   *now enjoy [yourself]*
Yet have I mete that were worthy   *I still have*
     A gret lord for to fech."   *fetch*
He broght a heron with a poplere,   *spoonbill*
305 Curlews, boturs, bothe in fere,   *bitterns; together*
     The maudlart and hur mech,   *mallard; mate*
And a wylde swan was bake.   *[that] was*
"Sich fowle con my slyng take;
     Theroff am I no wrech;   *cheapskate*
310 I bade felawes to my dynere   *invited*
And sithen thei wil not cum here,   *since*
     A devell have who that rech!   *whoever cares*

"Yif thou wilt ete, thou shall non wave;   *want to; pass up none of it*
But gif thou will any drynk have,
315   Thou most con thy play;   *learn; game*
When thou seest the cuppe anon,
But thou sei *passilodion*   *Unless; (see note)*
     Thou drynkis not this day.
Sely Adam shall sitt thee hende   *Good old; handy to you*
320 And onswere with *berafrynde*,   *(see note)*
     Leve upon my ley."   *Trust me*
The kyng seid that he wold lere: *wanted to learn*
"Me think it bourde for to here:
     Teche me, I thee pray."

325 "*Passilodyon*, that is this:
Whoso drynkis furst, iwys,
     Wesseyle the mare dele!   *Share out more liquor*
Berafrynde also, I wene,
Hit is to make the cup clene,   *empty*
330   And fylle hit efte full wele.   *again*
Thus shal the game go aboute,
And whoso falys of this route,   *fails in this custom*
     I swere be Seynt Mighell,
Get hym drynk wher he will,   *[Let] him get*
335 He getis non here (this is my skill)   *my view of what's right*
     Noght to another sele."   *till; occasion*

The kyng seid, "Let se that drynke;
I shall say right that I thynke:
   Me thirstis swyth sore."   *just what*
                                                       I'm very thirsty
340 The scheperde bade the cup fill;
The kyng to drynk hade gode will
   With passilodion more.

   ……………………………………
   "I con right wel my lore."   *know; lesson*
"Berafrynde," iseid Adam,
345 "Iwysse thou art a wytty man;   *Certainly; clever*
   Thou shalt wel drynk therfore."

Thus thei sate withoute strife,   *sat; disagreement*
The kyng with Adam and his wyfe,
   And made hym mery and glad.
350 The scheperde bade "the cuppe fill";
The kyng to drynke hade gode will;
   His wife did as he bade.
When the cuppe was come anon,
The kyng seid "passylodion"
355   When he the cuppe hade.
Hit was a game of gret solas;
Hit comford all that ever ther was;   *cheered*
   Therof thai were noght sade.

The scheperde ete till that he swatte,   *sweated*
360 And than nou erst he drew his hatt   *for the first time; pulled off*
   Into the benke-ende.   *Onto; bench-end*
And when he feld the drynk was gode,   *felt*
He wynkid and strokyd up his hode,   *pushed*
   And seid, "Berafrynde."
365 He was qwyte as any swan;   *white*
He was a wel begeten man,   *begotten*
   And comyn of holy kynde.   *descent*
He wold not ete his cromys drye: *crumbs*
He lovyd nothyng but it were trie,   *choice*
370   Nether fer ne hende.   *Of any kind*

Then seid the kyng in his reson,   *talk*
"Whoso were in a gode town,   *If someone*
   This wold ha costed dere,   *have*
In this maner to be fed
375 With alkyn dentey wel bested,   *every kind of delicacy; arranged*
   As we have had now here.
I shalle thee whyte, be hode myne: *requite; hood*
Now hade I lever a conyne   *rather; rabbit*
   Dight in my manere;   *Prepared*

380   But yif hit were of buk or doo,   *Unless it were of buck or doe*
       Ther is no mete i-lovyd soo,   *dish so well praised*
           And I come ther hit were."   *If; came where*

       The scheperde seid, "So mot thou the,   *As you hope to prosper*
       Con thou heyle a priveté?   *conceal a secret*
385   And thou shalt se gode game."
       "Ye!" seid the kyng, "Be my leuté,   *loyalty*
       And ellis have I mycul maugré   *Or else; blame*
           Yif hit be for my frame.   *Even if; to my advantage [to reveal it]*
       What man that wrye a gode frende,   *informs on*
390   Though he were right sibbe of my kynde,   *closely related to me by birth*
           He were worthy gret shame."
       Then seid Adam, "Thou seis soth;
       Yet I have a morsel for thi toth,   *tidbit to your taste*
           And ellis I were to blame."

395   He went and fett conyngis thre,
       Alle baken well in a pasty,
           With wel gode spicerye,   *spices*
       And other baken mete alsoo,
       Bothe of hert and of roo;   *roe deer*
400   The venyson was full trye.   *choice*
       "Sir," he seid, "asay of this: *try some*
       Thei were yisturday qwyk, iwysse,   *alive*
           Certan, withouten lye;
       Hidur thei come be mone-light.   *Hither*
405   Eete therof well aplight,   *truly*
           And schewe no curtasye."   *don't stand on ceremony*

       To the scheperd seid the kyng,
       "The forsters luf this over al thyng.
           Thou art alle thaire felawe: *ally*
410   To thaire profett thou con foulis slyng,
       And thei will venyson to thee bryng:
           Therof stande thei non awe.   *They aren't at all afraid of doing so*
       Were thou as perfete in a bowe,   *with*
       Thou shulde have moo dere, I trowe,
415   Soth to say in sawe.   *speech*
       Yet I rede that thou fande   *Again; advise; attempt*
       Than any forster in this land   *Rather than*
           An arow for to drawe."

       Then seid the scheperde, "Nothing soo: *Not at all*
420   I con a game worth thei twoo   *twice as much*
           To wynne me a brede: *piece of roast meat*
       Ther is no hert ne bucke so wode   *wild*

That I ne get without blode,
    And I of hym have nede.   *If*
425 I have a slyng for the nones   *purpose*
That is made for gret stonys;
    Therwith I con me fede.
What dere I take undur the side,   *hit*
Be thou siker he shall abide
430   Til I hym home will lede.   *carry*

"Conyngus with my nother slyng   *i.e., mine other*
I con slee and hame bryng,
    Sumtyme twoo or thre;
I ete thaim not myself alon:
435 I send presandes mony on,
    And fryndes make I me,   *I make myself friends*
Til gentilmen and yemanry.   *With landowners great and small*
Thei have thaim all; thei ar worthy —
    Those that ar privee.   *discreet*
440 Whatso thai have, it may be myne,
Corne and brede, ale and wyne,   *Grain*
    And alle that may like me.   *please me*

Do now gladly, Joly Robyne:
Yet shall thou drynk a draught fyne
445   Of gode drynk, as I wene;
Of Lanycoll thou shall prove: *From; try*
That is a cuppe to my behove;   *that suits me*
    Of maser it is ful clene.   *maple; pure*
Hit holdis a gode thrydendele   *third of a gallon*
450 Ful of wyne every mele;
    Before me it is sene.
Fil the cuppe," he seid anon,
"And play we passilodion,
    Sith no moo that we bene."   *Since there are no more of us*

455 When the drynk was filled,
The wife askid, "Who shuld begynne,
    The godeman, sir, or ye?"
"Take my geyst," seid Adam than,   *Choose*
"Sith he his gamme con;   *Since*
460   I wil that it so be."
The kyng toke the cuppe anon
And seid, "Passilodion!"
    Hym thoght it was gode gle.   *fun*
The sheperde seid "Certanly,
465 Berafrynd shalbe redy,
    Also mot I the."

He drank and made the cuppe ful clene,
And sith he spake wordis kene,   *then; sharp*
    That gamme was to here:
470 "This cuppe hit hat Lonycoll;   *is called*
I luf it wel, for it is holl;   *hollow*
    It is me lefe and dere;   *beloved*
Fil it efte to Joly Robyn;
Iwisse, he drank no bettur wyne
475   Of alle this seven yere!   *For*
To alle that wil my gamme play,
Fill it be the ee, I thee pray,   *copiously*
    My bourdis that wil lere."   *whoever wants to learn*

Then dranke oure kyng and toke his leve;
480 The sheperd seid, "Sir, not thee greve,   *don't be offended*
    And it thi wille be: *If*
I shalle the schew, Joly Robyn,
A litull chaumbur that is myne,
    That was made for me."
485 The kyng therof was ful glad,
And did as the scheperde bad:
    Moo bourdis wold he se.
He lad hym into a privé place
Ther venyson plenté in was,
490   And the wyne so claré.   *like clary*

Undur the erth it was dight,   *constructed*
Feire it was, and clene of syght,   *appearance*
    And clergially was hit wroght.   *skillfully; made*
The kyng seid, "Here is feyre ese:
495 A man myght be here wel at ese,
    With gamme yif he were saught."   *satisfied*
The kyng seid, "Gramercy, and have goday!"
The scheperde onswerid and said, "Nay,
    Yet ne gose thou nought;   *You don't go yet*
500 Thou shalle preve furst of a costrell tre   *taste; from a wooden keg*
That gode frendis send to me,   *sent*
    The best that myght be bought.

"Telle me now, whilke is the best wyne
Of Lonycoll, cuppe myne,
505   Als thou art gode and hynde?   *As; nice*
Play onys 'passilodion,'
And I shall onswer sone anon,
    Certes, 'Berafrynde.'   *Certainly*
This chambur hat Hakderne, my page;
510 He kepis my thyng and takis no wage,

In worde wher that I wende.   *Wherever in the world*
Ther is no man this place con wrye   *reveal*
But thiself, yif thou wilt sey,
 And than art thou unkynde.   *then you would be*

515 "Ther is no man of this contré
So mycull knowes of my priveté   *much; private business*
 As thou dose, Joly Robyn;
Whil that I liff, welcum to me;
Wyne and ale I dar hete thee,   *promise*
520 And gode flesshe for to dyne."
The kyng his stede he can stride,   *straddle*
And toke his leve for to ride;
 Hym thoght it was hye tyme.
The scheperde seid, "I will with thee goo:
525 I dar thee hete a foule or twoo,   *promise*
 Parauntur with a conyne."   *Perhaps*

The kyng rode softely on his way.
Adam folowyd, and wayted his pray: *lay in wait for*
 Conyngus saw he thre.
530 "Joly Robyn, chese thou which thou wylt;   *choose*
Hym that rennys er hym that sitt,   *or*
 And I shall gif hym thee."   *[to] you*
"He that sittis and wil not lepe:
Hit is the best of alle the hepe,   *group*
535 Forsoth so thynkith me."
The scheperde hit hym with a stone
And breke in two his brest-bon;
 Thus sone ded was he.

The kyng seid, "Thou art to alow: *praise*
540 Take hym als that rennyth now,   *also*
 And than con thou thy crafte."
"Be God," quod Adam, "here is a ston
That shalle be his bane anon."   *death*
 Thus sone his life was rafte.   *taken*
545 What fowle that sittis or flye,
Whether it were ferre or nye,   *far or near*
 Sone with hym it lafte.   *remained*
"Sir," he seid, "forsoth I trowe
This is bettur then any bowe,
550 For alle the fedurt schafte."   *feathered*

"Joly Robyn, brok wel my pray   *enjoy*
That I have wone here to day.
 I vouchesafe wele more.   *grant*

I pray thee telle it to no man

555 In what maner that I hit wan;   *won*
    I myght have blame therfore.

And gif thou do my errand of right,   *rightly*

Thou shalle have that I thee hyght,

    I swere be Goddis ore."   *mercy*

560 The kyng seid, "Take me thy tayle,   *Give; tally stick*

For my hors, I wolde not thee fayle,

    A peny that thou lore."   *lost*

The kyng to court went anon,

And Adam to his schepe con gon;

565   His dogge lay ther full stille.

Home er nyght come he noght;   *before*

New mete with hym he broght:

    For defaute wolde he not spill.   *lack; die*

"Wife," he seid, "be not sory:

570 I wil to courte certanly;   *will [go]*

    I shalle have alle my will.

Joly Robyn, that dynet with me,   *dined*

Hase behette me my moné,   *promised*

    As he can lawe and skill."   *knows the law and what is right*

575 "He is a marchande of gret powere:

Many man is his tresirere;   *treasurer*

    Men awe hym mony a pounde.

The best frend he had sith he was borne

Was the tother Edwart here beforne,   *other*

580   Whil he was holl and sounde.   *whole*

He hase a son is with the qwene;   *[who] is*

He may do more then other fyftene,

    He swerys be Seynt Edmonde.

Though he shuld gif of his catell,   *some of his goods*

585 I shalle have myne, everydell,   *every part*

    Of penys holl and rownde."   *pennies*

On morow when he shuld to court goo,

In russet clothyng he tyret hym tho,   *dressed himself then*

    In kyrtil and in curtebye,   *tunic; short coat*

590 And a blak furred hode

That wel fast to his cheke stode,   *firmly*

    The typet myght not wrye.   *[That] the scarf could not conceal*

The mytans clutt forgate he noght;   *rag mittens*

The slyng cumys not out of his thoght,   *comes*

595   Wherwith he wrought maystrie.   *performed great feats*

Toward the court he can goo;

His doghtur lemman met he thoo,   *daughter's lover*
    And alle his cumpanye.

He thoght more then he seyde.
600 Towarde the court he gaf a brayde,   *made a sudden movement*
    And yede a well gode pas.   *went quickly*
And when he to the yatis come,   *gates*
He askid the porter and his man
    Wher Joly Robyn was.
605 He was warned what he shuld seyn.[1]
Of his comyng he was fayne,   *glad*
    I swere be Goddis grace.
"Sir, I shall tel thee wher he is."
And than began thaire gammen, iwis,   *fun*
610   When he come forth in place.   *right there*

The kyng seid to erles tweyne,   *two*
"Ye shall have gode bourd, in certayne,
    Yif that ye will be stille,   *quiet*
Of a scheperde that I see
615 That is hidur come to me
    For to speke his wille.
I pray yow alle, and warne betyme,   *ahead of time*
That ye me calle Joly Robyne,
    And ye shalle lawgh your fille.
620 He wenys a marchand that I be.   *believes*
Men owe hym silver her for fe;   *here; livestock*
    I shalle hym helpe thertille.   *to [get] it*

"But a wager I dar lay
(And ye will as I yow say),   *If you will do*
625   A tune of wyne, iwysse: *barrel*
Ther is no lorde that is so gode,
Though he avayle to hym his hode,   *lower*
    That he wil do off his.   *doff*
Sir Raufe of Stafford, I pray thee,
630 Goo wete what his will be,   *find out*
    And telle me how hit is."
"Gladly, lord, so mot I the.
Whilke bourdis I wolde ful fayn se,   *Which*
    Of thyngus that fallis amysse."

635 And whan he to the herde came,
He seid, "Al hayle, godeman.

---

[1] *He [the porter] was warned what he [Adam] would say*

Whidur wiltow goo?"
He onsweryd as he thought gode
(But he did not off his hode
640   To hym never the moo),
"Joly Robyn, that I yondur see,
Bid hym speke a worde with me,
     For he is not my foo."   *foe*
Then onswerid that erle balde,   *bold*
645 "Take the porter thi staffe to halde,   *Give; hold*
     And thi mytens also."

"Nay, felow," he seid, "so mot I the,
My staffe ne shal not goo fro me.
     I will hit kepe in my hande.
650 Ne my mytans getis no man
Whil that I thaim kepe can,
     Be Goddis Sone Alweldande.   *Almighty*
Joly Robyn, that I yondur see,
Goo bidde hym speke a worde with me,
655   I pray thee, for Goddis sande.   *grace*
I wolde wete how hit is:
I am aferd my schepe go mysse   *amiss*
     On other mennys lande."

And when he to the kyng came,
660 Then seid the kyng, "Welcum, Adam,
     As to my powere!"   *To the best of my ability*
"Joly Robyn," he seid, "wel mot thou be!
Be God, so shuld thou to me   *as you would [be welcome] to me*
     On other stede than here.   *place*
665 I am commyn, thou wat wherfore;   *come; know why*
Thi travayle shal not be forlore: *effort; wasted*
     Thou knowis wel my manere."   *polite behavior*
"For God," seid the kyng tho,
"Thou shalbe sirvyd er thou goo;
670   Forthy make glad chere."   *So cheer up*

"Joly Robyn," he seid, "I pray thee
Speke with me a worde in priveté."
     "For God," quod the kyng, "gladly!"
He freyned the kyng in his ere   *asked*
675 "What lordis that thei were
     That stondis here thee bye?"
"The erle of Lancastur is the ton,   *the first*
And the erle of Waryn, Sir John,
     Bolde and as hardy;
680 Thei mow do mycull with the kyng: *They have much influence*

I have tolde hem of thi thyng."   *about your matter*
    Then seid he, "Gremercy!"   *Thank you*

The scheperde seid, "Sirs, God blesse yew!
I know yow not, be swete Jhesu!"
685   And swere a wel gret oth.
"Felaw," they seid, "I leve thee well: *believe*
Thou hase sene Robyn or this sell;   *before; occasion*
    Ye ne ar nothyng wrothe."   *not at odds*
"No, siris," he seid, "so mot I the,
690 We ar neghtburs, I and he;   *neighbors*
    We were never loth."   *hostile*
As gret lordis as thei ware,   *were*
He toke off his hode never the mare,
    But seid, "God save yow both."

695 The lordis seid to hym anon,
"Joly Robyn, let hym noght gon
    Till that he have etyn.
Hym semys a felow for to be.   *quite a guy*
Moo bourdis yet mow we se   *may*
700   Er his errand be gettyn."   *achieved*
The kyng to the scheperde con say,
"Fro me ne gost thou not away
    Tille we togedur have spokyn.   *together*
An errande I hyght thee for to done.
705 I wolde that thou were sirvyd sone,
    That hit be not forgetyn.

"Goo we togedur to the marshall,
And I myself shall tel the tale,
    The bett may thou spede."   *better; succeed*
710 "Robyn," he seid, "thou art trwe;
Iwis, it shalle thee never rew: *you will never regret it*
    Thou shalt have thy mede."   *reward*
To the hall he went, a ful gode pase,   *at a brisk pace*
To seke wher the stuarde was;
715   The scheperde with hym yede.   *went*
Long hym thought til mydday
That he ne were sirvyd of his pay;   *treated to his satisfaction*
    He wolde have done his dede.   *wanted to*

When he into the hall came,
720 Ther fande he no maner of man;   *found*
    The kyng hym bade, "Abyde.
I wil go aboute thi nede,
For to loke gif I may spede,   *see if I can succeed*

	For thing that may betide."	*No matter what may happen*
725	"Robyn, dwel not long fro me.	
	I know no man here but thee;	
	This court is noght but pride,	
	I ne can of no sich fare:	*know nothing of such carrying on*
	These hye halles, thei ar so bare!	
730	Why ar thei made so wyde?"	

	Then lowgh the kyng, and began to go,	*laughed*
	And with his marsshale met he tho.	
	He commaundit hym ayeyne.	*told him to go back*
	"Felaw," he seid, "herkyn a light,	*little*
735	And on myne errand go thou tyte,	*quickly*
	Also mot thou thynne:	
	A scheperde abides me in hall:	
	Of hym shall we lagh alle,	
	At the meyte when that we bene.	*food*
740	He is cum to aske four pounde;	
	Goo and fech it in a stounde,	*moment*
	The sothe that I may sene.	

	"Twey schelyng ther is more:	
	Forgete hem not, be Goddis ore,	*grace*
745	That he ne have alle his pay.	*deserts*
	I wolde not for my best stede	*horse*
	But he were sirvyd er he yede,	*Unless*
	Er then hye myddday.	*Before high*
	He wenys a marchande that I be;	
750	Joly Robyn he callis me,	
	For sirtan sothe to say.	
	Now sone to mete when I shall goo,	
	Loke he be noght fer me fro."	
	"Lorde," he seid then, "nay."	

755	Forthe the marshale can gon,	
	And brought the stuard sone anon,	
	And did adowne his hode.	*[the steward] put down*
	"Herstow, felow, hast thou do	*Do you hear*
	The thyng that I seid thee to,	
760	For the gode rode?"	*cross*
	"Sir," he seid, "it is redy;	
	I know hym not, be Oure Lady,	
	Before me thogh he stode."	
	"Goo, take yond man and pay betyme,	*choose that; promptly*
765	And bidde hym thonke Joly Robyn;	
	We shall sone have gamme gode."	

Forthe thei went all thre,
To pay the scheperde his moné
    Ther he stode in the halle.   *Where*
770 The stiward at hym frayned tho,
"What askis thou, felow, er thou goo?
    Telle me, among us alle."
"Sir," he seid, "so mot I the,
Foure pounde ye owe to me,
775   So fayre mot me befalle!
Twey schillyngis is ther odde: *Two; in addition*
I have wytnesse therof, be God,
    Within this castell wall.

"Hit is skorid here on a tayle;   *tally stick*
780 Have; brok hit wel withowt fayle: *enjoy*
    I have kepte hit lang enogh!"
The stiwarde: "Therof I ne rech: *care*
Iwisse, I have therto no mech!"   *match*
    At hym ful fast thei loogh;
785 "Ne were Joly Robyn, that I here se,   *If it were not for*
To-day ye gate no moné of me,   *would get*
    Made thou it never so towgh;   *No matter how difficult you made it*
But for his luf, go tel it here."   *count*
Then made the scheperde right glad chere,
790   When he the silver drowgh.   *obtained*

He did it up, the sothe to say,   *packed it up*
But sum therof he toke away
    In his hand ful rathe.   *promptly*
"Joly Robyn," he seid, "herkyn to me
795 A worde or tweyn in priveté
    Togedur betwene us bath.   *both*
I hight the yisturday seven shyllyng.
Have: brok it wel to thi clothyng.   *make use of it for*
    Hit wil do thee no skathe.   *harm*
800 And for thou hast holpyn me now,   *helped*
Evermore felowes I and thow,   *allies*
    And mycull thanke, sir, now have ye."

"Graunt mercy, sir," seid than he,   *Thank you*
"But silver shalt thou non gif me,
805   I swere be Seynt Martyne!"
"Be God," seid the scheperde, "yys!"
"Nay," seid oure kyng, "iwys,
    Noght for a tune of wyne.
For thi luf I wolde do more
810 Then speke a worde or twa the fore   *on your behalf*

Thou may preve sumtyme.   *demonstrate*
Yif thou be fastyng, cum with me
And take a morsell in priveté;
    Togedur then shalle we dyne."

815   "Nay, sir," he seid, "so God me spede!
To the kyngis meyte have I no nede.
    I wil therof no dele.   *part*
Ther is non of his proud meny   *retinue*
That hase alway so gode plenté   *such a large amount*
820   I have every sele."   *[As]; time*
The kyng bare wittnesse, and seid, "Ya!
But thou mygt onys, er thou ga,
    Etyn with me a mele.
The grettist lordis of this lande
825   Have bidde thee tary, I undurstonde,
    And therfore bere thee well."   *behave*

"For thi luff, Robyn, I wil gladly.
Today then mett I myne enmye,
    Forsothe as I thee tell:
830   He that be my doghtur lay.
I tolde thee of hym yisturday.
    I wolde he were in hell.
At my howse is alle the rowte.   *gang*
They wil do harme whil I am owte.
835   Full yvel then dar I dwell.   *Hardly*
Wold thou speke for me to the kyng,
He wolde avow me my slyngyng;   *approve*
    Thaire pride then shulde I fell."   *bring down*

Kyng Edwart onswerid agayne,
840   "I wil go to these erles twane
    That stode lang ore be me.   *long before*
Thai ar aperte of my knowyng.   *known to be of my acquaintance*
Thei shall speke for thee to the kyng,
    That wrokyn shal thou be.   *revenged*
845 In this courte thai ar twenty
At my biddyng to bidde redy   *ready to command*
    To do a gode jornay;   *day's fight*
When thou comys home, make no bost: *threats*
Thei shalbe takyn er thou it wost,   *before you know it*
850   Though thai were sech thre."   *three times as many*

Thus the kyng held hym with tale,   *kept him talking*
That alle that ever was in the sale   *hall*
    Of hym hade gret ferly.   *wonder*

Togedur thei yede up and down
855 As men that seid thare orison, *prayer*
But no man wist why.
The scheperde keppid his staf ful warme,
And happid it ever undur his harme *tucked; arm*
As he romyd hym by. *roamed*
860 He wold no man toke it hym fro
Til that he shulde to meyte goo,
Sich was his curtasy.

The kyng commaundit al his *his [people]*
That no man speke to hym amysse,
865 As thei wolde be his frynde. *friend*
When tablys were layd and clothis sprad,
The scheperde into the hall was lad
To begynne a bordis ende. *Sit at the head of a table*
His mytans hang be his spayre,
870 And alway hodit like a frere *[he was] still hooded; friar*
To meyte when he shulde wende.
And when the waytis blew lowde hym be, *musicians*
The scheperde thoght, "What may this be?"
He wende he hade herd a fende.

875 And alle that hym aboute stode
Wende that man hade bene wode, *crazy*
And lowgh hym to hethyng *laughed him to scorn*
For he so nycely yede in halle, *foolishly*
And bare a staffe among thaim alle,
880 And wolde take it nothyng. *give it up not at all*
The stwarde seid to Joly Robyn,
"Goo wesshe, sir, for it is tyme, *wash*
At the furst begynyng;
And for that odur Edwart love, *other*
885 Thou shalt sitte here above,
Instidde alle of the kyng." *Instead*

When he had wasshen and fayre isett, *nicely sat down*
The qwene anon to hym was fett, *fetched*
For sche was best worthy.
890 At every ende of the deyse *high table*
Sate an erle, withowt lese, *truly*
And a fayre lady.
The kyng commandit the stuard tho
To the scheperde for to goo
895 And pray hym specially
A tabul dormant that he begynne;

    "Then shal we lawgh, that be herein,
        Of his rybaudy."   *uncouth behavior*

    "Adam," he seid, "sit here down,
900   For Joly Robyn of this towne,
        He gifis thee gode worde.   *speaks well of you*
    And for thou art of his knoyng,   *acquaintance*
    We vouchsafe, olde and yong,
        That thou begynne the borde."
905   "Perdy," seid the scheperde, "nowe   *Gosh*
    Hit shal be thought, if that I mow,   *as far as I'm concerned*
        Hit is wel kept in horde.   *secret*
    But if I do Robyn a gode journé,   *Unless; day's work*
    Ellis mot I hangyt be
910   With a hempyn corde."

    And when the hall was rayed out,   *arranged completely*
    The scheperde lokid al aboute,
        How that hit myght bene.
    Surketis overal he con holde;   *Surcoats everywhere he beheld*
915   Of knyghtis and of persons bolde,
        Sich hade he non sene.
    The prince was feched to the borde
    To speke with the kyng a worde,
        And also with the qwene.
920   Then he frayned hym in his ere   *he [the king] asked*
    If he wolde "passilodion" lere,
        And "berafrende" bedene.   *together with it*

    "Lorde," he seid, "what may that be?
    I know it not, be Goddis tre.   *i.e., by the cross*
925   It is a new language."
    "I leve thee well," seid the kyng,   *believe*
    "Thou may not know al thyng:
        Thou therto ne has non age.   *You aren't old enough*
    Ther is a mon in this town
930   That will it preve gode reson   *sense*
        To kyng, squyer, and page.
    And gif thou wille gif any mede,   *if; recompense*
    I shal do thee to hym lede,
        Unto his scole a stage.   *school; grade*

935   "Hit is a scheperde that I of mene;   *speak*
    At his howse then have I bene
        Within this seven-nyght.
    A dosan knyghtis, and thai had cum with me,   *if*
    Thei shulde have had mete plenté

940	Of that I fonde redy dyght."	*prepared*
	Then he tolde hym alle the case,	
	Of passilodion, what it was,	
	And berafrynde, I plight.	*I assure you*
	"He sittis yonde, in a furred hode;	
945	Goo, bere hym here a golde ryng gode,	
	And that anon right,	*right away*

	"And thank hym mycul for Joly Robyn.	*much*
	He wenys that it be name myne,	
	Forsoth as I thee say.	
950	He wot I have a son here,	
	That is the quene lefe and dere:	*[to] the queen*
	I tolde hym so yisturday.	
	As ofte as thou wilt to hym gan,	
	Name passilodian,	
955	And wete what he will say."	*find out*
	"Lorde," he said, "I wil gladly:	
	I can hit wel and perfitely;	*know*
	Now have I lornyd a play."	*game*

	When he to the scheperde came,	
960	He seid, "Do gladly, gode Adam,	*Enjoy your food*
	And mycull gode hit thee doo.	*may it do*
	Micul thanke for Joly Robyn,	
	That thou did my lorde to dyne;	*had*
	And other ther is also:	*there's another thing*
965	Whi playes thou not passilodion	
	As thou did yisturday at home?	
	I wil onswer therto.	
	I know thi gamme to the ende,	
	For to say 'berafrynde,'	
970	As have I rest and roo."	*peace*

	Then loogh the herd, and liked ille,	*was uncomfortable*
	And seid, "Lefe childe, be stille,	
	For Goddis swete tre!	
	Go sei thi fadur he is to blame	
975	That he for gode dose me schame.	*in exchange for good does*
	Why has he wryed me?	*betrayed*
	Have I maugré for my god dede,	*If I have blame*
	Shall I never more marchand fede,	
	Ne telle my pryveté."	
980	He stroked up his hud for tene,	*pulled; hood; anger*
	And toke a cuppe and mad it clene.	*cleaned it out*
	A gret draught then drank he.	

The prynce seid, "That was wel done.
Hit shalbe filled ayeyn ful sone,
985   Alle of the best wyne.
Play passilodion, and ha no drede,   *have*
And have a gold ryng to thi mede,
        And were it for luf myne."   *wear*
"I wil it not, forsothe to sey: *want; truly*
990   Hit shulde not laste me halfe a day,
        Be Goddis swete pyne.   *suffering*
When it were brokyn, fare well he!   *may it fare well*
An hatte were bettur then sech thre   *A hat would be*
        For reyne and sonneschyne."   *rain; sunshine*

995   When the prince hade hym beholde,
He yede and sate hym where he wolde,   *wanted*
        As skille and reson is.   *right and reasonable*
And alle the lordyngis in the halle
On the herd thei lowgen alle   *laughed*
1000   When any cuppe yede amys.
When thei hade etyne and clothis draw,   *cleared the tablecloths*
And wasshen, as hit is landis lawe,   *the country's custom*
        Certan sothe iwysse,
Than dranke thai aftur sone anon,
1005 And played passilodion
        Tille ilke man hade his.   *each; his [drink]*

The lordis anon to chawmbur went.
The kyng aftur the scheperd sent;
        He was broght forth full sone.
1010 He clawed his hed, his hare he rent,
He wende wel to have be schent: *expected; ruined*
        He ne wyst what was to done.
When he French and Latyn herde,
He hade mervell how it ferde,   *how it was going*
1015   And drow hym ever alone.   *kept to himself*
"Jhesu," he seid, "for thi gret grace,
Bryng me fayre out of this place.
        Lady, now here my bone.   *prayer*

"What eyled me? Why was I wode,   *crazy*
1020 That I cowth so litell gode   *so little knew what was good for me*
        Myselven for to wrye?   *betray*
A, Lord God, that I was unslye!   *careless*
Alasse, that ever he come so nye,
        The sothe that I shulde seye!
1025 Wolde God, for His modurs luf,
Bryng me onys at myn abofe   *out on top*

I were out of theire eye,	*[So that]*
Shuld I never, for no faire spech,	
Marchande of my cowncell teche,	
1030 Soo aferde I am to dye."	
The kyng saw he was sory;	*distressed*
He had thereof gret myrth forthi,	
And seid, "Come nere, Adam;	*nearer*
Take the spices and drynk the wyne	
1035 As homely as I did of thyne,	*unpretentiously*
So God thee gif thedame."	*prosperity*
Fulle carfully in he yede;	*anxiously*
"Have I this for my gode dede?	
Me rewes that I here came."	*I'm sorry*
1040 He toke the wyne and laft the spice;	
Then wist thei wel that he was nyce.	*ignorant*
Wel carfull was that man.	
He ete the spyce, the wyne he drank,	*i.e., the king*
Oure kyng on the scheperde wanke	*winked*
1045 Prively with his eye.	
"Joly Robyn," he thoght, "wo thou be	
That tyme that I ever met with thee,	
Er ever that I thee seye.	*Or*
Be God," he thought, "had I thee nowe	
1050 Ther were yisturday I and thow,	
Paynes then shulde thou drye.	*endure*
I shulde chastis thee so with my slyng,	*chastise*
Thou shulde no moo tythyngis bryng,	
On horse though thou were hye."	
1055 The kyng commaundit a squyer tere,	*refined*
"Goo telle the scheperde in his ere	
That I am the kyng,	
And thou shall se sich cowntenence	
That hym had lever be in Fraunce,	*he had rather*
1060 When he heris of that tythyng.	
He has me schewid his priveté:	
He wil wene ded to be,	*expect*
And make therfore mournyng.	
Hit shalle hym meve al to gode:	*It will lead to nothing but good for him*
1065 I wolde not ellis, be the rode,	*I wouldn't want it any other way*
Nought for my best gold ryng."	
The squyer pryvely toke his leve	
And plucked the scheperde be the sleve	
For to speke hym with.	

1070 "Man," he said, "thou art wode!
     Why dose thou not down thi hode?
         Thou art all out of kith.   *You don't know how to behave*
     Hit is the kyng that spekis to thee,
     May do thee what his willis be,   *[Who] can*
1075   Berefe thee lym and lith;   *Deprive you of limb and limb*
     And gif thou have do any trespas,
     Fall on knees and aske grace,
         And he will gif thee grith."   *protection*

     Then was that herd a carful man,
1080 And never so sory as he was than,
         When he herd that sawe.   *speech*
     He wist not what hym was gode,
     But then he putte doun his hode;
         On knees he fel down lawe.   *low*
1085 "Lorde," he seid, "I crye thee mercy!
     I knew thee not, be Oure Lady,
         When I come into this sale.   *hall*
     For had I wist of this sorowe   *distress*
     When that we met yistur-morowe,
1090   I had not ben in this bale."   *trouble*

         NON FINIS SED PUNCTUS.   *(see note)*

ABBREVIATIONS: **MED**: *Middle English Dictionary*; **ODNB**: *Oxford Dictionary of National Biography*; **OED**: *Oxford English Dictionary*; **NCE**: *The New Catholic Encyclopedia*; **Whiting**: Whiting, *Proverbs, Sentences, and Proverbial Phrases*.

4 *lovys of melody*. This is an unusual use of the preposition *of* with an intransitive sense of *love*.

4–9 The syntax is very loose but can be understood this way: "May God grant a share of heaven's bliss (and shield their souls from peril) to all who love a song, who are worth telling tales of kings that are not vile at feasts and banquet."

19 *Con* (occasionally *can*) is sometimes used as a past tense marker in this poem: *con he mete* means "he met." But very often too the poet uses the word *con* meaning "know" or "learn."

35–36 *Thay take my bestis and don thaim slone, / And payen but a stik of tre.* "Thay," the king's servants, seize the shepherd's animals and have them butchered, giving in exchange a tally stick that the shepherd should theoretically be able to redeem for payment. The tally-stick system was to record the amount of debt: a stick would be scored with notches for each unit of debt, and then the stick split in half lengthwise. One half would be kept by the person selling goods, and the other half should have been given to the king's steward or other financial officer. The person owed money should have been able to turn up at court with his half of the stick, and when its notches matched or tallied with the notches on the half held by the steward, the steward should have paid the money owed. But the shepherd has apparently not been able to convert the tally stick into the money he is owed.

67 *Owe he.* "In the Northern dialect, in the present indicative (except for the second singular), the verb had no ending when it was immediately preceded or followed by a personal pronoun" (Mossé, *Handbook of Middle English*, §93 II).

73 *Seynt Edmonde*. St. Edmund was a king of East Anglia; he died in 870, martyred by invading Danes. His remains were eventually placed in the custody of monks in a location that is now known as Bury St. Edmunds. See "Edmund the Martyr, St.," *NCE*. Adam is swearing by a widely revered English king who died fighting against invaders of his kingdom. Ironically, as history turns out, the historical Edward III was just about to contribute to the de facto demotion of St. Edmund from national saint, when he chose St. George as patron saint of the Order of the Garter. But the cult of St. Edmund continued to flourish: he was, with John

the Baptist and Edward the Confessor, one of the patron saints of Richard II, as can be seen in the Wilton Diptych (though the angels carry a banner of St. George).

77   *Of hasill I mene that hit is.* Why does the shepherd complain that the stick is made of hazel? Perhaps because hazel sticks were rods of choice for beating people, and the shepherd feels that he is being abused; or perhaps because the hazel's flexibility makes it a comparatively flimsy and impermanent record-keeping device, an excuse of at least metaphorical force for the king's officers who fail to find confirmation of the king's debt to the shepherd.

85–87   The king asks the shepherd his name and where he lives so that he can follow through on his promise and therefore not be blameworthy.

102   *Whene she thar shuld be* is ambiguous: "when she was to be there," or "she was to be queen there." The whole passage is a series of cues that the speaker is Edward III: his father was Welsh (i.e., Edward II, the first English Prince of Wales); his mother is Isabel, who lived in the castle; as he told us before, he was born in Windsor; he was loved by Edward II; he travels overseas a good deal; and he has a son who is with the queen.

118   *undur.* Undern is one of the hours of the solar day, and therefore its clock time varies according to the time of year. More confusingly still, the term *undern* was applied in the Middle Ages to the third canonical hour (roughly, nine in the morning), the sixth canonical hour (noon), and even later. Here it must mean roughly nine in the morning.

121   *Seynt Thomas of Ynde.* The apostle Thomas was said to have traveled to India and proselytized there, where he was eventually martyred.

124   Why the name "Joly Robyn"? We do not have Robin Hood poems that survive from this early, but the epithet *Jolly* is used with *Robin* in later Robin Hood poems that we do have (*Robin Hood and the Tanner, The Jolly Pinder of Wakefield, Robin Hood and the Shepherd,* and *Robin Hood's Chase*), and it is possible that this is an early (and heavily ironic) adoption of the outlaw's name by a king who had a great deal of trouble with outlaws. The phrase *Joly Robyn* is used late in the fourteenth century by Pandarus in an expression of skepticism in Chaucer's *Troilus and Criseyde*, 5.1174–75:

> From haselwode, there joly Robyn pleyde,
> Shal come al that thow abidest here.

But both Chaucer and the *King Edward and the Shepherd* poet could be merely using the name *Robin* as one sometimes used in poetry for a peasant.

129   *Soo faire hym mot befalle.* Like the phrase *so mot he the*, a type more frequent in this poem, this simply strengthens the wish: "as he hopes for good things to happen to him."

141   *be Seynt Jame.* The more usual St. James to swear by is the apostle James, son of Zebedee. In the Middle Ages, Santiago de Compostela in Spain was a major pilgrimage site (as it still is, to a lesser degree); the remains of St. James were

said to have been returned there, to the scene of his proselytizing, after his martyrdom in Judea (see "James [Son of Zebedee], St.," *NCE*). The form "Jame" as opposed to "James" is common in medieval English, not a simple concession to rhyme: note line 146.

157–60   These lines are an allusion to the earlier wave of outlawry in the 1320s and 1330s (led by the Folville and Coterel gangs; see the introduction to *King Edward and the Shepherd*) and an acknowledgment of renewed activity. Edward's absence at Calais sparked a major rise in bandit activity in 1346 (Stones, "Folvilles of Ashby-Folville," p. 130), not long before a possible composition and performance date for the poem. At that time the only remaining Folville brother was Eustace (who, like the bandits in the poem, was a known robber and rapist), the others having died, for the most part, unapprehended despite the poem's allusion to previous capture and hanging at lines 157–58, and the historical attempt to pursue and prosecute the outlaws in 1332. It is notable that not only did Edward's absence enable Eustace but that Eustace had actually received a pardon in 1333 for service in Edward's Scottish campaign. In fact, the king pardoned Folvilles in 1327, 1329, and 1333, even though each pardon was preceded and followed by violent criminal behavior.

166   The plural "thei" and the violent home invasion of the context strongly suggest that this is a gang rape. Yet at line 597 the narrator mentions the daughter's "lemman," as if she merely had a lover among the robbers, and at 830 Adam speaks of "He that be my doghtur lay" as if, whether by rape or consent, only one man was involved. These three different possible scenarios trigger an extremely wide range of reactions among modern readers, from an appalled sympathy for the daughter to some resentment at her for enjoying herself with her lover while her parents are abused and humiliated. For us it is impossible to reconcile the passages or overlook their discrepancy from one another. But it is quite possible that these scenarios did not seem so grotesquely irreconcilable to the poet and his original audience, for whom the emotional point may have been sympathy with Adam, the man whose honor has been grossly violated by his daughter's involvement in illicit sexual acts, whether voluntary on her part or not.

193–204   This stanza is garbled and hard to reconstruct. French and Hale's footnote proposes an original rhyme on *benke/shenke* at lines 196–97: "An archery bank was a butt, a pyramidal mound of earth on which a paper bull's-eye was fixed; and shots which hit the mound and missed the bull's-eye counted as misses. The general sense may have been, 'I propose as terms that whoever first hits the bank (misses) is to order poured out for the other whatever he will drink'" (*Middle English Metrical Romances*, 2:957n196). This is a desperate reconstruction of a desperate passage. All that seems clear is that Adam is prepared to bet, both ale and his head (and maybe also a hawk, if the word *haut* is emended for rhyme; though why would a lowly peasant have a hawk?), on his winning a contest between any archer in the land and himself with his sling, with the object of the contest being to hit a target soonest; and he swears by his own death that he will take on the bet right away even in the shade.

225   *Seynt Gyle* provides a useful rhyme, but also has an interestingly apposite legend: his constant companion was a deer, which was then attacked by the king's hunters; one of their arrows missed the deer and wounded St. Giles, but he was ultimately befriended by the king himself.

263   *come to ryng*. Literally, "join the dance"; figuratively, be hunted by Edward.

264   *Therwith to make me a frende*. That is, to have meat to give away to gain others' favors in return.

268   *Wode has erys, fylde has sight*. This is a proverb cited by Whiting, F127: "Field has eyes and wood ears."

269   *forster*. The forester's job is to enforce forest law and to make sure that the game is protected from being taken by anyone but the king or his agents.

275–76 *A loge is dight / Full hye upon an hill* which serves presumably as a lookout from which the forester and his assistants can watch for poachers.

304–07 All these birds are waders (heron, spoonbill, curlew, bittern) or waterfowl (mallard, swan). They, and the crane of line 295, are precisely the sorts of bird that nobles would hunt with falcons or hawks when they went rivering, hunting along the banks of a river. That is what Edward is understood to be doing at the beginning of this poem:

> Oure kyng went hym in a tyde
> To pley hym be a ryver side
> In a mornyng of May.

The birds (especially swan) featured as showy prize dishes at medieval nobles' meals. Edward was particularly fond of rivering; he is represented in *Wynnere and Wastoure* as wearing a belt embroidered appropriately:

> Full gayly was that grete lorde girde in the myddis:
> A brighte belte of ble broudirde with fewles,
> With drakes and with dukkes — daderande tham semede
> For ferdnes of fawkons fete, lesse fawked thay were.
> And ever I sayd to myselfe, "Full selly me thynke
> Bot if this renke to the revere ryde umbestonde."
>   (lines 95–100)

In a note to line 100, editor Warren Ginsberg remarks, "Edward was known for his love of hawking." Wild swans, one of which Adam has had baked in line 307, belonged to the king. Later in Edward's rule (20 June 1356) he granted under his privy seal to his newly founded collegiate church at Windsor seven years' control over wild swans on the Thames: "to the warden and college of the king's free chapel of Wyndesore of all swans flying not marked within the water of Thames between Oxford and London Bridge, as fully as these should pertain to the king by reason of his right and prerogative" (*Calendar of the Patent Rolls*, 30 Ed.III., pt. 2, m. 20 [vol. 10, p. 406]). Adam has obviously been violating Edward's "right and prerogative."

306   *The maudlart and hur mech*. The term *mallard*, if it distinguishes the sex of the duck concerned, usually signals a male. But here the mallard is the female.

317   *passilodion*: This is a nonce word, attested only in this poem. *MED* gives it a derivation from Medieval Latin: "ML **passilūdium**, from **passum** 'raisin wine' & **lūdium** 'game, contest'; prob. a jocular coinage modeled on **hastilūdium**."

320   *berafrynde*. *MED* gives the sense "Bottom's up!" but with the qualifier "?Nonsense word." It's possible that we should understand the word as "barley-friend." *Bere* was the Middle English term for barley, a component of beer and malt liquors of various kinds. Both times the word occurs in rhyming position with an *–ende*.

321   *Leve upon my ley*. Literally, "Believe in my religious law."

325–36 The game is a simple one: the first player says "passilodion," drinks, and then refills the cup. The second replies with "berafrynde," empties the cup, and fills it again before returning it to the first person.

333   *Seynt Mighell*. The archangel Michael.

365–67 The implication of these lines stressing Adam's white skin, good origins, and holy descent may be (somewhat snidely) that he is the son of a priest (who has comparatively high social status, but who should be celibate and may not marry) rather than of a peasant.

370   *Nether fer ne hende*. Literally, "Neither far nor close."

404   *come be mone-light*. The implication is that the illicit venison was brought secretly to Adam at night.

446   *Lanycoll*. Adam's name for his drinking cup, a huge one made out of maple. Spelled Lonycoll at line 470, the word is an invented one. Possibly it is to be understood as a compound of *loan* (from Old Norse *lān*) and *accoll* meaning "embrace": because the cup is meant to be passed back and forth among drinkers, it is on loan and has to be returned, and because it is well loved for what it holds (Adam expresses his own love for the cup at lines 471–72), it is warmly embraced rather than just held.

457   *The godeman, sir, or ye?* This is odd, because Adam is most easily thought of as the goodman in this context, in the senses of the householder, the host. But the goodwife is unlikely to be asking the visitor who should get the cup first, and indeed Adam answers. So perhaps we are to understand that *goodman* applies to the merchant and is taken here in the sense of citizen of a town, a burgess.

468   *wordis kene*. But there is not really anything sharp about his words; the rhyme is more influential here than the meaning.

490   *wyne so claré*. Clary was a sweet mixture of wine, honey, and spices.

509   *Hakderne* is another of Adam's playful coinages. *Derne* means "secret"; *hak* may be a variant form of *hatch* (from Old English *hæc*), meaning "a small door." Adam's underground storage room is well hidden.

545   *What fowle that sittis or flye.* Note that the verb forms do not match. The form *flye* must be subjunctive (whatever bird that might fly), but the verb *sittis* is indicative (whatever bird that sits).

550   *For alle the fedurt schafte.* Bows and arrows are much more advanced technology than slings and stones: the arrowhead cuts, the feathered shaft stabilizes flight, and the bow is easier to aim. The historical Edward encouraged the use of the bow and arrow. In 1363 he was to make archery practice compulsory for all able-bodied men between sixteen and sixty years of age. English archers were critical to his victories on the Continent. In this poem he already champions the virtues of the bow, urging Adam to take up archery so that he can poach deer (lines 413–19), but Adam tells him he can kill deer by using the larger of his two slings (420–30). Here Adam closes the discussion by disparaging what he must see as unnecessary technology, the feathered shaft that stabilizes the flight of the arrow. If a man is as good with a sling as Adam has just demonstrated himself to be, why would he bother to change to a bow and arrows?

565   *His dogge lay ther full stille.* Adam's sheepdog is well trained and has been keeping the sheep safely in one place all day while its master is off drinking and hunting with Joly Robyn.

576   *Many man is his tresirere.* That is, many people owe him money.

579–80 The *tother Edwart*, Edward II, was whole and sound until his capture, deposition, and murder in 1326–27.

581   The first of Edward III and Queen Philippa's eight sons, Edward of Woodstock, now called the Black Prince, was born in 1330. He was the only one of the eight to have been created a prince, becoming Prince of Wales in 1343.

590   *a blak furred hode.* Frédérique Lachaud argues "that the idea of a strict hierarchical view of society expressed by the means of dress was a fourteenth-century phenomenon, which culminated in the sumptuary laws of the reign of Edward III" ("Dress and Social Status in England," p. 119). Here Adam's fur hood challenges the king's authority by violating a sumptuary ordinance set out by Edward III in 1337, which forbids any subject with less than £100 in earnings per year to "wear any fur . . . in or on any of his clothes, under pain of incurring the above-mentioned penalty [being punished at the 'king's will']." See F. E. Baldwin, *Sumptuary Legislation and Personal Regulation*, p. 31, quoting *Statutes of the Realm*, 11 Edward III c. 2, vol. I, pp. 280–81. But his russet clothing mentioned at line 588 is quite appropriate to his peasant status. Russet is homespun.

593   *mytans clutt.* "Mytans" is "mittens" or "mittens'," "clutt" is "clout" or "rag," but the word order is problematic and the sense is uncertain.

644   *Then onswerid that erle balde.* At the time that the story seems to be set, Sir Ralph Stafford was not yet an earl (see the introduction to the poem). At line 611 above, the king addresses two earls, and later we hear of those two as the earl of Lancaster and the earl of Warren; Stafford is addressed as "Sir Ralph of Stafford" and never referred to in the poem as earl of Stafford. The term *earl* is used anachronistically, perhaps introduced later than the time of the poem's composition.

647   *felow*. As a term of address, *fellow* would be used by people of high rank to people of low rank. Adam the Shepherd is oblivious to the social gaffe he is committing in calling Sir Ralph of Stafford, steward of the Royal Household (1327), seneschal of Aquitaine (1345), eventually a founding knight of the Garter (1348) and the first earl of Stafford (1350), "felow." See Carole Rawcliffe, 'Stafford, Ralph," *ODNB*. Adam is similarly oblivious to the social rules that require him to doff his hood or hat in the presence of a superior and those that require him to give up his weapons before entering the court.

662   *"wel mot thou be!"* A warm greeting, literally "May you be well."

677–78 The earl of Lancaster is Henry of Grosmont, second cousin to the king. Heir to a very powerful earldom, he gained even more power, land, and wealth by his services in war and diplomacy to Edward III. His father Henry became blind, so the younger Henry took over many of his political obligations from about 1330, when as a young man of roughly twenty he was knighted and took his father's place in parliament. Edward raised him to the status of earl in 1337, when he received one of his father's titles, earl of Derby. Then in 1345, he succeeded his father as earl of Lancaster. In the years leading up to the composition of the poem, his great victories were in the south of France, at Auberoche (1345) and at Poitiers (1346), and his service to Edward at the successful end of the siege of Calais (1347). Around 1347–48, the time during which the poem was written, he had probably begun construction of the magnificent Savoy Palace in London, using his profits from his campaigns. Edward made him a founding member of the Order of the Garter in 1349, and in 1351 raised his title to duke of Lancaster. One of his many services to the king was to stand hostage for Edward's debts in the Low Countries in 1340–41; it is because of his commitment of his own resources to Edward as security for a loan that we know about his gold statue of Tristram and Isolde (see Vale, *Edward III*, appendix 11), a possession that suggests not only his immense wealth but also his interest in literature. Later in life he was to compose the Anglo-Norman spiritual treatise called *Le Livre des seintz medicines*. See W. M. Ormrod, "Henry of Lancaster, first duke of Lancaster (c.1310–1361)," *ODNB*.

Edward's relations with John de Warenne, earl of Surrey, were rather different. Whereas Edward and Henry were about the same age, and both eager to establish their chivalric prowess on the battlefield and in tournament, John de Warenne was an older man. Born in 1286, he died in 1347, probably then just before the poem was written. At the time of the deposition of Edward II, John had urged the former king to abdicate but could not persuade him. John's service to Edward II led him into conflict with Thomas, then earl of Lancaster, Henry of Grosmont's uncle; John was even on the panel of judges appointed by Edward II to put Thomas to death. That John de Warenne and Henry of Grosmont feature together in this poem is a tribute to the harmony at the court of Edward III. John attended the coronation of the younger Edward and served on his regency council. In subsequent years he served Edward III in a number of administrative roles and some military ones. Though he was never as prominent as Henry of Grosmont, his service was in different forums: the Scottish wars rather than the French ones, administration in England rather than on the Continent.

For example, "In 1345 Warenne was one of the councillors appointed to advise the regent, Edward's second son, Lionel" (Scott L. Waugh, "Warenne, John de, seventh earl of Surrey (1286–1347)," *ODNB*, for the quotation and other information on John de Warenne). In the financial crisis of 1340, John stood up to the enraged king in Parliament about who should be present to advise him, but he was not usually confrontational. Edward rewarded him well and clearly considered him a valuable advisor. He died in late June of 1347. Perhaps it was the recentness of his death that prompted his inclusion as one of the figures of the poem.

736   *Also mot thou thynne.* That is, "also mot thou theen," "as you hope to prosper."

755   The marshal (who seems to be a domestic officer in charge of the arrangements for the feast rather than the officer of state, the marshall of England), has been given instructions to pass along to the steward (again, the steward seems to be a domestic officer rather than a high officer of state). At 756 the steward comes back to the king with him, lowers his hood respectfully in the king's presence at 757 (in contrast to Adam), and at 761 tells the king that the money is ready.

762   *I know hym not.* That is, "I can't tell who he is because I don't know him."

       be Oure Lady. "Our Lady" is the Virgin Mary.

775   *So fayre mot me befalle.* Another phrase underlining sincerity, literally "As I hope good things will happen to me."

782–83 Here is the flaw of the tally-stick system: if the steward does not want to pay the debt the king's household has incurred, it is easy enough to deny having a match to Adam's stick.

791–802 The notion of a shepherd tipping the king and advising him to put some money into new clothing would have been an amusing one. Edward paid careful attention to courtly display, for example, taking care that his lavish behavior on the Continent helped to bolster his grand claims to the throne of France.

805   *I swere be Seynt Martyne.* St. Martin of Tours was a fourth-century Roman soldier (see "Martin of Tours, St.," *NCE*). He is famous for cutting his cloak in half to share it with a naked beggar, an event that was followed by a vision of Christ and a dedication of the rest of his life to Christianity. The king would doubtless prefer to see himself as a benefactor, like St. Martin, rather than as someone who, according to modern conceptions, is taking a kickback. At any rate he would not care to see himself as someone whose cloak was the gift of a poorly dressed churl, a St. Martin in reverse.

806   *"Be God," seid the scheperde, "yys!"* The word *yes* here implies "to the contrary" like French *si*; simple agreement was signaled by *ay* or *yea*, as below (line 821), *ya*.

865   *As thei wolde be his frynde.* That is, friendship with the king is dependent on being polite to Adam the Shepherd.

869   *His mytans hang be his spayre.* His mittens hung beside his ?: The "spayre" (*MED* speier(e, *OED* † spare, *n.*^{2}) is evidently an opening in the clothing, in this case

predictably enough present that it can be identified as "his spayre" rather than "a spayre." I am tempted to think it might be the equivalent of a modern-day fly.

872   *And when the waytis blew lowde hym be.* The waits are wind musicians who are signaling mealtime. They are not necessarily trumpeters, and indeed since Adam thinks he has heard a fiend, perhaps they are playing bagpipes.

885   *Thou shalt sitte here above.* "Here above" would be at the high table, on the dais. Joly Robin is to occupy the seat of honor.

896   *A tabul dormant that he begynne.* Adam is being honored by being asked to take the head of a table dormant, a table that is a fixed piece of furniture rather than one of the trestle tables that would be set up for the less-important diners.

905–10   Adam is impressed with the reception Joly Robin has arranged for him and resolves both to keep the terms of their relationship secret and to pay Joly Robin back (or else, let Adam be hanged).

914   *Surketis overal he con holde.* The surcoats would display the heraldic arms of their wearers and so would make a colorful and impressive display. This also underscores the nobility of Adam's company.

934   *Unto his scole a stage.* The king proposes to have the prince taken to Adam for instruction.

970   *As have I rest and roo.* A phrase underlining sincerity, literally "As I hope to have rest and peace."

1000   *When any cuppe yede amys.* Everyone laughed at Adam when any cup, presumably that he was drinking from, went amiss.

1013   French lingered as the language of high culture at the court, and thus the language of much literature, such as Henry of Grosmont's *Livre des seintz medicines*. The role of Anglo-Norman heritage was reinforced at court by repeated royal marriages to French-speaking noblewomen, such as Edward II's to Isabella of France and Edward III's to Philippa of Hainault. And Latin continued to be an important third language, among clerics particularly. But English was widely used at court too. Edward may have adopted a French motto for his Order of the Garter ("Honi soit qui mal y pense," "Shame on him who thinks evil of it"), but he had several other mottoes in use for ceremonial occasions, and they were English ones: "It is as it is," "Syker as the wodebynd" (Vale, *Edward III*, p. 65), "Hay hay the wythe swan by goddes soule I am thy man" (Vale, *Edward III*, p. 175). Adam is disturbed, though, by hearing the other two languages used.

1018   The lady is, of course, the Blessed Virgin Mary, whom late medieval Christians reverenced as a kind intercessor who would intervene on their behalf.

1040–41   *He toke the wyne and laft the spice; / Then wist thei wel that he was nyce.* Adam has his own drinking customs, but he is not used to the court custom of drinking wine and eating spices after a meal. He drinks the wine but leaves the spices, betraying his lack of courtly polish.

1046–48   *"Joly Robyn," he thoght, "wo thou be / That tyme that I ever met with thee, / Er ever that I thee seye*. The lines are somewhat garbled grammatically, but the general sense that Adam regrets meeting Joly Robin is clear. "Wo is me" would be more idiomatic than, make more sense than, and work as well with the rhyme scheme as, "wo thou be."

colophon   *Non finis sed punctus*. "Not complete, but at an end." There is plenty of room for more text left on the page in the sole manuscript, but the exemplar from which the scribe was copying must have been lacking the last folio, probably no more than one since the plot is nearing its probable end.

COPY-TEXT: Cambridge University Library MS Ff.5.48, fols. 48v–56v.
ABBREVIATIONS: **MS**: manuscript, here referring to the copy-text.

title	There is no title in the MS.
1	MS reads: *God that sittis in Trinite*, in very large letters and underlined in red, like lines 226 and 377.
32	MS reads: *that I most fle fro my wony< >g*. Gap in MS.
66	MS reads: *A M £ pounde and mare*. £ is above the *M*.
74	MS reads: *Me is owand iiij li pounde*.
151	MS reads: *thei goo aboute be viij or nyn<.>e*.
178	MS reads: *had I helpe of sum lordyngis*. Emendation for rhyme.
181	MS reads: *ffor other iii felowes and I*.
226	MS reads: *Do way quod Adam let be that*, in very large letters and underlined in red, like lines 1 and 377.
278	MS reads: *But ride now forth in my blessyn*. The last letter is cut off.
293	MS reads: *ii peny ale he brouʒt with all*.
340–41	The stanza is defective and may have been so in the scribe's exemplar. Here the scribe has two lines that are perhaps borrowed from the next stanza, lines 350–51.
342	Two lines required by the stanza form are missing after line 342. No gap in MS.
375	MS reads: *With alkyn denteyth welbested*. Emendation for sense.
377	MS reads: *I shalle the whyte be hode myne*; in very large letters and underlined in red, like lines 1 and 226.
421	MS reads: *To wynne me a bridde*. Emendation for rhyme and sense.
436	MS reads: *And fy fryndes make I me*.
487	MS reads: *Moo bourdis wold he here se*.
512	MS reads: *This is no man this place con wrye*. Emendation for sense.
553	MS reads: *I vouchesafe wels more*. Emendation for sense, but the reading is uncertain.
589	MS reads: *In kyrtil and in surstbye*. Emendation for sense.
609	MS reads: *And than be thaire gammen iwis*. Emended for sense.
631–33	appear in the wrong order in the MS, thus:
	Whilke bourdis I wolde ful fayn se
	And telle me how hit is
	Gladly lord so mot I the.
	Emended for sense and stanza form.
683	MS reads: *the scheperde seid sir god blesse yew*. Emendation for sense.

185

740	MS reads: *He is cum to aske iiij pounde*.
789	The last two letters are cut off.
810	MS reads: *Then speke a worde or ii the fore*.
841	MS reads: *That stode lang ore be* ~~my~~ *me*.
911	MS reads: *And when the hall was rayed oght*. Emendation for rhyme and sense.
1015	MS reads: *And drow hym ever alove*. Emendation for sense and rhme.
1043	MS reads: *He ete the spyce, the wyne he dran*. End of the line cut off.
1060	MS reads: *When heris of that tythyng*. Emendation for sense.
1064	*Hit shalle hym meve al to gode*: French and Hale read: *Hit shalle hym mene al to gode*. The letters *u* and *n* are indistinguishable.
1086	MS reads: *I knaw the not be oure lady*. Emendation for sense.

JOHN THE REEVE: INTRODUCTION

MANUSCRIPT

John the Reeve appears on pp. 357–68 of the Percy Folio Manuscript (London, British Library, MS Additional 27879). That seventeenth-century manuscript, besides containing one of the later versions of *Jack and His Stepdame*, also contains *The Boy and the Mantle*, and a description of the manuscript and its history is to be found in the introduction to that poem. One scribe writes the whole of the manuscript, but it should be noted that his or her transcription of *John the Reeve* shows conservatism, preserving words and forms that are not the scribe's own: grammatical forms such as the northern imperative *brings* at line 707 and words such as archaic *outcept* (line 156), archaic or Scottish *pallett* (line 599), and archaic *ryke* (line 266). Final *e* on words like *soe* and *doe*, *mee* and *hee* is scribal, as is the occasional spelling *the* for *they*.

AFTERLIFE

John the Reeve appears, with different names as noted below, in the following early or otherwise useful editions:

1822. *John the Reeve*. David Laing, ed. *Select Remains of the Early Popular Poetry of Scotland*. Edinburgh: privately printed. I have not seen this edition.

1868. *John de Reeve*. John W. Hales and Frederick J. Furnivall, eds. *Bishop Percy's Folio Manuscript: Ballads and Romances*. London: N. Trübner. 2:550–94.

1885. *John the Reeve*. David Laing and John Small, eds. *Select Remains of the Ancient Popular and Romance Poetry of Scotland*, collected and edited by David Laing, Edinburgh; re-edited by John Small. Edinburgh: William Blackwood and Sons. Pp. 42–79.

1895. *John the Reeve*. David Laing and William Carew Hazlitt, eds. *Early Popular Poetry of Scotland and the Northern Border*, edited by David Laing, reedited by William Carew Hazlitt, 2 vols. London: Reeves and Turner. 1:250–83.

1985. *John the Reeve*. Melissa M. Furrow, ed. *Ten Fifteenth-Century Comic Poems*. New York: Garland. Pp. 177–234.

That it had an early circulation in Scotland is clear from the references to it in the early years of the sixteenth century. Gavin Douglas, in his *Palis of Honoure* (1501) sees "Johne the

reif" and "Raf Coilyear" in his magic mirror with the other great figures of world literature.[1]
William Dunbar mentions "Rauf Colyard and Johnne the Reif" in an address to the king (c.
1520).[2] And Sir David Lyndsay describes an archbishop as "dissagysit lyke Jhone the Raif"
in his *Testament of the Papyngo* (1530).[3] But despite these references, and David Laing's
inclusion of it among "early popular poetry of Scotland," a poem calling Edward I (the
Hammer of the Scots) "our king" (line 12) and referring to him with admiration is unlikely
to originate from Scotland.

REFERENCE TOOLS

John the Reeve is *NIMEV* 989.

It is addressed by Thomas Cooke in volume 9 (1993) of the *Manual*, section 24 Tales [12],
John the Reeve.

POET, POETRY, AND LANGUAGE

John the Reeve was committed to the Percy Folio Manuscript long after it was originally
composed. As discussed above in the Kings and Commoners Introduction, the poem must
have been composed between 1377 and 1461. The earliest citation in *MED* of the term
handful as a linear measurement (see *hondful*), as it is used in *John the Reeve* in lines 326 and
608, is in 1439, in a context that clearly marks it as a new concept: "'They were wonte to
mete clothe by yerde and ynche, now they woll mete by yerde and handfull' (*Rotuli
Parliamentorum* 5.30b)." Moreover, at lines 140–41 John distinguishes between ale (which
he drinks) and beer (which he does not). The two terms were synonymous in Middle English
until the introduction from the Low Countries of the use of hops in brewing (see *MED*, *ale*);
the old-fashioned drink was then called ale and the new drink with hops, beer. Beer was
imported into England in the fourteenth century, but only began to be made there, usually
by foreigners, in 1391 in London, and then gradually after 1400 in "other English towns,
but there were still very few of them outside London," according to Richard W. Unger. Not
until 1441 were beer-brewers established enough to begin to be regulated.[4] The date for the
composition of the poem therefore seems likely to be mid-fifteenth century rather than
much earlier.
    As to where it was composed, the second stanza connects the poem with Lancashire:

As I heard tell this other yere,
A clarke came out of Lancashire;
A rolle he had reading.

The story is set in and near Windsor (see lines 570 and 575), but there are many signs that
the poet's origins are farther north: the language, the choice of the bishop of Durham as a

[1] Douglas, *Palis of Honoure*, lines 1711–12.

[2] Dunbar, "To the King [Exces of thocht dois me mischeif]," line 33.

[3] Lyndsay, *Testament of the Papyngo*, from *Sir David Lyndsay: Selected Poems*, line 560.

[4] Unger, *Beer in the Middle Ages*, p. 99.

character, the swearing by St. William of York, and the perplexing assertion in the last stanza that John the Reeve lived in the "south west countrye," attributable only to an ignorance of exactly where Windsor is.

As for the language, any dialectal analysis of it is complicated by both the lapse of time between composition and manuscript, a lapse that would encourage scribal revision where forms have changed, and the poet's looseness in rhyming. In this poem there are rhymes on *nd/ng* (e.g., *wand/gange*, lines 346–47), *d/t* (e.g., *byte/syde*, lines 325–26), *th/f* (e.g., *wrothe/loffe*, lines 147, 150), and *wl/w* (e.g., *bowle/know*, lines 531, 534). There are also nonce inexact rhymes: *greeffe/office* (lines 205–06), *prime/line* (lines 559–60), *abacke/rappe* (lines 727–28). The poet sometimes rhymes on syllables that are normally unstressed (e.g., *bringe/likinge*, lines 3, 6). And there are repeated rhymes of long close *e* with long or short *i* (e.g., *hye/thee*, lines 88–89 and *mee/I*, lines 175–76).

Perhaps the most that can be said is that features of the language are compatible with a Lancashire origin. Lancashire is within the northern area where descendants of Old English long *a* still can appear with an *a* spelling in the late Middle English period (*LALME*, Q47), and in *John the Reeve* there are rhymes of descendants of Old English long *a* with long *a* from other sources: e.g., *dame/home* at lines 220–21, with *dame* from Old French, and *home* from Old English *hām*. A more restrictive rhyme is *abone/warrison* at lines 565–66. The area where the form *abone* appears for *above* is a much smaller one but does include Lancashire (*LALME* Q66). The rhyme *miss/penyles* (lines 276, 279), if we could rely on it to be an exact rhyme for the poet, would suggest an original *-lis* or *-lys* ending for *pennyless*, and *LALME* puts such endings in Derby, Lincolnshire, Northamptonshire, Lancashire, the East Riding of Yorkshire, and northern Middle English (Q277). This too works well with a Lancashire ascription but a loose rhyme would also be consonant with the poet's practice.

The poem is composed of six-line stanzas rhyming *aabccb*, usually with the *a* and *c* lines having four stresses and the *b* lines three but with variation. Occasionally the poet lengthens the stanza to *aabccbddb* (e.g., at lines 211–19). The tendency to reach for a rhyme or to use fillers like "as I trow" or "certaine" contributes to the general laxness of the poetry.

JOHN THE REEVE

God, through thy might and thy mercy,
All that loveth game and glee   *fun and games*
Their soules to heaven bringe.
Best is mirth of all solace;
5   Therfore I hope itt betokenes grace,   *indicates*
Of mirth who hath likinge.   *If a person likes mirth*

As I heard tell this other yere,
A clarke came out of Lancashire;   *clerk*
A rolle he had reading.
10   A bourde written therein he found   *funny story*
That sometime fell in England
In Edwardes dayes our king.

By east, west, north, and southe
All this realme well run hee cowthe,   *knew how*
15   Castle, tower, and towne.
Of that name were kinges three,
But Edward with the long shankes was hee,   *legs*
A lord of great renowne.

As the king rode ahunting upon a day
20   Three fawcones flew away;   *falcons*
He followed wonderous fast.
They rode upon their horsses that tyde.   *time*
They rode forth on every side;
The country they umbecast.   *went around*

25   From morning untill eveninge late
Many menn abroad they gate,   *far from home; got*
Wandring all alone.
The night came att the last;
There was no man that wist   *knew*
30   What way the king was gane,   *gone*

Save a bishopp and an erle free   *noble*
That was allwayes the king full nye.   *near*

And thus then gan they say,
"Itt is a folly, by St. John,
35   For us thus to ryde alone
Soe many a wilsome way: *wild*

"A king and an erle to ryde in hast,
A bishopp from his courte to be cast,   *driven out*
For hunting, sikerlye.   *certainly*
40   The whether happned wonderous ill: *weather*
All night wee may ryde with unskill,   *foolishly*
Nott wotting where wee bee."   *knowing*

Then the king began to say,
"Good Sir Bishopp, I you pray,
45   Some comfort, if you may."
As they stoode talking all about
They were ware of a carle stout.   *aware; sturdy peasant*
"Gooddeene, fellow," can they say.   *Good evening; they said*

Then the erle was well apayd.   *pleased*
50   "You be welcome, good fellow," hee sayd,
"Of fellowshipp wee pray thee."   *companionship*
The carle full hye on horsse sate.   *peasant*
His legges were short and broad,
His stirroppes were of tree;   *wood*

55   A payre of shooes were stiffe and store,   *sturdy; coarse*
On his heele a rustye spurre —
Thus forwardes rydeth hee.
The bishopp rode after on his palfrey: *small horse*
"Abyde, good fellow, I thee pray,
60   And take us home with thee."

The carle answered him that tyde,
"From me thou gettest noe other guide,   *no guide at all*
I sweare by sweete St. John."
Then said the erle, ware and wise,   *skilled*
65   "Thou canst litle of gentrise.   *courtesy*
Say not soe for shame."

The carle answered the erle unto,
"With gentlenesse I have nothing to doe,   *good breeding*
I tell thee by my fay."   *faith*
70   The weather was cold and even roughe;   *[the] evening*
The king and the erle sate and loughe,
The bishopp did him soe pray.

The king said, "Soe mote I thee,   *As I hope to prosper*
Hee is a carle, whosoever hee be:
75   I reade wee ryde him neere."   *advise; nearer*
They sayd with wordes hend,   *courteous*
"Ryd saftlye, gentle freind,   *slowly*
And bring us to some harbor."

Then to tarry the carle was lothe,
80   But rode forth as he was wrothe,   *as if; angry*
I tell you sickerlye.
The king sayd, "By Mary bright,
I troe wee shall ryde all this night   *believe*
In wast unskillfullye.   *wilderness foolishly*

85   "I feare wee shall come to no towne.
Ryde to the carle and pull him downe,
Hastilye without delay."
The bishopp said soone on hye,   *loudly*
"Abide, good fellow, and take us with thee,
90   For my love, I thee pray."

The erle said, "By God in heaven,
Oft men meete att unsett steven: *by chance*
To quite thee well wee may."   *pay you back*
The carle sayd, "By St. John,
95   I am affrayed of you eche one,
I tell you by my fay."

The carle sayd, "By Marye bright,
I am afrayd of you this night.
I see you rowne and reason.   *whisper; discuss*
100   I know you not and itt were day.   *even if*
I troe you think more then you say.
I am affrayd of treason.

"The night is merke: I may not see   *dark*
What kind of men that you bee.
105   But and you will doe one thinge —   *But if*
Swere to doe me not desease —   *harm*
Then wold I faine you please,   *gladly*
If I cold with anythinge."

Then sayd the erle, with wordes free,   *generous*
110   "I pray you, fellow, come hither to mee,
And to some towne us bringe.
And after, if wee may thee kenn   *see*

Amonge lordes and gentlemen,
Wee shall requite thy dealinge."   *repay; conduct*

115   "Of lordes," sayeth hee, "speake no moe:
With them I have nothing to doe,
Nor never thinke to have.
For I had rather be brought in bale   *suffering*
My hood or that I wold vayle   *before; lower*
120   On them to crouch or crave."   *cringe; beg*

The king sayd curteouslye,
"What manner of man are yee
Att home in your dwellinge?"
"A husbandman, forsooth, I am   *farmer*
125   And the kinges bondman;
Thereof I have good likinge."

"Sir, when spake you with our king?"
"In faith, never in all my living;
He knoweth not my name.
130   And I have my capull and my crofft,   *If; horse; field*
If I speake not with the king oft,
I care not, by St. Jame."

"What is thy name, fellow, by thy leave?"
"Marry," quoth hee, "John de Reeve.
135   I care not who itt heare.
For if you come into my inne   *dwelling place*
With beane-bread you shall beginne   *cheap, nasty bread*
Soone att your soupper,

"Salt bacon of a yeare old,
140   Ale that is both sower and cold —
I use neither braggatt nor bere.   *honeyed ale; beer*
I lett you witt withouten lett   *hesitation*
I dare eate noe other meate: *food*
I sell my wheate ech yeere."

145   "Why doe you, John, sell your wheate?"
"For I dare not eate that I gett;   *what; earn*
Therof I am full wrothe.
For I love a draught of good drinke as well
As any man that doth itt sell,
150   And alsoe a good wheat loffe.   *loaf*

"For he that first starveth John de Reeve,
I pray to God hee may never well cheeve,   *succeed*

Neither on water nor land,
Whether itt be sheriffe or king
155 That makes such statutinge: *decreeing*
I outcept never a one.   *except*

"For and the kings penny were layd by mine   *if*
I durst as well as hee drinke the wine
Till all my good were gone.
160 But sithence that wee are meitt soe meete,   *since; met so nicely*
Tell mee where is your receate: *accommodation*
You seeme good laddes eche one."   *servingmen*

The erle answered with wordes faire,
"In the kinges house is our repayre,   *usual dwelling place*
165 If wee bee out of the way."   *away from home*
"This night," quoth John, "you shall not spill,   *die*
Such harbour I shall bring you till: *to*
I hett itt you today.   *promise*

"Soe that yee take itt thankeffullye   *Provided that*
170 In Godes name, and St. Jollye,
I aske noe other pay.
And if you be sturdy and stout,   *surly; arrogant*
I shall garr you to stand without   *make*
For ought that you can say.

175 "For I have two neigbores won by mee   *[who] live near*
Of the same freeledge that am I: *independence*
Of o bandshipp are wee.   *one serfdom*
The bishopp of Durham the tone oweth;   *the one owns*
The erle of Gloster, whosoe him knoweth,   *whoever he is*
180 Lord of the other is hee.

"Wist my neighbors that I were thratt,   *If my neighbors knew; threatened*
I vow to God, they wold not lett   *hesitate*
For to come soone to mee.
If any wrong were to mee done
185 Wee three durst fight a whole afternoone,
I tell you sikerlye."

The king said, "John, tell us not this tale:
Wee are not ordayned for battell;   *armed*
Our weedes are wett and cold.   *clothes*
190 Heere is no man that yee shall greeve.   *will harm you*
But helpe us, John, by your leave,
With a bright feare and bold."   *fire*

"I' faith," sayd John, "that you shall want,   *In faith; lack*
For fuell heere is wonderous scant,
195   As I heere have yee told.
Thou getteth noe other of John de Reeve,
For the kinges statutes whilest I live
I thinke to use and hold.

"If thou find in my house paymen fine   *white bread*
200   Or in my kitchin poultry slaine
Peradventure thou wold say
That John Reeve his bond hath broken.
I wold not that such wordes weere spoken
In the kinges house another day,

205   "For itt might turne me to great greeffe.   *result in great trouble for me*
Such proud laddes that beare office   *servingmen with jobs at court*
Wold danger a pore man aye.   *harm; always*
And or I wold pray thee of mercy longe,   *before*
Yett weere I better to lett thee gange,   *go*
210   In twentye-naine devilles way."

Thus they rode to the towne.
John de Reeve lighted downe   *alighted*
Besides a comlye hall.
Four men belive came wight;   *at once; quickly*
215   They halted them full right   *properly*
When they heard John call.
They served him honestly and able   *respectably; ably*
And his horsse to the stable   *And [led]*
And lett noe tenne misfall.   *nothing annoying happen*

220   Some went to warne their dame
That John had brought guestes home.
Shee came to welcome them tyte,   *quickly*
In a side kirtle of greene.   *long gown*
Her head was dight all bydeene: *dressed in a little while*
225   The wiffe was of noe pryde.

Her kerchers were all of silke,   *kerchiefs*
Her hayre as white as any milke,
Lovesome of hue and hyde.   *Lovely; skin*
Shee was thicke and somedeale broad:
230   Of comlye fashyon was shee made,
Both belly, backe, and side.

Then John calld his men all,
Sayes, "Build me a fire in the hall,

And give their capulles meate.   *horses food*
235 Lay before them corne and hay.   *grain*
For my love rubb off the clay,
For they beene weary and wett.

"Lay under them straw to the knee,
240 ....
....
....
For courtyers comonly wold be jollye   *showy*
And have but litle to spend."

Then hee said, "By St. John,
245 You are welcome, every one,
If you take itt thankefullye.
Curtesye I learned never none,
But after mee, fellowes, I read you gone."   *advise you to go*
Till a chamber they went, all three.   *To*

250 A charcole fire was burning bright.
Candles on chandlours light: *candlesticks shine*
Eche freake might other see.   *man*
"Where are your sordes?" quoth John de Reeve.   *swords*
The erle said, "Sir, by your leave,
255 Wee weare none, perdye."

Then John rowned with the erle soe free: *whispered; noble*
"What long fellow is yonder," quoth hee,   *tall*
That is soe long of lim and lyre?"   *body*
The erle answered with wordes small,   *simple*
260 "Yonder is Peeres Pay-for-all,
The queenes cheefe fawconer."   *falconer*

"Ah ah," quoth John, "for Godes good,
Where gott hee that gay hood,
Glitering of gold itt were?   *as if it were*
265 And I were as proud as hee is like,   *If*
There is no man in England ryke   *kingdom*
Shold garr me keepe his gleades one yere.   *make; birds of prey*

"I pray you, sir, for Godes werke,
Who is yond in yonder serke,   *surplice*
270 That rydeth Peeres soe nye?"
The erle answered him againe,
"Yonder is a pore chaplaine,
Long advanced or hee bee.   *It will be a long time before he is promoted*

"And I myselfe am a sumpter man;   *driver of a packhorse*
275 Other craft keepe I none,   *trade*
I say you withouten miss."   *without fail*
"You are fresh fellowes to your a-pay,   *gorgeous; in your opinion*
Jolly jetters in your array,   *flashy strutters*
Proud laddes, and I trow, penyles."   *servingmen*

280 The king said, "Soe mote I thee,   *As I hope to prosper*
There is not a penny amongst us three
To buy us bread and flesh."   *meat*
"Ah ha," quoth John, "there is small charge,   *that matters very little*
For courtyers comonlye are att large,   *at liberty*
285 If they goe never soe fresh.   *Even if; fancily dressed*

"I goe girt in a russett gowne,   *clothed; coarse wool*
My hood is of homemade browne,   *brown cloth*
I weare neither burnett nor greene;   *fine wool cloth; green cloth*
And yett I troe I have in store
290 A thousand pounds and somedeale more,
For all yee are prouder and fine.   *more splendid; handsome*

"Therfore I say, as mote I thee,
A bondman itt is good bee,   *[to] be*
And come of carles kinne.
295 For and I bee in taverne sett,   *if*
To drinke as good wine I will not lett   *hesitate*
As London Edward or his queene."

The erle sayd, "By Godes might,
John, thou art a comly knight,
300 And sturdy in everye fray."   *brave*
"A knight!" quoth John, "Doe away for shame.
I am the kinges bondman.
Such wast wordes doe away.   *idle*

"I know you not in your estate.   *rank*
305 I am misnurtured, well I wott: *ill-bred; know*
I will not therto say nay.
But if any such doe me wrong,   *any such (i.e., a knight)*
I will fight with him hand to hand
When I am cladd in mine array."

310 The bishopp sayd, "You seeme sturdye.   *fierce*
Travelled you never beyond the sea?"
Jhon sayd sharplye, "Nay.
I know none such strange guise,   *custom*

But att home on my owne wise   *manner*
315   I dare hold the hye way.   *stand my ground on*

"And that hath done John Reeve scath,   *harm*
For I have made such as you wrath
With choppes and chances yare."   *jabs; exploits in the past*
"John de Reeve," sayd our king,
320   "Hast thou any armouringe,
Or any weapon to weare?"

"I vow, sir, to God," sayd John thoe,   *then*
"But a pikefforke with graines two —   *Just; pitchfork; prongs*
My father used never other speare —
325   A rusty sword that well will byte,
And a thwyttel a handffull syde   *knife four inches long*
That sharplye will share,   *cut*

"An acton and a habargyon a foote side;   *padded jacket; sleeveless coat of mail; long*
And yett peradventure I durst abyde
330   As well as thou, Peeres, for all thy painted geere."
Quoth John, "I reede wee goe to the hall,   *advise*
Wee three fellowes and Peeres Pay-for-all;
The proudest before shall fare."   *most splendid*

Thither they raked anon wright.   *went right away*
335   A charcole fyer was burning bright
With many a strang brand.   *massive log*
The hall was large and somedeale wyde:
There bordes were covered on everye syde;   *tables*
There mirth was commannde.   *enjoyment; starting*

340   Then the goodwiffe sayd with a seemlye cheere,   *welcoming face*
"Your supper is readye there."
"Yett watter," quoth John, "lettes see."
By then came Johnes neighbors two:
Hodgkin Long and Hob alsoe.   *Tall Roger; Robert*
345   The first fitt here find wee.   *section*

Second Parte

John sayd, "For want of a marshall I will take the wand.   *lack; bear*
Peeres Fawconer before shall gange: *go*
Begin the dish shall hee.   *food*
Goe to the bench, thou proud chaplaine;
350   My wiffe shall sitt thee againe: *facing*
Thy meate-fellow shall shee bee."   *dinner partner*
He sett the erle against the king.

They were faine att his bidding.   *well-pleased*
Thus John marshalled his meanye.   *arranged; company*

355   Then John sperred where his daughteres were.   *asked*
       "The fairer shall sitt by the fawconere:
       He is the best farrand man.   *most handsome*
       The other shall the sompter man have."   *packhorse driver*
       The erle sayd, "Soe God me save,
360   Of curtesye, John, thou can."   *have knowledge*

       "If my selfe," quoth John, "be bonnd,   *Even if I; in a state of serfdom*
       Yett my daughteres beene well farrand,   *attractive*
       I tell you sickerlye.   *truly*
       Peeres, and thou had wedded John daughter Reeve,   *if; John Reeve's daughter*
365   There were no man that durst thee greeve,
       Neither for gold nor fee."

       "Sompter man, and thou the other had,   *if*
       In good faith, then thou were made   *would be all set*
       Forever in this cuntrye.   *district*
370   Then, Peres, thou might beare the price.   *surpass all others*
       Yett I wold this chaplaine had a benefice,   *position in the Church*
       As mote I thrive or thee.

       "In this towne a kirke there is.   *church*
       And I were king itt should be his: *If*
375   He shold have itt of mee.
       Yett will I helpe as well as I may."
       The king, the erle, the bishopp can say,
       "John, and wee live wee shall quitte thee."   *if; repay*

       When his daughters were come to dease,   *the high table*
380   "Sitt farther," quoth John, withouten leaze,   *to tell the truth*
       "For there shalbe no moe.   *more [at the table]*
       These strange fellowes I doe not ken: *know*
       Peradventure they may be some gentlemen.
       Therfore I and my neighbors towe   *two*

385   "Att sidebord end wee will bee
       Out of the gentles companye.
       Thinke yee not best soe?
       For itt was never the law of England
       To sett gentles blood with bonnd;
390   Therfore to supper will wee goe."

       By then came in beane-bread,
       Salt bacon, rusted and redd,   *(see note)*

And brewice in a blacke dish.   *stew*
Leane salt beefe of a yeere old,
395 Ale that was both sower and cold: *sour*
This was the first service.   *course*

Eche one had of that ylke a messe.   *same; serving*
....
The king sayd, "Soe have I blisse,
400 Such service ner erst I see."   *never before; saw*
Quoth John, "Thou gettest noe other of mee
Att this time but this."

"Yes, good fellow," the king gan say,   *To the contrary*
"Take this service heer away,
405 And better bread us bringe,
And gett us some better drinke:
We shall thee requite as wee thinke,
Without any letting."   *delay*

Quoth John, "Beshrew the morsell of bread   *Damn*
410 This night that shall come in your head,
But thou sweare me one thinge: *Unless*
Swere to me by booke and bell
That thou shalt never John Reeve bettell   *speak against*
Unto Edward our kinge."

415 Quoth the king, "To thee my truth I plight,   *solemn promise I pledge*
He shall nott witt our service tonight
No more then he doth nowe,
Never while wee three live in land."
"Therto," quoth John, "hold up thy hand,   *To confirm*
420 And then I will thee troe."   *trust*

"Loe," quoth the king, "my hand is heere."
"Soe is mine," quoth the erle with a mery cheere,
"Therto I give God avowe."   *promise*
"Have heere my hand," the bishopp sayd.
425 "Marry," quoth John, "thou may hold thee well apayd,   *pleased*
For itt is for thy prow.   *advantage*

"Take this away, thou Hodgkin Long,
And let us sitt out of the throng,
Att a sidebordes end.
430 These strange fellowes think uncouthlye   *think of [as] strange*
This night att our cookerye,   *cooking*
Such as God hath us sent."

By then came in the paymen bread,   *white (refined) bread*
Wine that was both white and redd
435   In silver cuppes cleare.   *shining*
"Aha," quoth John, "our supper begines with drinke.
Tasste itt, laddes, and looke how yee thinke   *see what*
For my love, and make good cheere.

"Of meate and drinke you shall have good fare,
440   And as for good wine, wee will not spare,
I garr you to understand: *want (cause)*
For everye yeere, I tell thee thoe   *then*
I will have a tunn or towe   *cask; two*
Of the best that may be fonnd.   *found*

445   "Yee shall see three churles heere   *serfs*
Drinke the wine with a merry cheere.
I pray you, doe you soe.
And when our supper is all doone
You and wee will dance soone:
450   Lettes see who best can doe."

The erle sayd, "By Marry bright,
Wheresover the king lyeth this night
He drinketh no better wine
Then thou selfe does att this tyde."
455   "In faith," quoth John, "I had leever I died   *rather*
Then live ay in woe and pine.   *always; want; penance*

"If I be come of carles kinne,   *Even if*
Part of the good that I may winne,
Some therof shall be mine.
460   He that never spendeth but alway spareth,   *saves*
Comonlye oft the worsse he fareth:
Others will broake itt syne."   *enjoy; afterwards*

By then came in red wine and ale,
The bores head into the hall,
465   Then sheild with sauces seere,   *boar's flesh; various*
Capones both baked and rost,
Woodcockes, venison, without bost,   *exaggeration*
And dishmeate dight full deere.   *casseroles prepared at great cost*

Swannes they had piping hott,
470   Coneys, curlews, well I wott,   *Rabbits*
The crane, the hearne in fere,   *heron together*
Pigeons, partridges, with spicerye,   *spices*

Elkis, flaunes, with frumentye.   *Deer, flans (see note)*
John bade them make good cheere.

475   The erle sayd, "Soe mote I thee,   *prosper*
      John, you serve us royallye.
      If yee had dwelled att London,
      If King Edward where here,   *were*
      He might be apayd with this supper,   *pleased*
480   Such freindshipp wee have funden."   *found*

      "Nay," sayd John, "by Godes grace,
      And Edward wher in this place,
      Hee shold not touch this tonne.   *cask*
      Hee wold be wrath with John, I hope;   *believe*
485   Therefore I beshrew the sope   *curse; bread dipped in wine*
      That shall in his mouth come."

      Theratt the king laughed and made good cheere.
      The bishopp sayd, "Wee fare well heere."
      The erle sayd as him thought.   *how it seemed to him*
490   They spake Lattine amongst them there.
      "In fayth," quoth John, "and yee greeve mee mare,   *if; more*
      Full deere itt shalbe bought.   *dearly it will be paid for*

      "Speake English, everyche one,   *each one of you*
      Or else sitt still, in the devilles name:
495   Such talke love I naught.
      Lattine spoken amongst lewd men —   *laymen*
      Therin noe reason doe I ken;   *recognize*
      For falshood itt is wrought.   *deception; done*

      "Rowning, I love itt neither young nor old;   *Private conversation; not at all*
500   Therefore yee ought not to bee to bold,
      Neither att meate nor meale.
      Hee was false that rowning began;   *invented private conversation*
      Theerfore I say to you, certaine,
      I love itt never a deale.

505   "That man can nought of curtesye   *knows nothing*
      That letes att his meate rowning bee,   *at his table*
      I say, soe have I sele."   *happiness*
      The erle sayd right againe,
      "Att your bidding wee will be baine: *willing*
510   Wee thinke you say right weele."

      By this came up from the kitchin   *this [time]*
      Sirrupps on plates good and fine,   *Syrups; flat cakes*

Wrought in a fayre array.
"Sirres," sayth John, "sithe wee are mett
515 And as good fellowes together sett,
Lett us be blythe today.

"Hodgkin Long, and Hob of the Lath,   *of the Barn*
You are counted good fellowes both:
Now is no time to twine.   *depart*
520 This wine is new come out of France —
Be God, me list well to dance;   *By; it pleases me*
Therfore take my hand in thine.

"For wee will, for our guestes sake,
Hop and dance, and revell make,
525 The truth for to know."
Up he rose and drank the wine.
"Wee must have powder of ginger therein,"
John sayd, as I troe.

John bade them stand up all about,
530 "And yee shall see the carles stout
Dance about the bowle.   *[wine] bowl*
Hob of the Lathe and Hodgkin Long,
In fayth you dance your mesures wrang:
Methinkes that I shold know.

535 "Yee dance neither gallyard nor brawle,   *(see note)*
Trace nor true mesure, as I trowe,   *The right steps; rhythm*
But hopp as yee were woode."   *crazy*
When they began of foote to fayle,   *lose their footing*
They tumbled top over tayle,
540 And master and master they yode.   *first one on top, then the other; went*

Forth they stepped on stones store.   *massive*
Hob of the Lathe lay on the flore;
His brow brast out on blood.   *broke out bleeding*
"Ah ha," quoth John, "thou makes it tough.   *you make it look hard*
545 Had thou not falled wee had not lough: *fallen; laughed*
Thou gladdes us all, by the rood."   *cross*

John hent up Hobb by the hand,   *pulled*
Sayes, "Me thinkes wee dance our measures wronge,
By Him that sitteth in throne."
550 Then they began to kick and wince.   *kick*
John hitt the king over the shinnes
With a payre of new clowted shoone.   *newly studded shoes*

Sith King Edward was mad a knight   *Since*
Had he never soe merry a night
555   As he had with John de Reeve.
To bed they busked them anon;   *they got themselves ready*
Their liveryes were served them up soone   *(see note)*
With a merry chefe.   *fortune?*

And thus they sleeped till morning att prime   *the hour after sunrise*
560   In full good sheetes of line.   *linen*
A masse he garred them to have,
And after they dight them to dine   *got ready*
With boyled capons good and fine.
The duke sayd, "Soe God me save,
565   If ever wee come to our abone,   *to a higher position (see note)*
Wee shall thee quitt our warrison: *pay back; reward*
Thou shalt not need itt to crave."

Third Parte

The king took leave att man and may.   *maiden*
John sett him in the rode way:
570   To Windsor can hee ryde.
Then all the court was full faine
That the king was comen againe,
And thanked Christ that tyde.

The jerfawcones were taken againe   *gerfalcons*
575   In the forrest of Windsor, without laine: *to tell the truth*
The lordes did soe provyde.   *see to it*
They thanked God and St. Jollye.   *St. Julian*
To tell the queene of their harbery   *lodging*
The lordes had full great pryde.

580   The queene sayd, "Sir, by your leave,
I pray you send for that noble reeve
That I may see him with sight."
The messenger was made to wend
And bidd John Reeve goe to the king
585   Hastilye with all his might.

John waxed unfaine in bone and blood,   *grew reluctant to the bone*
Saith, "Dame, to me this is noe good,
My truth to you I plight."
"You must come in your best array."
590   "What too," sayd John, "sir, I thee pray?"   *For what reason*
"Thou must be made a knight."

"A knight!" sayd John. "By Marry myld,
I know right well I am beguiled
With the guestes I herbord late.   *recently*
595   To debate they will me bring.   *a fight*
Yett cast I mee for nothinge   *intend*
Noe sorrow for to take.   *harm*

"Allice, feitch mee downe my side acton —   *long padded jacket*
My round pallett to my crowne   *helmet for*
600   Is made of Millayne plate —   *[That] is*
A pitchforke and a sword."
Shee sayd shee was aferd   *afraid*
This deede wold make debate.   *cause a fight*

Allice feitched downe his acton syde.
605   Hee tooke itt for no litle pryde,   *considered it showing off not a little*
Yett must hee itt weare.
The scaberd was rent, withouten doubt:
A large handfull the bleade hanged out.   *A good four inches the blade*
John the Reeve sayd there,

610   "Gett lether and an aule, I pray: *awl*
Lett me sow itt a chape today   *scabbard*
Lest men scorn my geere.
Now," sayd John, "will I see
Whether itt will out lightlye   *come out easily*
615   Or I meane itt to weare."   *Before*

John pulled fast at the blade.
I wold hee had kist my arse that itt made:
He cold not gett itt out.
Allice held and John draughe: *pulled*
620   Either att other fast loughe,   *laughed hard*
I doe yee out of doubt.   *I tell you for sure*

John pulled att the scaberd soe hard
Againe a post he ran backward
And gave his head a rowte.   *blow*
625   His wiffe did laughe when he did fall,
And soe did his meanye all   *household*
That were there neere about.

Jhon sent after his neighbors both,
Hodgkine Long and Hobb of the Lath:
630   They were baene att his biddinge.   *willing*
Three pottles of wine in a dishe,   *half-gallons*

They supped itt all off, iwis,
All there att their partinge.

John sayd, "And I had my buckler,   *If*
635   There's nothing that shold me dare,   *hurt*
I tell you all in fere.   *together*
Feitch me downe," quoth he, "my mittons:
They came upon my handes but once
This two and twenty yare.

640   "Feitch mee my capull," sayd hee there.
His saddle was of a new manner,
His stirroppes were of a tree.   *made of wood*
"Dame," he sayd, "feitch me wine:
I will drinke to thee once syne.   *then*
645   I troe I shall never thee see.

"Hodgkin Long and Hob of the Lathe,   *the Barn*
Tarry and drinke with me bothe,
For my cares are fast commannde."   *coming*
They dranke five gallons verament.   *truly*
650   "Farwell fellowes all present,
For I am readye to gange."

John was soe combred in his geere   *hampered*
Hee cold not gett upon his mere   *mare*
Till Hodgkinn heave up his tail.   *heaved; butt*
655   "Now farwell, sir, by the roode."   *cross*
To neither knight nor barron good
His hatt he wold not vayle   *lower*
Till he came to the kings gate.
The porter wold not lett him in theratt,
660   Nor come within the walle,

Till a knight came walking out.
They sayd, "Yonder standeth a carle stout
In a rusticall arraye."
On him they all wondred wright,   *At; were struck by surprise right away*
665   And said he was an unseemelye wight,   *creature*
And thus to him they gan say:

"Hayle, fellow! Where wast thou borne?
Thee beseemeth full well to weare a horne.   *It suits you*
Where had thou that faire geere?
670   I troe a man might seeke full long,
One like to thee or that hee fonnd,   *before; found*
Tho he sought all this yeere."

John bade them kisse the devilles arse:
"For you my geare is much the worsse.
675   You will itt not amend;
By my faith, that can I lead.   *demonstrate*
Upon the head I shall you shred,   *prune*
But if you hence wende.   *Unless you get out of here*

"The devill him speede upon his crowne
680   That causeth me to come to this towne,
Whether he weare Jack or Jill.   *were*
What shold such men as I doe here,
Att the kinges manner?   *manor*
I might have bene att home still."

685   As John stoode flyting fast,   *taunting hard*
He saw one of his guestes come at the last.
To him he spake full bold,
To him he full fast rode;
He vayled neither hatt nor hood,
690   Sayth, "Thou hast me betold: *deceived*

"Full well I wott, by this light,
That thou hast disdaind mee right,   *treated me with contempt*
For wrath I waxe neere wood."
The erle sayd, "By Marry bright,
695   John, thou made us a merry night:
Thou shalt have nothing but good."

The erle tooke leave att John Reeve,   *of*
Sayd, "Thou shalt come in, without greefe.
I pray thee tarry and wait."
700   The erle into the hall went,
And told the king verament
That John Reeve was att the gate —
"To no man list hee lout —   *he chose to bow*
A rusty sword gird him about,
705   And a long fawchyon, I wott."   *curved sword*

The king said, "Goe wee to meate,
And brings him when wee are sett:
Our dame shall have a play."
"He hath ten arrowes in a thonge;   *leather strap*
710   Some are short and some are long.
The sooth as I shold say,

"A rusty sallett upon his crowne;   *headpiece*
His hood-were homemade browne.   *hood cloth*

	There may nothing him dare.	*daunt*
715	A thwyttill hee hath fast in his hand	*knife*
	That hangeth in a packe-band,	*packthread?*
	And sharplye itt will share.	*cut*

	"He hath a pouch hanging full wyde,	*wide open*
	A rusty buckeler on the other syde,	
720	His mittons are of blacke clothe.	
	....	
	Whosoe to him sayth ought but good,	
	Full soone hee wilbe wrothe."	

	Then John sayd, "Porter, lett mee in.	
725	Some of my goodes thou shalt win;	
	I love not for to pray."	*don't like to beg*
	The porter sayd, "Stand abacke.	
	And thou come neere, I shall thee rappe,	
	Thou carle, by my fay."	

730	John tooke his forke in his hend;	*pitchfork; hands*
	He bare his forke on an end:	
	He thought to make affray.	*intended; an attack*
	His capull was wight and cornefedd;	*quick; well-fed on oats*
	Upon the porter hee him spedd	*rushed*
735	And him can welnye slay.	*nearly killed*

	He hitt the porter upon the crowne:	
	With that stroke hee fell downe,	
	Forsooth, as I you tell.	
	And then hee rode into the hall	
740	And all the dogges, both great and small,	
	On John fast can they yell.	*barked*

	John layd about as he were wood,	*crazy*
	And four he killed as hee stood:	
	The rest will now beware.	
745	Then came forth a squier hend	*courteous*
	And sayd, "John, I am thy freind.	
	I pray you, light downe there."	

	Another sayd, "Give mee thy forke."	
	And John sayd, "Nay, by St. William of Yorke;	
750	First I will cracke thy crowne."	
	Another sayd, "Lay downe thy sword.	
	Sett up thy horsse. Be not affeard.	*Put your horse in a stable*
	Thy bow, good John, lay downe.	

"I shall hold your stirroppe of wood.
755 Doe of your pallett and your hoode   *Take off; headpiece*
     Ere they fall, as I troe.
     Yee see not who sitteth att the meate.
     Yee are a wonderous silly freake,   *ignorant*
     And also passing sloe."   *very slow*

760 "What devill!" sayd John. "Is yt for thee?   *Is it your hood?*
     Itt is my owne, soe mote I thee.
     Therfore I will that itt bide."   *intend*
     The queen beheld him in hast.
     "My lord," shee sayd, "for Godes fast,
765 Who is yonder that doth ryde?
     Such a fellow saw I never ere."
     Shee saith, "Hee hath the quaintest geere: *strangest*
     He is but simple of pryde."

     Right soe came John as hee were wood.
770 He vayled neither hatt nor hood:
     He was a folly freake.   *foolish*
     He tooke his forke as hee wold just.   *joust*
     Up to the dease fast he itt thrust.   *high table*
     The queene for feare did speake,

775 And sayd, "Lordes, beware, for Godes grace,
     For hee will frownte some in the face   *hit*
     If yee take not good heede."
     The laughed, without doubt,
     And soe did all that were about,
780 To see John on his steede.

     Then sayd John to our queene,
     "Thou mayst be proud, dame, as I weene,
     To have such a fawconer,
     For he is a well farrand man,   *handsome*
785 And much good manner hee can,   *knows*
     I tell you sooth in fere.   *together*

     "But, lord," hee sayd, "my good, it's thine,
     My body alsoe for to pine,   *torment*
     For thou art king with crowne.
790 But, lord, thy word is honourable:
     Both stedfast, sure, and stable,   *firm*
     And alsoe great of renowne.

     "Therfore, have mind what thou me hight   *promised*
     When thou were with me anight,   *at night*

795   A warryson that I shold have."   *reward*
       John spoke to him with sturdye mood: *stubborn spirit*
       Hee vayled neither hatt nor hood,
       But stood with him checkmate.   *as an equal*

       The king sayd, "Fellow mine,
800   For thy capones hott and good red wine
       Much thankes I doe give thee."
       The queene sayd, "By Mary bright,
       Award him as his right:
       Well advanced lett him bee."

805   The king sayd untill him then,   *to*
       "John, I make thee a gentleman.
       Thy manner place I thee give,
       And a hundred pounds to thee and thine,
       And every yeere a tunn of red wine,
810   Soe long as thou dost live."

       But then John began to kneele: *Only then*
       "I thanke you, my lord, so have I sele.   *as I hope for happiness*
       Therof I am well payd."   *pleased*
       Thee king tooke a coller bright   *neck chain*
815   And sayd, "John, heere I make thee a knight."
       That worshippe when hee sayd   *showed him that honor*

       Then was John evill apayd,   *displeased*
       And amongst them all thus hee sayd,
       "Full oft I have heard tell
820   That after a coller comes a rope:
       I shall be hanged by the throate.
       Methinkes itt goeth not well."   *things are not going well*

       "Sith thou hast taken this estate,   *status*
       That every man may itt wott
825   Thou must begin the bord."   *sit at the head of the table*
       Then John therof was nothing faine. *not at all happy about it*
       I tell you truth withouten laine,   *concealment*
       He spake never a word,

       But att the bordes end he sate him downe,
830   For hee had leever beene att home   *rather*
       Then att all their Frankish fare. *carrying on like the French*
       For there was wine, well I wott;
       Royall meates of the best sortes
       Were sett before him there.

835 A gallon of wine was put in a dishe.
John supped itt off, both more and lesse.
"Feitch," quoth the king, "such more."
"By my Lady," quoth John, "this is good wine.
Let us make merry, for now itt is time.
840 Christs curse on him that doth itt spare."

With that came in the porters hend
And kneeled downe before the king.
One was all berinnen with blood.   *dripping*
Then the king in hert was woe,
845 Sayes, "Porter, who hath dight thee soe?   *handled*
Tell on, I wax neere wood."
"Now in faith," sayd John, "that same was I,
For to teach him some curtesye,
For thou hast taught him noe good.

850 "For when thou came to my pore place
With mee thou found soe great a grace
Noe man did bidd thee stand without.
For if any man had against thee spoken
His head full soone I shold have broken,"
855 John sayd, "withouten doubt.

"Therfore I warne thy porters free,
When any man comes out of my countrye,   *district*
Another time lett them not be soe stout.   *arrogant*
If both thy porters goe walling wood,   *Even if; raging mad*
860 Be God, I shall reave their hood   *tear off*
Or goe on foote aboute.   *Or I will walk rather than ride*
But thou, lord, hast after me sent
And I am come att thy comandement
Hastilye, withouten doubt."

865 The king sayd, "By St. Jame,
John, my porters were to blame.
You did nothing but right."
He tooke the case into his hand: *matter*
Then to kisse hee made them gange.   *go*
870 Then laughed both king and knight.
"I pray you," quoth the king, "good fellows bee."   *friends*
"Yes," quoth John, "soe mote I thee,
We were not wrathe ore night."   *over*

Then the bishopp sayd to him thoe,   *then*
875 "John, send hither thy sonnes two:
To the schoole I shall them find;   *At; maintain*

And soe God may for them werke
That either of them have a kirke,   *church*
If fortune be their freind.

880   "Also send hither thye daughters both.
        Two marryages the king will garr them to have   *make*
        And wedd them with a ringe.
        Went forth, John, on thy way.   *Go*
        Looke thou be kind and curteous aye:
885   Of meate and drinke be neur nithing."   *never a miser*

        Then John took leave of king and queene,
        And after att all the court bydeene,   *as a group*
        And went forth on his way.
        He sent his daughters to the king,
890   And they were weded with a ringe
        Unto two squiers gay.

        His sonnes both hardy and wight,
        The one of them was made a knight,
        And fresh in every fray,   *vigorous; fight*
895   The other a parson of a kirke,
        Godes service for to worke,
        To serve God night and day.

        Thus John Reeve and his wiffe
        With mirth and jolty ledden their liffe: *jollity led*
900   To God they made laudinge.   *praising*
        Hodgikin Long and Hobb of the Lathe,
        They were made freemen bothe
        Through the grace of the hend king.

        John thought on the bishopps word
905   And ever after kept open bord
        For guestes that God him send,
        Till death feitcht him away
        To the blisse that lasteth aye,
        And thus John Reeve made an end.

910   Thus endeth the tale of Reeve soe wight —   *brave*
        God that is soe full of might
        To heaven their soules bring
        That have heard this litle story —
        That lived sometimes in the south west countrye
915   In Long Edwardes dayes our king.

                        Finis   *The End*

EXPLANATORY NOTES TO JOHN THE REEVE

ABBREVIATIONS: *MED*: *Middle English Dictionary*; *OED*: *Oxford English Dictionary*; *NCE*: *New Catholic Encyclopedia*; **Whiting**: Whiting, *Proverbs, Sentences, and Proverbial Phrases*.

title   The manuscript has *John de Reeve*, and the poem throughout refers to the central character as either John de Reeve or John Reeve, as if Reeve were only his surname, rather than indicating his station as well. I have changed the title since contemporary references are to John *the* Reeve (Douglas, Dunbar, and Lyndsay; see the introduction to the poem) but left the name unaltered elsewhere: it seems to me likely that the poem was originally inconsistent on this point.

9   *A rolle he had reading*. That is, he was reading a manuscript in the form of a long roll of parchment, rather than leaves folded and sewed together like a book. Formal documents tended to be kept on rolls, so the implication is that a story read by a clerk from a roll has historical authority.

17   *But Edward with the long shankes was hee*. Edward I (reigned 1272–1307), called "Longshanks."

33   *gan they say*. *gan* is a past tense marker in this poem. *Gan they say* means "they said."

34   *Itt is a folly, by St. John*. The probable reference is to St. John, the apostle said to be particularly loved by Christ in the account in the Gospel of John; medieval tradition considered John the apostle, John the evangelist, and John the author of the Book of Revelation to be the same person. But there were many other saints named John, including John the Baptist.

92   *Oft men meete att unsett steven*. A proverb, Whiting M210: "Men may meet at unset steven," people can meet at appointments that they have not set up.

94–104   The carle is clearly afraid of brigands and does not recognize the king, much like Adam the shepherd in the previous poem.

119   *My hood or that I wold vayle*. John refuses to show deference to lords by taking off his hood in their presence. True to his word here, he continues to resist doffing his hood, and the line "Hee vayled neither hatt nor hood" is a repeated comment on his later progress through the court (at lines 689, 770, 797). The doffing of the hood is an explicit point of contention in this poem, as it is in *King Edward and the Shepherd*.

126   *Thereof I have good likinge*. For a serf, the best owner was the king. The king's
            bondmen were subject to fewer taxes and restrictions.

132   *by St. Jame*. Probably St. James the Greater, the apostle, brother of John, whose
            shrine in Santiago de Compostela in Spain was one of the most important
            pilgrimage sites in the Middle Ages (see "James [Son of Zebedee], St.," *NCE*).
            But there are several other men named James mentioned in the New Testament.

134   *Marry*. A mild oath by the Virgin Mary, mother of Jesus.

140–41   *Ale that is both sower and cold — / I use neither braggatt nor bere*. "Until the
            introd[uction] of hops from the Low Countries (a1440), **ale** and **ber** are
            synonymous in M[iddle] E[nglish]" (from *MED ale*, def. 1). The distinction is
            that beer would be hopped, but ale would not. John drinks only the old-
            fashioned homemade ale.

143   *I dare eate noe other meate*. The obvious question is why John does not dare eat
            better food, especially since it is clear that he has a productive farm. Edward asks
            the question but gets an answer that does not help readers outside the historical
            context much. As a bondman, he would have been required to mill his wheat at
            a manorial mill and perhaps brew at a manorial brewing-house, and to pay for
            the privilege; perhaps he does not dare eat wheat bread because he ostensibly
            cannot afford to have his meal ground at the mill and will not risk being caught
            with a handmill. An alternative explanation is that John has run afoul of regula-
            tions fixing the prices of both bread and beer, if he has been selling them (see
            lines 148–49), and the fines incurred have persuaded him to have nothing to do
            with brewing or baking.

170   *St. Jollye*. St. Julian the Hospitaller, the patron saint of hospitality, whose tale is
            told in the *Legenda Aurea* and other medieval collections of saints' lives such as
            the *South English Legendary*. Briefly, as a boy he ran away from home in the hopes
            of escaping the prophecy that he would kill his parents. When they came seeking
            him years later, his wife hospitably housed them in the couple's own bed, and
            Julian, told that his wife was in bed with another man, returned home in a rage
            and killed the pair sleeping in their bed, only to discover that he had fulfilled
            the prophecy. He expiated his sin by founding hospitals and houses for travelers.

193–98   John is denying that he has been cutting fuel. He apparently lives in Windsor
            Forest, an area under Forest Law: penalties both for poaching deer and cutting
            wood in areas designated as the king's forest were severe.

196   *Thou getteth noe other of John de Reeve*. *Getteth* is the wrong form of the verb to go
            with the pronoun *thou*; the line should read *Thou gettest*. But the scribe of the
            Percy Folio manuscript is writing much later than the poem's time of composition,
            and I preserve his presentation of the poem except where it has to be corrected
            for rhyme or understanding.

199–202   Here John is apparently worried that he will be found to be too wealthy and
            suspected of skimming off the profits of the king's estate, as Chaucer's Reeve did
            to his lord.

210   *In twentye-naine devilles way.* The usual phrase is "in twenty devils' way." John's phrase is a humorous intensification of the expletive. The spelling *naine* for *nine* is unusual. It could represent a pre-seventeenth-century Scottish form *nayne*, it could simply be a mistake, or it could be a pseudo-archaism.

217   *They served him honestly and able.* Here *able* is being used as an adverb; this is a usage not attested anywhere else.

218   *And his horsse to the stable.* A verb of motion seems to be understood: "And they led his horse to the stable."

224–25   *Her head was dight all bydeene: / The wiffe was of noe pryde.* The point here seems to be that the goodwife did not spend a long time primping but instead came promptly to look after the guests.

226–31   Like conventional descriptions of a lovely heroine, the poem uses set comparisons and associations: *silk, white as milk, lovesome hue, made in comely fashion.* But it is quite unusual in applying them to a plump little old woman, whose hair rather than skin is white as milk. And it is very unusual in giving such a description of an elderly peasant woman in terms that are not the hideous inverse of descriptions of the young and courtly lady. John's wife Allice (named at line 598) is a pleasant-looking, well-dressed, but not ostentatious old woman.

260   *Peeres Pay-for-all.* Looked at from a sufficiently royalist point of view, the king is the one who pays for all, as taxes are collected for and disbursed by him.

265–67   The king's very rich clothing is the subject of John's comment here. John sees him as out of place, someone dressed so magnificently that it is surprising that he humbles himself to serve as a falconer.

311   *Travelled you never beyond the sea?* The implied question is "Have you been to war?"

342   *"Yett watter," quoth John, "lettes see."* Bringing water in for washing the hands was a regular ceremony before courtly meals but not to be expected in a serf's house.

346   *John sayd, "For want of a marshall I will take the wand."* Because John's household, unlike that of a great lord or the king, does not have a marshal experienced in protocol to seat those who are to dine, John will do it himself. A wand would be the marshal's symbol of office.

392   *Salt bacon, rusted and redd.* The bacon may be simply discolored (metaphorically rusted) or the scribe may not have recognized the word *reested.* *Reested* would mean either that the bacon was cured (and thus be a neutral term) or that the bacon was rancid (and thus contribute to the gathering sense that the meal is unpleasant).

412   *Swere to me by booke and bell.* Swearing "by book and bell" was in reference to those used in the Mass.

419   *"Therto," quoth John, "hold up thy hand."* John is getting his guests to swear not to tell on him, and they raise their hands to confirm their promise. See *MED hond(e* (n.)1c. (a).

433   *paymen bread. Pandemain (OED)* or *pain-demeine (MED)*, a white bread made with refined flour, more expensive than wholegrain breads and therefore far more apt to be on a noble's or prosperous merchant's table than a peasant's. Here it is probably being used for trenchers, slabs of bread, sometimes toasted for greater firmness, to serve as dinner plates.

473   *Elkis, flaunes, with frumentye.* Frumenty was a dish made of wheat simmered in milk, sweetened and spiced. Elks were probably not the large animal now called elk but a smaller member of the deer family (*OED elk*[1]). Of the foods mentioned from lines 464 to 473, the boar and venison would have been poached illegally from the forest; the wildfowl were not protected by Forest Law but would have been poached from some lord's warren.

527   *"Wee must have powder of ginger therein."* It was customary in courtly circles to take wine with spices in it after a meal.

535   The galliard was a dance popular in the sixteenth century but possibly too late to be the one originally mentioned in this poem. The brawl (or bransle) too was a popular dance in the sixteenth century.

557   *Their liveryes were served them up soone.* Their allotment of something is being given to them just before bed, but it is not clear from the context what. It might be candles, or perhaps it is the voidee, the service of wine and spices at the very end of a social occasion, just before heading home or to bed. But the voidee is more or less implied above, at line 527.

561   *A masse he garred them to have.* John's household lacks very little that a royal or baronial court would have, including apparently a chaplain and a chapel in which he can have Mass said on the premises.

565   *If ever wee come to our abone. Abone* is a northern form of *above.*

600   *Is made of Millayne plate.* Milan was famous for its steel and armor.

601   *A pitchforke and a sword.* As a bondman, John is not entitled to carry a sword.

604   *Allice feitched downe his acton syde.* But the context calls for her to fetch him his sword, not his "jacket long." There must be some corruption in the text here. Compare line 607 and its use of "scaberd."

637   *"Feitch me downe," quoth he, "my mittons."* Rather than an armed knight's chain-mail gloves, John's mittens are heavy cloth ones, used to protect a workman's hands from thorns and brush when he is hedging and the like.

668   *Thee beseemeth full well to weare a horne.* That is, like the devil, but also like a forester. The men of the court, seeing John's mittens, and his gear, take him for a forester, responsible for both trees and game in the king's forest. John responds, at line 677, by offering to prune them. Legally, John is not allowed to carry bow and arrows in an area under Forest Law, but as we see below, he is carrying them.

676   *By my faith, that can I lead.* John can show from his experience how harmful the courtiers are to the peasantry.

749 *And John sayd, "Nay, by St. William of Yorke."* William Fitzherbert, consecrated archbishop of York in 1143, deposed in 1147, restored in 1153, and dead within weeks, perhaps poisoned. The party opposed to him accused him of simony. Miracles were said to have occurred at his tomb, and he was canonized in 1227 (see "St. William," *NCE*). The oath by St. William of York, not a widely venerated figure like the apostles or St. Julian, suggests that the origins of the poem are not far from York.

764 *for Godes fast*. The queen is swearing by Christ's fast of forty days (Matthew 4:2).

819–21 *Full oft I have heard tell / That after a coller comes a rope: / I shall be hanged by the throate*. This is an earlier use of the proverb (after a collar comes a rope) than those cited in the proverb dictionaries. The saying implies that those raised to knighthood (with the collar signifying their rank) are then in danger of a halter taking the place of the collar because of their eminence: obscurity is safer.

838 *By my Lady*. That is, by the Virgin Mary.

860 *Be God, I shall reave their hood*. The porters at the king's castle would likely be armed; John may be threatening to take their hoods off (as people have been urging him to take off his own), but in this case their hoods are probably chain-mail.

875 John's sons are introduced here, though we met his two daughters at the feast. The bishop proposes to educate them so that they may eventually become beneficed priests, each eventually with a parish of his own. This is his way of compensating John for his kind wishes at lines 371–76 that the bishop, apparently a poor chaplain, might receive a benefice.

880–82 Here the bishop proposes to address the other major issue of the well-being of John's family. The daughters must be married to provide for their futures, and the bishop promises that the king will sponsor their marriages, thus ensuring that the women will marry well and be set for life financially.

TEXTUAL NOTES TO JOHN THE REEVE

COPY-TEXT: London, British Library MS Additional 27879 (the Percy Folio Manuscript), pp. 357–68.

ABBREVIATIONS: **MS**: manuscript, here referring to the copy-text; **OED**: *Oxford English Dictionary*.

title	MS: *John De Reeue*. Below the title is written: *--in 3 parts--*.
1	The opening word *God* appears in large letters, the same size as the title, in the left margin.
22	MS spelling *the* has been changed to *they* for the pronoun here and in lines 76, 182, 211, 217, 539, 556, 741, 756, and 778.
24	MS: *The country they out cast*. Emendation for sense.
38	MS: *A bishopp from his coste to be cast*. Emendation for sense.
41	MS: *All night wee may ryde vnskill*. Emendation for grammar.
95	MS: *I am affraye of you eche one*. Emendation for grammar.
115	MS: *Of lordes sayet hee speake no more*. Emendation for rhyme (*more* to *moe*) and sense (*sayet* to *sayeth*).
137	MS: *With beffe and bread you shall beginne*. Emendation for sense, to correspond to line 391 below. Probably in a prior MS *beue* was misread for original *bene*.
146	MS: *ffor dare not eate that I gett*. Emended for sense.
155	MS: *That makes such statuinge*. Emendation for sense.
161	MS: *Tell mee where is your recreate*. Emendation for sense.
174	MS: *ffor ought that I you can say*. I is canceled, and *you* added both above the line and in the margin to the left.
178	MS: *The Bishopp of Durham this towne oweth*. Emendation for sense.
192	MS: *With bright a ffeare and bold*. Emendation for sense.
199	MS: *If thou find in my house payment ffine*. Emendation for sense.
215	MS: *They halted them ffull swift*. Emendation for rhyme.
232	MS: *Then ^ calld his men all*. In the margin: *John*.
233	MS: *Sayes build me a ffore in the hall*. Emendation for sense.
239–41	These lines are missing in the MS; no gap.
242	MS: *ffor courtyes comonly wold be Jollye*.
247	MS: *Curtesye I learned ne<..>r none*. Blot in MS.
276	MS: *I say you withouten miste*. Emendation for rhyme and sense.
277	MS: *You are ffresh ffellowes in your appay*. Emended for idiom.
284	MS: *ffor courtyes comonlye are att large*.

326	MS: *And a handffull a thyttille syde*. Emended for sense.
335	MS: *A charcole ffyer burning bright*. Emendation for sense.
338	MS: *there bordes werer covered on euerye syde*.
339	MS: *There mirth was comanded*. Emended for sense and rhyme; for form compare line 648.
344	MS: *Hobkin Long and Hob alsoe*. *Hodgkin* is his name elsewhere in the poem.
heading	In the MS, the large heading *2nd Parte* appears extending from the margin into the text area, beside bracketed and indented lines 346—54 (a complete stanza).
370–71	MS: *Then Peres thou might beare the prize* *Yett I wold this chaplaine had a benefize* The scribe has not recognized the older idiom *to bear the price*, "to surpass all others," and has changed the last word of line 370, then altered the word *benefice* in line 371 to give a pseudo-rhyme.
372	MS: *As mote I tharve or thee*. Emendation for sense.
381	MS: *ffor there shalbe no more*. Emendation for rhyme and sense.
385	MS: *Att side end bord wee will bee*. Emendation for sense.
393	MS: *And brewish in a blacke dish*; added above the line: *ice*.
398	This line is missing in the MS, no gap.
400	MS: *Such service nerest I see*. Emendation for sense.
416	MS: *He shall nott witt our service*. Conjectural emendation for rhyme.
426	MS: *For itt is for thy power*. Emendation for sense and rhyme.
427	MS: *Take this away, thou Hobkin Long*. Compare note to line 344.
429	MS: *a sword sidebordes*.
433	MS: *by then came in the payment bread*. Emendation for sense.
441	MS: *I goe you to understand*. Emendation for sense.
455	MS: *Infaith quoth John soe had leever I did*. Emendation for sense and rhyme.
456	MS: *Then live ay in woe and payne*. Emendation for sense and rhyme.
462	MS: *others will broake itt ffine*. Emendation for sense.
466	MS: *Capones both baked and rosted*. Emendation for rhyme.
470	MS: *Coneys curleys well I wott*. Emendation for sense.
473	MS: *Elkis fflounes with froterye*. Emendation for sense and rhyme.
480	MS: *Such ffreindshipp wee haue ffounde*. Emendation for rhyme.
485	MS: *Therefore I beshrew the soape*. Emendation for sense.
486	MS: *That shall come in his mouth*. Emendation for rhyme.
491	MS: *Infayth quoth John and yee greeve mee <....>*. Emended for rhyme.
493	MS: *speake English everye eche one*. Emendation for sense.
497	MS: *therin noe reason ffind I can*. Emendation for rhyme.
499	MS: *rowing I loue itt neither young nor old*. Emendation for sense.
505	MS: *That man can of curtesye*. Emendation for sense.
514	MS: *Sirrah sayth John sithe wee are mett*. Emendation for sense.
519	MS: *Now is no time to thrine*. Emendation for sense.
535	MS: *Yee dance neither gallyard nor hawe*. But there is no medieval dance called the hawe known to me. Emendation for sense and approximate rhyme (with probable form *trawe*).
543	MS: *His brow brast out of blood*. Emendation for idiom.
544	MS: *Ah ha Quoth John thou makes good game*. Emendation for rhyme.

545	MS: *Had thou not ffalled wee had not laught*. Emendation for rhyme.
558	MS: *With a merry cheere*. Emendation for rhyme.
559	MS: *And thus they sleeped till morning att prine*.
566	MS: *Wee shall thee quitt our varrison*.
heading	In the MS, the large heading *3rd Parte* appears extending from the margin into the text area, beside bracketed and indented lines 571–79. This placement ignores the stanza form.
568	MS: *The king took leave att man and mayde*. Emendation for rhyme.
578	MS: *To tell the queene of their harbor*. Emendation for rhyme.
602	MS: *Shee sayd shee was affrayd*. Emendation for rhyme (probably on original *swerd*).
604	MS: *acton* p̶<.̶>̶y̶d̶e̶ *syde*.
610	MS: *gett lether and a nayle John can say*. Emendation for sense (leather stitching is done using an awl, not a nail). *OED awl*: "In 15–17th c. a mistaken division of *an awl* as *a nawl* gave the form with initial *n*." Second emendation conjectural: *John can say* makes sense and rhymes, but repeats the sense of line 609.
614	MS: *hether itt will out lightlye*. Emendation for sense.
619	MS: *Allice held and John* t̶o̶u̶g̶h̶e̶ *draughe*.
632	MS: *They supped itt all off as I wis*. Emendation to restore idiom.
637	MS: *Feitch me downe quoth he my gloues*. Emendation for rhyme and sense (compare line 720). The rhyme on mittons/once was probably originally on *eyns* or *anes* forms of both words.
638	MS: *They came but on my handes but once*. Emendation for sense.
639	MS: *22*. The normal way of expressing that numeral would have been "two and twenty" throughout the Middle Ages.
644	MS: *I will drinke to thee once againe*. Emendation for rhyme.
654	MS: *till hodgkinn heave vp behind*. Emendation for rhyme (although it is possible that there are lines missing after 654 and there should be two stanzas rather than one of unusual length).
682	MS: *What shold such men as I doe [h]ere*. The *h* is unreadable.
688	MS: *To him he ffast ffull rode*. Emendation for sense.
693	MS: *ffor wrat I* a̶x̶e̶ *waxe neere wood*. Emendation for sense.
699	MS: *I pray thee tarry a while*. Emendation for rhyme.
713	MS: *His hood were made home browne*. Emendation for sense.
715	MS: *A thyttill hee hath fast in his hand*.
716	MS: *that hangeth in a peake band*. Emendation for sense.
721	This line is missing in the MS; no gap.
730	MS: *John tooke his forke in his hand*. Emendation for sense and rhyme.
735	MS: *And him had welnye slaine*. Emendation for rhyme.
747	MS: *I pray you, light downe heere*. Emendation for rhyme.
754	MS: *I shall hold your stirroppe*. Emendation for rhyme.
759	MS reads: *And alsoe* <...> *passing sloe*.
762	MS: *Therfore I will itt weare*. Emendation for rhyme (although it is possible that there are three lines missing after 762 and there should be two stanzas rather than one of unusual length).
766	MS: *Such a fellow saw I never yore*. Emendation for rhyme.

771	MS: *He was a ffaley freake*. Emendation for sense.
776	MS: *For hee will frowte some in the face*. Emendation for sense.
787	MS: *But lord hee sayd my good itt thine*. Emendation for sense.
790	MS: *But lord thy word is honour*. Emendation for sense and rhyme.
794	MS: *When thou with me a night*. Emendation for sense.
812	MS: *I thanke you my lord as I haue soule*. Emendation for idiom and rhyme.
816	MS: *With worshippe when hee sayd*. Emended for sense.
822	MS: *Methinkes itt doth not well*. Emended for sense.
829–34	The rhymes in this stanza (*downe/home* and *wott/sortes*) are poor and suggest corruption of the text.
838	MS: *good* ⟵...⟶ *wine*.
843	MS: *was all berinnen with blood*. Emendation for sense.
857	MS: *When any man out of my countrye*; *out* is added above the line, with a caret. Emended for sense.
858	MS: *another lett them not be soe stout*. Emended for sense.
861	MS: *or goe on foote boote*. Emended for sense and rhyme.
874	MS: *Then they bishopp sayd to him thoe*. Emendation for sense.
	the. MS: *they*.
897	MS: *to god serue night and day*. Emended for sense.
903	MS: *through the grace of the king hend*. Emended for sense and rhyme.
904	MS: *then thought on the bishopps word*. Emended for sense.

The King and the Hermit: Introduction

Manuscript and Scribe

The King and the Hermit appears on fols. 157r–161v of Oxford, Bodleian Library, MS Ashmole 61. The poem is incomplete. As we have it, its last line appears at the bottom of fol. 161v and the following leaf of the manuscript, the last one, is blank. See the introduction to *Sir Corneus* in the current collection for a discussion of the scribe Rate and the Leicestershire origins of the language of the manuscript. It should be noted that Rate uses abbreviations frequently and flexibly: a raised *u* can mean *ou*, *ur*, even *nour*, or just *r*; a raised *a* can mean *ra* or just *a*. He uses the grapheme *y* for both thorn and the vowel, sometimes distinguishing the vowel by an accent mark. I have represented his consonantal *y* with *th*.

Afterlife

The King and the Hermit appears, with different names as noted below, in the following early or otherwise useful editions:

1814. *The Kyng and the Hermyt.* [J.J.] C[oneybeare], ed. In *The British Bibliographer*, ed. Sir Egerton Brydges and Joseph Haslewood. Volume 4. London: R. Triphook. Pp. 81–95.

1829. *The Kyng and the Hermyt.* Charles Henry Hartshorne, ed. *Ancient Metrical Tales*. London: W. Pickering. Pp. 293–315.

1864. *The Kyng and the Hermyt.* William Carew Hazlitt, ed. *Remains of the Early Popular Poetry of England*. London: John Russell Smith. 1:11–34.

1905. *König Eduard und der Einsiedler: eine mittelenglische Ballade*. Albert Kurz, ed. Dissertation, Universität Erlangen-Nürnberg. Erlangen: von Junge und Sohn.

1985. *The King and the Hermit.* Melissa M. Furrow, ed. *Ten Fifteenth-Century Comic Poems*. New York: Garland. Pp. 237–69.

2008. *King Edward and the Hermit.* George Shuffelton, ed. *Codex Ashmole 61: A Compilation of Popular Middle English Verse*. Kalamazoo, MI: Medieval Institute Publications. Pp. 401–13.

REFERENCE TOOLS

The King and the Hermit is *NIMEV* 1764.

It is addressed by Thomas Cooke in volume 9 (1993) of the *Manual*, section 24 Tales [15], *The King and the Hermit*.

POET, POETRY, AND LANGUAGE

The dating of the poem is difficult. It is close kin to *King Edward and the Shepherd*, notably in its use of the drinking game; it is probably later than that poem and is obviously earlier than the manuscript, which has been dated around 1500. Unlike *King Edward and the Shepherd*, *The King and the Hermit* does not have specific topical references, at least not ones that are evident at this distance. Line 13, "Yt befelle be god Edwerd deys," inasmuch as it implies that there is no possibility of confusion with the current monarch, also implies a date between 1377 (the death of Edward III) and 1461 (the accession of Edward IV), or conceivably after the death of Edward IV in 1483. The language of the poem is consonant with a time between these dates but does not help to make the dating more precise.

Given its language, the poem must be either from the North or from the northern Midlands. It is clearly from within the northern area where Old English or Old Norse long *a* can be retained as long *a* in Middle English (*LALME*, Q47). These sets of rhymes must all be on long *a* for the poet: *skath/bothe* (lines 244–45); *gate/late/state/hate* (lines 444, 447, 450, 453); *sore/were/ther/fare* (lines 516, 519, 522, 525); and *name/home* (lines 448–49).[1]

The vocabulary of the poem, too, reflects a northerly origin: *hopys* (in the sense "suppose" at lines 412, 418), *hyng* (line 261), *hend* (as plural of *hand*, line 415), *at* (for *that*, line 71), *trayst* (line 88), *leyke* (line 367), *spyre* (line 446), and *bos* (line 277). I have emended the beginning of line 277 to "Us bos" from "Bo be," and I think that emendation is correct since *bos* is not a form of *behoves* that is attested from Leicestershire and it is likely to have confused Rate, a Leicestershire scribe. If *bos* is what the poet wrote, then the field of origin for the poem is further restricted: *LALME* (Q80) attests *bos* in one manuscript from each of Derby and Lincolnshire and *bose* and *bous* as minority forms (used less than a third of the time by each of two scribes), one from the West Riding of Yorkshire and the other from Lancashire.

The stanza of *The King and the Hermit* is the twelve-line tail-rhyme stanza familiar from some contemporary romances: *aabccbddbeeb*, with the longer lines usually having four stresses and the shorter lines three. In one instance, an apparently undamaged stanza has only nine lines (lines 121–29). In another, the rhyme scheme is apparently *aabccbddeffe* (lines 430–41), but the sequence *sene/bene/thre/be* can be normalized if the first two infinitives are read without an *-ne* ending. In general this poet is comparatively precise in his rhyming. The rhyme *huntyng/tyme* (lines 208–09) is a rare exception, and as such may be suspected of being a corruption. But at lines 400–01, the rhyme *yate/therate* depends on an artificial lengthening of the short *a* of *at* under stress, and the rhymes *hale/stale/schall* (lines 468, 471, 474) probably depend on a similar lengthening in *schall*.

---

[1] See my earlier edition, *Ten Fifteenth-Century Comic Poems* (pp. 241–42), for more detailed analysis of these rhymes.

THE KING AND THE HERMIT

	Jhesu that is hevyn kyng,	*heaven's*
	Yiff them all god endyng	*Give; a good end*
	(Yf it be thi wyll)	
	And yif them parte of hevyn gam	*a share in the delight of heaven*
5	That well can calle gestes same	*summon guests together*
	With mete and drinke to fylle.	*food*
	When that men be glad and blyth,	*happy*
	Than wer solas god to lyth,	*entertainment; listen to*
	He that wold be stylle.	*If everyone would be quiet*
10	Of a kyng I wyll you telle,	
	What aventour hym befelle,	
	He that wyll herke thertylle.	*If people will listen to it*

	Yt befelle be god Edwerd deys —	*in good Edward's days*
	Forsoth, so this romans seys:	*Truly*
15	Herkyns, I wyll you telle.	*Hearken*
	The kyng to Scherwod gan wend	*went to Sherwood*
	On hys pleyng for to lend	*recreation; stay a while*
	....	
	For to solas hym that stond,	*entertain himself; time*
20	The grete hertes for to hunte	*harts*
	Yn frythys and in felle,	*woods; high moorland*
	With ryall festes and feyr ensemble,	*assembling*
	With all the lordes of that contré;	
	With hym ther gan thei duell.	*they dwelt*

25	Tyll it befell upon a dey	
	To hys fosterse he gan sey,	*foresters*
	"Felous, wher is the best?	*Fellows*
	In your playng wher ye have bene,	
	Wer have ye most gam sene	
30	Of dere in this forest?"	
	They ansuerd and fell on kne,	
	"Overall, lord, is gret plenté	*plenty*
	Both est and west.	
	We may schew you at a syght	*show*

35 Two thousand dere this same nyght
  Or the son go to reste."   *Before*

 An old foster drew hym nere.
 "Lystins, lord, I saw a dere   *Listen*
  Under a tre.
40 So gret a hed as he bare,   *head [of antlers]; carried*
 Sych one saw I never are: *Such a one; before*
  No feyrer myht be.
 He is mour than other two   *bigger than any two others*
 That ever I saw on erth go."
45 Than seyd the kyng so fre,   *noble*
 "Thy waryson I wyll thee yeve   *reward; give*
 Evermour whyll thou doyst lyve,
  That dere thou late me se."   *[If]; let*

 Upon the morne thei ryden fast
50 With hundes and with hornes blast:
  To wodde than are thei wente.
 Nettes and gynnes than leyd he.   *traps*
 Every archer to hys tre,   *[went] to; tree*
  With bowys redy bent.
55 The blew thrys, uncoupuld hundes;   *They; released*
 They reysed the dere up that stondes,   *at that moment*
  So nere thei span and sprent.   *raced and sprang*
 The hundes all, as thei wer wode,   *crazy*
 They ronne the dere into the wode.
60 The kyng hys hors he hent.   *took*

 The kyng sate onne a god courser.   *powerful horse*
 Fast he rode after the dere:
  A rechasyd hym ryght fast.   *He chased him back to the woods*
 Both thorow thyke and thine
65 Thorow the forest he gan wyn   *made his way*
  With hundes and hornes blast.
 The kyng had folowyd hym so long
 Hys god sted was ne sprong: *nearly foundered*
  Hys hert away was past.
70 Horn ne hunter myght he non here.   *nor; none hear*
 So ranne the hundes at the dere   *that*
  Awey was at the last.   *[Got] away*

 The kyng had folowyd hym so long,
 Fro mydey to the evynsong,   *midday; evensong*
75 That lykyd hym full ille.   *pleased him not at all*
 He ne wyst wer that he was,   *did not know where*
 Ne out of the forest for to passe,   *Nor [how] to get out of the forest*

And ther he rode all wylle.   *astray*
"Whyle I may the deylyght se
80   Better is to loge under a tre,"
He seyd hymselve untylle.   *to himself*
The kyng cast in hys wytte,   *considered*
"Yyff I stryke into a pytte,   *go; hole in the ground*
Hors and man myght spylle.   *be destroyed*

85   "I have herd pore men call at morow   *in the morning*
Seynt Julyan send them god harborow   *shelter*
When that they had nede,
And yit when that thei wer trayst   *when they were still trustful*
And of herborow wer abayst,   *perplexed for*
90   He wold them wysse and rede.   *guide; advise*
Seynt Julyan, as I ame trew knyght,
Send me grace this iche nyght   *very*
Of god harbour to sped.   *succeed in getting*
A yift I schall thee gyve: *gift*
95   Every yere whyll that I lyve,
Folke for thi sake to fede."

As he rode, whyll he had lyght.   *for a time*
And at the last he hade syght
Of an hermytage hym besyde.
100   Of that syght he was full feyn,   *glad*
For he wold gladly be in the pleyn,   *clearing*
And theder he gan to ryde.   *thither*
The hermytage he fond ther;
He trowyd a chapell that it wer.   *thought*
105   Than seyd the kyng that tyde,   *time*
"Now, Seynt Julyan, a bonne hostel,   *a good lodging*
As pylgrymes trow full wele.   *believe*
Yonder I wyll abyde."

A lytell yate he fond ney: *gate; nearby*
110   Theron he gan to call and cry
That within myght here.   *That [anyone] within*
That herd an hermyte ther within.
Unto the yate he gan to wyn,   *make his way*
Bedyng his prayer.   *Praying*
115   And when the hermyt saw the kyng,
He seyd, "Sir, gode evynyng."
"Wele worth thee, Sir Frere.   *Happiness befall you*
I pray thee I myght be thi gest,
For I have ryden wyll in this forest,   *astray*
120   And nyght neyghes me nere."   *approaches*

The hermyte seyd, "So mote I the,   *As I hope to prosper*
For sych a lord as ye be,   *such*
   Y have non herbour tyll.   *suitable to*
Bot if it wer never so pore a wyght   *creature*
125 Y ne der not herbour hym a nyght
   Bot he for faute schuld spyll.   *For inevitably he would die for want of food*
Y won here in wyldernes   *live*
With rotys and ryndes among wyld bestes   *roots; bark*
   As it is my Lordes wylle."

130 The kyng seyd, "I thee beseche
The wey to the tounne thou wold me teche.
   And I schall thee behyght   *promise*
That I schall thi travell quyte   *labor recompense*
That thou schall me not wyte   *blame*
135   Or passyth this fortnyght.   *Before; two weeks*
And if thou wyll not, late thi knave go   *let; servant*
To teche me a myle or two   *guide*
   The whylys I have deylyght."   *while*
"By Seynt Mary," seyd the frere,
140 Schorte sirvys getys thou here,   *Scant*
   And I can rede aryght."   *If; tell correctly*

Than seyd the kyng, "My dere frend,
The wey to the towne if I schuld wynd,   *go*
   How fer may it be?"
145 "Syr," he sayd, "so mote I thryve,   *as I hope to thrive*
To the towne is myles fyve
   From this long tre.   *tall*
A wyld wey I hold it wer,   *consider it to be*
The wey to wend (I you suere),   *swear*
150   Bot ye the dey may se."   *Unless*
Than seyd the kyng, "Be Godes myght,   *By*
Ermyte, I schall harbour with thee this nyght,   *Hermit*
   And els I wer we."   *Or else I would be miserable*

"Methinke," seyd the hermyte, "Thou arte a stout syre.   *Seems to me; arrogant lord*
155 I have ete up all the hyre   *wages*
   That ever thou gafe me.
Were I oute of my hermyte wede   *hermit's habit*
Of thi favyll I wold not dred   *trickery*
   Thoff ther wer sych thre.   *Though; three such [as you]*
160 Loth I wer with thee to fyght: *Reluctant*
Y wyll herbour thee all nyght
   And it behovyth so be.   *must*
Sych gode as thou fyndes here, take,   *goods*

And aske thyn in for Godes sake."   *ask for; lodging*
165   "Gladly, sir," seyd he.

      Hys stede into the hous he lede: *led*
      With lytter son he gan hym bed.   *straw*
         Met ne was ther non: *Food*
      The frere he had bot barly stro —   *only barley straw*
170   Two thake-bendesfull, without mo,   *bundles; more*
         Forsoth it was furth born.   *Truly; forth*
      Befor the hors the kyng it leyd.
      "Be Seynt Mayre," the hermyte seyd,   *By; Mary*
         "Other thing have we non."
175   The kyng seyd, "Garamersy, frer.   *Thank you*
      Wele at es ame I now here.   *ease*
         A nyght wyll son be gon."

      The kyng was never so servysable: *ready to serve*
      He hew the wode and keped the stable.   *tended*
180   God fare he gan hym dyght   *He made comfortable conditions for himself*
      And mad hym ryght well at es,
      And ever the fyre befor hys nese   *nose*
         Brynand feyr and bryght.   *Burning*
      "Leve ermyte," seyd the kyng,   *Dear*
185   "Mete, and thou have anything,   *Food, if*
         To soper thou us dyght.
      For sirteynly, as I thee sey,   *certainly*
      I ne hade never so sory a dey
         That I ne had a mery nyght."

190   The kyng seyd, "Be Godes are,   *grace*
      And I sych an hermyte were   *If*
         And wonyd in this forest,   *lived*
      When fosters wer gon to slepe,
      Than I wold cast off my cope   *friar's cape*
195   And wake both est and weste   *work all night*
      Wyth a bow of hue full strong   *yew*
      And arowys knyte in a thong: *bundled; strip of leather*
         That wold me lyke best.   *please me*
      The kyng of venyson hath non nede:
200   Yit myght me hape to have a brede   *happen that I would; roast*
         To glad me and my gest."   *cheer*

      The hermyte seyd to the kyng,
      "Leve sir, wer is thi duellyng?   *dwelling*
         Y praye thou wolde me sey."
205   "Sir," he seyd, "so mote I the,
      Yn the kynges courte I have be

Duellyng many a dey,
And my lord rode on huntyng
As grete lordes doth many tyme
210   That yiff them myche to pley.   *commit themselves much*
And after a grete hert have we redyn   *ridden*
And mekyll travell we have byden   *much labor; undergone*
    And yit he scape awey.   *escaped*

"Todey erly in the morenyng
215 The kyng rode on huntyng,
    And all the courte beden.   *as a group*
A dere we reysed in that stondes   *at that moment*
And ganne chase with our hundes:
    A feyrer had never man sene.
220 Y have folowyd hym all this dey
And ryden many a wylsom wey: *uncertain*
    He dyd me trey and tene.   *trouble; hardship*
I pray you, helpe me I wer at es.   *[so that] I*
Thou boughtes never so god sirvese   *gained*
225   In sted ther thou hast bene."   *any place where*

The ermyte seyd, "So God me save,
Thou take sych gode as we have: *goods*
    We schall not hyll it with thee."   *hide; from*
Bred and chese forth he brought.
230 The kyng ete whyles, hym thought; *for a [long] time, it seemed to him*
    Non other mete saw he.   *food*
Sethen thyn drynke he dreughe.   *Then weak; drew*
Theron he had sone inoughe.   *enough*
    Than seyd the kyng so fre,   *noble*
235 "Hermyt, pute up this mete tyte.   *quickly*
And if I mey I schall thee quyte   *repay*
    Or passyd be these monethys thre."   *Before*

Than seyd the kyng, "Be Godes grace,
Thou wonnys in a mery place!
240   To schote thou schuldes lere.   *shoot; learn*
When the fosters are go to reste   *gone*
Somtyme thou myght have of the best,   *some of the best*
    All of the wylld dere.
Y wold hold it for no skath   *harm*
245 Thoff thou had bow and arowys bothe   *Though*
    Allthoff thou be a frere.   *Although*
Ther is no foster in all this fe   *estate*
That wold sych herme to thee; *Who wishes you the harm that you imagine*
    Ther thou may leve here."   *In that case; feed yourself*

250 The armyte seyd, "So mote thou go,   *hermit*
   Hast thou any other herand than so   *errand than that*
    Onto my lord the kynge?[1]
   Y schall be trew to hym, I trow,   *expect*
   For to weyte my lordes prow   *look out for; profit*
255 For dred of sych a thing.
   For iff I wer take with sych a dede,   *caught in*
   To the courte thei wold me lede
    And to preson me bryng;   *prison*
   Bot if I myght my raunson gete,   *Unless; get my ransom*
260 Be bond in prison and sorow grete
    And in perell to hyng."   *danger of hanging*

   Then seyd the kyng, "I wold not lete, *[If I were you] I would not refrain*
   When thou arte in this forest sette,   *situated*
    To stalke when men are at rest.
265 Now, as thou arte a trew man,
   Iff thou ought of scheting can, *know anything about shooting*
    Ne hyll it not with thi gest.   *hide; from*
   For, be Hym that dyghed on tre,   *died; (i.e., the cross)*
   Ther schall no man wyte for me,   *know because of*
270 Whyll my lyve wyll lest.   *last*
   Now hermyte, for thi professyon,   *by your vows*
   Yiff thou have any venison,
    Thou yiff me of the best."

   The ermyte seyd, "Men of grete state,
275 Oure ordyr thei wold make full of bate   *strife*
    Aboute schych mastery.   *such feats*
   Us bos be in prayer and in penans,   *It behooves us; penance*
   And arne therine by chans *we are in it [the forest] by chance*
    And not be archery.   *because of*
280 Many dey I have her ben
   And flesche mete I ete non   *I ate no flesh*
    Bot mylke of the ky.   *Except; cows*
   Warme thee wele and go to slepe,   *well*
   And I schall lape thee with my cope,   *wrap*
285 Softly to lyghe.   *lie*

   "Thou semys a felow," seyd the frere.   *a regular guy*
   "Yt is long gon seth any was here   *ago since anyone*
    Bot thou thyselve tonyght."
   Unto a cofyr he gan go   *chest*

---

[1] Lines 251–52: That is, *"Do you have any other reason for coming here besides talking me into violating Forest Law so that I can be fined by the king?"*

290	And toke forth candylles two,	
	And sone thei wer ilyght.	*lighted*
	A cloth he brought, and bred full whyte,	
	And venyson ibake tyte.	*baked quickly*
	Ayen he yede full ryght:	*Back again; went directly*
295	Venyson isalt and fressch he brought,	*salted*
	And bade hym chese wheroff hym thought	*choose whatever he liked*
	Colopys for to dyght.	*To make fried slices from*
	Well may ye wyte, inow thei had.	*know, enough*
	The kyng ete and made hym glad	
300	And grete laughtur he lowghe:	*laughed*
	"Nere I had spoke of archery	*If it were not that*
	I myght have ete my bred full dryghe."	*dry*
	The kyng made it full towghe.	*gave him a hard time about it*
	"Now Crystes blyssing have sych a frere	
305	That thus canne ordeyn our soper	*prepare*
	And stalke under the wode bowe.	*bough*
	The kyng hymselve, so mote I the,	
	Ys not better at es than we,	
	And we have drinke inowghe."	*If*
310	The hermyt seyd, "Be seynt Savyour,	*the holy Savior*
	Y have a pote of galons foure	
	Standing in a wro.	*nook*
	Ther is bot thou and I and my knave:	
	Som solas schall we have	
315	Sethyn we are no mo."	*more*
	The hermyte callyd hys knave full ryght —	
	Wylkyn Alyn, forsoth, he hyght —	*was called*
	And bad hym belyve go,	*quickly*
	And taught hym prively to a sted	*showed him secretly to a place*
320	To feche the hors corne and bred,	*grain and bread*
	"And luke that thou do so."	*see that*
	Unto the knave seyd the frere,	
	"Felow, go wyghtly here.	*swiftly*
	Thou do as I thee sey.	
325	Besyde my bed thou must goo	
	And take up a sloughte of strawe	*layer*
	Als softly as thou may.	
	A howvyd pote, that stondes ther,	*lidded*
	And Godes forbot that we it spare	*God forbid*
330	To drynke to it be dey.	*until it is day*
	And bryng me forth my schell,	*cup*
	And every man schall have hys dele,	*share*
	And I schall kenne us pley."	*teach*

     The hermyte seyd, "Now schal I se
335 Yff thou any felow be
       Or of pley canst ought."   *know anything about play*
     The kyng seyd, "So mote I the,
     Sey thou what thou wyll with me:
       Thy wyll it schall be wrought."   *done*
340 "When the coppe commys into the plas,   *cup comes; place*
     Canst thou sey 'Fusty bandyas'
       And thinke it in thi thought?
     And thou schall her a totted frere   *tipsy*
     Sey 'Stryke pantner'
345   And in the cope leve ryght nought."

     And when the coppe was forth brought,
     Yt was oute of the kynges thought,
       That word that he schuld sey.
     The frere seyd "Fusty bandyas."
350 Than seyd the kyng, "Alas, alas."
       Hys word it was awey.
     "What! Arte thou mad?" seyd the frere,
     "Canst thou not sey 'Stryke pantener?'
       Wylt thou lerne all dey?
355 And if thou efte forgete it ons,   *again; once*
     Thou getes no drinke in these wons   *this dwelling*
       Bot yiff thou thinke upon thi pley."   *Unless you pay attention*

     "Fusty bandias," the frere seyd,
     And yafe the coppe sych a breyd   *jerk*
360 That well nygh off it yede.   *nearly; went*
       The knave fyllyd it up and yede in plas.   *went to [his] place*
     The kyng seyd "Fusty bandyas":
       Therto hym stod gret nede.   *To do it he had great need*
     "Fusty bandyas," seyd the frere,
365 "How long hast thou stond here   *stood*
       Or thou couth do thi dede?   *knew how*
     Fyll this eft and late us leyke,   *again; play*
     And betwen rost us a styke,   *in the interval; steak*
       Thus holy lyve to lede."

370 The knave fyllyd the coppe full tyte   *quickly*
     And brought it furth with grete delyte;
       Befor hym gan it stand.
     "Fusty bandyas" seyd the frere;
     The kyng seyd "Stryke pantener"
375   And toke it in hys hand,
     And stroke halve and more;   *And drank up half and more*
       "Thys is the best pley, I suere,   *swear*

That ever I saw in lond.
Y hyght thee, hermyte, I schall thee yeve,   *assure*
380 Y schall thee quyte, if that I lyve,   *[That] I; pay back*
   The gode pley thou hast us fonnd."

Than seyd the ermyte, "God quyte all,
Bot when thou commys to the lordes haule   *hall*
   Thou wyll forgete the frere.
385 Bot wher thou commyst, nyght or dey,
Yit myght thou thinke upon the pley
   That thou hast sene here.
And thou com among jentyllmen
The wyll laugh and thou hem it ken,   *They; if; teach*
390   And make full mery chere.
And iff thou comyst here for a nyght,
A colype I dere thee behyght,   *slice of fried meat I dare; promise*
   All of the wyld dere."

The kyng seyd, "Be Hym that me bought,   *By Him who redeemed me*
395 Syre," he seyd, "ne thinke it nought,
   That thou be thus forgete.
Tomorow sone when it is dey
I schall quyte, iff that I may,
   All that we have here ete.
400 And when we com to the kynges yate,
We schall not long stond therate: *at it*
   In we schall be lete.
And by my feyth, I schall not blyne   *hesitate*
Tyll the best that is therine   *therein*
405   Betwenn us two be sete."

Th'ermyte seyd, "Be Hym that me bought,
Syre," he seyd, "ne thynke it nought.
   Y suere thee by my ley,   *faith*
Y have be ther and takyn dole,   *handouts*
410 And have hade many merry mele,   *meal*
   Y dare full savely sey.   *safely*
Hopys thou I wold for a mase   *Do you think that; delusion*
Stond in the myre ther and dase   *mud; act stunned*
   Nehand halve a dey?   *Nearly*
415 The charyté commys thorow sych menys hend,   *charity [that] comes; hands*
He havys full lytell that stond at hend   *[of it] who stands nearby*
   Or that he go awey.   *Before*

"Hopys thou that I ame so preste   *willing*
For to stond at the kyng yate and reste
420   Ther pleys for to lere?   *behavior; learn*

Y have neyghbors her nygh-hand: *nearby*
I send them of my presente   *as my gift*
  Sydes of the wyld dere.
Of my presantes thei are feyn: *glad*
425 Bred and ale thei send me ageyn.   *in return*
  Thusgates lyve I here."   *In this way*
The kyng seyd, "So mote I the,
Hermyte, me pays wele with thee: *you please me well*
  Thou arte a horpyd frere."   *bold*

430 The kyng seyd, "Yit myght thou com sum dey   *Nevertheless*
Unto the courte for to pley,
  Aventourys for to sene.
Thou wote not what thee betyde may
Or that thou gon awey: *Before*
435   The better thou may bene.   *You may be better off*
Thoff I be here in pore clothing,
Y ame no bayschyd for to bryng   *not abashed*
  Gestys two or thre.   *Guests*
Ther is no man in all those wonys   *the whole dwelling*
440 That schall myssey to thee onys,   *say nasty things; once*
  Bot as I sey, so schall it be."

"Sertes," seyd the hermyte than,
"Y hope thou be a trew man: *think*
  I schall aventour the gate.   *risk the trip*
445 Bot tell me fyrst, leve syre,
After what man schall I spyre,   *ask*
  Both erly and late?"
"Jhake Flecher, that is my name:
All men knowys me at home.
450   I ame at yong man state.   *My status is a young man's*
And thoff I be here in pore wede   *clothing*
Yn sych a stede I can thee lede   *place*
  Ther we schall be made full hate."   *warm*

"Aryse up, Jake, and go with me,
455 And more off my privyté   *private business*
  Thou schall se somthyng."
Into a chambyr he hym lede:
The kyng saughe aboute the hermytes bed
  Brod arowys hynge.   *hang*
460 The frere gaff hym a bow in hond.
"Jake," he seyd, "draw up the bond."   *string*
  He myght oneth styre the streng.   *hardly stir*
"Sir," he seyd, "so have I blys,   *as I hope for the happiness of heaven*

| | Ther is non archer that may schet in this | *shoot this* |
| 465 | That is with my lord the kyng." | |

	An arow of an elle long,	*A forty-five-inch-long arrow*
	In hys bow he it throng,	*thrust*
	And to the hede he gan it hale.	*pull*
	Ther is no dere in this foreste	
470	And it wold onne hym feste	*land*
	Bot it schuld spyll his stale.	*urine*
	"Jake, seth thou can of flecher crafte,	*since; know*
	Thou may me es with a schafte."	*help*
	Than seyd Jake, "I schall."	
475	....	
	....	
	....	

	"Jake, and I wyst that thou wer trew,	*if*
	Or and I thee better knew,	*Or if*
480	Mour thou schuldes se."	
	The kyng to hym grete othys swer:	*oaths*
	"The covenand we made whyleare,	*a while before*
	I wyll that it hold be."	*held*
	Tyll two trowys he gan hym lede:	*To; trees*
485	Of venyson ther was many a brede.	*roast*
	"Jake, how thinkes thee?	
	Whyle ther is dere in this forest,	
	Somtyme I may have of the best	
	The kyng wytesave on me.	*[That] the king would confer*

490	"Jake, and thou wyll of myn arowys have,	*if*
	Take thee of them, and sum thou leve,	*[some] of*
	And go we to our pley."	
	And thus thei sate with "Fusty bandyas,"	
	And with "Stryke pantener" in that plas,	
495	Tyll it was nerehand dey	*close to*
	When tyme was com ther rest to take.	
	On morn thei rose when thei gan wake.	
	The frere began to sey,	
	"Jake, I wyll with thee go	
500	Yn thi felowschype a myle our two,	*or*
	Tyll thou have redy wey."	*an easily followed path*

	"Ye," seyd the kyng, "mekyll thanke,	*Yes; many thanks*
	Bot when we last nyght togeder dranke,	
	Thinke what thou me behyght:	*promised*
505	That thou schuld com som dey	
	Unto the courte for to pley	

What tyme thou se thou myght."   *When you saw you could*
"Sertes," seyd the hermyte than,
"Y schall com, as I ame trew man,
510   Or tomorow at nyght."   *Before*
Ather betaught other gode dey.   *Each one bid the other*
The kyng toke the redy wey:
    Home he rode full ryght.

Knyghtes and squyres many mo,
515   All that nyght thei rode and go,
    With sygheng and sorrowyng sore.   *sighing*
They cryghed and blew with hydoys bere,   *cried; hideous clamor*
Yiff thei myght of ther lord here,   *[To see] if they might*
    Wher that ever he were.   *Wherever he might be*
520   When the kyng his bugyl blew,   *bugle*
Knyghtes and fosters wele it knew,
    And lystind to hym ther.
Many men that wer masyd and made,   *dazed; crazed*
The blast of that horn made them glad:
525   To the town than gan thei fare.   *they went*

EXPLANATORY NOTES TO THE KING AND THE HERMIT

ABBREVIATIONS: *MED*: *Middle English Dictionary*; *OED*: *Oxford English Dictionary*.

1   *Jhesu that is hevyn kyng.* This text often has genitives with no inflectional ending.

13   Unlike *John the Reeve*, *The King and the Hermit* does not name which Edward is being spoken of; and unlike *King Edward and the Shepherd*, *The King and the Hermit* is not at all specific about contemporary people or events. The only identifier we have for which Edward is meant is the phrase in line 13: "be god Edwerd deys." The phrase implies that the poem is set in the past, so not in the time of a contemporary king Edward. The adjective *god* more or less eliminates the deposed Edward II, in comparison to his much more successful father or son. If the poem is late enough, the Yorkist king Edward IV is a possible target for the allusion (reigned 1461–70 and again 1471–83), and the northern origins of the poem are compatible with widespread support of the Yorkists in the North. And Edward IV did enjoy hunting in his royal forests and had new apartments in Nottingham Castle that would have made a stay there while hunting in Sherwood Forest an attractive proposition (see Ross, *Edward IV*, pp. 9, 55, 148, 261, 271, 354 for the hunting, p. 272 for the apartments). But Edward I was a hunter too (Prestwich, *Edward I*, pp. 115–17), as was Edward III. Froissart reports that during his 1359 expedition in France, the king had for his personal use thirty mounted falconers and their loads of birds and sixty couples of big hounds and as many coursing dogs, with which he went either hunting or wild-fowling every day (Froissart, *Chronicles*, ed. Brereton, p. 165).

     Of the various Edwards, Edward III is the one most likely to have been looked back upon by everyone, of whatever faction, as "god Edwerd." But what king is understood to be referred to here is very much dependent on the time and politics of the reader. A sixteenth-century somewhat analogous chapbook poem, *King Edward IV and the Tanner of Tamworth*, is explicit in its title (which may however be editorial) about which King Edward it is who goes out hunting and meets a suspicious and surly tanner, trades horses with him, and eventually rewards him with lands, but the poem itself never specifies its protagonist beyond "King Edward." That poem is closely analogous to a fifteenth-century poem, *The King and the Barker*, from Cambridge University Library MS Ee.4.35, in which the king is never named. Similarly a seventeenth-century poem, *The Pleasant Ballad of King Henry II and the Miller of Mansfield*, specifies only in its (editorial?) title which King Henry goes hunting in Sherwood Forest, is lost, and takes lodging with a suspicious and surly miller who eventually warms up to him and feeds him venison. For the poets in question, the main value in choosing an

237

Edward or a Henry as protagonist may be that there are several of them, safely in the past, and there is therefore no need for historical detail beyond the contrast between the richly dressed king and the commoner he meets and, in most cases, the general knowledge of poaching practices and regulations.

16   *The kyng to Scherwod gan wend. Gan* is a past tense marker in this poem; *gan wend* means "went." Sherwood Forest in Nottinghamshire once covered a much larger area than it does now. The area was a royal forest, and like other royal forests, protected from hunting except by the king and those he explicitly authorized. The territory of a royal "forest" included not just woodland but also open land and wetland, a variety of habitats. A bureaucracy of foresters existed to patrol and protect the forest and the wildlife. Modern tradition remembers Robin Hood as one inhabitant of and poacher in Sherwood Forest, this poem tells of another, but there were poachers in all the royal forests of England.

63   The manuscript reads: "A ro chasyd hym ry3t fast." This makes no sense: a deer would not be chasing the king. But neither would the king be chasing a roe, the smallest of the three species of deer in England at the time (red, fallow, and roe). It would be a red deer (a hart) that would be impressively large and carry a large set of antlers. "A" must signify "he" (not usual in this scribe's writing, but all the more likely then that it would confuse him in a source text), and "ro chasyd" should be read as "rechasyd" (as it is by Albert Kurz in his edition).

69   *Hys hert away was past.* Probably "the horse's spirit was broken" but could be "the hart had escaped."

85–87 *I have herd pore men call at morow / Seynt Julyan send them god harborow / When that they had nede.* St. Julian the Hospitaller was the legendary patron saint of hospitality. Edward tells us that he has heard poor men calling on Julian in the morning (presumably before setting off on a journey, or perhaps these are homeless men) to send them a good lodging when they need one. Middle English literature has other instances of travelers calling on St. Julian for lodging when they are, like Edward here, stranded and in need of shelter. Sir Gawain thanks "Jesus and sayn Gilyan" on his first glimpse of Hautdesert and goes on to petition them, "Now bone hostel . . . I beseche yow yette" (line 776) in *Sir Gawain and the Green Knight*. For further information, consult the introduction to *The Life of St. Julian the Hospitaller in the "Scottish Legendary" (c. 1400)*, edited by E. Gordon Whatley, with Anne B. Thompson and Robert K. Upchurch, in *Saints' Lives in Middle English Collections* (Kalamazoo, MI: Medieval Institute Publications, 2004), pp. 307–15.

106   The manuscript reads: "Now seynt Julyan a bonne vntyll," here emended for sense and rhyme. The conventional plea to St. Julian was for "bon hostel," "good lodging." Compare Chaucer's *House of Fame*, line 1022 ("Seynt Julyan, loo, bon hostel"), and line 776 of *Sir Gawain and the Green Knight*.

107   *As pylgrymes trow full wele.* That is, pilgrims believe that Julian provides "a bonne hostel."

117   *Wele worth thee, Sir Frere.* The hermit is apparently a friar of either the Carmelite or Augustinian order. Both orders had their origin in eremiticism, but both, soon after their arrival in England, moved towards communal life in larger towns. Nevertheless, the early foundations were in isolated areas, the hermit's life was the ideal underlying both orders, and it was possible to have a small priory in an outlying area with only a single friar. For information on both orders, see Knowles, *Religious Orders in England*, 1:194–204, 2:144–51.

122–23   *For sych a lord as ye be, / Y have non herbour tyll. For* is a conjunction here, and *tyll* a preposition. The two lines together mean "For I have no shelter appropriate for such a lord as you are."

139   Mary, the Virgin Mother of Jesus, was the most familiar and the most frequently invoked of all the saints. If there is a particular aptness to her invocation here and at line 173 below, it is that she too was rather famously treated with minimal hospitality in her hour of need, when she was turned away from the inn in Bethlehem.

140   *Schorte sirvys getys thou here.* That is, no service at all. This is probably a reference to the customary service owed by a tenant to a lord. Here and below at lines 154–56 the hermit is emphasizing (ironically, as his guest is after all the king) that he doesn't have any duty to his pushy and unwanted guest.

155–56   The hermit's irony is scathing in the face of the stranger's declaration that he intends to stay overnight.

178–79   George Shuffelton aptly remarks, "The king . . . performs his chores before dinner with the enthusiasm of a visitor to a dude ranch" (*Codex Ashmole 61*, p. 592).

193–94   Probably the rhyme is on the forms *slape* and *cape*.

213   *scape.* This is an unusual form of the past tense, which should be *scaped*, or if the strong verb form, *scope*.

224   *Thou boughtes never so god sirvese.* That is, "you have never gained such good compensation as you will by helping me." The form of the verb "boughtes" is an impossible one: it was incorrect in every dialect area of England to have an *–es* ending on a past tense strong verb such as *buy*. But could this be some form of hypercorrection, with a southern scribe trying to reproduce what he imagines to be a northern dialect form, since *–es* is a normal ending in the present tense for the second person singular in the North?

232   *Sethen thyn drynke he dreughe.* "Then he [probably the hermit] drew [from a cask] thin drink." The thin drink is probably weak beer.

286   The hermit has a change of heart between the stanzas.

292–95   The richness of this food and its presentation are in striking contrast to the hermit's professed poverty. Candles, a tablecloth, and fine white bread for trenchers were all extravagances for rich men's tables. Baked venison implies both that the hermit has been poaching deer in the royal forest and that he has access to the services of someone with an oven and fuel (probably also illegally gathered from the royal forest) to stoke it. See lines 421–25 for an explanation for the hermit's wealth.

320   *To feche the hors corne and bred.* Bread made of beans or pease, sometimes bran and chaff, was baked specifically for horse fodder.

328   *A howvyd pote, that stondes ther.* The word *howved* is unattested in *OED* or *MED*; Hazlitt reads *hownyd*, a form for *honeyed*. I take *howuyd* as meaning "lidded," related to *houve*, a substantive meaning "cap" or "head covering."

329–30 *And Godes forbot that we it spare / To drynke to it be dey.* That is more literally, "And [it is] God's prohibition that we refrain from [emptying] it, to drink until it is day."

341–45 *Fusty bandyas* and *stryke pantner* or *pantnever* appear to be nonsense syllables, but they can be resolved into the following components:

> fusty: smelling of the cask
> ban: bon, or good
> dias, dyas: medicines
> stryke: drink up
> pant: gasp
> ner: never

"This is a good fusty medicine." "Drink it up at one gulp."

The principal oddity is the component *strike*. It is nowhere beyond this poem attested as a verb meaning "drink up," although it seems to mean exactly that in line 376 (which *MED* cites in def. 10b).

The game seems to be slightly more demanding than the drinking game in *King Edward and the Shepherd*. Whenever the servant fills the cup and puts it in the designated place, the first to call "Fusty bandias" gets to drink, and can continue till the other calls out "Strike pantner," when he in turn gets the cup and finishes the drink in it.

369   The hermit tends to use heavy irony. The consumption of excessive amounts of meat and liquor would not constitute "holy life," but the diet of roots and bark he claims to follow at line 128 would certainly be ascetic deprivation enough to be holy.

409–11 *Y have be ther and takyn dole, / And have hade many merry mele, / Y dare full savely sey.* After the mocking echo of the last lines, the hermit is now exercising a heavy irony. As becomes clear in the next lines, very little food is distributed to the poor at the king's court, and he is unwilling to hang around half a day waiting for it when he has a sweet system of exchange with his neighbors worked out at home.

422   *presente.* The rhyme on *nygh-hand* depends on the northern form *presand.*

423   *Sydes of the wyld dere.* A side of deer is half the animal split the length of the backbone, a more manageable size for a household to deal with at a single time than the whole carcass.

434   *Or that thou gon awey. Gon* is an impossible form of the verb *go* in the second person singular subjunctive. My guess is that the poet originally used the verb

gang(en) or *gong(en)* in the phrase "or that thou gong awey," and that a subsequent scribe tried to make sense of an unfamiliar verb by converting it partway to a more southern form, choosing the synonymous similar verb *go(n)* but not adjusting the ending appropriately.

436   *Thoff I be here in pore clothing.* Unlike the king in *John the Reeve*, this king is apparently dressed in shabby clothes. But they must be only relatively shabby (hunting clothes fit for a king), because the hermit recognizes him immediately as a great lord (see line 122). Of course the excellent horse and trappings would be an additional clue.

448   *Jhake Flecher.* "Jake the Arrow-maker." As Shuffelton points out, "The lengthy description of the hunt at the outset of the tale and King Edward's choice of pseudonyms . . . only emphasize the common bonds between the poacher/ host and his royal guest. Hermits, unlike peasants, were essentially outside the bounds of class" (*Codex Ashmole 61*, pp. 591–92). That makes *The King and the Hermit* different from the other king and commoner poems, in that the hermit is not a peasant.

471   *Bot it schuld spyll his stale.* A deer will often empty its bladder when frightened or wounded.

525   The manuscript breaks off here, but from the other king and commoner stories certain aspects of the ending are predictable. As in *Rauf Coilȝear* (*RC*), the king finds his way back to court on his own. The next day the hermit decides to follow his guest to court and take him up on his offer of hospitality there, despite his misgivings, as in *King Edward and the Shepherd* (*KS*), *John the Reeve* (*JR*), and *RC*. Once there, he runs into conflict with the porter (as in *JR*) but on the king's instructions, does get into the hall, where he is uneasy at feeling himself very out of place and where courtiers laugh at him. Eventually he spots his guest, is made to feel terrified of reprisals for his poaching when the man proposes to play the drinking game in front of the king's courtiers, reproaches him, and only then discovers that his guest has been the king (roughly as in *KS*). Because in this story the antagonist is a hermit friar, it is unlikely that the ending can involve the king's knighting the (often) reluctant man and giving him lands and riches (as in *JR* and *RC,* and roughly as in the later *King Edward IV and a Tanner of Tamworth* and the much later *Pleasant Ballad of King Henry II and the Miller of Mansfield*). But there is undoubtedly some comparably rich reward for his hospitality, perhaps advancement in the Church.

TEXTUAL NOTES TO THE KING AND THE HERMIT

COPY-TEXT: Oxford, Bodleian Library, MS Ashmole 61 (Bodley 6922), fols. 157r–161v.
ABBREVIATIONS: MS: manuscript, here referring to copy-text.

title	No title appears in the MS. Instead the words "Amen quod Rate" appear above the poem, running from within the left margin.
14–15	In the right margin of the MS, canceled, appear these words: *ffor soth as the / romans seys*.
15	MS: *Herkyng I wyll ȝou telle*. Emendation for sense.
18	This line is missing in the MS; no gap.
32	MS: *Ouer all lord is gret plete*. Emendation for sense.
50	MS: *With hundes and with honnes blast*. Emendation for sense.
59	MS: *They ronne the dere as thei wer wode*. The line as it stands in the MS partly repeats line 58. Conjectural emendation.
69	MS: *Hys hert away was s past*.
88	MS: *And yit whe that thei wer trauyst*. Emendations for sense (*when, trayst*) and rhyme (*trayst*).
99	MS: *Off an hermyte <...> hym besyde*. But the hermit is inside his hermitage, as we learn below (line 112); it must be the building in a clearing that the king spots. Emendation for sense.
103	MS: *An hermytage he fond ther*. Emended for sense (since after the emendation to line 99, this is the second mention of the hermitage).
109	MS: *A lytell ȝate he fond ner*. Emendation for rhyme.
116	MS: *He seyd sir gode euyn*. Emendation for rhyme.
124	MS: *Bot if it <illegible...> pore a wyȝht*.
129 ff.	The stanza form calls for three more lines.
135	MS: *Or passyȝh this fortnyȝt*. Emendation for sense.
152	MS: *Ermyte I schall herabour with the this nyȝht*. Emendation for sense.
170	MS: *Two thake bendes full without no*. Emendation for better sense.
173	The saint's name is blurred: What I read as "mayre" is read "mayry" by Kurz and Shuffelton, and "Mary" by Hazlitt. At line 139 of the poem, the name is spelled *Mary*.
193	MS: *When fosters wer gon to slep<.>*. The last letter is blurred.
195	MS: *And wake beth est and weste*.
215	MS: *The kyng rode on hutyng*.
220	MS: *Y haue <..>lowyd hym all this dey*. There is a blot before "lowyd."
224	MS: *Thou boughtes never so god siruege*. Emendation for rhyme.
228	MS: *We schall we not hyll with the*. Emendation for sense.
275	This line is followed by the following canceled line: *And on to prison bryng*.

277	MS: *Bo be in prayer and in penans*. Emendation for sense.
318	MS: *And bad hym be lyue and go*. Emendation for sense.
334	MS: *The hermyte seyd now scha<.> i se*. The last letter of *shal* is blurred.
360	MS: *That well ny3 of iyede*. Emended for sense.
361	MS: *The knaue fyllyd and vp it 3ede in plas*.
367	MS: *ffyll this eft and late vs lyke*. Emendation for sense.
374	MS: *The kyng seyd stryke pantneuer*. Emendation for rhyme.
423	MS: *Be sydes of the wyld dere*. Emendation for sense.
438	MS: *Yiftys two our thre*. Emendation for sense.
466	MS: *An arow off an elle lond*. Emendation for sense.
467	MS: *In hys low he it throng*. Emendation for sense.
474 ff.	After line 474, three lines are missing from the stanza. No gap in MS.
490	MS: *Jake and thou wyll ~~ha~~ of myn arowys haue*.
507	MS: *When tyme thou se thou myght*. Emendation for sense.
516	MS: *With sygheng and sorrowyg sore*.
525	The poem breaks off here, at the end of a leaf. There is one more leaf in the MS, but it is blank.

❦ BIBLIOGRAPHY

A number of resources are referred to by abbreviation throughout this book:

ATU = Uther, Hans-Jörg. *The Types of International Folktales: A Classification and Bibliography, Based on the System of Antti Aarne and Stith Thompson.* 3 vols. Helsinki: Suomalainen Tiedeakatemia, 2004.

DOST = Craigie, William A., et al., eds. *A Dictionary of the Older Scottish Tongue from the Twelfth Century to the End of the Seventeenth.* 12 vols. Chicago: University of Chicago Press; Aberdeen: Aberdeen University Press; and Oxford: Oxford University Press, 1937–2004.

LALME = McIntosh, Angus, M. L. Samuels, and Michael Benskin, eds., with the assistance of Margaret Laing and Keith Williamson. *A Linguistic Atlas of Late Mediaeval English.* 4 vols. Aberdeen: Aberdeen University Press, 1986.

Manual = Severs, J. Burke, Albert E. Hartung, and Peter G. Beidler, eds. *A Manual of the Writings in Middle English, 1050–1500.* 11 vols. New Haven: Connecticut Academy of Arts and Sciences, 1967–2005.

MED = Kurath, Hans, and Sherman M. Kuhn, eds. *Middle English Dictionary.* Ann Arbor: University of Michigan Press, 1954–2000.

NCE = *The New Catholic Encyclopedia.* Ed. Berard L. Marthaler et al. Second ed. 15 vols. Detroit, MI: Thomson/Gale, 2003.

NIMEV = Boffey, Julia, and A. S. G. Edwards. *A New Index of Middle English Verse.* London: British Library, 2005.

ODNB = *Oxford Dictionary of National Biography.* Oxford: Oxford University Press, 2004; online ed., Jan. 2008.

OED = *The Oxford English Dictionary.* Second ed. Oxford: Oxford University Press, 1989.

RSTC = Pollard, A. W., and G. R. Redgrave. *A Short-title Catalogue of Books Printed in England, Scotland, and Ireland and of English Books Printed Abroad 1475–1640.* Second ed., Rev. W. A. Jackson, F. S. Ferguson, and Katharine F. Pantzer. 3 vols. London: Bibliographical Society, 1976–91.

Whiting = Whiting, Bartlett Jere, with the collaboration of Helen Wescott Whiting. *Proverbs, Sentences, and Proverbial Phrases from English Writings Mainly before 1500.* Cambridge, MA: The Belknap Press of Harvard University Press, 1968.

The Anglo-Norman Text of "Le Lai du cor." Ed. C. T. Erickson. Oxford: Basil Blackwell, 1973.

Arber, Edward, ed. *A Transcript of the Registers of the Company of Stationers of London, 1554–1640.* 2 vols. New York: Peter Smith, 1950.

Baldwin, F. E. *Sumptuary Legislation and Personal Regulation in England.* Baltimore, MD: Johns Hopkins University Press, 1926.

The Bannatyne Manuscript: National Library of Scotland, Advocates' MS.1.1.6. Introduced by Denton Fox and W. A. Ringler. London: Scolar Press in association with the National Library of Scotland, 1980.

Bawcutt, Priscilla. "Scottish Manuscript Miscellanies from the Fifteenth to the Seventeenth Century." *English Manuscript Studies 1100–1700* 12 (2005), 46–73.

Birrel, Jean R. "The Medieval English Forest." *Journal of Forest History* 24 (1980), 78–85.

Blanchfield, Lynne S. "The Romances in MS Ashmole 61: An Idiosyncratic Scribe." In *Romance in Medieval England*. Ed. Maldwyn Mills, Jennifer Fellows, and Carol Meale. Cambridge: D. S. Brewer, 1991. Pp. 65–87.

———. "Rate Revisited: The Compilation of Narrative Works in MS Ashmole 61." In *Romance Reading on the Book*. Ed. J. Fellows et al. Cardiff: University of Wales Press, 1996. Pp. 208–20.

Bloch, R. Howard. *Medieval Misogyny and the Invention of Western Romantic Love*. Chicago: University of Chicago Press, 1991.

Boffey, Julia. *Manuscripts of English Courtly Love Lyrics in the Later Middle Ages*. Cambridge: D. S. Brewer, 1985.

Boffey, Julia, and Carol Meale. "Selecting the Text: Rawlinson C.86 and Some Other Books for London Readers." In *Regionalism in Late Medieval Manuscripts and Texts: Essays Celebrating the Publication of "A Linguistic Atlas of Late Mediaeval English."* Ed. Felicity Riddy. Cambridge: D. S. Brewer, 1991. Pp. 143–69.

Boffey, Julia, and A. S. G. Edwards. *A New Index of Middle English Verse*. London: British Library, 2005.

Bolte, Johannes, and Georg Polívka. *Anmerkungen zu der Kinder- und Hausmärchen der Brüder Grimm*. Second ed. 1914. Rpt. Hildesheim: Georg Olms, 1963.

Brewer, Derek. "The International Medieval Popular Comic Tale in England." In *The Popular Literature of Medieval England*. Ed. Thomas J. Heffernan. Knoxville: University of Tennessee Press, 1985. Pp. 131–47.

———. "The Comedy of Corpses in Medieval Comic Tales." In *Risus Mediaevalis: Laughter in Medieval Literature and Art*. Ed. Herman Braet, Guido Latré, and Werner Verbeke. Louvain: Louvain University Press, 2003. Pp. 11–29.

———, ed. *Medieval Comic Tales*. Second ed. Cambridge: D. S. Brewer, 1996.

Brown, Carleton. *English Lyrics of the XIIIth Century*. Oxford: Clarendon, 1932.

Busby, Keith. "Conspicuous by Its Absence: The English Fabliau." *Dutch Quarterly Review* 12 (1982), 30–41.

Calendar of the Patent Rolls: Edward III. Vol. 10. London: Anthony Brothers, 1909.

Cartwright, Jane. "Virginity and Chastity Tests in Medieval Welsh Prose." In *Medieval Virginities*. Ed. Ruth Evans, Sarah Salih, and Anke Bernau. Toronto: University of Toronto Press, 2003. Pp. 56–79.

Chaucer, Geoffrey. *The Riverside Chaucer*. Third ed. Gen. ed. Larry D. Benson. Boston: Houghton Mifflin, 1987.

Cooke, Thomas, with Peter Whiteford and Nancy Mohr McKinley. "Middle English Comic Tales." In *A Manual of the Writings in Middle English 1050–1500*. Ed. J. Burke Severs, Albert E. Hartung, and Peter G. Beidler. 11 vols. New Haven: Connecticut Academy of Arts and Sciences, 1967–2005. 9:3138–3328, 3472–3592.

Cowan, Ian Borthwick. *Medieval Religious Houses, Scotland*. London: Longman, 1976.

Craigie, W. A., et al., eds. *A Dictionary of the Older Scottish Tongue from the Twelfth Century to the End of the Seventeenth*. 12 vols. Chicago: University of Chicago Press; Aberdeen: Aberdeen University Press; and Oxford: Oxford University Press, 1937–2004.

Curtius, Ernst Robert. *European Literature and the Latin Middle Ages*. Trans. Willard R. Trask. New York: Pantheon Books, 1953.

de Beaulieu, Marie-Anne Polo. *La Scala coeli de Jean de Gobi*. Paris: Édition du Centre national de la recherche scientifique, 1991.

Dobson, E. J. *English Pronunciation 1500–1700*. Second ed. 2 vols. Oxford: Clarendon Press, 1968.

Douglas, Gavin. *The Palis of Honoure*. Ed. David Parkinson. Kalamazoo, MI: Medieval Institute Publications, 1992.

Downing, Janay Y. "A Critical Edition of Cambridge University MS Ff. 5. 48." Ph.D. dissertation, University of Washington, 1969.

Dunbar, William. *William Dunbar: The Complete Works*. Ed. John Conlee. Kalamazoo, MI: Medieval Institute Publications, 2004.

Farmer, David Hugh. *The Oxford Dictionary of Saints*. Oxford: Clarendon, 1978.

Ferguson, George. *Signs and Symbols in Christian Art*. Oxford: Oxford University Press, 1954.

French, Walter Hoyt, and Charles Brockway Hale, eds. *Middle English Metrical Romances*. New York: Prentice-Hall, 1930. Rpt. in two vols. New York: Russell and Russell, 1964.

Froissart, Jean. *Chronicles*. Trans. Geoffrey Brereton. Harmondsworth: Penguin, 1968.

Furrow, Melissa M. *Ten Fifteenth-Century Comic Poems*. New York: Garland, 1985.

———. "Comic Tales." In *Medieval England: An Encyclopedia*. Ed. Paul E. Szarmach, M. Teresa Tavormina, and Joel T. Rosenthal. New York: Garland, 1998. Pp. 203–04.

———. "The Middle English Fabliaux and Modern Myth." *ELH* 56 (1989), 1–18.

Gaunt, Simon. "Genitals, Gender, and Mobility: The *Fabliaux*." In *Gender and Genre in Medieval French Literature*. Cambridge: Cambridge University Press, 1995. Pp. 234–85.

Ginsberg, Warren, ed. *Wynnere and Wastoure and The Parlement of the Thre Ages*. Kalamazoo, MI: Medieval Institute Publications, 1992.

Goldstein, R. James. "*The Freiris of Berwik* and the Fabliau Tradition." In *The European Sun: Proceedings of the Seventh International Conference on Medieval and Renaissance Scottish Language and Literature, 1993*. Ed. Graham Caie, Roderick J. Lyall, Sally Mapstone, and Kenneth Simpson. East Linton: Tuckwell Press, 2001. Pp. 267–75.

Goodall, Peter. "An Outline History of the English Fabliau after Chaucer." *AUMLA: Journal of the Australasian Universities Language and Literature Association* 57 (1982), 5–23.

Görlach, Manfred. *The Textual Tradition of the South English Legendary*. Leeds: University of Leeds, 1974.

Griffiths, J. J. "A Re-examination of Oxford, Bodleian Library, MS Rawlinson C. 86." *Archiv für das Studium der neueren Sprachen und Literaturen* 219 (1982), 381–88.

Hart, W. M. "The Fabliau and Popular Literature." *PMLA* 23 (1908), 329–74.

Hines, John. *The Fabliau in English*. London: Longman, 1993.

Hoccleve, Thomas. *The Regiment of Princes*. Ed. Charles R. Blyth. Kalamazoo, MI: Medieval Institute Publications, 1999.

Jack, R. D. S. "*The Freiris of Berwik* and Chaucerian Fabliau." *Studies in Scottish Literature* 17 (1982), 145–52.

Jordan, Richard. *Handbook of Middle English Grammar*. Trans. and rev. Eugene Joseph Crook. The Hague: Mouton, 1974.

Kellogg, Alfred L., and Robert C. Cox. "Chaucer's May 3 and Its Contexts." In *Chaucer, Langland, Arthur: Essays in Middle English Literature*. Ed. Alfred L. Kellogg. New Brunswick, NJ: Rutgers University Press, 1972. Pp. 155–98.

Kelly, Kathleen Coyne. *Performing Virginity and Testing Chastity in the Middle Ages*. London: Routledge, 2000.

Kieckhefer, Richard. *Magic in the Middle Ages*. Second ed. Cambridge: Cambridge University Press, 2000.

Knowles, Dom David. *The Religious Orders in England*. 2 vols. Cambridge: Cambridge University Press, 1955–56.

Koble, Nathalie, ed. *"Le Lai du cor" et "Le Manteau mal taillé," Les dessous de la Table Ronde*. Paris: Éditions rue d'Ulm, 2005.

Kooper, Erik, ed. *Sentimental and Humorous Romances*. Kalamazoo, MI: Medieval Institute Publications, 2006.

Lachaud, Frédérique. "Dress and Social Status in England before the Sumptuary Laws." In *Heraldry, Pageantry and Social Display in Medieval England*. Ed. Peter Coss and Maurice Keen. Woodbridge: Boydell, 2003. Pp. 105–24.

Lee, Brian S. "Seen and Sometimes Heard: Piteous and Pert Children in Medieval English Literature." *Children's Literature Association Quarterly* 23 (1998), 40–48.

Lewis, C. S. *English Literature in the Sixteenth Century, Excluding Drama*. Oxford: Clarendon Press, 1954.

Lindahl, Carl. "Jacks: The Name, the Tales, the American Traditions." In *Jack in Two Worlds*. Ed. William Bernard McCarthy. Chapel Hill: University of North Carolina Press, 1994. Pp. xiii–xxxiv.

Luick, Karl. *Historische Grammatik der englischen Sprache*. 1914–40. Rpt. Oxford: Basil Blackwell, 1964.

Lupack, Alan, ed. "The Tale of Ralph the Colier." In *Three Middle English Charlemagne Romances*. Kalamazoo, MI: Medieval Institute Publications, 1990. Pp. 161–204.

Lydgate, John. *Lydgate's Fall of Princes*. Ed. Henry Bergen. 4 vols. Washington, DC: Carnegie Institution of Washington, 1923–27.

Lyndsay, David. "The Testament and Complaynt of our Soverane Lordis Papyngo." In *Sir David Lyndsay: Selected Poems*. Ed. Janet Hadley Williams. Glasgow: Association for Scottish Literary Studies, 2000. Pp. 58–97.

MacDonald, Alasdair A. "The Cultural Repertory of Middle Scots Lyric Verse." In *Cultural Repertoires: Structure, Function, and Dynamics*. Ed. Gillis J. Dorleijn and Herman L. J. Vanstiphout. Louvain: Peeters, 2003. Pp. 59–86.

Malory, Thomas. *The Works of Sir Thomas Malory*. Ed. Eugène Vinaver. 3 vols. Rev. P. J. C. Field. Third ed. Oxford: Clarendon Press, 1990.

Matheson, Lister M. "Appendix: The Dialects and Language of Selected Robin Hood Poems." In *Robin Hood: The Early Poems, 1465–1560: Texts, Contexts, and Ideology*. Newark: University of Delaware Press, 2007. Pp. 189–210.

McCracken, Peggy. *Romance of Adultery: Queenship and Sexual Transgression in Old French Literature*. Philadelphia: University of Pennsylvania Press, 1998.

McIntosh, Angus, M. L. Samuels, and Michael Benskin, eds., with the assistance of Margaret Laing and Keith Williamson. *A Linguistic Atlas of Late Mediaeval English*. 4 vols. Aberdeen: Aberdeen University Press, 1986.

Morgan, Gwendolyn A. *Medieval Balladry and the Courtly Tradition: Literature of Revolt and Assimilation*. New York: Peter Lang, 1993.

Mossé, Fernand. *A Handbook of Middle English*. Trans. James A. Walker. Baltimore, MD: Johns Hopkins University Press, 1968.

Muscatine, Charles. *The Old French Fabliaux*. New Haven: Yale University Press, 1986.

Nelson, Marie, and Richard Thomson. "The Fabliau." In *A Companion to Old and Middle English Literature*. Ed. Laura Cooner Lambdin and Robert Thomas Lambdin. Westport, CT: Greenwood Press, 2002. Pp. 255–76.

Newlyn, Evelyn S. "The Political Dimensions of Desire and Sexuality in Poems of the Bannatyne Manuscript." In *Selected Essays on Scottish Language and Literature: A Festschrift in Honor of Allan H. MacLain*. Ed. Steven R. McKenna. Lewiston, NY: Edwin Mellen Press, 1992. Pp. 75–96.

Ohlgren, Thomas H. "'lewed peple loven tales olde': *Robin Hood and the Monk* and the Manuscript Context of Cambridge, University Library MS Ff.5.48." In *Robin Hood: The Early Poems, 1465–1560: Texts, Contexts, and Ideology*. Newark: University of Delaware Press, 2007. Pp. 28–67.

Orme, Nicholas. "Children and Literature in Medieval England." *Medium Ævum* 68 (1999), 218–46.

Ormrod, W. M. "For Arthur and St George: Edward III, Windsor Castle, and the Order of the Garter." In *St George's Chapel Windsor in the Fourteenth Century*. Ed. Nigel Saul. Woodbridge: Boydell, 2005. Pp. 13–34.

Parsons, Ben, and Bas Jongenelen. "A Play of Three Suitors: A Neglected Middle Dutch Version of the 'Entrapped Suitors' Story (ATU 1730)." *Folklore* 119 (2008), 58–70.

Pollard, A. W., and G. R. Redgrave. *A Short-title Catalogue of Books Printed in England, Scotland, & Ireland and of English Books Printed Abroad 1475–1640*. Second ed., ed. Rev. W. A. Jackson, F. S. Ferguson, and Katharine F. Pantzer. 3 vols. London: Bibliographical Society, 1976–91.

Prestwich, Michael. *Edward I*. Berkeley: University of California Press, 1988.

Rawcliffe, Carole. "Stafford, Ralph, First Earl of Stafford (1301–1372)." *Oxford Dictionary of National Biography*. Ed. H. C. G. Matthew and Brian Harrison. Oxford: Oxford University Press, 2004.

Ritchie, W. Tod, ed. *The Bannatyne Manuscript Writtin in Tyme of Pest, 1568*. 4 vols. Scottish Text Society new series 22–23 and 26, and third series 5. Edinburgh: William Blackwood and Sons, 1928–34.

Robbins, Rossell Hope. "The English Fabliau: Before and after Chaucer." *Moderna Språk* 64 (1970), 231–44.

Robertson, D. W., Jr. "Chaucerian Tragedy." *ELH* 19 (1952), 1–37.

Rosenblüt, Hans. "Von einem varnden Schüler." In *Fastnachtspiele aus den fünfzehnten Jahrhundert*. Ed. Adelbert von Keller. Darmstadt: Wissenschaftliche Buchgesellschaft, 1965. Pp. 1172–76.

Ross, Charles. *Edward IV*. Berkeley: University of California Press, 1974.

Salisbury, Eve. *The Trials and Joys of Marriage*. Kalamazoo, MI: Medieval Institute Publications, 2002.

Schenck, Mary Jane Stearns. *The Fabliaux: Tales of Wit and Deception*. Amsterdam: John Benjamins, 1987.

Severs, J. Burke, Albert E. Hartung, and Peter G. Beidler, eds. *A Manual of the Writings in Middle English, 1050–1500*. 11 vols. New Haven: Connecticut Academy of Arts and Sciences, 1967–2005.

Shakespeare, William. *Hamlet*. Ed. G. R. Hibbard. Oxford: Clarendon Press, 1987.

Shuffelton, George, ed. *Codex Ashmole 61: A Compilation of Popular Middle English Verse*. Kalamazoo, MI: Medieval Institute Publications, 2008.

Sir Gawain and the Green Knight. Ed. J. R. R. Tolkien and E. V. Gordon. Second ed. Rev. by Norman Davis. Oxford: Clarendon Press, 1967.

Smith, Thomas. *Catalogue of the Manuscripts in the Cottonian Library 1696*. Ed. C. G. C. Tite. Cambridge: D. S. Brewer, 1984.

Snell, Rachel. "The Undercover King." In *Medieval Insular Romance: Translation and Innovation*. Ed. Judith Weiss, Jennifer Fellows, and Morgan Dickson. Cambridge: D. S. Brewer, 2000. Pp. 133–54.

Speake, Jennifer, ed. *Oxford Dictionary of Proverbs*. Oxford: Oxford University Press, 2003.

Stones, E. L. G. "The Folvilles of Ashby-Folville, Leicestershire, and Their Associates in Crime, 1326–1347." *Transactions of the Royal Historical Society*, fifth series 7 (1957), 117–36.

Taylor, Archer. "Dane Hew, Munk of Leicestre." *Modern Philology* 15 (1917–18), 221–46.

"Les Trois amoureux de la croix." In *Recueil de Farces (1450–1550)*. Ed. André Tissier. Geneva: Droz, 1997. Pp. 115–81.

Unger, Richard W. *Beer in the Middle Ages and the Renaissance*. Philadelphia: University of Pennsylvania Press, 2007.

Uther, Hans-Jörg. *The Types of International Folktales: A Classification and Bibliography, Based on the System of Antti Aarne and Stith Thompson*. 3 vols. Helsinki: Suomalainen Tiedeakatemia, 2004.

Vale, Juliet. *Edward III and Chivalry*. Woodbridge: Boydell, 1982.

Vickers, Kenneth H. *Humphrey, Duke of Gloucester*. London: Archibald Constable, 1907.

Walsh, Elizabeth. "The King in Disguise." *Folklore* 86 (1975), 3–24.

Whatley, E. Gordon. "The Life of St. Julian the Hospitaller in the *Scottish Legendary* (c. 1400): Introduction." In *Saints' Lives in Middle English Collections*. Ed. E. Gordon Whatley, with Anne B. Thompson and Robert K. Upchurch. Kalamazoo, MI: Medieval Institute Publications, 2004. Pp. 307–15.

Whiting, Bartlett Jere, with the collaboration of Helen Wescott Whiting. *Proverbs, Sentences, and Proverbial Phrases from English Writings Mainly before 1500*. Cambridge, MA: The Belknap Press of Harvard University Press, 1968.

William of Pagula. *The Mirror of King Edward III*. Trans. Cary J. Nederman. In *Medieval Political Theory: A Reader: The Quest for the Body Politic, 1100–1400*. Ed. Cary J. Nederman and Kate Langdon Forhan. London: Routledge, 1993. Pp. 200–06.

Williams, Gordon. *A Dictionary of Sexual Language and Imagery in Shakespearean and Stuart Literature*. London: Athlone, 1994.

Woodbridge, Linda. *Vagrancy, Homelessness, and English Renaissance Literature*. Urbana: University of Illinois Press, 2001.

Wright, Glenn. "Churl's Courtesy: *Rauf Coilȝear* and Its English Analogues." *Neophilologus* 85 (2001), 647–62.

———. "The Fabliau Ethos in the French and English *Octavian* Romances." *Modern Philology* 102 (2005), 478–500.

🌿 GLOSSARY

ABBREVIATIONS:

a: adjective

adv: adverb

art: article

BM: *The Boy and the Mantle*

comp: comparative

conj: conjunction, conjunctive

dem: demonstrative

DH: *Dane Hew, Munk of Leicestre*

DOST: *Dictionary of the Older Scottish Tongue*

FB: *The Freiris of Berwik*

imp: imperative

impers: impersonal

indef: indefinite

int: interjection

irreg: irregular

JR: *John the Reeve*

JS: *Jack and His Stepdame*

KH: *The King and the Hermit*

KS: *King Edward and the Shepherd*

LP: *The Lady Prioress*

n: noun

n.: note

MED: *Middle English Dictionary*

OED: *Oxford English Dictionary*

pa: past

pers: person

phr: phrase

pl: plural

poss: possessive

ppl: participial

pple: participle

prep: preposition

pres: present

pron: pronoun

refl: reflexive

SC: *Sir Corneus*

sing: singular

t: tense

TB: *The Tale of the Basin*

v: verb

vbl: verbal

Some entries in the glossary are simply equivalencies (e.g., ermyte = hermit *KH* 152, 184, etc.), meant to help readers who might not recognize the familiar word in the unfamiliar spelling. But a typical definition entry will include one or more spellings of the word as it appears in the text, then label the part of speech, give a definition, and identify the first place that the word appears with that definition in one or two poems. There may then be further definitions; if the word occurs with a variety of meanings, usually only those that are not the normal modern meanings will be given. Closely related parts of speech (i.e., adjective and adverb) may be treated within the same entry. Some entries will be followed by an additional entry form in square brackets. This is to give readers a point of departure for research when a modern form of the word is not obvious or does not exist. These entry forms are usually from the *OED*, but with words from *The Freiris of Berwik*, *DOST* entry forms are also given where they differ from the *OED*.

The alphabetical order of this glossary is modified in places where *y* may represent the modern *i*, though the entries for *yche* and *ys* have been placed under both *i* and *y* for ease of access. It may also be useful for readers unfamiliar with fifteenth-century English to remember some other common late medieval spellings and grammatical forms. Final *e* in some of these texts is virtually random: it appears where it should not and does not where, historically, it should. Consonants may be unexpectedly doubled after usually long vowels and single after short ones. The symbols *ei* and *ey* often appear where modern spelling has *ai* or *ay*. Scottish and northern texts may have the following grammatical forms: final *-and* for the ending of the present participle (e.g., cumand = coming); final *-it* (or *-yt*) for the weak past tense and past participle (e.g., cryit = cried); final *-is* (or *-ys*) for the plural ending of nouns or the third singular present tense ending of verbs (e.g., dedis = deeds, thynkys = thinks). In the Scottish *Freiris of Berwik* initial *quh-* would have the spelling *wh-* in more modern texts, and final *-cht* would be *-ght*.

This glossary omits entries which occur only once and need no further treatment than the marginal gloss provides.

abacke, abak *a*: back, off, away *FB* 329, *JR* 727

abyde *v*: await defiantly *JR* 329; **abod** *pa t*: endured *LP* 226

abod *pa t* see **abyde**

abofe, abone *quasi-n*: position above one's current one *KS* 1026, *JR* 565 [*form of the adverb* "above"]

aboute, abowte about *JS* 102, *SC* 88, etc.

aby(e) *v*: atone, make restitution for *DH* 149, *KS* 142

adrad, adred *pa pple*: frightened *JS* 287, *LP* 76

aferd, afeard, affeard *pa pple*: afraid *LP* 141, *JR* 602, etc. [afear]

af(f)ray, effray *n*: alarm, fright *LP* 224, *FB* 367, etc.; attack *JR* 732

after me(e) *prep phr*: according to the instructions of *LP* 120; in my opinion *JR* 248

again(e), ageyn *adv*: in response *FB* 168, *KH* 425, etc.; back *JR* 572, *KH* 294, etc.

againe, ageyn(e), agene *prep*: opposite to *JR* 350; against *JS* 371, *SC* 192, etc.

against *prep*: opposite to *JR* 352

ageyn *adv* see **again**

ageyn(e) *prep* see **againe**

agon *pa ppl*: departed *JS* 165 [ago]

alhaill *adv*: entirely *FB* 98; *a*: entire *FB* 127 [*OED* all-whole, *DOST* alhale, alhail]

all(e) *a*: every *TB* 125, *SC* 15, etc.; *n*: everything *TB* 55, *LP* 55, etc.

almerie, almery *n*: cupboard *FB* 217, 268 [*OED* ambry, *DOST* almery]

als *adv*: as *KS* 505, *KH* 327, etc.; also *FB* 25, *KS* 540, etc.

also as *KS* 27, 93, etc.

amang among *FB* 31, 172, etc.

amerveylid *pa pple*: surprised, astonished *JS* 416 [amarvel]

among(e) *adv*: from time to time *TB* 30, *JS* 253; meanwhile *LP* 48, *SC* 12; at the same time *JS* 260

and *conj*: if *LP* 65, *KH* 141, etc.; even if *JR* 100; **and el(li)s**: or else *KS* 387, *KH* 123, etc.

-and the northern, and particularly Scottish, ending of the present participle, e.g., cumand (coming) *FB* 45

and if *conj*: if *DH* 18, *JR* 172, etc.

ane *indef art, a*: a, an, one *FB* 6, 40, etc.; **a one** *FB* 10, *KS* 296

annon(e) see **anon**

annwch(e) enough *FB* 301, 419

an(n)on(e) *adv*: at once *TB* 93, *JS* 57, etc.; anon as *conj phr*: as soon as *TB* 179

a-pay *n*: satisfaction *JR* 277

appaid, apayd(e) *ppl a*: satisfied *JS* 426, *DH* 181, etc.; pleased *JR* 49 [apaid]

apnit see **hapnit**

apon see **upon**

appaid see **apayd**

ar(r)aye *n*: attire, dress *JS* 291, *JR* 663, etc.; state of things *JS* 297 [array]

are, ore *n*: grace *KS* 744, *KH* 190, etc.; mercy *KS* 559, 744 [ore]

arraye see **araye**

as(s)ay, asey *v*: venture *TB* 192; assail *DH* 17; test *SC* 148, *KS* 287, etc.; feel *DH* 87

as(s)tere *v*: restrain *JS* 101, 359, etc. [a- + steer; *unattested*]

astent(t) *v*: stop *JS* 174, 387 [astint]

astere see **as(s)tere**

attour *prep*: over *FB* 534 [atour]

aught *pa t* see **owe**

aventour, awnter *v*: (ad)venture *FB* 450, *KH* 444

aventour, aventure *n*: adventure *LP* 225, *KH* 11, etc.

awen, awne, awin own *LP* 67, *SC* 50, etc.

awnter *v* see **aventour**

bad *pa t*: bid *JS* 74, *FB* 210, etc.

baine, baene *a*: ready, willing *JR* 509, 630

baith *a*: both *FB* 105, 108, etc.; (of three things) *FB* 181 [*DOST* bathe, baith]

bald(e) see **bold**

bale *n*: suffering, pain *JS* 3, *JR* 118, etc.

banadicitie see **benedicité**

bare bore *TB* 100, *JS* 49, etc.

baskefysyke *SC* 116 (see n).

bauld see **bold**

be *prep* see **by**

beden(e), bydeene *adv*: one after another *BM* 140; in a little while *JR* 224; together *JR* 888, *KH* 216, etc.

bedyng *pres pple*: praying *KH* 114 [bid]

beforn(e), befoir before *FB* 107, *SC*

23, etc.

beggyd *pa pple*: located *LP* 147 [big]

begyen begin *LP* 27

begin, begynne *v*: sit at the head of *SC* 200, *KS* 868, etc.

begynne see **begin**

beglued *pa pple*: deluded *LP* 199 [beglue]

behette see **behyght**

behyght *v*: promise *KH* 132, 392; *pa t KH* 504; **behette** *pa pple KS* 573

beit *v*: make a fire *FB* 133 [*OED* beet, bete, *DOST* bete, beit]

belive, belief, belyfe, belyve, blyffe *adv*: at once, immediately, quickly *TB* 44, *LP* 231, etc.

bene be *FB* 369, *KH* 435, etc.

benedicité, banadicitie *interj*: expressing astonishment, Bless us! *JS* 301, *FB* 369, etc.

bening *a*: benign *FB* 403 [*DOST* bening]

beseeme *v*: befit, suit *BM* 44, *JR* 668

beshet *v*: shut in *JS* 143 [beshut]

beshrew *v*: curse *JR* 409, 485; **beshrewyd** *pa pple*: treated badly, abused *LP* 200

besyd *adv*: close *FB* 296, 479, near *KH* 99

besines *n*: diligence *FB* 403 [*OED* business, *DOST* besines]

bestrood *v*: strode across *LP* 228 [*pa t* bestride]

bet see **bett**

betaught *v*: bid *KH* 511 [*pa t* beteach]

bethought *v refl*: considered *LP* 45; resolved *LP* 46; *pa pple LP* 13 [*pa t* bethink]

bett(e), bet *a*: better *TB* 55, *KS* 709, etc.

bettell *v*: slander *JR* 413; **betold** *pa pple*: deceived *JR* 690

betold *pa pple* see **bettell**

bette see **bett**

byd bide *FB* 97, 101, etc.

bydand biding *FB* 132, 494

bydeene *adv* see **bedene**

byden *pa pple*: endured *KH* 212 [bide]

byn are *TB* 2, *LP* 3, etc.

blee *n*: complexion, face *BM* 50, 78, etc.

blyffe *adv* see **belive**

blyn(n)e *v*: cease, desist *JS* 312, *KS* 38; hesitate *KH* 403 [blin]

bliss(e), blis, blys *n*: gladness, joy *KS* 5, *JR* 909; **soo have I bliss**: as I hope for [the] happiness [of heaven] *TB* 61, *KH* 463, etc.

blyth(e), blithe *a*: happy *FB* 54, *SC* 232, etc.

blithe, blithly *adv*: cheerfully *TB* 89, 102, etc.

blowen *pa pple*: spread around, proclaimed *LP* 86 [blow]

boiss see **bo(i)ss**

bok, bok(k)e, bucke *n*: buck, male deer *LP* 38, *KS* 380, etc.

bold(e), bald(e), bauld *a*: strong, fierce *JR* 192; audacious *FB* 252; to be bold; to take the liberty *LP* 115, *JR* 500 [*DOST* bald]

bolte *n*: arrow *JS* 85, 92

bond *n*: string *KH* 461; obligation *JR* 202

bond(e), bown *pa pple*: bound, shackled *KS* 157, *KH* 260, etc.; under obligation *DH* 30; **bond** *pa t*: bound, shackled *JS* 344

bondman *n*: serf *JR* 125, 293, etc.

bord(e) *n*: table *TB* 33, *SC* 25

borowe see *JS* 180n.

borrow(e) *n*: town *LP* 30, 237 [borough]

bos *v impers*: [it] is necessary for *KH* 277 [*OED* see bus, *v third pers sing contracted form of* behoves]

bo(i)ss *n*: leather wine bottle *FB* 157, 354, etc. [*DOST* bos]

bost(e) *n*: clamor *LP* 213; without boast; without exaggeration *JS* 284, *JR* 467; threats *KS* 848 [boast]

bot see **but**

botkin *n*: bodkin, dagger *FB* 176

[*DOST* boitkin, botkin]

bought *v*: redeemed *KH* 394, 406; *pa pple*: atoned for *JR* 492 [buy]

bourd(e), bowrd *n*: idle tale, joke *SC* 4, *JR* 10; funny custom *KS* 214; fun *KS* 223, 323, etc.

boure see **bowre**

bown *pa pple* see **bond**

bowrd *n* see **bourd**

bowre, boure *n*: inner room *KS* 126, 290 [bower]

braggat *n*: drink made of honey and ale *JR* 141 [bragget]

braid, brayde, brey(e)d *n*: moment *DH* 182; sudden movement, jerk *TB* 184, *KH* 359, etc.

braid, brayd *v*: grabbed *BM* 34; broke into speech *SC* 97; **brayed up** *v phr*: burst into action *LP* 139 [*pa t*: **braid**]

brak(e), breke broke *LP* 143, *FB* 533, etc.

brand *n*: sword *DH* 94; burning piece of wood *JR* 336

brast(e) *v*: break *JR* 543 [burst]

brawle *n*: French dance *JR* 535 (see n.)

brede *n*: (piece of) roast meat *KS* 421, *KH* 200, etc.

bredir see **brether**

brey(e)d *n* see **braid**

breke *n*: underpants *LP* 166 [breek]

breke *v* see **brake**

brether(n), brethir, bredir *n*: brothers, brethren *DH* 5, *SC* 231, etc.

brewice *n*: broth, or bread soaked in broth *JR* 393 [brewis]

bribour *n*: vagabond *DH* 149 [briber]

bright *a*: beautiful *JR* 82, 97, etc.

bring *v*: escort, accompany *DH* 174, *JR* 111, etc.; forth brought *v phr*: expressed, brought to light *LP* 12

britled *v*: cut to pieces *BM* 173 [*pa t*: brittle]

broake, brok *v*: enjoyed the use of *KS* 246, *JR* 462, etc.

broch *n*: taper *LP* 40 [broach]

brocht brought *FB* 69, 161, etc.

brode *adv*: broadly, extensively *LP* 86 [broad]

broder brother *TB* 45

brok see **broake**

browne *n*: brown fabric *JR* 287, 713

bruder brother *FB* 46, 263 etc.

bucke see **bok**

buck(e)ler *n*: small round shield *JR* 634, 719

bugyll-horn, bugyl(l) *n*: horn of a wild ox used as an instrument *KH* 520; used as a drinking vessel *SC* 22, 38, etc.

buk(e) book *FB* 322, 495, etc.

burd board *FB* 216, 374, etc.

burde *n* see *FB* 149–50n.

burdoun *n*: stout staff *FB* 531 [*OED* bourdon, *DOST* burdoun]

bure bore *FB* 42, 550

burges *n*: city merchant *LP* 30, 41, etc.

but, bot *conj*: unless *JS* 203, *LP* 49, etc.; *adv*: only, just *JR* 323, *KH* 169, etc.; neither more nor less than *LP* 140, *FB* 343

but *prep*: without *JS* 191, *FB* 96, etc. [*DOST* bot]

but (g)if, but yif, bot (g)if, bot yiff *conj*: unless *TB* 26, *KS* 380, etc.

bute *n*: use, avail *FB* 363 [*OED* boot, *DOST* bute]

by, be *prep*: on the course of *TB* 174, *KH* 13, etc.; before *TB* 180; because of *KH* 279; on *JS* 383

by and by *adv phr*: right away *JS* 250, *DH* 138, etc.

caitife *n*: wretch, villain *DH* 189, 208

calltrape *n*: usually a foot trap or snare, but see *LP* 196n. [caltrop]

can, con *v*[1]: have knowledge of *KS* 343, *JR* 360, etc.; learn *KS* 315; **couth, cowth(e), cold** *pa t*: knew *TB* 16, *SC* 28, etc.; could *SC* 30, *KH* 366, etc.

can, con *v*[2]: began to, proceeded to, did *TB* 36, *JR* 48, etc.; **cowld** *irreg pa t*: did *FB* 34, 75, etc.

capul *n*: horse *JR* 130, 234, etc.

care *n*: suffering *TB* 223, *LP* 176, etc.; attention *LP* 174

carle *n*: bondman *JR* 47, 52, etc.

cas(e) *n*: occurrence *LP* 14, *DH* 244, etc.; matter *JR* 869

cast *v*: intend *JR* 596; *pa t*: considered *KH* 82; **castin** *pa pple*: dug *FB* 10

caste *n*: shot from a sling *KS* 191, 245

castin *pa pple* see **cast**

catell *n*: livestock *KS* 34; property *KS* 156, 584

cauld *a*: cold *FB* 251, 255

certain(e), serten *adv*: certainly *LP* 101, *DH* 173, etc.

certes, certis, sertes *adv*: certainly *JS* 294, *KS* 162, etc.

chalmer, chambyr, cha(u)mbur, chaumber, chawmbur chamber *FB* 138, *KS* 1007, etc.

chance, chans(e), chaunce *n*: a mischance *TB* 165, *SC* 105, etc.; exploit *JR* 318; destiny *KH* 278

chandlour *n*: candlestick *JR* 251 [chandler]

chans(e) see **chance**

chapelery *n*: scapular, short cloak *JS* 251

chapmon *n*: peddler *TB* 143 [chapman]

charcole charcoal *JR* 250, 335

chaste(n) *n*: train, correct by discipline *JS* 30, *BM* 145

chaumber, chaumbur see **chalmer**

chaunce *n* see **chance**

chawmbur see **chalmer**

cheere, cheir, chere, chier *n*: fun *DH* 37, *KH* 390, etc.; food *DH* 239; facial expression *JS* 369, *JR* 340, etc.; enjoyment *FB* 418; **with a good chere** *phr*: cheerfully, with a good will *JS* 411

cheeve *v*: succeed *JR* 152 [cheve]

cheir, chere, chier see **cheere**

chyre chair *FB* 183, 216 (see n.)

clam climbed *FB* 541 [*DOST pa t* clim]

clathis *n*: bedclothes *FB* 104 [*DOST* clath]

clawcht *v*: snatched up *FB* 549 [*OED* cleek, *DOST pa t* cleke]

cleithe *v*: clothe *FB* 143 [*OED* clead, *DOST* cleith, cleth(e)]

clething *n*: clothing *FB* 538 [*OED* cleading, *DOST* clething]

cloiss *a*: hidden *FB* 474, 477, etc. [*DOST* clos, clois]

cloiss *v*: close, fold up *FB* 216 [*DOST* close, clois]

close *n*: farmyard *JS* 141; enclosed field *DH* 277

closit *pa pple*: enclosed *FB* 120, 211 [close]

clowte *n*: clout, heavy blow *TB* 198; rag *JS* 274

cock(e)s *n*: God's [a weakened form] *TB* 208, *DH* 262

coft *pa pple*: redeemed *FB* 101 [*OED* coff; *DOST* copen]

cokwold, cuchold, cukolde, kokwold cuckold *SC* 13, 31, etc.

cold *pa t* see **can** *v*[1]

com came *LP* 33, *SC* 70, etc.

combred *pa pple*: hampered *JR* 652 [cumber]

comly(e) *a*: seemly *LP* 57, *JR* 213, etc. [comely]

commannde *pres pple*: coming *JR* 339, 648

compenabull *a*: companionable *SC* 110 [companable]

con see **can**

coney, cunyng, conyne, conyng(e) *n*: rabbit *FB* 135, *JR* 470, etc. [*OED* cony, *DOST* cuning]

connyng *n*: expert *LP* 3 [cunning]

consayet *n*: notion *LP* 12 [conceit]

cons(s)ell, co(u)nsail counsale, councell *n*: private business *LP* 85; secret *TB* 172; advice *DH* 104,

136, etc.; **kepe consell, counsale kepe** *phr*: observe secrecy *LP* 95 [counsell], *FB* 311

counsail *v*: advise *DH* 215

counsail, counsale *n* see **consell**

convay *v*: remove secretly *DH* 105 [convey]

conyne, conyng(e) see **coney**

cop(e) cup *FB* 388, *KH* 340, etc.

cope *n*: long cloak, esp. a friar's *KH* 194, 284

corse *n*: body *LP* 112, 118, etc.

coste *n*: customary behavior (see *JR* 38n.)

costrell *n*: vessel for holding liquid *KS* 500 [costrel]

councell *n* see **consell**

couth *pa t* see **can** *v*[1]

cowd, cowld *irreg pa t* see **can** *v*[2]

cowle, cowll *n*: garment with a hood worn by a religious *LP* 57, *FB* 509

cowth(e) *pa t* see **can** *v*[1]

crabitly *adv*: crossly *FB* 230 [*OED* crabbedly, *DOST* crabitly]

cracched *v*: scratched *JS* 247 [cratch]

crave, craif *v*: demand by right *LP* 91; ask for *DH* 78, *FB* 305, etc.; beg *SC* 112, *JR* 120, etc.

creill *n*: creel, wicker basket *FB* 160, 356 [*DOST* crele, creill]

creip, crepe creep *JS* 266, *FB* 209, etc.

croun *n*: coin, the French ecu *FB* 303 [*OED* crown, *DOST* croun(e)]

crowt *v*: push *BM* 114 [crowd: *unattested sense*]

cukolde, cuchold see **cokwold**

cunyng see **coney**

cure *n*: charge (laid upon one) *FB* 348, 477; care *FB* 403

curtassy, curtesye, curtasy(e) *n*: courtly manners *SC* 174, *JR* 247, etc.

curteous, curtesse *a*: having courtly manners *TB* 80, *BM* 3, etc.; **curteouslye, courteslye** *adv FB* 57, *JR* 121

curtesse see **curteous**
curtesye see **curtassy**

dame, deme *n*: mother *LP* 147; lady
  JS 32, *FB* 72, etc.
dare *n*: hurt *JR* 635; daunt *JR* 714
  [dere]
dase *v*: be stupefied, bewildered *KH*
  413 [daze]
deal, dele, dell *n*: bit *JR* 504, *KH*
  332, etc.; **never a dele, no dell**
  not a bit *JS* 14, *KS* 150, etc.
dealinge *n*: conduct *JR* 114
dease, dese *n*: dais, high table *SC*
  210, *JR* 379, etc.
debate, debait *n*: physical fight, strife
  JR 595, 603; resistance *FB* 456,
  512
ded did *LP* 227, 240
deere *adv*: at great cost *JR* 468, 492
  [dear]
deid *a*: dead *FB* 92, 548 [*DOST* dede,
  deid]
deid *n*: deed *FB* 1 [*DOST* dede, deid]
deir *v*: harm *FB* 462, 472 [*OED* dere,
  DOST dere, deir(e)]
dele *n* see **deal**
dele *v*: share out *KS* 327
delyverly, deliverlie *adv*: quickly *FB*
  250, 292, etc. [deliverly]
dell *n* see **deal**
deme see **dame**
demyd *n*: considered *LP* 140, 156 [*pa
  t* deem]
dengerous *a*: haughty *FB* 55
  [dangerous]
dentey *n*: delicacy *KS* 375; **denteis** *pl*
  FB 425 [*OED* dainty, *DOST*
  daynté]
der(e) dare *KH* 48, 125, etc.
dese see **dease**
desease, disese *n*: harm *JR* 106;
  uneasiness *TB* 27 [disease]
desyrand *pres pple*: asking for *FB* 262
  [desire]
desire, desyre *v*: ask for *JS* 108, *FB*
  66, etc.

devyiss *n*: command *FB* 379, 474; **at
  all devyiss** *phr*: entirely *FB* 243
  [*OED* device, *DOST* devis(e)]
dicht *v* see **dight**
dyghed died *SC* 251, *KH* 268
dight, dicht, dyght *v*: prepare *FB*
  122, *KH* 180, etc.; *pa t*: dressed *LP*
  136; got ready, prepared *JR* 562;
  pa pple: dressed *SC* 78, *JR* 224;
  handled *JR* 846; prepared *KS*
  379, 940; built, constructed *KS*
  275, 491
dyscuryd *pa pple*: made known *LP*
  130 [discover]
dyses *n*: decease *LP* 237
disese see **desease**
dispyte *n*: indignation *SC* 34;
  outrage *FB* 466 [despite]
dissagyiss *v*: disguise *FB* 454 [*DOST*
  disagyse]
diverse, dyvers(e) *adv*: different *JS*
  384, *KS* 44, etc.
do(e) of *v phr*: take off *KS* 628, *JR*
  755
doe away *v phr*: stop *JR* 301;
  abandon *JR* 303
done do *TB* 127, *KS* 113, etc.
doo *n*: doe *LP* 38, *KS* 380
dorge, dyrge dirge *LP* 93, 137, etc.
dowte, doute doubt *JS* 99, *SC* 234,
  etc.; fear *KS* 62
draught, drawght, draght *n*: drink
  KS 444, *JR* 148, etc.; move in a
  game *TB* 60 (see n.), *SC* 118
dred *a*: afraid *LP* 203
dred(e) *n*: dread *TB* 177, *KS* 986, etc.
durst *v*: dare *JR* 158; dared *TB* 34,
  FB 84, etc.
dwel(l) *v*: delay *BM* 22; linger *TB* 3,
  KS 725, etc.

effeiritlie *adv*: fearfully *FB* 412 [*OED*
  effeiredly, *DOST* efferitly]
effray *n* see **affray**
eft(e) *adv*: again *KS* 330, *KH* 355, etc.
eftir after *FB* 59, 389
eik, eke *adv*: also *JS* 248, *FB* 23, etc.

[*OED* eke, *DOST* eke, eik]

eyre heir *TB* 10, 68

eysell *n*: vinegar *JS* 2 [eisell]

eiss see **ese**

eit ate *FB* 70; eat *FB* 259

eke see **eik**

ellis *adv*: otherwise *TB* 2 [else]

empere *n*: supreme command *JS* 438 (see note)

endewed *n*: invested with property *LP* 238 [*pa t* endued]

ensemble *n*: assembling *KH* 22 [*MED* ensemble]

er or *TB* 198, *KS* 120, etc.

er(e) *adv*: before *JR* 766; *conj*: before *TB* 161, *JR* 756, etc.

ermyt(e) hermit *KH* 152, 184, etc.

erst *adv*: earlier; **ner erst, nou erst**: never before *KS* 360, *JR* 400

es *v*: help *KH* 473 [ease]

es(e), eiss *n*: comfort, advantage *TB* 29, *FB* 70, etc. [ease]

estate *n*: status, rank *JR* 304, 824

ete(n) ate *TB* 127, *JS* 77, etc.; eaten *KH* 155

even *n*: evening *DH* 39, *JR* 70, etc.

even, evin *adv*: exactly *FB* 379; equally *FB* 393; **evin with that** just then *FB* 76, 190 [*OED* euen, *DOST* evin, ewin]

evermoo, evermour, evermore *adv*: *emphatic form*: ever *TB* 80, *SC* 23, etc.

everychon(e) every one, each one *JS* 143, *SC* 65, etc.

evil(l) *a*: bad, rough *DH* 100, *FB* 93, etc.; *adv*: badly *JS* 22, *FB* 48; ill *JR* 818

evin *adv* see **even**

evynsong *n*: canonical service for sunset *KH* 74 [evensong]

fadur father *KS* 97, 974, etc.

fayer, fayre *adv*: directly, straight *LP* 111; nicely *KS* 1017 [fair]

fayle *v*: miss (a step) *JR* 538; **fayle of**: miss *JS* 89 , *KS* 245

fain(e), fayn(e), feyn, fane *a*: well-pleased *FB* 543, *JR* 353, etc.; glad under the circumstances *JS* 281; *adv*: gladly *FB* 458, *JR* 107, etc.

fair *v* see **fare**

fayre see **fayer**

fairly, ferly *n*: wonder *FB* 370, *KS* 853 [*OED* ferly, *DOST* farly]

fall(e) *v*: come to pass, occur *KS* 634; **foule mot yow falle** may evil befall you *TB* 182

fallow see **fellow**

fand *v*: provided *FB* 365 [*pa t* find]

fane see **fain**

fansy *n*: inclination *DH* 8 [fancy]

fare *n*: doings *LP* 216; mode of proceeding *TB* 146; food *JR* 439; comfort *KH* 180; carrying on, pomp *KS* 728, *JR* 832

fare, fair *v*: do, get on *TB* 57, *FB* 258, etc.; **faris** *impers third sing*: happens *TB* 72; **ferd(e)** *pa t*: did, got on *TB* 55, *KS* 1014; behaved *JS* 242; went *KS* 10;

farforth *adv*: far *JS* 24, *LP* 100

farrand *a*: handsome *JR* 357, 784

fast(e) *adv*: readily *LP* 47; strongly, vigorously *FB* 191, *JR* 616, etc.; earnestly *FB* 553, *SC* 88, etc.; firmly, fixedly *TB* 139, *FB* 78, etc.; steadily *FB* 229; *a*: firmly attached *TB* 154

faute, fawt *n*: fault *LP* 6; want of food *KH* 126

fawconer(e) *n*: keeper and trainer of hawks *JR* 261, 347, etc. [falconer]

fawt see **faute**

fay(e), feyth *n*: faith *JS* 179, *DH* 35, etc.; **in gode fay, in good faye** in truth *TB* 148, *JS* 202, etc.; **by my fay(e), be my fay(e)** truth to tell, literally "by my faith" *JS* 179, *DH* 35, etc.

fech(e) see **fett**

fe(e) *n*: estate in land *KH* 247; money *LP* 242, *JR* 366; **in fee** by heritable right *LP* 239; livestock

KS 621

feyn see **fain**

feynd fiend *FB* 555

feir see **fere**

feyth see **fay**

felaw(e) see **fellow**

fele *a*: many *JS* 224, *SC* 240, etc.

fellone, felloun *a*: fierce, terrible *FB* 193, 530 [*OED* felon, *DOST* felloun]

fellow(e), fallow, felaw(e), felou, felow(e) *n*: agreeable companion *TB* 78, *FB* 258, etc.; title of address for a servant *KH* 323; regular guy *JR* 257, *KH* 286, etc. [*OED* fellow, *DOST* fallow]

fend(e) fiend *LP* 126, *KS* 874, etc.

ferd *pa t* see **fare**

fere, feir *n*: company; **in fere, in feir** together *FB* 105, *JR* 471, etc.

ferly see **fairly**

fest *n*: gathering for pleasure or sports *KH* 22 [feast]

fett *n*: feet *LP* 106, 164

fett(e), fet, fech(e) *v*: fetch *KS* 291; *pa t*: **fetched** *DH* 301, *SC* 211, etc.; *pa pple SC* 38, *KS* 888, etc. [fet]

fylde field *JS* 193, *KS* 268

filosophie *n*: magic *FB* 386 [philosophy]

find *v*: maintain; **find to schoole**: maintain while at school *JR* 877

fine, fyne *a*: consummate, supreme *SC* 185; handsome *JR* 291

fitt, fytte *n*: section of a poem *JR* 345; stave of music *JS* 354, 413

fle(e) *v*: fly *JS* 234; **lait fle** let fly *JS* 173, *FB* 530 [*OED* fly, *DOST* fle]

flecher *n*: arrowmaker *KH* 472 [fletcher]

flee see **fle**

flure *n*: *FB* 404, 478, etc., see *FB* 404 (see n.)

flyting *pres pple*: chiding, wrangling *JR* 685

fond(e), fonnd found *KS* 941, *KH* 103, etc.

fonnd *v*: attempt, try *SC* 150 [fand]

for *conj*: because *JS* 23, *SC* 107, etc.; **for God** *prep phr*: as God knows, by God *JS* 332, *KS* 94, etc.

forlore *pa pple*: lost *LP* 220; wasted *KS* 666 [forlese]

forsoth(e), forsooth, forsuth *adv*: truly *JS* 20, *LP* 10, etc.

forster see **foster**

forsuth see **forsoth**

forteyned *pa pple*: happened *SC* 168 [fortune]

foster, forster *n*: forester, huntsman *KS* 269, *KH* 37, etc.

fowle *adv*: badly *LP* 144, 158 [foul]

fra *prep*: from *FB* 61, 83, etc. [*OED* fro, *DOST* fra]

franyt *v*: asked, made inquiries *FB* 553 [*OED* *pa t* frayne, *DOST* *pa t* frain(e)]

fre see **free**

freake see **freke**

fre(e) *a*: noble, of gentle birth *DH* 19, *JR* 31, etc.; generous *SC* 106; (of an offer) readily given *JR* 109; *adv*: nobly, honorably *LP* 240

freeledge *n*: freedom, independence *JR* 176 [freelage]

freir friar *FB* 24, 29, etc.

freke, freake *n*: man *JS* 37, *JR* 252, etc.

frere friar *JS* 182, *KH* 139, etc.

freryry *n*: brotherhood *SC* 215 [frary]

fressch, fresch(e), fresse, fresh *a*: healthy looking or youthful *LP* 28; full of vigor *JR* 895; gaily attired *FB* 6, *JR* 277, etc.

frumentye *n*: dish of hulled wheat boiled in milk *JR* 473 (see n.)

ful(l), fulle *adv*: very *TB* 20, *KH* 100, etc.

furth forth *LP* 136, *FB* 68, etc.

ga go *FB* 216, *KS* 233, etc.

gaf(f)(e), gaif *v*: gave *JS* 73, *FB* 82, etc.; **ne gaff** did not care *JS* 50 [*pa t* give]

gaist guest *FB* 233, 561

gall(e) *n*: bile *JS* 2, 437; spirit to resent injury *SC* 96, 107, etc.

galland *n*: fine gentleman *FB* 6 [*OED* gallant, *DOST* galland]

galle see **gall**

gam(m)(e) *n*: fun *TB* 5, *JR* 2, etc.; jest *SC* 247; amorous play *DH* 31; delight *KH* 4

gan(ne) *v*: began (to) *LP* 21, *KH* 218, etc. [*pa t* gin]

ganand *ppl a*: appropriate *FB* 248 [*OED* gainand, *DOST* ganand]

gang(e) *v*: go *FB* 524, *JR* 209, etc.

ganne see **gan**

gape *n*: breach in a hedge or thicket *LP* 177 [gap]

gar(r) *v*: cause (one to do) something *FB* 312, *JR* 173, etc.; **gart, garred** *pa t FB* 209, *JR* 561

garamersy see **gramercy**

garr see **gar**

garr see **gargat(e)** got *FB* 482, *JR* 26, etc.

garred see **gar**

gart see **gar**

gate *n*: road or journey *KH* 444

gate see **yate**

gentle *n*: one of gentle birth *JR* 386, 389

gentrise *n*: kindness, courtesy *JR* 65 [gentrice]

gest guest *KH* 5, 118, etc.

gesttyng *vbl n*: tale-telling, recitation *LP* 1 [gest *v*]

gett *v*: earn *JR* 146 [get]

geve give *JS* 69, 228; given *JS* 79

gif *conj*: if *TB* 149, *FB* 84, etc. [northern and Scottish form]

gyff(e), gyfe, gif *v*: give *JS* 80, *KS* 80, etc.

gyle *n*: trick, wile *SC* 177, *KS* 12, etc. [guile]

gyn(n)e *n*: trick, *TB* 85; device *SC* 148: **gynnes** *pl*; traps *KH* 52 [gin]

gird, girt *pa pple*: fastened *JR* 704; clothed *JR* 286 [gird]

gyse see **guise**

gytyrn *v*: to play on the gittern, an instrument like a guitar *TB* 81 [gittern]

glade *v*: rejoice *TB* 120; cheer *KH* 201

gle(e) *n*: fun, entertainment *TB* 5, *SC* 203, etc.; musical instrument *JS* 314, *SC* 249, etc. [glee]

gleade *n*: bird of prey, *usually*, a kite *JR* 267 [glede]

glee see **gle(e)**

glent *v*: moved aside quickly *LP* 177 [*pa t* glent]

glour *v*: stare with eyes wide open *FB* 334; **glowrit** *pa t FB* 330 [*OED* glower, *DOST* glowr]

glowrit *pa t* see **glour**

gluder *v*: flatter *FB* 34 [*OED* glother, *DOST* gluther]

gode see **good**

godeman see **goodman**

godewyf(e) see **goodwiff**

gois(s) goes *FB* 187, 499

go(o) *v*: be in a specific condition *TB* 181, 182; walk *JS* 406

gode see **good**

godeman see **goodman**

godewyf(e) see **goodwiff**

gone go *DH* 102, *JR* 248, etc.

goo see **go**

good(e), gode *n*: money *LP* 91; goods *KS* 283, *KH* 163, etc.

goodman, godeman, gudman *n*: male head of a household *TB* 36, *JS* 31, etc.; host of an inn *FB* 59, 83, etc. [*DOST* gud(e)man]

goodwiff(e), goodwyf(e), godewyf(e), gudwyf(e) *n*: female head of a household *TB* 152, *JS* 25, etc. [*DOST* gud(e)wife]

goule *a*: red *BM* 41 [gules]

governaunce, govirnance *n*: behavior *JS* 417; deed(s) *FB* 362, 392 [governance]

grace *n*: fortune *JS* 381; favor *FB* 510, *JR* 5, 904

graithly *adv*: properly, really *FB* 447
  [*OED* gradely, *DOST* graithly]
gramercy, gramarcy garamersy,
  gremercy *int*: thanks *JS* 78, *DH*
  86, etc.
graunt *v*: agree, consent *LP* 134, *KS*
  84 [grant]
gre(e)ffe, greif *n*: harm, trouble *JR*
  205, 698, etc.; offense, displeasure
  SC 133 [grief]
gre(e)ne, gr(e)yne *n*: green clothing
  or cloth *FB* 149, *SC* 222, etc.; tree
  or plant *LP* 157
gre(e)ve, greif *v*: trouble *DH* 46, *JR*
  365, etc.; harm *JR* 190; offend *KS*
  480 [grieve]
greffe, greif *n* see **greeffe**
greif *v* see **greeve**
greyne see **greene**
gremercy see **gramercy**
grene see **greene**
gret(t)(e) great *TB* 177, *LP* 53, etc.
grett *n*: gravel *LP* 157 [grit]
greve see **greeve**
greyne see **greene**
gryne see **greene**
gryse *v*: shudder, tremble with
  horror *LP* 151; **grose** *pa t LP* 206
  [grise]
grit great *FB* 4, 23, etc.
grose *pa t* see **gryse**
gud(e) good *FB* 18, 51, etc.; **gudly**
  goodly *FB* 20
gudman see **goodman**
gudwyf(e) see **goodwife**
guise, gyse *n*: custom, habit *TB* 171,
  JR 313, etc. [*DOST* gys(e]

habargyon *n*: sleeveless coat of mail
  JR 328 [habergeon]
hacche *n*: half door *JS* 394 [hatch]
hafe, haif see **have**
hairtfullie *adv*: heartily *FB* 294 [*OED*
  heartfully, *DOST* hartfully, hairt-]
hairtly *a*: affectionate *FB* 244; *adv*:
  heartily *FB* 279, 402 [*OED*
  heartly, *DOST* hartfully, hairtly]

halde see **hold**
hale *v*: pull *KS* 198, *KH* 468
hall(e) *n*: large public room in a
  substantial house *TB* 180, *JS* 144,
  etc.
haly holy *FB* 36, *KS* 69, etc.
hame home *FB* 36, *KS* 432, etc.
handf(f)ull *n*: measure of four inches
  in length *JR* 326, 608
hap *n*: luck *FB* 536
hape *v*: chance, occur *KH* 200
(h)apnit happened *FB* 371, 526, etc.
harbo(u)r, harborow, herborow,
  herbour *n*: shelter, lodging *JR*
  78, *KH* 86, etc.; *v*: shelter, lodge
  KH 152, 161; **herbord** *pa t JR* 594
  [harbour]
harbry(e), harbery, herbrye *n*:
  shelter, lodging *FB* 81, *JR* 578,
  etc.; *v*: shelter *KH* 152 [*OED*
  harboury, *DOST* herbery]
hardely *adv*: boldly *FB* 490 [*OED*
  hardily, *DOST* hardely]
harnes(se) *n*: genitals *TB* 209, 214
hat *v* see **hight**
hate *a*: warm *KH* 453 [hot]
have, hafe, haif *v*: have; *imperative
  absolute*: take this *BM* 25, *JR* 424,
  etc.
he high *FB* 12, 22
hecht see **hight**
he(e)de *n*: heed, careful attention to
  TB 176, *JR* 777, etc.
hem them *JS* 42, *KS* 186, etc.;
  hemself(e) themselves *JS* 101,
  356
hend, hynde *a*: courteous, gracious
  KS 505, *JR* 76, etc.
hend *n*: hands, *northern form JR* 730,
  KH 415, etc.
hend(e) *adv*: near *KS* 319; **at hend** at
  hand *KH* 415; **neither far ne
  hende** neither far nor near *KS*
  370
hent(e) *v*: take *DH* 74; *pa t*: took,
  mounted *JS* 236, *KH* 60; *pa pple*:

seized *LP* 178; grabbed *TB* 98, *JR* 547

hepe *n*: group *JS* 360, KS 534, etc.

herbord *pa t* see **harbour**

herborow, herbour see **harbour**

herbry *v*: lodge *FB* 85, 233; **herbryt** *pa t FB* 50 [*OED* harbry, *DOST* herbry]

herbrye see **harbry**

herke hark *JS* 325, *KH* 12

herkyn(s), herkynes harken *SC* 2, *KS* 734, etc.

hert *n*: courage *KH* 69 (see n.) [heart]

hertly *adv*: heartily, cordially *FB* 165 [*OED* heartly, *DOST* hertly]

het see **hight**

het(e), hett *v* see **hight**

hether hither *DH* 55, 58, etc.

hett see **hight**

hett *a*: hot *FB* 41, 169 [het]

hevy *a*: doleful *JS* 369, *FB* 418 [heavy]

hicht *n*: height *FB* 12, 15; haughtiness *FB* 82 [*OED* height, *DOST* hicht]

hid(d)er hither *TB* 91, *FB* 202, etc.

hye, hygh(e) *a*: high *TB* 159, *KS* 120, etc.

hye *v*: hasten, go quickly *JS* 267, *DH* 137, etc.

hy(e), hyghe *n*: haste; **in hy(e), in hyghe, on hye** in haste *TB* 159, *SC* 74, etc. [hie, hy]

hye *n*: high; **on hye** *adv*: loudly *JR* 88 [high]

hygh(e) *a*: high *LP* 225, *SC* 210, etc.

hight, hyght(e), hecht, het(e), hett, hat *v*: promise, vow *JR* 168, *KH* 504, etc.; order, command *LP* 64, *BM* 18; assure *KH* 379; is called *KS* 92, 470, etc.; **hyght** *pa t*: promised *JS* 105, *KS* 167, etc.; was called *SC* 246, *KH* 317, etc.; **hote** *ppl inf KS* 79, 243

hyld held *JS* 259, 398

hyll *v*: hide *KH* 228, 267

him, hym himself *FB* 524, *KH* 180, etc.

hynde *a* see **hend**

hyne *n*: lad, boy *JS* 12 [hind]

hyng(e) hang *KH* 261, 459

hyre *n*: wages, reward *FB* 246, *KH* 155

hit it *TB* 21, *KS* 10, etc.

hold(e), halde held *TB* 14, *KS* 645, etc.

hop(e) *v*: suppose, think *JR* 484, *KH* 443; **hopys** *second pers sing KH* 412, 418, etc.

hopys *second pers sing* see **hope**

hore *a*: gray with age *SC* 155 [hoar]

hore *n*: slime *KS* 177 [hore]

hote *ppl inf* see **hight**

horpyd *a*: bold *KH* 429 [orped]

howvyd see *KH* 328n.

hunde hound *KH* 50, 55, etc.

husband(e), husbond *n*: manager of a household *TB* 12; married man *TB* 19, *DH* 23, etc.; farmer *FB* 237, *KS* 152

yche, iche each *SC* 181, *KH* 92; **ychon** each one *SC* 206

ylke *a*: same (thing) *JR* 397

ilke *a*: each, every *KS* 125, 1006

ilkone *pron*: each one *FB* 421, *KS* 187

in(ne) *n*: dwelling-place *JR* 136; lodging *KH* 164

inowgh(e), inow(e), inoughe enough *JS* 51, *KH* 233, etc.

intill *prep*: in *FB* 52, 111, etc.

into *prep*: into the possession of (by will) *LP* 238; in *FB* 1, 7; onto *KS* 361

invy *n*: hostility *FB* 338 [envy]

ys his *LP* 135, *LP* 144, etc.; is *LP* 8, *SC* 5, etc.

ische *v*: issue *FB* 130 [*OED* ish, *DOST* isch(e]

iwys(se), iwis(se) *adv*: certainly *TB* 59, *KS* 474, etc. [iwis]

jerfawcon *n*: large falcon *JR* 574

journé, jorney, jornay *n*: day's work *JS* 284, *KS* 908; day trip *KS* 18;

day's fight *KS* 847

just *v*: joust *DH* 286, *JR* 772

keep(e) see **kepe**

ken(n), kenn(e) *v*: know (a person) *JR*
382; see *JR* 112; recognize *FB*
236, *JR* 497; teach *KH* 333, 389;
kend *pa t*: gave instructions *FB*
109; knew *FB* 154

kend *pa t* see **ken**

kepe, keep(e) *v*: practice *JR* 275;
guard, preserve *LP* 241, *KS* 274,
etc.; tend *JR* 267; **keepest** *second
pers sing*: observe with formality;
kepyth *third pers sing*: tend *JS* 38;
preserve *LP* 241; **keped** *pa t*:
tended *KH* 179

kind, kynd(e) *n*: form *FB* 447, 459;
nature *TB* 73, *FB* 471; family *KS*
390; species *KS* 261; *a*: well born
BM 3

kirke(e) *n*: church *FB* 23, *JR* 373, etc.

kirtle, kirtill, kyrtell, kyrtil *n*: man's
tunic *SC* 142, *BM* 5, etc.; a
woman's gown *FB* 143, *JR* 373, etc.

knave *n*: male servant *KH* 136, 313,
etc.

knaw know, identify *FB* 231, *SC* 81,
etc.

kokwold see **cokwold**

lad *n*: serving-man *JR* 206, 279, etc.

lad(de) led *TB* 41, *KS* 165, etc.

laine *n*: concealment *JR* 828;
without(e) laine to tell the truth
JR 575

lang long *FB* 152 , *KS* 781, etc.

late, lat(t) let *FB* 556, *KH* 48, etc.

law(e) low *FB* 546, *KS* 1084

lawgh laugh *KS* 12, 619, etc.

leaze, les(e) *n*: falsehood *KS* 288;
**withouten leaze, withouten les,
withowt lese** to tell the truth *SC*
207, *JR* 380, etc. [lease]

leef, lefe, leve *a*: beloved, dear *JS*
298, *KS* 215, etc. [lief]

leever, leevur see **lever**

leffe *n*: friend *SC* 134; *adv* [lief]

leir see **lere**

lemmane *n*: lover *FB* 181, *KS* 597

lenger longer *JS* 219, 234, etc.

lere, leir *v*: learn *FB* 308, *SC* 1, etc.

les(e) see **leaze**

lese *v*: lose *TB* 209, 214; **lesyst** *second
pers sing LP* 133 [leese]

les(s)yng *n*: lie *LP* 48, *SC* 18, etc.
[leasing]

lesyst *second pers sing* see **lese**

lessyng see **lesyng**

lett(e), let *n*: hindrance; **withoute(n)
let(e)** without hesitation, without
pause *TB* 105, *DH* 58, etc.

lett(e), lete *v*: delay, hinder *JS* 396,
KH 262, etc. [let *v*²]

letting, lettynge *pres pple*: delay *JS*
327, *JR* 408

leughe laughed *SC* 44

leve *a* see **leef**

le(e)ver, levir, leevur *comp a*: rather
FB 282, *JR* 455, etc.; *adv*: rather
TB 141 [*OED* liever, *DOST* levar,
levir]

levyd *v*: abandoned, forsook (a
practice) *TB* 218 [*pa t* leave]

levir see **lever**

lewd, lewed *a*: bad, worthless *LP* 202;
uneducated *JR* 496

lewh laughed *JS* 253

ley *n*: faith *KS* 321, *KH* 408

libberla *n*: staff, cudgel *FB* 482 [*OED*
libberla, *DOST* libber-lay]

light, lyght(e) see **lite**

lightly, lyghtely, lightley *adv*:
quickly *DH* 59; easily *JS* 93, *JR*
614

like *a*: likely *DH* 21; **is like** has the
appearance of being *JR* 265

like, lyke *impers v*: pleases *KS* 442,
KH 198

likinge *vbl n*: pleasure *JR* 126

lyre *n*: body *JR* 258 [*MED* lire]

lyst(e) *n*: desire, longing *LP* 36, 49
[list]

list, lystyth *impers v*: [it] pleases *JS*

231, *JR* 521; [it] pleased *TB* 128;
ye list, list hee (used personally):
you please, he pleased *DH* 80, *JR*
703, etc.

lite, lyte, light, lyght(e) *n*: little, not
much *TB* 53, *KS* 734; *a*: small *JS*
95, 226

lyve *n*: life *JS* 86, *KH* 270; **on lyve**
alive *TB* 19

liveryes *n*: allotment *JR* 557 (see n.)
[livery]

loffe love *LP* 108, *SC* 218

loke see **look**

loogh laughed *KS* 55, 784, etc.

look(e), loke, luke *v*: take care, make
sure *JS* 194, *DH* 60, etc.; consider
JR 437

long *a*: tall *JR* 257, *KH* 147

lording, lordyng *n*: *SC* 202, *KS* 178,
etc.

lorne *pa pple*: lost *JS* 308, *KS* 283

lost(e) *pa pple*: wasted *JS* 16, 21;
destroyed *JS* 379, *LP* 148

loth *a*: pleasant; hostile *KS* 691; **me
were loth, lothe I were** it would
be unpleasant for me *LP* 3, *KH*
160, etc. [loath]

louff, loufe love *LP* 34, 50

lough(e) laughed *JS* 175, *JR* 71, etc.

lout *v*: bow *JR* 703; **lowt** *pa t* *FB* 336

lowgh(e), lowgen laughed *JS* 106, *KS*
999, etc.

luf(e) love *FB* 152, *KS* 788, etc.

luge lodge *FB* 49; **lugit** lodged *FB*
235

luke see **look**

lust *n*: desire, appetite *JS* 56, *DH* 95

lusty *a*: handsome *FB* 6; lustful *DH* 7

ma *n* see **mo**

ma *v* see **may**

mayne see **mane**

mair more *FB* 119, 223, etc.

maist most *FB* 18, 244, etc.

maistrye see **mastery**

maistrys mistress *TB* 162, 163

mall *n*: hammer (weapon) *DH* 202

[maul]

manar, manner *n*: country residence
FB 52, *JR* 683, etc. [*OED* manor,
DOST maner, -ar]

mane, mayne *n*: bread of mane =
pane pain-demaine, the finest
kind of bread *FB* 160, 219, etc.
[maine]

manner see **manar**

mark *n*[1]: target *JS* 90

mark *n*[2]: money of account, equal to
eight ounces of silver *LP* 236, *BM*
84

marshall *n*: officer in charge of the
arrangement of ceremonies, esp.
the seating plan *KS* 707, *JR* 346,
etc.

mastery, maistrye *n*: feat(s) *KS* 238,
KH 276

may, ma *v*: have power *JS* 130, *JR* 93,
etc.; can *JS* 42, *FB* 280, etc.; **mowe**
second pers pl: may *TB* 6

meanye *n*: company of persons *JR*
354; household *JR* 626 [meinie]

measure, mesure *n*: dance *JR* 533,
548; melody, tune *JS* 98; rhythm
JR 536

meate, meit, meyte, mete *n*: food,
meal *SC* 61, *JR* 234, etc.

mede see **meed**

medyll middle *JS* 405, *LP* 178

meed(e), mede *n*: wage, reward *DH*
43, *KS* 712, etc.; bribe *KS* 237;
(un)to meede as a reward *BM* 84,
192

meete, mete, meit *adv*: in a fit or
proper manner *JR* 160; *a*:
appropriate *JS* 87, *FB* 261

meit *a* and *adv* see **meete**

meit, meyte *n* see **meate**

**mekyll, mycul(l), mykell, mekle,
mikill, micul(l)** *a*: much *FB* 207,
KH 212, etc.

merth see **myrth**

mesure see **measure**

mete *adv* see **meete**

mete *n* see **meat**

methe *n*: alcoholic drink made of honey and water *LP* 210 [mead]

meve see **move**

myche much *SC* 28, *KH* 210

micht might *FB* 16, 492, etc.

micul(l), mycul(l) see **mekyll**

midday, mydey *n*: mid-day *KS* 120, *KH* 74, etc.

mydyll erd *n*: middle earth, the world *LP* 161 [middle-erd]

mykell see **mekyll**

myld(e) *a*: kind, considerate, gentle *JS* 434, *JR* 592, etc.

mildam *n*: the damned up water above a mill *DH* 214, 219

mylde see **myld**

myr(e) *n*: piece of swampy ground *FB* 536, *LP* 186

myrth, merth, mirth *n*: enjoyment *SC* 224, *KS* 1032; musical entertainment *JS* 419; *pl*: entertainments, diversions *LP* 202

mitton, mytan, myten *n*: protective hand covering for a hedger or the like *JR* 637, 720; mitten *KS* 646, 593, etc. [mitten]

mo(o), ma more *KS* 414, *JR* 115, etc.; more (in number) *FB* 359; more persons *SC* 253, *JR* 381, etc. [*OED* mo, *DOST* ma]

modur mother *KS* 98, 1025

moir more *FB* 108, 375, etc.

mone *n*: moon *LP* 35, *FB* 381, etc.

mone *v*: must *FB* 478

moné *n*: money *TB* 64, *KS* 119, etc.

moo see **mo**

mor(r)ow *n*: morning *TB* 174, *LP* 68, etc.

most(e) must *TB* 113, *KS* 32, etc.

mot(e), mott, mut *v*: may *TB* 182, *DH* 128, etc.; must *TB* 114, *KS* 909 [mote]

move, meve *v*: proceed *LP* 9, *KS* 1064; mention *LP* 13

mow(e) may *KS* 680, 906 etc.

mow(e) *second pers pl* see **may**

mut see **mot**

na no *FB* 16, 79, etc.

ne *conj*: nor *TB* 33, *KS* 16, etc.; *adv¹*: not *TB* 64, *JS* 294, etc.

ne *adv²*: nearly *KH* 68 [nigh]

neer never *LP* 232

neghtbur neighbor *KS* 70, 690

nehand nygh-hand

neir see **ner**

neirhand see **nerehand**

ner, neir ne'er, never *FB* 318, *JR* 400

nerehand, neirhand *adv* + *prep*: close at hand *FB* 479; close to *KH* 495 [*OED* nearhand, *DOST* nere hand]

new *adv*: newly *JR* 520, 552

ny see **nye**

nyce *a*: foolish, stupid *TB* 146, *KS* 1041, etc.; nycely *adv*: foolishly *KS* 878

ny(e) *adv*: *KS* 1023, near *JR* 32, etc.; nearly *JR* 270 [nigh]

nygh-hand, nehand *adv*: nearby *KH* 421; nearly *KH* 414 [nigh hand]

noble *n*: gold coin, worth ten shillings in the late fifteenth century *DH* 36, 79

nobull *a*: splendid *SC* 139, 250 [noble]

nocht, no(u)ght *n*: nothing *TB* 16, *BM* 116, etc.; *adv*: not *TB* 92, *FB* 39, etc.; not at all *KH* 395 [*OED* nought, *DOST* nocht]

nons, for the *phr*: "on this occasion," but usually a mere tag with little or no meaning *JS* 188, *DH* 261, etc. [nonce]

nother *a*: other *KS* 78, 431 [nouther]

nother, nouther *adv*: neither *LP* 157, *KS* 230, etc.

nothing, nothyng *adv*: not at all *FB* 538, *KS* 95, etc.

nought see **nocht**

oftetymes, ofttymes, oft time *adv*: often *DH* 180, *FB* 412, etc.

on one *TB* 19, *LP* 200

oneth see **unneth**

ons, onys once *KS* 114, *KH* 355, etc.

ony any *FB* 54, 151, etc.

or *conj*: before *DH* 276, *JR* 119, etc.

ordeyn *v*: prepare *KH* 305;
ordayned, ordeynd *pa pple*:
armed *JR* 188; ordered to be set
up *SC* 50

ore over *BM* 82, *KS* 841

ore *n* see **are**

oriso(u)n *n*: prayer *KS* 855; oration
FB 326

other *n*: another one, one another *LP*
162, *SC* 44, etc.; **others** *poss pron*:
another one's *JS* 389

ought *n*: anything *SC* 208, *JR* 174,
etc.

our over *FB* 323, 496, etc.

out of *prep*: beyond *LP* 25, *JR* 621,
etc.

owe *v*: own *JR* 178; **aught** *pa t*: bore
(good will) *SC* 218

ower our *LP* 58, 113, etc.

owttoure, outtour *prep*: over *FB* 509,
532, etc. [*OED* out-over, *DOST*
out-our]

paymen *n*: white bread *JR* 199, 433

parsaving *vbl n* see **persaving**

part *n*: share (see *FB* 278n.)

pass *v*: go on, proceed *FB* 37, *KH* 77,
etc.

pay *n*: satisfaction *KS* 717; deserts *KS*
41, 745, etc.

peradventure, paraunter *adv*:
perhaps *KS* 526, *JR* 201, etc.

perdy(e) *int*: by God, certainly *KS*
905, *JR* 255, etc.

persaving, parsaving *vbl n*:
perception *FB* 175, 339

person parson *TB* 6, *LP* 29, etc.

pertrik partridge *FB* 159, 359, etc.

pet(t) see **pytt**

pikefforke *n*: pitchfork *JR* 323, 601
[pickfork]

pine, pyne *n*: suffering *KS* 152, 991;
penitential suffering caused by
hunger *JR* 456

pine, pyne *v*: torment *JR* 788

pistill *n*: spoken story; *also*, extract
from an apostolic letter *FB* 184
[*OED* pistle, *DOST* pistil(l)]

pytt(e), pet(t) *n*: hell *LP* 185; grave
LP 105, 146 [pit]

place, plase *n*: convent, religious
house *LP* 18, *DH* 121, etc.

play, pley crafty proceeding *DH* 268;
diversion *JR* 708; delight *SC* 20,
54, etc.; game *KS* 288, *KH* 377,
etc.

playn see **pleyn**

playng see **pleyng**

plase see **place**

playntie plenty *FB* 349

pleyn, playn *n*: clearing *JS* 53, *KH*
101

pleyng, playng *n*: sport *KH* 17, 28
[playing]

pleynte *n*: complaint *JS* 185, 268
[plain]

pleiss *n*: pleasure *FB* 408 [*OED*
please, *DOST* (plese), pleis]

pleiss please *FB* 441, 469

pleyt see **plight**

plenté plenty *KS* 489, *KH* 32, etc.;
aplenty *KS* 939

plight, plyght, pleyt *v*: pledge *JS*
262, *JR* 415, etc.; assure *SC* 13, *KS*
943

pluver plover *FB* 360, 377

polax *n*: battle-ax *DH* 195, 202 [pole-
ax]

posterne *a*: private, side or back
(entrance) *TB* 126; *n*: private gate
FB 129

potener *n*: pouch *BM* 21 [pautener]

practik *n*: artful contrivance *FB* 307,
319 [practic]

precedent *n*: head *LP* 58 [president]

preisit *v*: hurried *FB* 524 [*pa t* pres]

prelet prelate *LP* 29; **preletlyk** like a
prelate *FB* 183

preste *a*: willing *KH* 418; **preste to**
ready for *JS* 48

preve see **prove**

prevely see **privily**

previe, prevy see **privé**

pride, pryde *n*: ostentation *JR* 605; pomp, magnificence *SC* 87, *KS* 727, etc.

prime *n*: the first hour of the day after sunrise *JR* 559

privé, prevy, previe *a*: secret, clandestine *FB* 129, *KS* 439, etc.

privily, prively, prevely, pryvely *adv*: stealthily, secretly *DH* 273, *KH* 319, etc.

privyté, priveté, pryveté *n*: thing kept secret *KS* 384; private business *KS* 516, *KH* 455, etc.; **in priveté** confidentially, in private *KS* 64, 672, etc.

proud, prowd *a*: splendid *FB* 148, 180, etc.; **proudest** most splendid *JR* 333

prove, preve *v*: test, try *FB* 319, *KS* 446, etc.; **provyd** *pa pple*: found by experience *LP* 20

prow *n*: advantage, profit *JR* 426, *KH* 254

prowd see **proud**

purveance, purviance *n*: supply of food *FB* 384, *FB* 414 [purveyance]

quha who *FB* 117, 125, etc.

quhair where *FB* 4, 105, etc.

quhairfoir wherefore; because of which *FB* 18, 406

quhairin *n*: see *FB* 523 (see note)

quhat what *FB* 86, 91, etc.

quhatevir whatever *FB* 416, 475, etc.

quhatkin *a*: whatever *FB* 320 [whatkin]

quhen when *FB* 15, 56, etc.

quhylis *adv*: sometimes *FB* 331, 334, etc.

quhilk which *FB* 2, 103, etc.

quhill *conj*: till, until *FB* 37, 205, etc.

quhyt white *FB* 24, 144, etc.

quyt quite *LP* 171, *FB* 558

quyt(e), quite, quitt(e), white *v*: repay *FB* 199, *JR* 378, etc.; **quit** *pa pple*: paid *DH* 265; **quitted** *pa t*: acquitted *BM* 158

rafte *pa pple*: taken *TB* 142, *KS* 544 [reave]

raiss rose *FB* 252, 521

rakand *pres pple*: going quickly *FB* 420 [rake]

rakyl *n*: chain, fetter *LP* 138, 154

rappe *n*: breaking of wind *JS* 119, 170

raste *v*: rushed *TB* 166 [*pa t* rase]

rax *v*: rouse, stretc.h *FB* 504, 520

read(e) see **rede**

receate, ressett *n*: accommodation *FB* 511, *JR* 161 [receipt]

rech *v*: care, want to do something *TB* 48, *KS* 312, etc. [reck]

red *adj*: frightened *FB* 410 [rad]

rede *n*: scheme, plan *JS* 340

rede, read(e), reed(e) *v*: advise, counsel *JS* 27, *JR* 75, etc.; read *DH* 10; tell, speak *KH* 141; guess *KS* 96; **redd** *pa pple*: expounded the significance *SC* 121 [rede]

redy *a*: easily followed (of a route) *KH* 501, 512

reed(e) *v* see **rede**

reeve *n*: bailiff, overseer *JR* 134, etc.

ren(ne) run *DH* 305, *KS* 155, etc.; **renning** running *DH* 62

rent *n*: revenue, income *LP* 40; property yielding income *SC* 195

rent *pa t* and *pa pple* see **rentt**

rentt *v*: break *LP* 173; **rent** *pa pple JR* 607; **rent** *pa t JS* 250, *KS* 1010 [rend]

repair, repayre *n*: usual dwelling place *JR* 164; concourse of people to a place *FB* 106

reson *n*: narrative *LP* 5 [reason]

ressett see **receate**

rewll *v*: restrain (yourself) *FB* 473; rewlyd *pa pple*: guided *LP* 62 [rule]

ryall royal *JS* 257, *KH* 22

ryght, right, richt *n*: justifiable claim *LP* 113, *JR* 804, etc.

ryght, (w)right, richt *adv*: straight,
directly *JS* 320, *DH* 310, etc.; in a
proper manner *JR* 215;
altogether, quite *TB* 106, *FB* 120,
etc.; just *LP* 64, *BM* 134, etc.; *a*:
direct *JS* 401

rynnyng running *LP* 138

ryve *adv*: promptly, speedily *TB* 20,
JS 85, etc. [rife]

rode see **rood**

ronne ran *KH* 59, run *LP* 202

rood(e), rode, rud *n*: Christ's cross
FB 302, *JR* 546, etc.

round(e) *adv*: on all sides *TB* 190, *FB*
542, etc.

route, rowte *n*¹: disorderly crowd *TB*
197, *JS* 404, etc.; group *SC* 227,
231; gang *KS* 833 [rout]

route *n*²: process of a drinking ritual
KS 332 [*MED* route]

row(e) *n*: (up)on a row(e): all together
TB 190, *JS* 126; one after the
other *JS* 137

rown *v*: whisper *FB* 184, *JR* 99;
rowned *pa t JR* 256 [round]

rowning *n*: private conversation *JR*
499, 506

rowte *n*¹ see **route**

rowte *n*³: blow *JR* 624 [rout]

rud see **rood**

rudd *n*: complexion *BM* 51, 79, etc.
[rud]

russet(t) *n*: coarse woolen cloth *KS*
588, *JR* 286

rusted *pa pple*: rust-colored see *JR*
392 [rust; *influenced by* reested]

sa so *FB* 231, 249, etc.

sain, sayn say *JS* 32, *DH* 177, etc.

sair see **sore**

sall shall *FB* 74, 204, etc.

salvyd *v*: healed *LP* 243 [*pa t* salve]

sam(m)e *adv*: together *SC* 140, *KH* 5,
etc.

samyn(e) *a*: same *FB* 125, 435, etc.
[samen]

samme see **sam(m)e**

sanct saint *FB* 36, 287

sande *n*: grace *TB* 13, *KS* 655

saw(e) *n*: proverb *TB* 21; story *SC* 12;
speech *TB* 191, *KS* 1081, etc.

scape, scapyd *v*: escaped *LP* 207, *KH*
213; *pa pple*: *LP* 162, 190 [*pa t*
scape]

scath, skath(e) *n*: harm *JR* 316, *KH*
244, etc. [scathe]

schaw show *FB* 506

schelyng shilling *KS* 82, 743

schent see **shent**

schet(e) *v*: shoot *KS* 189, *KH* 464

schew(e) show *KS* 406, *SC* 4, etc.

scho she *FB* 55, 211, etc.

scor(e)n *v*: mock *JR* 612; disdain *LP*
184; **scornyd** *pa pple*: *SC* 184

se(e), sey *v*: saw *LP* 150, *JR* 400, etc.
[*pa t* see]

seere, seir *a*: various *FB* 307, *JR* 465
[sere]

sey *n*: sea *FB* 8, 308

sey *v* see **see**

seid(e), seyd(e) said *JS* 112, *KS* 24,
etc.

seik seek *FB* 26, 62

seir see **seere**

sekyrly see **sikerly**

sele, sell *n*: happiness *JR* 507, 813;
occasion *KS* 336, 687, 820

seme *v*: appears *JS* 290, *KH* 286;
semyd *pa t impers*: it was suitable
for (someone) *LP* 138 [seem]

sen *conj*: considering (that) *FB* 163,
469

send *v*: grant *DH* 326, *BM* 194, etc.

senne *adv*: from that time onwards
SC 252

serten *adv* see **certain**

sertes see **certes**

service, servys(e), sirvese, sirvys *n*:
performance of a servant's duties
KH 224; payment for such
performance *KH* 140; religious
service *TB* 173, *LP* 98; the hours
of the breviary *DH* 150; course of
food *JR* 396, 400, etc.

serwand servant *FB* 440, 445

seth see **sythe**

sethen *adv*: then *KH* 232 [sithen]

sethen, sethyn, sithen *conj*: since *KS* 311, *KH* 315, etc. [sithen]

share *v*: cut *JR* 327, 717 [cut]

sheede *v*: spill *BM* 181; **shedd** *pa t BM* 183 [shed]

sheild *n*: meat cooked in boar skin *JR* 465 [shield]

shent, schent *pa pple*: ruined, disgraced *DH* 134, *KS* 1011, etc.

sherwly see **shrewdly**

shete shoot *JS* 84, 230, etc.

shevell, shevyll shovel *TB* 189, 200, etc.

shew(e) show *JS* 353, *LP* 233

shewed shown *LP* 201

shope *v*: created *LP* 210 [*pa t* shape]

showyll shovel *LP* 103

shread *v*: prune *JR* 677; *pa pple*: cut to shreds *BM* 40 [shred]

shreeven *pa pple*: confessed *TB* 123 [shrive]

shrewd(e), shrewed, shrewed, shrewid *a*: bad, vile *JS* 297, *DH* 268, etc.; vigorous *DH* 22

shrewdly, sherwly *adv*: severely *DH* 46; grievously *LP* 145

sic *a*: such *FB* 88, 200, etc.

sich, sych(e), soch such *SC* 101, *KH* 163, etc.

side, syde *a*: long *JR* 223, 326, etc.

sidebord *n*: table at the side of a hall *JR* 385, 429

syer see **sire**

sikerlye, sykerly, sykerlyke, sekyrly *adv*: certainly, without doubt *SC* 17, *JR* 39, etc.; **siker** *a*: certain, sure *KS* 429

silly *a*: ignorant *FB* 34 (see n.), *JR* 758, etc.

silwer silver *FB* 128, 145

sympyll, simple *a*: deficient in mental powers *LP* 12; free from pride *JR* 768

syn(e) *adv*: afterwards *FB* 220, *JR* 462, etc.; then *FB* 11, *JR* 644, etc.

sire, syer *n*: person of importance *LP* 187, *SC* 19; sirres *pl JR* 514

sirvys, sirvese see **service**

syth(e) *n*: times *SC* 233, 240; **sithes, sithis** *pl*: times KS 62, 134

sythe, sith(e), seth *conj*: since *JR* 514, *KH* 287, etc.; *adv*: then, afterwards *LP* 134

sithen see **sethen**

sithence that *conj phr*: considering that *JR* 160

skath(e) see **scath**

skerlet, skerlyt *n*: rich cloth *SC* 222; *as a*: *SC* 142 [scarlet]

skyll *n*: case, reason *SC* 102; **in what skyll** *phr*: by what reason *SC* 152

slech *v*: assuage *TB* 46 [sletch]

slo slay *DH* 193, **slone** slain *KS* 35

smache *n*: slight suggestion *TB* 25 [smatch]

soch see **sich**

solas, solace *n*: entertainment *SC* 1, *JR* 4, etc.

solas *v*: entertain *KH* 19 [solace]

some *indef pron* see **sum**

somedeale, somedele *adv*: somewhat *JS* 432, *JR* 229, etc.

sompter see **sumpter**

soon(e), son(e) *adv*: early *DH* 110, *KH* 397; without delay *LP* 86, *JR* 183, etc.; quickly *DH* 101, *JR* 855, etc.

sooth, soth(e), ssoth, swth, suth *a*: true *TB* 7; *n*: truth *FB* 373, *SC* 51, etc.

sore *a*: bitter *KH* 516

sore, sair *adv*: intensely, painfully, badly *JS* 67, *FB* 554, etc.

sory *a*: painful *TB* 165; distressed *KS* 1031 [sorry]

sorrow, sorowe *n*: harm, distress *LP* 77, *JR* 597, etc.

sorowe see **sorrow**

soth(e) see **sooth**

sower sour *JR* 140, 305

sowy(e)d sewed *LP* 66, 155

sowld should *FB* 124, 411, etc.

sowp *v*: sweep *FB* 220 [*OED* soop]

sowsit *pa pple*: pickled *FB* 254 [souse]

space *n*: time *FB* 323, 497, etc.

spake spoke *DH* 199, *BM* 131, etc.

span *v*: ran quickly *KH* 57 [*pa t* spin]

spare *v*: avoid effort *TB* 99, *SC* 230; save *JR* 460; **sparyd** *pa t*: avoided *LP* 157, 160

speciall *n*: sweetheart, mistress *TB* 197 [special]

speed *n*: fortune *DH* 100, 151

speed, sped(e) *v*: succeed, prosper *BM* 194, *KS* 137, etc.; cause one to succeed *JS* 131, *KS* 815; **sped of** succeed in getting *KH* 93; **spedd** *pa t*; *refl*: rushed *JR* 734 [speed]

spicery *n*: spices *KS* 397, *JR* 472

spill, spyll(e) *v*: perish, be destroyed, die *JR* 166, *KH* 84, etc.

spyre *v*: ask *KH* 446 [speer]

sport *n*: entertainment *JS* 257, *FB* 117; amorous dalliance *FB* 170

sport *v*: amuse oneself *FB* 185; **sportit** *pa t*: *FB* 395

sprent *v*: sprang *KH* 57 [*pa t* sprent]

sprong *pa pple*: foundered *KH* 68 [spring]

ssoth see **sooth**

stalke *v*: walk stealthily *LP* 122, *KH* 264, etc.

stane stone *FB* 9, 522, etc.

start, sterte, stertit *v*: leapt, jumped *JS* 368, *FB* 347, etc. [*pa t* start]

state *n*: rank *KH* 274, 450

sted(e) *n*[1]: place *KS* 664, *KH* 225, etc. [stead]

sted(e) *n*[2]: large horse *KS* 746, *KH* 68, etc. [steed]

steir *n*: movement *FB* 476 [stir]

stent *v*: stop *JS* 356 [stint]

stere see **styre**

sterte, stertit see **start**

still(e), styll(e) *adv*: quietly, silently *TB* 175, *LP* 122, etc.

styll stile *LP* 160, 228

still(e), styll(e), stil *a*: silent *JS* 261, *KH* 9, etc.

styre, stere *v*: begin to move *LP* 123, *KH* 462, etc.; bestir (oneself) *LP* 112 [stir]

stod(e), stodyn stood *SC* 143, *KH* 363, etc.

stond(e) see **stound**

stone *n*: stone missile, pellet *JS* 168, *KS* 188, etc.

store, sture *a*: massive *JR* 541; coarse *JR* 55; stern *FB* 347 [stout]

store *n*: reserve *JR* 289; food collected for future use *DH* 252

stound(e), stond(e) *n*: a time, a while, a moment *JS* 363, *KH* 19, etc.; **(in) that sto(u)nde(s)**: at that moment *TB* 206, *KH* 56, etc.

stout, stowt *a*: proud, arrogant *JR* 172, *KH* 154, etc.; formidable, menacing *FB* 196, *JR* 47

stowp *n*: cup, tankard *FB* 66, 256 etc.

stowt see **stout**

straight, strait, streyte *adv*: upright *DH* 113, 139; immediately *JS* 368, *DH* 126, etc.; *adj*: narrow *FB* 12

straik *n*: slap *FB* 341 [stroke]

strait, streyte see **straight**

strife, stryfe stryff *n*: trouble, pain *DH* 208; contention *DH* 96, *KS* 347, etc.

stryk(e) *v*: go *KH* 83; hit *FB* 490, 529; **stroke(d)** *pa t*: drank up *KH* 376; pulled *KS* 980 [strike]

stro straw *FB* 172, *KH* 169

stroke(d) see **stryk** *pa t*

studeing *vbl n*: studying, meditating *FB* 331, 346

sturdy(e) *a*: stern, rough *JR* 172, 796; impetuously brave *JR* 300

sture *a* see **store**

subteltie *n*: cunning *FB* 385; trick *FB* 17

suffisance *n*: sufficient supply *FB* 391 [sufficience]

sum *adv*: a little, somewhat *FB* 265 [some]

sum, some *indef pron*: someone, somebody *TB* 115, *JR* 776 [some]

sumdel *n*: some part *TB* 46, *KS* 283 [somedeal]

sumpter, sompter *n as a*: driver of a packhorse *JR* 274, 358, etc.

sumthing *adv*: somewhat *FB* 55, 484

supped *v*: drank *JR* 632, 837 [*pa t* sup]

sure *a*: safe, secure *DH* 69; **surer** *comp*: more secure *BM* 19; *adv*: securely *DH* 303

suth see **sooth**

swa so *FB* 51, 463, etc.

sware, swere swore *JS* 256, *LP* 35, etc.

swete *v*: work hard *TB* 38 [sweat]

swetyng *n*: sweetheart *TB* 112 [sweeting]

swett *n*: sweetheart *LP* 67, 108 [sweet]

swynke *v*: toil *TB* 38 [swink]

swyth(e) *adv*: very *KS* 339; quickly *TB* 106, 111 [swith]

swth see **sooth**

tach *n*: fault, bad habit *TB* 24 [tache]

tail(l), tayle *n*: backside *JR* 654; **top our taill, top over tayle** *phr*: head over tail *FB* 565, *JR* 539

tane taken *BM* 69, 133, etc.

teche *v*: show someone the way, guide *KH* 131, 137; **taught** *pa t* *KH* 319

tell till *LP* 45, *LP* 131

ten(n)e *n*: pains taken *LP* 42; hardship *KH* 222; something annoying *JR* 219; anger *KS* 980 [teen]

tenid *pa pple*: annoyed *JS* 158 [teen]

tenne see **tene**

tha *dem pron* see **tho**

thaym them *TB* 128, *KS* 2, etc.

thair(e) their *FB* 3, *KS* 409, etc.

thake-bendesfull *n*: amount that could be held by the band of twisted straw normally used to hold a bundle of straw for thatching *KH* 170 [thank + bend

+ full]

tham(e) them *TB* 158, *FB* 15, etc.

than(e) then *LP* 67, *FB* 60, etc.

thay they *JS* 403, *KS* 35, etc.

the *pron*: they *JR* 756, *KH* 55, etc.

the *v* see **the(e)**

there *v*: dare *LP* 51 [dare]

theder thither *LP* 116, *KH* 102, etc.

the(e) *v*: thrive, prosper *JR* 372, *KH* 121, etc.

then than *TB* 141, *LP* 7, etc.

therat(e), theratt *adv*: thereat, at it *SC* 53, *JR* 487, etc.

theron *adv*: immediately after that *DH* 308, *KH* 110, etc.

thertille, thertylle *adv*: *KS* 622, *KH* 12

thertoo *adv*: besides *TB* 81, 123

therwith, therwyth *adv*: thereupon *JS* 62, *LP* 236, etc.

they the *JR* 875; thy *LP* 219, 233

theym them *JS* 3, 4

thider thither *TB* 175, 176

think(e), thynk(e) *v¹ impers*: (it) seems (to) *JS* 291; **thoght, thought** *pa t* *DH* 193, *KS* 463, etc.

think(e) *v²*: intend *FB* 433, *JR* 198, etc.; **thoughth** *pa t* *JS* 184

thir *a*: these *FB* 34, 118, etc.

this *adv*: in this way, thus *FB* 131, 415, etc.

tho, tha *dem pron*: those *JS* 361, 397, etc.; *dem a*: those *FB* 279

tho(o) though *LP* 191, *JR* 672

thoo, tho(e) *adv*: after that, thereupon, then *JS* 154, *JR* 322, etc.

thoch though *FB* 484

thocht thought *FB* 152, 343, etc.

thoff though *KH* 245, 436, etc.

thoght *v¹ pa t* see **thynke**

thoght *n*: thought *TB* 90, *KS* 42, etc.

thol *v*: endure without complaint *FB* 198; **tholit** *pa* t: allowed *FB* 226 [thole]

thone then *FB* 283

thong(e) *n*: narrow strip of leather *JR*

709, *KH* 197

thoo *adv* see **tho**

thore there *DH* 224, *KS* 174

thoro(w), thrught *prep*: through *JS* 139, *KH* 64, etc.; by means of *TB* 12, *SC* 105, etc. [thorough]

thouh though *JS* 95

thoughth *v*² *pa t* see **thynke**

thrast *v*: push violently *DH* 213 [threst]

thratt *pa pple*: threatened *JR* 181 [threat]

thry(is)s thrice *FB* 336, *KH* 55

thristit *v*: thrusted *FB* 134; squeezed *FB* 168 [thrust]

throng *v*: thrust *KH* 467 [*pa t* thring]

throw through *FB* 176, 411, etc.

thrught see **thoro**

thwyttel, thwyttill *n*: knife *JR* 326, 715 [thwittle]

tyde *n*: time *JS* 265, *KH* 105, etc.

tyll till; *prep*: to *FB* 140, *KH* 484 etc.; for *KH* 25

tyret *v*: dressed *KS* 588; **tyryd** *pa pple* *LP* 127 [tire]

tyrit tired *FB* 38, 227

tyte *adv*: quickly, soon *JR* 222, *KH* 235, etc.

to *prep*: for *JR* 599; till *KH* 74, 330

togyder together *FB* 201, 441, etc.

toke see **tooke**

tome *n*: opportunity *JS* 395 [toom]

ton(e) the (first) one *TB* 10, *JR* 178

tooke, toke *v*: gave *JS* 154; tooke ... for: considered *JR* 605

to-raged *pa pple*: very ragged *JS* 272 [to- + rag]

to-rente *pa pple*: torn in pieces *JS* 272 [to- + rend]

tother other (of two) *TB* 11, *KS* 104, etc.; other's *KS* 197

totted *a*: tipsy *KH* 343 [totty *a*²]

toute, towte *n*: buttocks *TB* 199, *SC* 120, etc.

towe two *JR* 384, 443

towgh(e) tough *KS* 787, *KH* 303

towoke *v*: awoke completely *LP* 96

[to- + wake]

travayle *n*: labor, effort *KS* 666 [travail]

travell *n*: labor, trouble *FB* 65, *KH* 133, etc. [travel]

travell *v*: travel *FB* 39; **travellit, travelled** *pa t*: labored *FB* 274; traveled *JR* 311

trey *n*: trouble, vexation *KH* 222 [tray]

treserer, tresirere treasurer *KS* 47, 576

trest trust *FB* 432 [*OED* trest]

trie, trye *a*: "choice," superior *KS* 369, 400

trifull *n*: false or idle tale *TB* 1 [trifle]

troch trough *FB* 328, 498, etc.

troe see **trow**

troich trough *FB* 206

trow(e), troe *v*: believe, think *JS* 82, *JR* 83, etc.; expect *KS* 131, *KH* 253

trowth *n*: faith *JS* 107, 257, etc. [troth]

truth *n*: solemn promise *JR* 415, 588

tunn *n*: large wine cask *JR* 443, 810 [tun]

turss *v*: be off *FB* 511 [truss]

tusche *n*: rich green cloth (see *FB* 149–50n.) [tissue]

twa two *FB* 29, *KS* 75, etc.

twane, twayen *a*: two *KS* 840 [twain]; *n*: pair, couple *LP* 159 [twain]

tway, twey(e) *a*: two *FB* 99, *KS* 743, etc. [tway]

twayen see **twane**

twey(e) see **tway**

twine, twyn *v*: separate, disjoin *TB* 136; depart *JR* 519

uder, udir other *FB* 33, 415, etc.

umbecast *v*: went round *JR* 24 [*pa t* umbecast]

uncoupuld *v*: released (dogs) from being fastened in couples *KH* 55 [*pa t* uncouple]

undernom *pa pple*: reproved, rebuked *LP* 3 [undernim]

unneth, oneth *adv*: hardly, scarcely *JS* 274, *KH* 462, etc. [uneath]

unskill *n*: folly *JR* 41

unskillfullye *adv*: foolishly, ignorantly *JR* 84

untill *prep*: to *FB* 466, *JR* 806

unto *prep*: until *LP* 68

uphent *v*: raised *TB* 108 [*pa t* uphend]

upo(u)n, apon *prep*: upon *LP* 77, *FB* 2; **apon a boke** from a book *LP* 98

upryss *second pers*: rise up *FB* 501; **uprais** *pa t FB* 322 [uprise]

upstert *v*: jumped up *TB* 152, 161 [*pa t* upstart]

use *v*: observe or comply with (a law) *JR* 198; **usyd, usit** *pa pple*: accustomed *LP* 11, *FB* 30

vayle *v*: take off (a hat) *JR* 657, 797, etc.; lower (a hood) *JR* 119, 689, etc. [vail]

verament *adv*: really, truly *TB* 110, *DH* 300, etc.

vilany, vilony, vylony *n*: disgrace *SC* 35, 171; wicked conduct, vile deed *KS* 143; [villainy]

voyed *v*: go away *LP* 132 [void]

wayn see **wane**

wait *pres t* see **wit**

wald see **wold**

wan won *BM* 189, *KS* 555, etc.

wane, wayn *n*: expedient *FB* 415, 521

want *v*: lack *FB* 398; **wantit** was lacking *FB* 378; lacked *FB* 114 [want]

ware *a*: aware *BM* 153, *JR* 47; prudent *TB* 219, *JR* 64

ware were *KS* 692

ware, were *n*: commodities *SC* 110, *KS* 63, etc.; cloth *JR* 713

warne *v*: inform *JR* 220, 857, etc.

warrand *v*: protect *FB* 480; undertake, pledge oneself *FB* 492 [warrant]

warrison, war(r)yson *n*: reward *JR*

566, *KH* 46, etc.

wast *n*: uninhabited and uncultivated country *JR* 84

wast *a*: idle, vain *JR* 303

wast were *BM* 106, *JR* 667

watt *pres t* see **wit**

wayiss ways *FB* 79, 106, etc.

wede, weed(e), weed(es) *n*: clothing, garments *JR* 189, *KH* 157, etc.

weend *v* see **wend**

weele well *BM* 174, *JR* 510

weill well *FB* 9, 178, etc.

wele well *KS* 330, *KH* 107, etc.

wele happiness, prosperity *KH* 117 [weal]

wench(e) *n*: female servant *TB* 158, 195

wend(e), weend, wynd(e) *v*: go *LP* 172, *KS* 511, etc.; go off, depart *KS* 47, *JR* 678, etc.; twist *JS* 275, 374; **went** *sing imp*: go *JR* 884; *pa t*: winded *LP* 37

wend(e) *pa t* see **wene**

wene *v*: think, believe *KS* 95, 445, etc.; expect *KS* 1062; **wend(e), went** *pa t*: believed *JS* 209, *KS* 876; expected *SC* 178, *KS* 1011 [ween]

went *pa t* see **wene**

went *sing imp* see **wend**

wer where *KH* 29, 203, etc.

were *n* see **ware**

werke work *KS* 38, *JR* 268, etc.

wern *v*: refuse a request, deny something *SC* 114 [warn]

werryed *a pple*: made war upon *BM* 154 [warray]

wete see **wyte**

wesche, wesshe *v*: wash *SC* 207, *KS* 882; **wasshen** washed *KS* 887

wex(e), woix *v*: grew, became *JS* 164, *FB* 421, etc. [*pa t* wex]

whyle *n*: time *LP* 94, *SC* 180, etc.; **whyles** for a long time *KH* 230; **the whylys** while *KH* 138

whyleare *adv*: a while before *KH* 482 [whilere]

white see **quyt**

wicht *a* see **wight**

wicht, wight, wyght *n*: person *FB*
514; creature *FB* 467, *KH* 124,
etc. [wight]

wife *n*: woman *TB* 145; *pl*: wyffis *FB*
34, 35

wight, wicht *a*: strong, stout *FB* 11,
JR 893, etc.; quick *JR* 733; brave
JR 911; *adv*: quickly *JR* 214

wight, wyght *n* see **wicht**

wyghtly *adv*: swiftly *KH* 323

wyiss see **wise**

wyll(e) *adv*: astray *KH* 78, 119 [will]

wilsome, wylsom *a*: lonely, wild,
dreary *FB* 390, *JR* 36; leading
astray *KH* 221

win, winne, wynne *v*: make one's way
KH 65; capture *FB* 17, *SC* 172;
earn *LP* 23, *JR* 458; steal or fetch
TB 86; get *FB* 95, 195

wynd(e) see **wend**

winne, wynne see **winwynnit** *v*:
dwelt, resided *FB* 51 [*pa t* win *v²*]

wise, wyiss *n*: manner *FB* 177, *JR*
314, etc.

wysse *v*: guide *KH* 90 [wis]

wist, wyst *pa t* see **wit**

wyte *v*: blame *JS* 58, *KH* 134

wyte, wit(t), wete *inf v*: find out *FB*
345, *JR* 142, etc.; **watt, wot(t),
wait, wost, wo(o)te** *pres t*: know *LP*
83, *FB* 342, etc.; knows *FB* 61, *JR*
825, etc.; **wyst, wist** *pa t*: knew *LP*
27, *JR* 29, etc. *subj JR* 181

with *prep*: by *FB* 267, *JR* 594, etc.;
from *KH* 228, 267

withall *adv*: likewise, as well *JS* 256,
FB 13, etc.

without *conj*: unless *DH* 20, 104, etc.;
prep: outside of *FB* 52

witt see **wit**

wo(e) *a*: grieved, miserable *FB* 418,
JR 845, etc.

wode see **wood**

wodman *n*: madman *JS* 242
[woodman]

woe see **wo**

woid see **wood**

woix see **wex**

wold(e), wald *v*: want *KS* 277, *JR* 201,
etc.; wish *JS* 29, *KH* 248, etc.; *pa t*:
wanted to *SC* 189, *BM* 126, etc.

won *v*: dwell, stay *JS* 187, *JR* 175,
etc.; **wonyd** *pa t KH* 192

wonder *a*: wonderful *SC* 82

wo(u)nder, woundir *adv*: very *JS* 255,
FB 35, etc.

wonyng *n* see **wonnyng**

won(n)yng *n*: dwelling *KS* 32, 87

wonys see **wons**

won(y)s *pl n*: dwelling, *pl form sing
concordance and meaning KH* 356,
439 [wone]

wont(e), wunt *pa pple*: accustomed *TB*
127, *DH* 40, etc. [wont]

wood, wo(o)de, woid *a*: insane *JS*
282, *FB* 330, etc.; violent *KS* 185;
wild *KS* 422

woote *pres t* see **wit**

worshippe, worshype *n*: honor *JR*
817; good name *LP* 92

wot(e), wott *v pres t* see **wit**

wounder, woundir *adv* see **wonder**

wrath(e), wrothe *a*: very angry *JR* 80,
484, etc.; **wrother** angrier *SC* 68
[wroth]

wrech *n*: miser *TB* 45, *KS* 309
[wretc.h]

wright *adv* see **ryght**

wrocht, wroght see **wrought**

wronge *v*: clasped and twisted (the
hands) *JS* 254 [*pa t* wring]

wrothe see **wrath**

wro(u)ght, wrocht *v*: did, performed
TB 17, *DH* 206, *KS* 595; made *TB*
101, *DH* 160; *pa pple*: done *TB* 89,
KH 339, etc.; made *FB* 13, *BM* 54,
etc. [work]

wrye *v¹*: reveal, betray *KS* 389, 512,
etc.; **wryed** *pa t KS* 976 [*OED v¹*
wray]

wrye *v²*: cover up *KS* 592 [*OED v²*
wry]

ws us *FB* 96, 200, etc.

wunt see **wont**

yait see **yat(e)**

yare see **youre**

yat(e), yait, yet(t), gate *n*: gate *TB* 126, *FB* 276, etc.

yche, iche each *SC* 181, *KH* 92; **ychon** each one *SC* 206

ye *adv*: yes *LP* 196, *KH* 502, etc. [yea]

yede see **yode**

yeer(e) year *DH* 32, *JR* 144, etc.

yeft gift *JS* 104

yeir, yere year *FB* 30, *KH* 595, etc.

yet(t) gate *FB* 47, 191, etc.

yet(t) see **yate**

yet(t), yit, yeit *adv* + *conj*: again *TB* 63, *FB* 538; in addition, also *JR* 342; at length *KH* 88; nevertheless *FB* 303, *SC* 94, etc.

[yet]

yif(f), yeve *v*: give *KH* 2, 379, etc.; make over in discharge of an obligation *KH* 46; devote (oneself) *KH* 210; **yef** grant *JS* 119

y(i)f(f) if *LP* 118, *KS* 113, etc.

yift gift *KH* 94

yys yes *KS* 806

yit *adv* see **yet**

yode, yede, yude *pa t*: went *JR* 540, *KH* 294, etc. [*pa t* go]

yone yon *FB* 102, 197, etc.

yong man *n*: yeoman *KH* 450 [young man]

youre, yare *adv*: for a long time *LP* 217; in the past *JR* 318

ys yes *JS* 334; his *LP* 135, 144, etc.; is *LP* 8, *SC* 5, etc.

yude see **yode**

MIDDLE ENGLISH TEXTS SERIES

Stanzaic Guy of Warwick, edited by Alison Wiggins (2004)

Saints' Lives in Middle English Collections, edited by E. Gordon Whatley, with Anne B. Thompson and Robert K. Upchurch (2004)

Siege of Jerusalem, edited by Michael Livingston (2004)

The Kingis Quair and Other Prison Poems, edited by Linne R. Mooney and Mary-Jo Arn (2005)

The Chaucerian Apocrypha: A Selection, edited by Kathleen Forni (2005)

John Gower, *The Minor Latin Works*, edited and translated by R. F. Yeager, with *In Praise of Peace*, edited by Michael Livingston (2005)

Sentimental and Humorous Romances: Floris and Blancheflour, Sir Degrevant, The Squire of Low Degree, The Tournament of Tottenham, and The Feast of Tottenham, edited by Erik Kooper (2006)

The Dicts and Sayings of the Philosophers, edited by John William Sutton (2006)

Everyman and Its Dutch Original, Elckerlijc, edited by Clifford Davidson, Martin W. Walsh, and Ton J. Broos (2007)

The N-Town Plays, edited by Douglas Sugano, with assistance by Victor I. Scherb (2007)

The Book of John Mandeville, edited by Tamarah Kohanski and C. David Benson (2007)

John Lydgate, *The Temple of Glas*, edited by J. Allan Mitchell (2007)

The Northern Homily Cycle, edited by Anne B. Thompson (2008)

Codex Ashmole 61: A Compilation of Popular Middle English Verse, edited by George Shuffelton (2008)

Chaucer and the Poems of "Ch," edited by James I. Wimsatt (revised edition 2009)

William Caxton, *The Game and Playe of the Chesse*, edited by Jenny Adams (2009)

John the Blind Audelay, *Poems and Carols*, edited by Susanna Fein (2009)

Two Moral Interludes: The Pride of Life and Wisdom, edited by David Klausner (2009)

John Lydgate, *Mummings and Entertainments*, edited by Claire Sponsler (2010)

Mankind, edited by Kathleen M. Ashley and Gerard NeCastro (2010)

The Castle of Perseverance, edited by David N. Klausner (2010)

Robert Henryson, *The Complete Works*, edited by David J. Parkinson (2010)

John Gower, *The French Balades*, edited and translated by R. F. Yeager (2011)

The Middle English Metrical Paraphrase of the Old Testament, edited by Michael Livingston (2011)

The York Corpus Christi Plays, edited by Clifford Davidson (2011)

Prik of Conscience, edited by James H. Morey (2012)

The Dialogue of Solomon and Marcolf: A Dual-Language Edition from Latin and Middle English Printed Editions, edited by Nancy Mason Bradbury and Scott Bradbury (2012)

Croxton Play of the Sacrament, edited by John T. Sebastian (2012)

🖉 COMMENTARY SERIES

Haimo of Auxerre, *Commentary on the Book of Jonah*, translated with an introduction and notes by Deborah Everhart (1993)

Medieval Exegesis in Translation: Commentaries on the Book of Ruth, translated with an introduction and notes by Lesley Smith (1996)

Nicholas of Lyra's Apocalypse Commentary, translated with an introduction and notes by Philip D. W. Krey (1997)

Rabbi Ezra Ben Solomon of Gerona, *Commentary on the Song of Songs and Other Kabbalistic Commentaries*, selected, translated, and annotated by Seth Brody (1999)

John Wyclif, *On the Truth of Holy Scripture*, translated with an introduction and notes by Ian Christopher Levy (2001)

Second Thessalonians: Two Early Medieval Apocalyptic Commentaries, introduced and translated by Steven R. Cartwright and Kevin L. Hughes (2001)

The "Glossa Ordinaria" on the Song of Songs, translated with an introduction and notes by Mary Dove (2004)

The Seven Seals of the Apocalypse: Medieval Texts in Translation, translated with an introduction and notes by Francis X. Gumerlock (2009)

The "Glossa Ordinaria" on Romans, translated with an introduction and notes by Michael Scott Woodward (2011)

🖋 DOCUMENTS OF PRACTICE SERIES

Love and Marriage in Late Medieval London, selected, translated, and introduced by Shannon McSheffrey (1995)

Sources for the History of Medicine in Late Medieval England, selected, introduced, and translated by Carole Rawcliffe (1995)

A Slice of Life: Selected Documents of Medieval English Peasant Experience, edited, translated, and with an introduction by Edwin Brezette DeWindt (1996)

Regular Life: Monastic, Canonical, and Mendicant "Rules," selected and introduced by Douglas J. McMillan and Kathryn Smith Fladenmuller (1997); second edition, selected and introduced by Daniel Marcel La Corte and Douglas J. McMillan (2004)

Women and Monasticism in Medieval Europe: Sisters and Patrons of the Cistercian Reform, selected, translated, and with an introduction by Constance H. Berman (2002)

Medieval Notaries and Their Acts: The 1327–1328 Register of Jean Holanie, introduced, edited, and translated by Kathryn L. Reyerson and Debra A. Salata (2004)

John Stone's Chronicle: Christ Church Priory, Canterbury, 1417–1472, selected, translated, and introduced by Meriel Connor (2010)

🖋 MEDIEVAL GERMAN TEXTS IN BILINGUAL EDITIONS SERIES

Sovereignty and Salvation in the Vernacular, 1050–1150, introduction, translations, and notes by James A. Schultz (2000)

Ava's New Testament Narratives: "When the Old Law Passed Away," introduction, translation, and notes by James A. Rushing, Jr. (2003)

History as Literature: German World Chronicles of the Thirteenth Century in Verse, introduction, translation, and notes by R. Graeme Dunphy (2003)

Thomasin von Zirclaria, *Der Welsche Gast (The Italian Guest)*, translated by Marion Gibbs and Winder McConnell (2009)

Ladies, Whores, and Holy Women: A Sourcebook in Courtly, Religious, and Urban Cultures of Late Medieval Germany, introductions, translations, and notes by Ann Marie Rasmussen and Sarah Westphal-Wihl (2010)

🖋 VARIA

The Study of Chivalry: Resources and Approaches, edited by Howell Chickering and Thomas H. Seiler (1988)

Studies in the Harley Manuscript: The Scribes, Contents, and Social Contexts of British Library MS Harley 2253, edited by Susanna Fein (2000)

The Liturgy of the Medieval Church, edited by Thomas J. Heffernan and E. Ann Matter (2001; second edition 2005)

Johannes de Grocheio, *Ars musice*, edited and translated by Constant J. Mews, John N. Crossley, Catherine Jeffreys, Leigh McKinnon, and Carol J. Williams (2011)

🖋 TO ORDER PLEASE CONTACT:

Medieval Institute Publications
Western Michigan University
Kalamazoo, MI 49008-5432
Phone (269) 387-8755
FAX (269) 387-8750
http://www.wmich.edu/medieval/mip/index.html

Typeset in 10/13 New Baskerville
and Golden Cockerel Ornaments display
Designed by Linda K. Judy
Manufactured by McNaughton & Gunn, Inc.

Medieval Institute Publications
College of Arts and Sciences
Western Michigan University
1903 W. Michigan Avenue
Kalamazoo, MI 49008-5432
http:/ /www.wmich.edu/medieval/mip

 WESTERN MICHIGAN UNIVERSITY